Charismatic Christianity
as a Global Culture

Studies in Comparative Religion
Frederick M. Denny, General Editor

Charismatic Christianity as a Global Culture

Edited by Karla Poewe

University of South Carolina Press

Published in Columbia, South Carolina, by the
University of South Carolina Press

Manufactured in the United States of America

Library of Congress Cataloging-in-Publication Data

Charismatic Christianity as a global culture / edited by Karla Poewe.
    p.   cm.
Includes bibliographical references and index.
ISBN 0–87249–996–0 (alk. paper)
   1. Pentecostalism.   I. Poewe, Karla O.
BR1644.C43 1994   94–6874
270.8′2—dc20

To Irving Hexham
Husband and Colleague

Contents

**III. Cases: Turning Orality into Literary Narrative—
The Making of Pentecostal and Holy Spirit History**

IV. Charismatic Christian Thought

General Editor's Preface

Generally speaking, comparative religion has been, from a Western viewpoint, the study of "other" religions, that is, non-Christian traditions. It is rare to find course offerings on Christianity in North America that go beyond historical, literary (e.g., New Testament), doctrinal-theological, and, increasingly, feminist approaches. Social scientific treatments of such things as Christian communities and leadership roles are available, but they tend to be narrow in scope.

Charismatic Christianity as a Global Culture is a rarity in the literature about the tradition. By treating what many would consider marginal, idiosyncratic, and even odd varieties of Christian experience and witnessing as a mainstream dimension extending back to Pentecost, the book informs, surprises, and delights. The emphasis throughout is on charismatic Christianity as both global and, from the standpoint of personal piety, normative. The editor and her colleagues present various aspects of their subject, sometimes in frank disagreement with each other. But throughout there is a concern for presenting data in a manner that transcends "dry academic discourse." There is a sense of strong engagement in most of the book that is a far cry from the usual "Enlightenment Rationalist Fundamentalism" (Ernest Gellner) of detachment and condescension of non-believers studying believers. We have in *Charismatic Christianity as a Global Culture* a series of discourses that combine anthropology, sociology, history, theology, religious studies, and missiology in a rich, variegated fabric of academic approaches to the "global tapestry" that is charismatic Christianity.

Frederick Mathewson Denny

Preface

Perhaps the best way to introduce this volume is to say a few words about the terms used in the title. The first and most important term, *charismatic*, refers to the gifts of the Holy Spirit, which are said to be available to Christians who have surrendered their lives to Christ. These gifts are listed in Romans 12:6–8 and in 1 Corinthians 12:8–10. The most popular gifts are those of speaking in tongues (Kelsey 1981), healing, prophecy (Hill 1989), and discernment (Kelsey 1978). From the perspective of North American charismatics, and more important, from the perspective of the American press, a popular charismatic movement developed in the 1960s. It was said to involve primarily baby boomers, to have followed upon an earlier Pentecostal movement, and to have spread from America to the rest of the world.

The term *global* refers to the unbound spatial, temporal, institutional, and linguistic reach of charismatic Christianity. The latter has become a global culture or way of life based on perceptions and identities that are transmitted worldwide through high-tech media; international conferences, fellowships, and prayer links; and megachurches.

The metaphor of a tapestry, taken from Edith Schaeffer's 1981 book, aptly expresses the global dimension of charismatic Christianity. It highlights the fact that the latter consists of many small and large revival and renewal movements dating back several centuries. It also dispels the notion that charismatic and Pentecostal movements are american inventions that were foisted upon the rest of the world by the Christian Right (see chapters three, four, and eight of this volume).

The tapestry metaphor for global culture itself is not new. As Fritz Kramer (1986: 10) points out, Bronislaw Malinowski talked about culture as woven. He was against conceptualizing culture as a system and wanted to capture the texture of lifeways. According to Kramer, Malinowski's contribution was not only his espousal of participant observation but his espousal of a genre of writing that wove the stories of individuals, their poetry, their myths, and their beliefs, into his "scientific" account. This genre has been attempted by various contributors to this volume (most notably in chapters seven and eight).

But where Malinowski concentrated on the culture of a single people, we concentrate on a culture that covers the span of time from the first century A.D. to the present and is found in indigenized form in all parts of the world. It is a global culture because it transcends national, ethnic, racial, and class boundaries, but it does not transcend, or rarely transcends, other world religions. It cannot do so because at the core of this global culture is the story of Pentecost: of Jesus, the Christ, who upon his death and resurrection sent his faithful followers the Holy Spirit to comfort, inspire, and empower them.* The genius of charismatic Christians, as Michael Polanyi said about Columbus in another context (1964: 277), lies in taking this story "literally and as a guide to practical action." The study of the surprising consequences of being guided by, and taking literally, this story is what the volume is about.

Naturally, the book cannot be a definitive history and description of this global culture. What we purport to do, rather, is to show that looking at charismatic expressions of Christianity as a global culture is not only possible, it also frees us of many preconceptions and denigrating biases, and suggests alternative methods of study.

In sum, charismatic Christianity is a *global* culture because it is experiential, idealistic, biblical, and oppositional. Being experiential, it is not tied to any specific doctrine nor denomination. Being idealistic, it embraces the whole person and the whole world (Stoeffler 1973: 16, 19). Being biblical, it places the "Word" above politician, government, or any other worldly authority. Being oppositional, it is always potentially in tension with the establishment, which includes church, government, university, ethnic, class, and racial structures. What Stoeffler (1971) wrote about Pietism applies equally to the charismatic movement: it has "no one system of theology, no one integrating doctrine, no particular type of polity, no one liturgy, no geographical homogeneity" (13).

Karla Poewe

---

*Charismatics are people who see themselves as having surrendered their lives to Christ. They are baptized in the Holy Spirit and, therefore, exercise one or several of these gifts. When genuine, they "literally reproduce the traits of primitive piety" (Gordon 1905 : 38). The word charismatic is retained even though some Christians, who are appalled by the abuses and excesses of televangelists, have ceased to use it as a term of self-reference. Televangelists, who are a relatively new breed of spiritual entrepreneurs, have used glossy marketing to transform genuine religion into expensive television illusions. Abuse has occurred because American televangelists operate in a relatively free, unmonitored, and unregulated religious market. As of this writing a new generation of evangelical Christians has surfaced who value mega churches, integrity, and the charismatic spirit without using charismatic self-referentially. In Germany, some of these young people are forging links, for example, between Pietists, who continue to be especially prominent in the Württemberg are, and the charismatics of Mike Bickle's Metro Vineyard Fellowship in Kansas. Linkages are created through rather inconspicuous prayer networks.

Acknowledgments

This work began in Africa and from there moved to Canada, the United States, Germany, and Britain. Impressed by the international aspect of charismatic Christianity, I called together several scholars from different disciplines and countries to write chapters for a book that would draw attention to two outstanding characteristics of Pentecostal and charismatic Christianity: the distinctive pattern of thought of the movements' followers and the globality of the movements. I thank the Social Sciences and Humanities Research Council of Canada (SSHRCC) and various faculties and departments of the University of Calgary for funding the conference, held May 9–11, 1991, in which each scholar read his or her chapter. I also thank members of the Calgary community who added their financial support, especially the Ranaghan Foundation, Father Mohan of the Catholic School Board, and Gordon Donaldson.

Without the openness and patience of numerous charismatic Christians, especially the many scientists, evangelists, prophets, and founders of independent churches whom we interviewed, this research could not have moved forward. To you I extend my greatest thanks and to you too I apologize for the unavoidable limitations and incompleteness of this work.

I thank colleagues who showed an interest in this work and who encouraged its completion. Among them Lawrence Sullivan, director, Center for the Study of World Religions, Harvard, and Ed Bruner, department of Anthropology, University of Illinois, Urbana. Special thanks go to Irving Hexham, religious studies, University of Calgary. Not only is he a wonderful husband, he is also an exciting colleague and co-researcher. My kindest thanks go also to Richard Roberts, formerly of Lancaster University, for giving me an opportunity to present a paper on the topic of charismatic Christianity. I thank Harvey Cox, whom I have never met, for recognizing my ongoing work in a review-article. I thank David Stoll and Stephen Glazier for their helpful suggestions and gracious criticisms. I thank Merlin Brinkerhoff, who helped with the conference and developed an increasing interest in the study of Pentecostals and charismatics. The participation of Johannes Fabian, Patricia Fortuny

Loret de Mola, and Jim Houston was appreciated, as was the interest of Andrew Strathern. Appreciation must also be extended to Jean-Guy Goulet, Graham Watson, Josie and Alan Smart, and Usher Fleising, all of the University of Calgary, for showing a cautious but growing interest in this subject matter. I am grateful to Michael Hahn of Marburg University, Germany, for a listening ear and for accompanying me and my husband on some of our visits to churches in Germany. I wish to remember Frank Manning, department of anthropology, the University of Western Ontario, who was keen to participate but who sadly passed away before activities on the project commenced.

On the more unromantic side I thank Geraldine Dyer, of the University of Calgary, for helping substantially with the conference organization. Thanks go especially to Avril Dyson, who, at a most difficult time, processed this manuscript. Harold Dyson too must be thanked, and also Rob Lagore. The latter supplied me with various videos and journals to keep me informed of scandals and exposés.

Finally, I thank my immediate family for their patience and love. Jeremy Hexham, my stepson, must be singled out for the many cups of camomile tea that he brewed and brought to my basement study to keep my stomach and brain working in unison.

Without the strategic grant from SSHRCC for research on scientists in the charismatic Christian fold, this work would not have begun. It should be noted, however, that the contributors to this volume and I take full responsibility for the views expressed here and, yes, for the inevitable shortcomings.

Charismatic Christianity
as a Global Culture

Introduction
The Nature, Globality, and History
of Charismatic Christianity

Karla Poewe

This book is about the history, spread, and characteristics of Pentecostal and charismatic Christianity. Unlike their forerunners, British
Puritanism and Methodism, German Pietism, American Holiness, and
Canadian Latter Rain, Pentecostalism and charismatic Christianity are
still growing (see Barrett 1982, Burgess, McGee, and Alexander 1988:
810–30; Kelley 1977; Hollenweger 1988; Stoll 1990a; Martin 1990; Finke
and Stark 1992; Synan 1971; Riss 1987). This growth continues even
though Pentecostalism became a mainline denomination some decades
ago and charismatic Christianity has been denomination-like since the
late 1970s.[1] Although their growth has ceased, or at least slowed, in North
America (see chapter eight), it continues on a comparatively large scale
in Latin America, Africa, South Korea (see chapters two, three, four, and
seven), and on a smaller scale in Europe, the Far East, Southeast Asia, and
even Eastern Europe (see Kepel 1991; Ross and Hampel 1992).

Pentecostalism and the charismatic movement suffer from the academic biases discussed by Finke and Stark (1992).[2] In brief, charismatic
Christianity does not measure up to scholars' notions about "intellectual
progress," "progressive refinement," "religious ideas" (4–5), and political correctness (251).[3] "Political correctness" is a particularly popular
measuring rod used in South Africa and Latin America to dismiss and
denigrate independent Pentecostal and charismatic activities, especially
as it conflicts with their keen sense for religious business and investment
(Finke and Stark 1992: 17; Martin 1990; Stoll 1990; de Soto 1989: 4; Poloma
1989: 215–31; Poewe 1993a). Using left-liberal politics, the African National Congress (ANC), and "written" liberation theology as their measuring rod, scholars and mainline Christians denigrate the business
acumen and the wide-ranging political predilections of charismatics

(Poewe 1993b).[4] While radical-liberation theologians and their mainline sympathizers dismiss the new church charismatics, new church charismatics, including South African blacks, South African Indians, and so-called "coloreds," do not dismiss liberation theology. These issues are discussed as they relate to countries other than the United States in chapters two, three, and four of this volume. In order to place these issues in a relative context, I will here address definitions, theory, and the special attractiveness of charismatic Christianity.

DEFINITIONS AND THE NORTH AMERICAN VERSION OF THE HISTORY OF THESE MOVEMENTS

Since a very useful dictionary (Burgess, McGee, and Alexander 1988) and many articles and books exist that define and give a history of the charismatic and Pentecostal movements (Dayton 1987; Quebedeaux 1983; Synan 1971, 1975; Harrell 1975, 1981, 1985), I shall confine my defining and historical comments to a brief overview. I start this overview from an American perspective because students who are new to this subject matter will find it more familiar. Later comments and chapters in the book, however, point precisely away from America. The aim is to begin the process of realizing a global perspective so that we do not lose sight of the impact of the rest of the world on us (E. Wolf 1982; Wallerstein 1974, 1987; Featherstone 1990: 2, 4).

As said above, the term *charismatic Christianity* is meant to encompass all Christianity, from its beginning in the first century, that emphasized religious or spiritual experiences and the activities of the Holy Spirit. Here I am not alone (Gordon 1905; Stoeffler 1973).[5] John Wimber, the founder of the Vineyard Movement who defines charismatic Christianity in terms of "signs and wonders," goes back to patristic times to find similar expressions of Christianity among such church fathers as Ignatius, Hermas, Polycarp, and the Montanists, moving forward to include an unbroken stream of Catholics and Protestants into the present (Wimber and Springer 1985). More specifically for purposes here, I use the term *charismatic Christianity* to include present-day Pentecostalism, the charismatic, renewal, and third wave movements, African Independent Churches (AICs), independent Pentecostal churches, and the New Independent Churches (NICs) or ministries worldwide. Distinctions between North American Pentecostals, Fundamentalists, and charismatics are made in chapter five.[6]

From the North American perspective, the immediate forerunners of the charismatic, or renewal, movement were the healing evangelists, including Bill Branham (Weaver 1987), Kathryn Kuhlman (Buckingham 1979), Oral Roberts (Harrell 1985), and many others (Harrell 1975).[7]

While many of these evangelists had Pentecostal backgrounds, they started independent ministries which were non- or adenominational. Independent ministries became especially popular in the late 1970s.

An important nondenominational organization that appealed especially to business and, generally, working men was the Full Gospel Businessmen's Fellowship International (FGBMFI). It was founded by Demos Shakarian (1913–1993), a millionaire dairy farmer from California whose ethnic background was Armenian.[8] In an interview with me he emphasized that Armenian spirituality inspired him to bring men into churches that were then (following World War II) primarily attended by women (Shakarian 1989).

The charismatic, or neo-Pentecostal movement, as it was called early on, affected especially Pentecostals and independents. The first person to make an impact on mainline or historic churches was David du Plessis (1905–1987). For our purposes, two things are interesting about du Plessis. First, he responded to a prophecy that the Englishman Smith Wigglesworth (1859–1947) spoke over him in South Africa in 1936. Second, du Plessis was deeply affected by the spirituality of black South African Christians for whom healing, tongues, dreams, and visions were simultaneously and quintessentially African and Christian. While Wigglesworth was a product of and remained Pentecostal, du Plessis moved beyond Pentecostalism to reach mainline and nondenominational churches. Du Plessis's work and that of William J. Seymour (1870–1922), a black American, caution us in our claim that charismatic Christianity is solely an American Christian Right product subverting religious expressions across the world (Gifford 1988; for a balanced view see Stoll 1990a). This point is taken up in various chapters in this volume.

A mainline Christian who had great influence on the charismatic renewal of mainline churches was Agnes Sanford (1897–1982), who spent her youth in China. Sanford, and Kenneth McAll, also born in China (in 1910), concentrated on healing memories (McAll 1990; McAll 1985). Unfortunately, McAll is a neglected figure in charismatic history, perhaps because he is explicit about the impact of Chinese religious beliefs on his theology and healing practices. Nevertheless, McAll, Sanford, and the Order of St. Luke brought many Anglicans and Episcopalians into the charismatic movement primarily through their emphasis on healing.

Soon Presbyterians (through James Brown [1912–1987]) and Lutherans (through Harald Bredesen [1918–]) became involved. The "real beginning" of the charismatic renewal, however, is associated with the Episcopal priest Dennis Bennett (1917–), who announced publicly on Passion Sunday, 1960, that he had received baptism in the Holy Spirit and spoke in tongues (Bennett 1970; Sherrill 1965).

Bennett's bold announcement is seen as the real beginning. When Bennett changed congregations, Jean Stone (1924–), who also experienced the baptism in the Holy Spirit, saw to it that Bennett's story reached *Newsweek* and *Time*. In other words, "the beginning" is an American media event, and has nothing to do with the actual history of worldwide charismatic Christianity. This fact will be borne out by later chapters in this volume. In a sense, like Finke and Stark, so we too argue that there is no beginning, certainly not in one specific spot in the world. Rather there is, as they argue, a "long, slow, and consistent increase in religious participation" over the centuries that is characterized by shifts in the "religious economy" and that involves "the rising and falling fortunes of religious firms" (1992: 274).

The significant role played by the media in North America in the making of charismatic Christian history is astonishing, and charismatic Christians learned quickly to use the media, which usually concentrated on the negative aspects of the movement, to their own advantage.[9] Following a significant rise in charismatic assemblies and television networks, the *Wall Street Journal,* on May 19, 1978, announced that "religious broadcasting" had become "big business" (Frankl 1987: 12). By the 1970s numerous Christian centers and ministries televised their services. In 1959 Pat Robertson (1930–) began to build what became the sophisticated Christian Broadcasting Network (CBN) in Virginia Beach. In 1973, Paul Crouch (1934–) formed the Trinity Broadcasting Network with Jim Bakker (1940–) and Tammy Bakker (1942–). Crouch also made inroads into Canada, where George Hill, of Victory Outreach Ministries, Calgary, is still struggling to televise in the more regulated Canadian broadcasting market. David Mainse (1936–) of Toronto and Bernice Gerard of Vancouver have managed to televise their programs for years. The former, while quite independent, has released his programs to Crouch's TBN and other American television stations.

The 1970s also saw the rise of popular and scholarly charismatic literature written by charismatic Christians themselves. Dissemination took place primarily through Logos International, Fleming H. Revell, the Catholic Paulist Press, and more recently Mercer University Press. Much of the literature was focussed on healing and was written by such well-known charismatics as Jimmy Carter's sister, Ruth Carter Stapleton (1930–1983), Barbara Shlemon (1936–), Agnes Sanford (1897–1982), Leanne Payne (1932–), Briege McKenna (1946–) and the Canadian Joan James (1986; 1990). Healing is an area in which women, as well as Catholic and Episcopal priests and scholars, excel (for example, Linn and Linn 1974; Kelsey 1986). Another woman, Cindy Jacobs (1991), has written on intercessory prayer, an area in which women play a prominent role. The volume of publications, first on healing, then on prophecy, and now on intercession, reflect charismatic thinking about these phenomena as sequential movements "of the Spirit." Overall, the enthusiasm for publishing had simultaneously to do with inspiring and influencing others, keeping tap on charismatic developments, and ensuring that major figures and processes have a place in history (see chapters seven and eight of this volume).

Finally, in keeping our focus on North America, we might describe the decade between the late 1970s and late 1980s as one of consolidation through the establishment of numerous fellowship networks or charismatic-Pentecostal streams. Each fellowship involves hundreds, and sometimes more than a thousand, affiliated churches. Most are from the same country, though some include affiliated churches from abroad. A megachurch, which is like a city within a city and is thus a major employer for its school, university, clinic, old age complex, hospital, broadcasting network, or publishing house, is the core organization with which several hundred smaller churches affiliate.[10]

Some megachurches, Earl Paulk's Chapel Hill Harvester, for example, function much like international corporations. Their literature, tapes, and videos are exported to Latin American, African, Asian and/or European markets. Likewise, large churches abroad export their products to various countries, including North America. Fellowships are vital because their international conference programs maintain the sense that charismatic Christianity is still a movement, or rather several movements, despite considerable institutionalization. Networks also give a sense of the diversity of political and Christian views. This is not only important in the United States; it is of crucial importance in South Africa and Latin America, as we see in chapters two and three.

Fellowship networks exist in many countries. I have observed several in South Africa, Germany, Britain, and Canada. Since these structures are relatively loose and ever changing, I mention only one American fellowship here, the International Communion of Charismatic Churches, which is led by an international team of bishops: Bishops John Meares and Earl Paulk of the United States, Bishop Robert McAlister of Brazil, Bishop Benson Idahosa of Nigeria, as well as Bishop Herro Blair from the Caribbean. This network and their affiliated churches tends to be interracial. In the United States, these churches are effectively involved in local-level politics, especially politics concerning black ghettos (Idahosa 1990; McAlister 1990; Meares 1990; Paulk 1989). In Brazil and Nigeria involvement in politics has reached all levels. The Chapel Hill church also serves as a center for the arts, especially music, from classical to rap, and dance, from folk to ballet.[11]

Fellowships and networks are impermanent structures. They are sometimes not much more than relationships based on friendships. Many new ones have probably emerged since this writing. In the language of our time, they say something about marketing new expressions of charismatic Christianity, diversifying religious firms, and circulating funds.

Given the holistic orientation of charismatic Christianity, it is not surprising to learn that most fellowships have overseas connections. For example, the publications of Christian Growth Ministries, especially those of its founders Bob Mumford (1930–), Derek Prince (1915–), Don Basham (1926–1989), and Charles Simpson (1937–) were mentioned by founders of South African independent churches, especially the leaders of the International Fellowship of Christian Churches, Ray McCauley (1949–) and Ed Roebert (1939–) (McCauley 1987; Roebert 1987, 1989). The Vineyard Movement had some contact with the young South African Johweto program, a program of black-white cooperation centered on white Johannesburg and black Soweto. West Canadian churches, especially Langley, led by Gary Best, and North Delta, formerly led by Ken Blue and the Canadian psychiatrist John White, sought links with Vineyard of California. It is not the case that American networks always force themselves on the rest of the world.[12] Rather, it is often the case that networks that rise spontaneously in various other countries seek contact with America. Both Paulk and Meares, for example, were inspired by South Africa's Nicolas Bhengu, whom they knew personally (Bhengu's work is described in Sundkler 1961, 1976).

In many ways, 1987 was a turning point for the charismatic movement. It was the year in which the first sexual and financial scandals involving the Bakkers, Swaggart, and others made front-page news. Many of these ministries were underpinned by the "prosperity gospel," a spiritual economic philosophy especially associated with Kenneth Hagin; consequently, Hagin, along with the various major ministry networks associated with him, and the "prosperity gospel" came under severe attack.[13] The next two years were a time of serious soul searching.

CHINA: A LINK TO ANTHROPOLOGY, JESUITS, PIETISTS, AND CHARISMATICS

Since 1989, fellowships whose economies are based on the modest practice of "faith prayer," or "faith and prayer," have increased their activities.[14] Curiously enough, it is precisely these fellowships that attract well-educated followers and place a high emphasis on education, art, and learning from other cultures (see Poewe, chapter eleven of this volume). Further conjoined with faith prayer and education is a fascination for the Far East and Southeast Asia. What do the various Asian ministries, the Vineyard movement of the United States and Canada, and the New Covenant Ministries International of South Africa and Australia have in common? And what is faith prayer? To answer these questions we have to weave new threads into the charismatic tapestry, threads that take us back into sixteenth-century Spain and Italy, sixteenth- and seventeenth-century China, seventeenth- and eighteenth-century Germany, and nineteenth-century Britain. Finally, one of these threads leads directly to the history of anthropology.

While Hollenweger, in chapter nine of this volume, mentions the evangelical and Catholic roots of charismatic Christianity and concentrates on its black roots, I must here say some words about the first two and add another, the Asian root. Specifically, the roots of present-day independent ministries, and of faith missions in previous centuries, are found among Pietists and Jesuits.

P. Matteo Ricci (1552–1610), a Jesuit and eminent missionary scientist who established a scientific apostolate in China, and August Hermann Francke (1663–1727), the German founder of the Pietist movement, established several traditions that, in different combinations, are part of the discourse and practice of charismatics to this day.[15] These include a practical spirituality equally comfortable with visions and service; a sensitivity to cultural relations; an emphasis on science, literature, and education generally; and the founding of various institutions, including orphanages, houses to reclaim prostitutes, schools, colleges, missions, hospitals, even a system of banking for the poor (Catherall 1978: 531; Clouse 1978: 780; Poewe, chapter eleven of this volume). The currently popular discourse of spiritual warfare, for example, can be traced back to the Spanish founder of the Society of Jesus (Jesuits), Ignatius of Loyola (1491–1556), who was a soldier before he became a Jesuit.

Metaphorically speaking, four kinds of roots nourished the idea and practice of faith missions through the centuries. They are: Catholic evangelical priests who became Lutheran Pietists, for example, Johannes Gossner (1773–1858); devout Jesuit scientists who founded the modern Chinese church, for example, P. Matteo Ricci (1552–1610);[16] the Halle Pietists whose educational institutions and practices became influential worldwide through August Hermann Francke (1663–1727) and were carried forward by, for example, Karl Friedrich Gützlaff (1803–1851); and early Enlightenment philosophers who, inspired by the China mission, developed the idea of *Kulturmission* (cultural mission), for example, Gottfried Wilhelm Leibniz (1646–1716) (Merkel 1920). To show just how direct some of these links are, I shall say something about each of these roots. I shall also show how some of these roots shaped anthropology.

Johannes Gossner is a pivotal figure because he is generally regarded as the father of faith missions (Gordon 1905). Like his predecessors of Catholic and Pietist traditions, he founded schools, an asylum, a hospital, and a mission. His innovation, however, was to base the mission on faith and prayer "in total dependence on God," rather than on the deliberate solicitation of funds. Taught and influenced by Jesuits who were very evangelical, Gossner left Catholicism to become a Lutheran Pietist.[17] He had direct contact with the Pietist Ludwig Harms (1808–1865), who sent agricultural missionaries to South Africa and, more importantly, with Gützlaff and James Hudson Taylor (1832–1905), both missionaries to China who relied on faith and prayer. In short, early Jesuits-cum-Pietists established a discourse, a style of service, and a set of institutions that still have currency. Importantly, in their approach to missions they developed the major methods of anthropological research (see Poewe, chapter eleven of this volume). To that story, we turn presently.

In chapters one and eleven of this volume, André Droogers and I describe parallels between this experiential form of Christianity and social-science approaches to the study of religions. Are these parallels pure coincidence?

For some time now prominent German ethnologists have argued against the myth that Bronislaw Malinowski invented participant observation (Kramer 1986: 8–9; Kohl 1987: 44; Mühlmann 1984: 45). They argued instead that the founders of the three most important methodological approaches in anthropology (systematic comparison, participant observation, and mirroring, or reflexivity), were three Jesuit missionaries: Joseph François Lafitau (1670–1740), Ricci, and Louis le Comtes (1656–1729). Of these, the last two, but especially Ricci, are important to our study. Both were missionaries to China and both invented methods that are enjoying a renaissance in anthropology. Furthermore, their methods were, indeed continue to be, practiced by charismatic Christians with China links.

P. Matteo Ricci did not leave behind any published works, but it is well known from his correspondence with Chinese literati that he practiced participant observation (*teilnehmende Beobachtung*) in the extreme (see Bettray 1955: 276–90 for examples). He adopted the clothing, mannerisms, and food habits of the Chinese scholars among whom he lived. More important, he penetrated Chinese history and culture in such depth that, from a Western perspective, he is often called the second discoverer of China (Mühlmann 1984: 45; Bettray 1955: xxviii; Lyall 1978: 217, 845; Latourette 1970). Like Placide Tempels (1959) in Africa, so Ricci too saw the importance of "responsible syncretism" (see chapter nine of this volume).[18] He contemplated grafting Christianity onto Confucianism because the latter, he argued, was consistent with the Christian faith (Lyall 1978: 217).

From all appearances Ricci's participant observation impressed Gützlaff. Like Ricci, Gützlaff became a missionary to China and adopted Chinese dress, mannerisms, and food habits. Also like Ricci, he studied Chinese thought and on one occasion returned to Germany to recruit scientist missionaries (Latourette 1970: 253–55). Gützlaff publicized Ricci's method in numerous articles and tracts. Through these he influenced the Welsh missionary Timothy Richard (1845–1919), who followed Ricci's model, adapting Christianity to the Chinese culture of the literati (Lyall 1978: 846).

Gützlaff was an optimistic and fascinating speaker. The historian of the Berlin Mission Society, Professor D. Julius Richter (1924), describes how Gützlaff started an awakening movement (*Erweckungsbewegung*) among German missionaries of various societies to various countries (82). He also inspired the formation of various Chinese societies, including a Women's Society for China (*Frauenverein für China*) (Richter 1924: 509–11, 504–5). Combining faith prayer with the idea that missionaries should be scholars, Gützlaff left a deep mark on the Rheinische and Berlin Missionsgesellschaft.[19]

More important for the China faith mission is the fact that the Englishman James Hudson Taylor, founder of the China Inland Mission, adopted his methods from Gützlaff. Taylor's followers, for example the Cambridge educated C. T. Studd (1862–1931), continued these methods in China and took them to Africa. Taylor and Studd, in turn, directly influenced the work of Edith Schaeffer (1914–) and her husband Francis Schaeffer (1912–1983) in Switzerland, as well as charismatic Christian leaders in South Africa. Furthermore, the books of Taylor, Studd, and the Schaeffers are read in some charismatic circles. Finally, Taylor, Studd, and the Prussian-born Georg Müller (1805–1898) started "revivals," especially in American universities, where students received the "Holy Ghost" (Grubb 1933: 100–3; Taylor 1911: 87–89).

Gützlaff, who studied in Halle, best unites some of Ricci's methods with those of Pietism. The reason is that Pietists, especially Francke, had ample opportunity to select or discard different aspects of the Jesuit China mission experience. That Francke could do so had not only to do with his and other Pietists' contacts with Catholics; it also had to do with the fact that Francke discussed the China mission extensively with the Enlightenment philosopher Leibniz. In the end, Francke rejected Leibniz's idea of *Kulturmission*, but that was not the end of the discussion. Their thoughts inspired radical Pietists, some of who, for example Graf Nilolaus Ludwig von Zinzendorf (1700–1760), took Leibniz's ideas in the direction of nondenominationalism (Wallmann 1990: 110; Latourette 1970: 210; Merkel 1920; Steinecke 1902).

ACCOMMODATION: THE CONNECTING LINK
AMONG FAITH PRAYER, PARTICIPANT
OBSERVATION, AND MIRRORING

Before I run too far ahead of myself, I must say why faith prayer is a thread in the charismatic tapestry much like that of participant observation and, for that matter, like le Comtes's method of mirroring. According to Ricci, it will be remembered, faith prayer is a method of accommodation and accommodation is the essence of participant observation (Bettray 1955). It is accommodation, however, first to God and then, through the Holy Spirit, to others, and vice versa. It is based on "surrender" and "receptivity" (Poewe 1989, 1992). The success of this method, furthermore, is mirrored in the responses that the charismatic Christian receives from those cultural others with whom he or she interacts (Pullinger 1980: 62). But seeing one's actions mirrored by the responses of others to them means that the other makes us aware of the peculiarity of our actions. And this reflexivity is close to what le Comtes meant by mirroring. Transposing this lesson to scholars, le Comtes suggested that scholars of foreign cultures should present their findings in such a manner as to show that the ethnographic "other," for example the Chinese, find our customs and actions as peculiar as we find theirs (Mühlmann 1984: 45).[20]

Those who look carefully will see that mirroring is used especially among charismatic Christians who practice faith prayer. Only now we are no longer surprised that the threads of mirroring, participant observation, and faith prayer should intertwine. Thus the prayers of Chinese, and later, Africans, for Studd's healing make him aware of the narrow-mindedness or predilections of Western Christians who would not allow it (Grubb 1933: 164).[21] Jackie Pullinger's book (1980), written in a popular style, exemplifies mirroring. Working with Chinese addicts, she is constantly made aware of her hitherto unquestioned predilections that now, however, limit her spiritual and practical progress. Mirroring brings out the full meaning of these predilections, freeing her to make responsible choices concerning them. Is it surprising that the work of these Christians, most recently that of Pullinger, who follows in the footsteps of Ricci, Gützlaff, Müller, Taylor, and the Schaeffers, among others, enchants present day charismatics?

The Schaeffers, whose influence on the American and Canadian Vineyard movement and on the South African and Australian New Covenant Ministries fellowship is direct, knew of Taylor, Gützlaff, and Müller. Gützlaff, it will be remembered, and Müller studied at Halle, where they learned of Ricci. What is important for us is that all of these

men started their own nondenominational missions: Gützlaff founded
the Chinese Union and is considered the grandfather of the China Inland
Mission; Taylor founded the China Inland Mission; Müller founded the
orphanage houses at Ashley Down, near Bristol; Studd founded the
Heart of Africa Mission; the Schaeffers founded L'Abri; and, I might add,
in the 1970s Pullinger founded homes to reclaim addicts in Hong Kong.[22]

All of these men, as well as Pullinger, were well educated and
therefore made a deep impression on students and, generally, the young
(Grubb 1933; Pierson 1984; Taylor 1911). They all started faith missions.
They lived by faith and prayer, making themselves dependent "on God
alone for supplies" (Taylor 1911: 88; Pullinger 1980). Also important is
the fact that various other current charismatic Christian beliefs and
practices were part of their missions. Gützlaff prayed "for the outpouring of the Spirit of God upon China" (Taylor 1911: 88). They organized
prayer meetings and associations in Britain, Continental Europe, and
America (Taylor 1911: 89). They depended upon "the Holy Spirit to
illuminate the Word" (Grubb 1933: 53). They were generous givers who
trusted, often with great humor, that God would "give an hundredfold"
in return (62).[23] Finally, visions, voices, and dreams (67, 69), prophetic
words (70), baptism in the Holy Spirit (71), and healing (90) were seen as
evidence of an active God. (See also Pullinger 1980).

Most recently, the philosophy of "faith prayer" was explicitly used
and developed by the Schaeffers at L'Abri.[24] This is not surprising since
both knew of Taylor and Müller. Edith Schaeffer, who was born in China,
is of British-American descent. At the time of her birth her parents served
in the China Inland Mission and knew Hudson Taylor personally.
Francis Schaeffer was of Prussian-American descent. Apparently, Georg
Müller is known to Edith and Francis only through his written works,
although it is curious that Francis Schaeffer's immediate Prussian ancestors lived in the German-populated parts of America where Müller was
a frequent speaker between 1877 and 1887.

According to Edith Schaeffer their works and lives have been "lived
by prayer" in "four specific realms": financial and material needs were
made known only to God in prayer, not by sending out pleas for money;
they prayed to God to bring the right people and "keep all others away";
they prayed "that God will plan the work," and that the plan will be
unfolded "day by day, rather than planning the future in some clever or
efficient way in committee meetings"; they prayed that "God will send
the workers of His choice" so that one avoids looking "for workers in the
usual channels" (1969: 16). This philosophy of praying that God look
after financial and material needs, bringing the right people, planning
the work, and bringing needed workers, when taken literally by people

who were imbued with a vision of service, had astounding consequences of which Müller's orphanages, Taylor's China Inland Mission, the Schaeffers' L'Abri, and Pullinger's homes for addicts are but few examples.

Worldwide ministries that are, as said, the heirs of this approach, are Paul Yonggi Cho's Korean ministry, Vineyard of the United States and Canada, and the New Covenant Ministries of South Africa and Australia.[25] Members of Vineyard and the New Covenant Ministries visit the Far East and Southeast Asia regularly and frequently.[26] And there can be little doubt that they bring increasingly more of Asia to the West.

Charismatic Christianity reverses emphases that we have taken for granted: the centrality of the rational, of calculated doing, of articulate verbal skills, of doctrine, and of things Western. It does not deny nor reject these things. Rather it comes to *them* in unexpected ways. A charismatic Christian comes from the nonrational to the rational, from happening to doing, from experience to talk, from sign to metaphor, from spiritual gifts to utility, from receptiveness to action, from demonstration to theology, from indigenization to globalization. It is often the African, the Chinese, the Latin American who leads the Western nominal Christian to experience the Holy Spirit and tongues. For the devoted charismatic Christian, tongues, not exegesis, is the explicit language of worship, healing, and turning people around (Pullinger 1980: 62; but see also chapter eight of this volume).[27] And yet, these people are eminently rational, sometimes scientists, often businessmen. To get to the bottom of this turn of thought has been the thrust of much of my own work (Poewe 1989, chapter eleven of this volume).

FINKE AND STARK'S THEORY AND
THE IMPORTANCE OF GENERATIONS

The religious-economy model of Finke and Stark is based, appropriately enough, on the "history of human actions and human organizations, not the history of ideas" (1992: 5). The transformation of actions into organizations is the first surprising characteristic about a form of Christianity that purports to emphasize holiness and the gifts of the Holy Spirit, especially when these gifts are revealed to individuals through dreams, visions, inner prompting; in short, through what I have called the passive or receptive imagination (Poewe 1989). But from its inception among Pietists and Jesuits, there is nothing passive about charismatic Christianity (Stoeffler 1973). Simply put, this form of Christianity is so convincing that charismatic Christians act out their gifts and revelations. Many become religious entrepreneurs, even against their will. They realize in action what is revealed to them in dreams. They build large corporations. These building goals, and beyond that, the goals to turn around cities, nations, and the world, motivate and actively involve hundreds and thousands of their congregants. The Holy Spirit story, without question, motivates sacrifice (Stoeffler 1973: 5) and this in so positive a manner as to make the very sacrifice a reward.[28]

Finke and Stark argue against the idea "that the decline of the liberal Protestant churches was a product of the sixties" (1992: 247) and that it had something to do with the baby boom generation. Instead, they point out that the "liberal decline" and "conservative growth" is a "long, steady trend." It is not related to explanations about cultural crises, especially the cultural crisis of the 1960s (239–51; see also McLoughlin 1978; Wuthnow 1988). Not only does the early history of charismatic Christianity support this view, the ages of founders and the succession of generations do as well.

Revivals, generally, and the renewal, neo-Pentecostal, and charismatic movements of the 1960s and 1970s are Protestant ways of recruiting the next generation, expanding its "markets," if you like, and "testing the market" for new products. If Finke and Stark's discussion of Catholic recruitment problems is correct (1992: 259), then Catholics too recruit periodically in "Protestant ways." Treating renewal as recruitment, explains something that puzzled me throughout my years of researching the charismatic movement and the formation of independent churches. I mean the curious fact that all the prominent leaders of the charismatic and renewal movements of the 1960s did not belong to the baby boom generation but to one or two generations before.

In fact, generations of founders succeed one another systematically. From Arndt the Pietist born in 1555 to Ricci the Jesuit born 1552 we move forward through several generations of brilliant Pietists and Jesuits to the meeting of the two traditions in Gossner, born in 1773. Gossner made explicit the idea of faith mission, which was carried forward with enthusiasm by Müller (born 1805), Gützlaff (born 1803), and Harms (born 1808). With these men, and hundreds like them, it spread into England, China, and South Africa. Taylor (born 1832) combined the participant-observation method of Ricci with the faith mission organization of Gossner and took it to China, and his disciple Studd (born 1862) took the same combination to Central Africa. Because all of these men were well educated, they made a deep impact on university students in Britain, Germany, and the United States.[29] In the meantime, numerous movements, given ever new names, were started in England and the United States. Unfortunately, when these movements originated among Chinese, Indians, and Africans, they were often dismissed with terms like millenarian, separatist, syncretistic, sect-like, and so on.

At the turn of this century we start again with the birth of David du Plessis in 1905, Demos Shakarian in 1913, and Derek Prince in 1915. We then have quite a few prominent evangelists, prophets, and apostles born in the 1920s, 1930s, and 1940s. Even the latter are, strictly speaking pre–baby boomers. Furthermore, there are continuous generational links to the younger founders of churches and fellowship networks. Thus, in South Africa, for example, Dudley Daniels, born in the 1940s, is in an apostolic relationship with the two young church founders Chris Wienans and Rob Rufus, born in the 1950s (Wienans 1987). Or there is John Wimber, born in 1934 (who encouraged leaders in Canada), Ken Blue and Gary Best, born in the late 1940s and 1950s respectively (Best 1990; Blue 1990), and Paul Mbete (1962–) and Bushy Venter (1955–) in South Africa, born in the 1950s and 1960s (Mbete 1989; Venter 1989), and Mike Bickle, of Kansas, born in the 1950s (Bickle 1990). In short, this generational continuity is present in all major independent churches that I researched in four countries. It can be taken as further evidence of a continuous historical process. Even the emphasis on the Holy Spirit, which appears to be such an outstanding feature of the charismatic phenomenon of the last three decades, can be traced back continuously. There is, for example, the fascinating book *The Holy Spirit: A Study* (1916), written by the Canadian Methodist bishop Wilson T. Hogue between 1884 and 1890. On pages xi and xii, Hogue lists other authors who in turn influenced him. These include the seventeenth-century Puritan John Owen, who published on the Holy Spirit, and from him forward to include people from England, Scotland, and the United States.

ORGANIZATION OF THE BOOK

I. Methods and Models

In chapter one, André Droogers raises a burning question, namely, how social-science scholars can study a phenomenon that, so far at least, has been presented as "the opposite of science" and as not subject to "scientific verification." While I, in chapter eleven, show that charismatic Christian thought is in fact not the opposite of science, Droogers tackles the problem by looking at the researcher-researched dynamics. To that end, he constructs a simple heuristic model based on external and internal symbolic and social structures. The model allows us to see how scholars who operate wholly within structures that are external to those of believers tend to see religiosity, generally, or a religiosity different from their own, specifically, as somehow deviant. Consequently, they find it necessary to transform religion into social and economic functions or otherwise voice severe criticisms. By contrast, scholars who conduct their study from within the structures of believers prefer to see religiosity as normal. To them, religion is of interest in its own right.

Because chapter one is written in a somewhat inaccessible social-science (rather than historical and narrative) style, I think it advisable to provide additional background material before proceeding to an outline of chapter two.

People in religious studies hold that there are three methodological positions from which to make sense of other people's religious beliefs and practices. These are methodological theism, atheism, and agnosticism.[30] The last mentioned method (the term was coined by T. H. Huxley in the nineteenth century), is generally favored. All three terms are linked to the Enlightenment and the advance of science. They became popular at a time, from the seventeenth century forward, when most philosophers started with Christianity and rejected it. All three methodological positions, even theism, which holds that God (or divinity in general) exists and works in the world, are centered on reason or on reason and the material condition. What Enlightenment thinkers opposed were traditions that held that we can also know through revelation and religious experiences. Perhaps because this generation tends to be illiterate in Christianity, these ways of knowing have once again gained currency. More curiously still, they have gained currency simultaneously among social scientists as well as Pentecostals and charismatics.

As said, agnosticism allows social scientists to argue that since religious beliefs can neither be proven nor falsified, we can at least take them seriously when they are believed by those whom we study. But what about our own beliefs? Do we take them seriously? Do they affect our research and writing? Whether we take them seriously or not can we assume that they do not play a role in our research? Can we feel safe that our determination to take seriously only the belief of the people we study will prevent bias?

During our discussion of these chapters at the conference at which they were initially presented, it became quite clear that indifference toward one's own belief (or nonbelief), whether it was that of a Catholic and Pentecostal or of an ex-Catholic and ex-Pentecostal, was more ideal than real. Seemingly neutral in their written work, some ex-Catholic and ex-Pentecostal scholars were surprisingly passionate about matters with which they could or could not agree, because these matters disturbed their nonbelief. Was their written work neutral or did they use a neutralizing rhetoric to hide passionate disbelief?

There was, however, another position. There were people who could, with great ease, shift in and out of their own and other people's symbolic universe.[31] Furthermore, that they could do so had something to do with experience. Looking first at practitioners of this experiential form of Christianity, it is quite clear that we must take seriously their claim that they have moved beyond "belief" to "knowing." The importance of "knowing" rather than "believing" was not only mentioned, for example, by North American aboriginals (Goulet 1991), and by African charismatic Christians (Poewe 1989), but also by scientists who are charismatic Christians (see Poewe, chapter eleven of this volume). Not surprisingly, therefore, the nature of this knowing, including its potentially negative implications, also comes up in chapters eight and ten, written by Stanley Johannesen and Gerard Roelofs.

Moreover, looking at scholars we discover that they too can not be divided simply into believers and nonbelievers. The dynamic of discussion made it quite clear that several scholars had transcended this dichotomy, possibly because they experienced something of the sort, or something analogous to, that which was experienced by the people they researched. While religious belief is important to some and anathema to others, it seems to be the case after all that indifference, distance, or benign neglect is possible. Curiously, though, it seems to be more possible among those who accept that experience and revelation, and not only reason, are also ways of knowing.

This said, we are now ready to move on. We know that many Pentecostal and charismatic practices have been disreputable. In earlier footnotes I described some eminently justified concerns. I also made reference to books whose sole aim was to criticize this form of Christianity. Some criticisms of charismatic Christianity, however, are methodologically weak and otherwise deceptive. Consequently, they prevent rather than help our understanding of this phenomenon and, like deadwood, must be removed.

In chapter two, therefore, Irving Hexham and I handle some popular criticisms of, specifically, South African charismatic Christianity. We do so by exposing the biases and poor methods that inform much of this literature and suggest an alternative approach, one more explicitly global. For obvious reasons, in South Africa perhaps more so than elsewhere, researchers start their work on the topic with a wish. They wish that independent charismatic churches would speak the politically correct rhetoric that the researcher favors. As will be pointed out in later chapters, however, the politically correct position—be it that of the establishment or of the radical left and right—is precisely the position from which charismatics walked away. As David Martin points out in chapter three, Pentecostalism is a "walkout from all social antecedents." Certainly in South Africa charismatic Christians have walked away from both apartheid and its violent alternative.

II. Regional Overviews and Variations

While chapters one and two alert us to the problems scholars have with this topic, and while the authors give us further hints of what makes this form of Christianity global, namely, that it is being based on "known" things, we must now turn to the section that deals with Pentecostalism in different regions of the world. Here the major themes discussed earlier are reiterated in a new form. In chapter three, David Martin points out, for example, that Western scholars ignore the very broad "geological shift in religious identification" because they still work with the dated assumption that "political and economic spheres are primary realities" that inform all else. The all else, which includes charismatic Christianity, is said to be reactionary. This blind assumption leads to other equally blind ones, especially the claim that Pentecostalism is always financed and directed from outside. Bringing light into this darkness, Martin shows how the truly global is also quintessentially local. Postulating the thesis that Pentecostalism is a "walkout" from "all that belongs to the status quo," he shows how "small people" create their own space in which they fuse traditions and forge new religious links. These turn out to be creative strategies of survival.

What is global are traditions that reach across national boundaries, take on local color, and move on again. Thus, in chapter four, Mark R. Mullins shows how Pentecostalism remained stagnant in Japan and even Korea until it shed its Western associations and became "shamanized." As in Southern Africa, where healing, tongues, prayer, dreams, mountain tops, and ancestors had to be worked into narrative theologies, so in Korea (and on a much smaller scale in Japan and China) Pentecostalism did not take off until this theological indigenization took place. One wonders, however, what is meant by indigenization when urban and rural folk from different continents demand that the same sorts of religious rituals and experiences be incorporated into Pentecostal forms of Christianity. It is not always clear which is the correct perspective, that of the scholar who sees indigenization of what was Western, or that of the African and Korean founder who claims to be taking back what originated in his part of the world in the first place (Shembe 1987; Cho 1990). To complicate things further, W. J. Hollenweger suggests that the things we most associate with indigenization may simply be basic aspects of any oral, as opposed to written, culture (Hollenweger 1979a).

Now that we have an understanding of regional diversity, we return to North America to define, and distinguish between, Pentecostalism and fundamentalism. In chapter five, Russell P. Spittler argues that Pentecostalism and fundamentalism have separate historical roots and, in North America at least, Pentecostalism has sometimes been the target

of fundamentalism. The difference between Pentecostalism and fundamentalism points to another distinction that is also implicit in other
chapters, namely, that between experiential and interpretive literalism.
Literalism is usually associated with fundamentalism and narrowness of
mind. But experiential literalism is inclusive and open, while interpretive
literalism is exclusive and closed. According to Spittler, it is especially the
practice of biblical or interpretive literalism that has given rise to some
"curious theological deviations" and consequently to various kinds of
Pentecostalism.

III. Cases: Turning Orality into Literary Narrative—The Making of Pentecostal and Holy Spirit History

Given the tendency of fundamentalists to accuse charismatic Christians of heresy, it is not surprising to learn that charismatics worldwide
seek their own ancestry and vision of Christianity. In chapter six, Charles
Nienkirchen discusses how these Christians construct prophetic histories. We also learn that these constructions or reconstructions vary in
different parts of the world. In the West, the emphasis has tended to be
on the restoration of something, the return to something, or the dismantling of dead traditions. In the non-West, by contrast, the emphasis has
tended to be on indigenization, contextualization, and cultural reconstruction. In the West, argues Nienkirchen, prophetic historians have
postulated the fall of the church from the first to the sixteenth century,
with restoration beginning with Luther. Thereafter, we see a global
recovery of such truths as holiness, healing, and, sometimes,
premillennialism through John Wesley of England, Johanne Blumhardt
of Germany, and Dorothea Trüdel of Switzerland, to name but a few. Just
how differently charismatic genealogies are constructed in Africa we see
in chapter seven.

The next three chapters, by Nancy Schwartz, Stanley Johannesen,
and W. J. Hollenweger, return to the question whether scholars can
understand what the Holy Spirit does, in the first instance, for the
African, and in the other two for anyone, including the North American.
The question has special importance when the scholar does not have, nor
want, the religious sensibility of the people he studies. The anthropologist Schwartz, who formulates this question at the end of chapter seven,
gives two answers. The first, and only answer I shall discuss here,
underpins the whole chapter. It essentially argues that we can understand another religious sensibility by letting their "voices into our dry
academic discourse." At the conference during which this chapter was
first presented, these "voices" did not persuade a Western Christian,
however, from asking whether Legio Maria, an African Catholic charis-

matic movement, was Christian at all. Why do most Western Christians fail to recognize Christianity in Legio? Why do others, Schwartz and Hollenweger among them, not have this problem?

The answer to the first question has something to do with the freedom that these movements grant "the work of the Holy Spirit" and the narrative style they use to describe it. Not only do we see Legios use metonyms as they look for worldwide coincidences and linkages in their construction of a Spirit- inspired global history.[32] Much of this history is told in the oblique fashion of an allegory, where talk of their history is talk about the work of God (especially as Mary, Christ, and Spirit), and vice versa. It is a talk, furthermore, that requires of the Western listener that he shift from analysis to narrative and use more than the usual powers of perception. Legio members seem to tell three kinds of stories in one: stories of their founder in Kenya, stories of the Bible, and stories of the Holy Spirit, who shows Legios how the story of Africa is also a biblical story and one of humanity in toto.

When the missionary arrives, now from a Pentecostal institution that has become relatively wealthy and mainline, he converts the narrative language of the non-West into the conceptual language of the West. The language of dreams, visions, and experiences that manifests the Spirit is transformed into the language of computers, techniques, and professional jargon that manifests Western know-how.

In chapter eight Johannesen, who is an ex-Pentecostal and an academic historian, describes a third-generation suburban Pentecostal church in Canada in terms of what he calls a "Pentecostal perception." It is a perception he understands but does not share. This perception, he argues, is intrinsic to the Pentecostal social life and can be derived empirically from it. He distinguishes between his perception and that of a Pentecostal by examining a phrase that both he and a Pentecostal might have voiced upon participating in the same meeting. The phrase is "That was a real Pentecostal meeting," and he uses it to show how he and they see this same "reality" differently. He sees "reality" empirically from within the symbolic and social structure of academia. They see the same "reality" metonymically, as a sign that they "know" to be part of a greater invisible "reality" beyond. As Johannesen says, the heart of Pentecostal discourse is a "social perception" to which the only response is "Praise the Lord."

But why does Johannesen reduce the perception to a social perception? Why does he not call it a religious or spiritual perception? The answer is twofold. First, and as per Droogers's model, he makes his argument from within the social and symbolic structure external to that of the believer. Second, he wants to argue that there is a homology between Pentecostal practice and modern life, with the key to this homology being the practice of praise. Since, to Johannesen, modern life is primarily an absence, Pentecostalism, which is one possible adaptation to modern life, is therefore a substitution for this absence. Furthermore, since Johannesen does not entertain the idea of the a priori existence of God, since he cannot find a Durkheimian God in modern life because it is defined as a social absence, and since, finally, he cannot find God in the narratives of suburban Pentecostals because the narrative tradition is dead among them, he argues that Pentecostals create their God out of their emotions and feelings during prayer. Pentecost is therefore a substitution of a made-up reality for a missing reality.

No Marxist could have given a finer description of alienation. And no one but an ex-Pentecostal would have been able to describe the lurid beauty of a church-death: of a suburban church that is so global as to have no memory, no specificity, no links to its dead, no sense of boundaries, and hence no sense of the sacred. So ensconced is Johannesen in his written academic culture that he finds no bridge to the synaesthetic techniques, tongues, and multisolitary praises that constitute the oral culture of the people he researched. Unable to grant them their most basic assumption, that God works through them in the everyday, he sees in their activities but the last twitching of a decapitated corpse. His chapter stands as an icon of Pentecostal failure, unpleasant to ponder, too powerful to ignore.

The question as to why some Christians and scholars see Legios as Christian while others do not is not easily answered. Hollenweger of course has made it a matter of method to switch between analytical and narrative, oral and written, modes of communication and cultures (see his 1979a, 1979b, 1988b). His narrative and intercultural theological approaches enable him to see similarities of content and construction between African Christian and biblical stories. He recognizes African Christian beginnings in orality, notes their transition to literacy, and their maturation in Christianity. Indeed, these same processes can be seen in North America daily. But it must be said of both Schwartz, who is Jewish, and Hollenweger, who is Christian, that faith and belief are not issues for them. Consequently, both surrender themselves to dialogue. They experience with others their beliefs.

In chapter nine, Hollenweger argues that independent Pentecostal churches confront us with our narrowness: the narrowness of the scholar who must despiritualize religion to conform with colleagues' expectations of conducting a scientific work; the narrowness of the theologian who is unwilling to accommodate his exegesis to the oral narrative style of the majority in his church; the narrowness of the missionary and lay

Christian who is afraid to learn something about the Gospel that is in contradiction to what he thought the Gospel was. From there Hollenweger proceeds to discuss primarily one of the five roots, the black oral one, of Pentecostalism. Remembering a similar rootedness in Korea and China, however, I wonder whether one should not simply call this the shamanic root of Pentecostalism. Hollenweger seems to hint at something like this when he argues that "the Holy Spirit" is already present in a situation before the missionary arrives.

IV. Charismatic Christian Thought

But is Pentecostalism to blame for the kind of church-death that Johannesen portrays and Hollenweger fears? To answer this question we must look more closely at charismatic patterns of thought. This is what Gerard Roelofs does in chapter ten. His study of Roman Catholic Charismatics in Antwerp, Belgium, and my study of charismatic scientists in South Africa, North America, and Britain, build on one another despite some disagreements. Roelofs argues that the essence of charismatic Christian thought consists of charismatic experiences and their articulation, of surrender to God, who makes things happen, and of the reinterpretation of life and its consequent healing. It is a thought pattern, in short, that relies heavily, if not exclusively, on the use of signs or metonyms.

Roelofs's chapter raises a possible controversy, for while he worries about the likely closure of metonymic thinking, I argue for its openness. How are these contradictory views possible? In my opinion, the answer has something to do with what Roelofs hints at but perhaps does not adequately explore: the irony that, against all academic expectations, symbolic interpretations of the Bible can lead to sterility and routinization while literal interpretations can lead to new discoveries and breakthroughs. Roelofs's worry that metonymical thought patterns may end in stereotypical expressions raises an important question. How? The answer, I believe, has something to do with the conversion of these patterns of thought into symbolic jargon—the conversion of life experiences into stereotypical "commodified texts" or politically correct metaphors.[33] It is a conversion, furthermore, that is part of the process of routinization. As Johannesen's study shows only too well, when experiences of the sacred become but vague memories or are lost to memory altogether, and when new experiences are actively discouraged, then charisma has not only been routinized, but the church itself has "died."

Perhaps charismatic Christians, certainly the scientists whom I interviewed in chapter eleven, understood this all too well. Hence we find among them, as among many American blacks, the pattern of multiple or sequential affiliation, so that even when the institutions become sterile the individual's or community's spiritual development continues. More important, the discussion of scientists who are charismatic Christians in chapter eleven shows that conducting science and "knowing" God through the Holy Spirit is intimately connected to metonymic patterns of thought that are grounded in one and the same epistemology. While Johannesen argued that the "reality" of the people he studied was nothing other than the "quotidian flow" of the everyday embellished by an attitude of "make belief," the reality of these scientists who are charismatic Christians is one "which is expected to reveal itself indeterminately in the future" (Polanyi 1964: 10). It is a reality, furthermore, that is based on taking something literally until it yields a new discovery or revelation. These charismatic Christians and scientists, in other words, experience the world as entirely open. It is a world in which ever and again something is expected to happen sola gratia that will yield new revelations (see here Hollenweger on Kimbanguism 1979a).

The scientists I interviewed became charismatic Christians following proleptic experiences; that is, experiences that were so shattering that they changed the basic assumptions on which their work and lives were based. Not only did these experiences initiate a paradigm shift, they were also responsible for the scientists' openness to globality. It is a globality, as will be seen, that has much to do with revelation, local adaptation, and liminality.

NOTES

1. Pentecostalism is taken to be a mainline denomination in the sense that it has become an established *type* of Christianity that, given its numbers and popularity, can no longer be said to be peripheral.

2. Likewise, Gordon points out that Pietism, Mysticism, Puritanism, Methodism, and Brethrenism "are the names given in derision to those renewals of Pentecost, those revivals of primitive spirituality which have repeatedly appeared in the Church of Christ" (1905: 46). Regarding Pietism see Martin Brecht (1993: 4) and Johannes Wallmann (1990: 8). Wallmann refers to Pietism as a seventeenth- and eighteenth-century renewal movement (7).

3. Leaders of Puritanism, Methodism, Pietism, and Pentecostalism argued selectively against certain Enlightenment ideas and, consequently, were often portrayed as being anti-intellectual. Recent work by Brecht (1993) on Pietism, for example, shows that this was not the case. See also the exceptional work of Ernest Stoeffler (1973) and Wallmann (1990). In Germany, where ministers of mainline churches are required to have university degrees, the nature of theological education is a matter of controversy to this day. About the Arndt and Spener schools of Pietism see Wallmann (1990) and Brecht (1993). Arndt and Spener were university professors intent on basing theology on a "living belief," and a "true and active Christianity" taught by professors

who personally "experienced" this life transforming religiosity (Wallmann 1990:15). Their effort to found theology taught in secular universities on active belief, rather than intellectual theism, agnosticism, or atheism, earned Pietists the erroneous reputation of being anti-intellectual. At the age of eighteen, for example, Spener wrote a dissertation in which he criticized Thomas Hobbe's *De Cive*. As for political correctness, see especially the difficult course that German Pentecostals followed in the mid and late 1930s between the naive hope that Hitler intended to usher in an era of peace, and the reality that Pentecostal conferences were forbidden and some leaders were shadowed by the Gestapo (Fleisch 1983:345, 353). Finally, like our volume, the first of Brecht's four promised volumes also seeks to establish the "global reach" of Pietism.

4. It is fascinating to remember that mainline Christian denigration and/or persecution of renewed evangelicals or charismatics, in the broad sense, has a long history going back to medieval mystics (Brecht 1993; Wallmann 1990). The work of the Jesuit missionary Louis le Comtes (1656–1729) was banned by the Catholic church. German Pietists of the seventeenth and eighteenth centuries like Spener (1635–1705), Francke (1706–1790), and the Prussian Schwartz (1726–1760), a missionary to India, were denigrated by the church that they sought to renew. Francke was also pressured to leave his university post at Leipzig (Gordon 1905: 43–45; Stoeffler 1973). The Methodists of nineteenth-century Britain did not fare much better. These men, therefore, started independent missions to serve orphans or other countries, such as India and China. The pattern would repeat itself into the present. As for those who created scandals, historians left them out of their accounts or mentioned "rumors" about their private lives, for example, Madame Guyon (1648–1717) (compare Wallmann 1990: 35 with Sellers 1978: 445).

5. Gordon (1905) traces Catholic and Protestant movements inspired by primitive piety of the first century to Columba, the sixth-century apostle to the Scots, to Raymond Lull, the thirteenth-century missionary to the Mohammedans, and to the Pietists and Methodists. Throughout, he pinpoints all the ingredients that recent scholars thought to be unique to the charismatic movement. Gerhard Tersteegen (1697–1769) translated the lives of Catholic mystics into German specifically for the Pietist renewal movement and Johann Henrich Reitz published *Historie der Wiedergeborenen* (A History of the Born Again) between 1698–1717. The born again were Catholic mystics. Tersteegen held that there were more genuine evangelicals in the Catholic than in the evangelical churches of his time (Wallmann 1990: 35). J.Ruysbroeck (1293–1381), a Flemish mystic and ordained priest, influenced Johann Tauler (c.1300–1361), Gerard Groote (1340–1384), and Florentius Radewijns (1350–1400). The last two mystics taught a practical piety and founded Brethren of the Common Life. Thomas a Kempis (1380–1471), a Catholic mystic who is very popular with charismatic Christians today, was educated in a school run by the Brethren of the Common Life. Tersteegen researched these biographies over twenty years (1733–1753) and published them in three volumes, *Auserlesene Lebens-Beschreibungen Heiliger Seelen* (Selected Biographies of Holy Souls) (Wallmann 1990:35; Brecht 1993). Three things stand out: the

emphasis on a practical piety; that charismatics stand on the shoulders of generations of Pietists and Catholic mystics (Brecht 1993: 3); and that education based on a "vital Christianity" played a major role in preserving and spreading the tradition.

6. The most precise and lucid distinctions between Fundamentalists, charismatics, and Pentecostals are made by Stephan Holthaus (1993). His superb work is the first extensive analysis of American and German fundamentalism using works written in both German and English.

7. Richard Quebedeaux (1983: 145) distinguishes between the charismatic and renewal movements. The charismatic movement referred first and foremost to the restoration of the charismata, or gifts of the Spirit, to the whole contemporary Body of Christ, including Pentecostals, mainliners, and independents. By calling it a renewal movement emphasis is placed on relating spiritual gifts to "institutional Christian renewal." The distinctions are not very useful except to Christians who do not like the term "charismatic" because it has become associated with excesses of the movement. Other terms have been used, for example, "neo-Pentecostalism," to refer to the fact that the Pentecostal experience was taken up by members of mainline churches making it respectable, or "Spirit-filled," to characterize Christians who experienced baptism in the Spirit and spoke in tongues. I retain the inclusive term *charismatic*.

8. Where possible I indicate the year of birth or birth and death of major charismatic figures. The year of birth becomes part of the argument about the continuity of this type of Christianity.

9. Unfortunately, many televangelists have been less than honest. In 1991 Diane Sawyer, of the television news magazine "Prime Time," using hidden cameras, undertook a four-month investigation of three major televangelists. An impressive and competent report, it showed that W. V. Grant relied on stage- magician tricks, Larry Lea on impression management, and Robert Tilton on state of the art marketing and gimmickry to "rake in" big money. Steve Wilson, of the "Inside Edition" program, did an exposé of Benny Hinn, who relied on the spectacular. Not only did these reports expose deceit, cynicism, and greed. They also showed a "Robin Hood" attitude toward the media. In this instance, however, what televangelists took from the rich and gave to the poor was the big televised show. Following their exposure, all thumped their noses at television journalism. Even a ditty was composed: "Whose report will you believe? We will believe the report of the Lord, For his report says I am healed, I am free, Victory." Media exposés have not been sensitive, however, to the question of how one translates a Holy Spirit–based religion into television images, nor to the question of whether a theologically responsible syncretism of television culture and charismatic Christianity is even possible. In chapter nine, W. J. Hollenweger discusses the problem of translating oral, narrative patterns of thought into written, conceptual ones. Televangelism poses another problem, that of translating back and forth among spiritual experiences, television images, and American folk language and culture.

10. Note how, on a smaller scale and in accordance with the times, this pattern was first established by August Hermann Francke (1663–1727) of Halle. Francke was responsible for the founding of various institutions, including "a school for the poor, an orphanage, a hospital, a widows' home, a teachers' training institute, a Bible school, book depot, and Bible house." Francke "wrote the story of his activities in an account entitled *Pietas Hallensis: or a Public Demonstration of the Footsteps of a Divine Being Yet in the World, in an Historical Narration of the Orphan House and Other Charitable Institutions at Glaucha near Halle in Saxony*" (Clouse 1978: 780). To understand the influence of Francke's educational institutions beyond Halle see Wallmann 1990: 69–73, 76–79. Francke also had some influence in North America through the Puritan Cotton Mather, with whom he corresponded (Clouse 1978: 77).

11. Other fellowships in the United States include the International Convention of Faith Ministries, led by Happy Caldwell and Terry Mize, which was formed in 1979 and emphasizes leadership training; the Charismatic Bible Ministries, formed by Oral Roberts in 1986, which includes Pentecostal and nondenominational churches and which consolidated the remains of Oral Roberts's empire (Harrell 1985); the Fellowship of Covenant Ministries and Conferences, formed by Charles Simpson in 1987, which succeeded Christian Growth Ministries after that ministry fell into disrepute over the issue of shepherding charismatic pastors; the National Leadership Conference, formed in 1979 by Ken Sumrall; and two relatively new organizations, the youthful Vineyard Fellowship of John Wimber, with its emphasis on "signs and wonders," and the People of Destiny International, founded by Larry Tomczak and C.J. Mahaney. Vineyard, of which more shortly, is particularly attractive to the young and to academics. The People of Destiny serves a Catholic constituency (Burgess, McGee, and Alexander 1988: 142–43).

12. During our research in South Africa, Irving Hexham and I learned that some leaders of fellowships discouraged ties with American Christians. According to them, Americans take rather than give. We were told that British charismatic leaders like Gerald Coates, for example, always arrive in South Africa to give. Coates has given thousands of Rands to individuals in need. Americans, so said some leaders, come and take.

13. The prosperity gospel is also called "Word of Faith" and "Positive Confession." It has been severely criticized by Christian scholars from Sweden, Norway, and the Netherlands. English-language works on this issue include those of D. R. McConnell (1988) and Bruce Barron (1987). McConnell was at the time working on his Ph.D. at the Free University of Amsterdam. A recent popular criticism of megaministries and televangelists was published by Hank Hanegraaff (1993), president of the Christian Research Institute, a fundamentalist California-based organization founded by Walter Martin.

14. The sharp, sometimes unfair attack on the prosperity gospel has something to do with the fact that the seeming opposition between faith prayer and prosperity gospel parallels the Ulfilas versus Francis Xavier dichotomy. According to Gordon, Francis Xavier (1506–1552), Jesuit missionary to the East Indies and Japan, was a "soldier of hierarchy," Ulfilas a "disciple of the

Holy Ghost" (1905 : 37). Ulfilas trusted in spiritual regeneration, Xavier in"sacraments" and "ecclesiastical rites" (39). The first, inspired by the Holy Spirit, started "evangelical missions," the second, respectful of hierarchy, engaged in "ecclesiastical conquest by means of arms and diplomacy and persecution" (1905: 37).

15. Francke was of course influenced by earlier Pietists, especially Johann Arndt (1555–1621) through his book *True Christianity*, and Philipp Jakob Spener (1635–1705), who emphasized fasting and prayer, conversion or the new birth, and renewal of Lutheranism. With Spener's help Francke became professor of oriental studies at the University of Halle. Francke, who was a superb educator, grounded his theology in religious experience (Stoeffler 1973: 11–12). Like many of the present-day founders whom I interviewed, Francke combined vision and pragmatism, science and art, local involvement and world mission, and cultivation of friendships, with an international political elite and helping the poor; all was centered on religious and moral renewal of the individual, church, state, and education (Stoeffler 1973: 1–37).

16. Also mentioned must be Pompilio Ruggieri, Johann Terrence Schreck, Johann Adam Schall, all said to have been men of brilliance and vision (Dunne 1962; Latourette 1929).

17. There were other Pietist-Jesuit links, for example, Spener and Count von Zinzendorf (Stoeffler 1973; Erb 1983). One can speak of a cross-fertilization between Catholicism and charismatic Protestantism into the present. I do not hold with the view that the latter threatens the former with extinction.

18. Ricci, however, would not have used the term "syncretism" at all. "Responsible syncretism" is the consequence of a deep and sensitive understanding of people's beliefs and customs. Many of these beliefs and customs then become part of an indigenized Christianity, provided that they do not contradict the existence of a personal, usually triune God. See especially the mutual accommodation between Ricci and Chinese followers vis-à-vis ancestors and burial practices (Bettray 1955: 292).

19. Gützlaff's method was not lost on Alexander Merensky (1837–1918), missionary to South Africa, who argued that *"Der Missionar hat die heilige Pflicht..., (die) sittlichen Anschauungen des Volkes, unter dem er arbeitet, zu schonen, ja zu achten"* (van der Heyden 1991: 266; roughly translated: it is the duty of missionaries not only to care for, but to respect, the moral/ethical views of the people among whom they work). Merensky's ethnographic, historical, and narrative writings are detailed and often brilliant. He was (in the Christian and Weberian sense) a charismatic figure who is largely misinterpreted in the English-speaking world (van der Heyden 1991; Poewe 1993a).

20. George F. Marcus and Michael M. J. Fischer (1986) point out that this is precisely what anthropologists have failed to do. I have tried to use mirroring, reflection, and reflexivity to some extent in my pseudonymous book (Cesara 1981) and in Poewe 1985. The first book, however, was written in the context of my rebellion against Christianity. Marcus and Fischer and James Clifford (1986), among others, seem to think that these methods and the changes in

ethnographic writing are relatively new. In fact, they are a revival of something old in a postmodern context.

21. Studd's reflexivity and mirroring comes through despite his biographer's (Norman Grubb 1933) much narrower and biased mind. One must separate Grubb's comments from Studd's, which are quoted. Studd clearly engaged in meaningful dialogues with Chinese and Africans. They were his equals and contemporaries. He talked with chiefs and people about the things of God. He was also sensitive enough to note which songs hit "their sorrows" (Grubb 1933: 167).

22. L'Abri is a shelter that the Schaeffers founded in Switzerland. Its purpose was to sort out the befuddled Christianity of adults and youth by demonstrating and teaching that God is really there, in truth (Schaeffer 1969: 28). This was precisely Spener's and Francke's message. The fame of L'Abri spread by word of mouth, as is usual in the largely oral culture of charismatic and evangelical Christians.

23. Some of these men gave away large inheritances to other missions and missionaries in need. For example, Müller bailed out Taylor, Studd distributed his substantial inheritance from his father to Dwight Lyman Moody (1837–1899), who started the Moody Bible Institute in Chicago, to Müller for his orphanages, and to Booth Tucker, of the Salvation Army in India, among several others. Studd, in turn, received money from other unknown donors, and so on, ad infinitum.

24. The Schaeffers are usually said to be charismatic evangelicals. Their books are read widely by leading, well- educated charismatics of, especially, the Vineyard movement and South Africa's Glenridge church, among others. At least that is where we noticed it.

25. I am aware that while faith prayer underpinned Yonggi Cho's ministry, his operation has grown to such an extent that he is accused of having abandoned this approach. His financial philosophy now looks more like a Koreanized version of Kenneth Hagin's and Robert Schuller's prosperity gospel. His more than 650,000 followers tithe and give generously beyond tithing, "believing" that God will return what they give many times over.

26. The apostolic team of the New Covenant Ministries International-Australia and South Africa have relating churches in Hong Kong, Singapore, Ipoh, and Kuala Lumpur, Malaysia, and in Mussoree, India.

27. My fieldwork in 1987, 1989, and 1990 indicates that inspired songs, especially those I observed in Glenridge, South Africa, and Langley, Canada, are also important aspects of the language of worship.

28. Like the European visitors Finke and Stark talk about (17), many charismatic founders and evangelists use "economic language" to describe their ventures. Let me quote from two of numerous interviewed founders. Carel Cronje (1944–), the founder of Teen Challenge South Africa and of the Invisible Church, recalled his founding days as follows:

> So it was actually a business venture that gave me my first start. . . .
> There was a sociological development, you know, God is not removed
> from social and economic realities. Teen Challenge was a movement

into the market place, but now the market place was coming to church. That is the way I saw it. (Cronje 1987)

Theo Wolmarans (1948–) founded Christian City in Johannesburg. It is one of several South African megachurches. Explaining his church corporation he said:

We believe a lot in prayer, organization, and good management principles. All of my staff have been to leading companies for training. Last year alone I spent R28,000.00 in training them. Included in management is training not only of staff and pastors but also of the people. . . . In order to harness thousands of people to work for Jesus without any remuneration . . . , we train up members in the church to do ten main tasks: to be deacons, counsellors, in the prayer team, home church leaders, area leaders, fishers of men, which is the evangelism team, elders in the church, to run the music ministry, the children's ministry, and youth leaders. These are voluntary offices in the church. People enter programs and progress in golf-course fashion through a number of holes. When they finish they get a graduate certificate and go into an office. . . . As you probably know, it's an adaptation of the Yonggi Cho model. (Wolmarans 1989)

29. One thinks of British Methodists, and, in the United States, of the likes of Jonathan Edwards.

30. Methodological theism starts with the assumption that the existence of God can be shown through the use of reason. It is an assumption that can be said to have underpinned, for example, the work of the German Catholic priest and anthropologist Wilhelm Schmidt (see Brandewie 1990). Atheism negates the existence of God, gods, or anything godly. This assumption informed the work of Marx, Nietzsche, and Freud, for example. Scholars who base their work on this assumption tend to explain religion away or explain it from economic, social, ecological, political, or psychological perspectives. Methodological agnosticism starts with the assumption that one cannot know whether gods are or are not. Consequently, if one must look at religion, one should heed Huxley, who advised following reason as far as it can take you. Since rationalism, empiricism, or falsification cannot help with the question about the existence of natural and supernatural reality, we can at least take other people's beliefs seriously. As different as the three positions are, they share an emphasis on reason. If religious-studies scholars favor methodological agnosticism, it is because agnosticism seems to encourage tolerance and suspension of disbelief.

31. This included Christians, non-Christians, or ex-Christians. See, for example, chapters seven, eight, and nine.

32. Metonym is a figure of speech (a way of saying something) which allows one to interpret an event or a happening as a sign that the whole of which this event is a part also caused it. It should be kept in mind that my definition (see especially chapter eleven) is somewhat different from the usual one, which simply says that metonym "designates one thing by an object closely associated

with it (e.g., the "King" is called the "crown") (see Horner 1988: 447). Droogers (in chapter one) and Roelofs (in chapter ten) say they use metonym in my sense, but in fact do not or usually do not. My use of metonym is based on charismatic practice and a theory of rhetoric that argues that rhetoric is most effective when it imitates life, nature, or when figures "*demonstrate feeling*" and are "signs of a state of mind in the speaker" (Vickers 1989: 304, 303). As Cicero purportedly said: "For nature has assigned to every emotion a particular look and tone of voice and bearing of its own" (quoted in Vickers 1989: 66). In the case of happenings in the charismatic fold, for example, when charismatics are prayed over and fall down, which is referred to as "resting in the spirit," this event is interpreted as a sign that the Holy Spirit, who caused their falling, is working in their spirit and life. This small event is therefore a part of and caused by a much larger whole, namely God's presence. The causal aspect, which is important to what I call metonymic pattern of thought, is usually ignored. It is because of this neglect that I emphasized the importance of metonym (Poewe 1989), even though charismatics otherwise symbolize like any other human being.

33. Symbol here refers to metaphor. It should be remembered, however, that symbol is often used to refer to both metaphor and metonym. Thus Avery Dulles sometimes talks about a symbol as "a sign pregnant with a plenitude of meaning which is evoked rather than explicitly stated" (1992: 132). This usage, a symbolic sign, resembles what I mean by metonym. As I relate metonym and revelation, so he relates symbolism and revelation.

I

Methods and Models

Chapter 1

The Normalization of Religious Experience
Healing, Prophecy, Dreams, and Visions

André Droogers

ABSTRACT

The normalization model of religious experiences is a means of highlighting the fact that the interests of some social scientists have come to parallel in significant ways those of Pentecostals. Where this convergence occurs, it reflects an epistemological shift away from naive realism to existential holism. Secular scholars, scholars of diverse faiths, and Pentecostals who are uncomfortable with certain religious expressions can use this model to gauge how they, as observers, arrive at their judgment of why and in what sense religious experiences are or are not normal.

NORMALIZATION: PENTECOSTALISM

The term normalization suggests two things: that something abnormal has become normal and accepted; and that something formerly excluded or ignored is being included and given attention. What is it that has been accepted and made normal by Pentecostals? And what was formerly ignored but is now given attention? Quite simply, the answer is the desire to experience integrity and wholeness (Fernandez 1986a: 188-213; McGuire 1985: 276; Poewe 1989). This experience is contrasted with a life lived in fragmented or plural contexts.

The first kind of fragmentation that Pentecostals want to end is that of body from mind. It is their belief based on experience that mind, body, and spirit become one through healing, prophecy, dreams, and visions. Consequently, these practices are introduced into normal religious service and become part of normal religious practice.

Pentecostal acceptance of religious experiences to restore an individual's sense of wholeness represents a critique of Western culture. It does so for two reasons. First, Pentecostals oppose the generally accepted pluralization of one reality into many realities. They are uncomfortable with the fact that the experience of life has become partial and individuals have become "dividuals" (Fernandez 1986a: 188; 1986b: 160). Put simply, they oppose radical relativism. Second, Pentecostals oppose conceptual, if not moral, dualism. They tend to be particularly uncomfortable with the attitude of favoring one of a pair of opposites above the other; for example, reason above emotion, the profane above the secular, the mind above the body, and society above the individual.

It is this Western tendency to emphasize one of these poles above the other that is responsible for the fragmentation or pluralization of experience. For example, the sacred may be experienced in church (a defined space), and on Sunday morning (a defined time), but not in the restaurant, bedroom, or university. In North America, the secularization of healing is only stopped during revivals. Dreams and visions are assigned to the field of psychotherapy. Modern medicine isolates body from mind, the individual from her social context, and the patient's religious convictions from medical treatment. Morality and ethics are contextualized, theology and preaching rationalized, and clergy and laity divided.

On the whole, Pentecostals want to unite what others have divided. John Wimber's definition of power evangelism exemplifies this attitude. He talks about "a presentation of the gospel that is rational but also transcends the rational" (1985: 46). To Pentecostals unlimited choice between alternatives are symptoms of moral chaos. Most would prefer a more narrow and committed way of life, a life in which the choices are centered on the struggle for an authentic Pentecostal religious experience.

While Pentecostal churches can petrify (see Johannesen, chapter eight of this volume), they are dynamic as long as this struggle for authentic experiences, for experiences that can be read as signs that God is active in each individual life, continue. The process of signification, of viewing happenings as metonyms, as part of and caused by an active God (Poewe 1989), is responsible for the paradoxical coexistence of narrowness and openness in Pentecostalism (see Poewe, chapter eleven of this volume). Even the Pentecostal sense of wholeness is paradoxical: it *is* and it is also yet to be.

This dynamism has interesting consequences. Opting for wholeness also means that Pentecostals, once they have taken advantage of what David Martin (1990) calls "free social space," subsequently tend to limit it. Pentecostals do not subscribe to Thomas Jefferson's tolerant and pluralist view that it does not matter whether your neighbor believes in one or in twenty gods. As far as the future of humanity is concerned, most Pentecostals have some form of theocracy in mind. In a sometimes ambitious manner, they make plans for the evangelization of the world. Because Latin America has been Catholic for almost five centuries does not mean that one day it cannot be evangelical (Stoll 1990a: xiii, 42–67, 308; see also Martin, chapter three of this volume). Pentecostal expansion, therefore, should not only be explained in social and political terms, but also in terms of the ideal as defined by Pentecostals themselves. In other words, Pentecostal ideals might throw new light on their political practices.

At this point, the question should be raised as to whether the Pentecostal proposal also presents a solution to the dichotomy between individual and society. Here the Pentecostal position is rather complicated. Opting for the rehabilitation of the body, the sacred, and the emotion is not matched by an equally clear rehabilitation of either the individual or society. In Western culture, it seemed superfluous to rehabilitate the individual. Moreover, Pentecostals reflect society's dominant individualism. They have been accused of one-sided individualism, based on personal conversion.

Nor have Pentecostals worked society into the whole scheme of things since society is viewed as evil. Instead, they seem to have reduced their social field from society as a whole to their own church or, at most, the Pentecostal movement. In other words, society is only important as material for change. While Pentecostalism expands across the world, it attempts to do so on its own terms. Here too, therefore, Pentecostals surrendered to a new form of one-sidedness.

Yet, wholeness is not totally absent from the Pentecostal view of society. A special aspect of the relation between the individual and social dimension in Pentecostalism is the return of the religious initiative to people who had been denied access to the religious means of production. The exclusive monopoly of the clergy was broken by a formerly excluded laity. Furthermore, it was broken by individuals who had dreams and visions and were inspired by a dramatic religious experience. In that sense as well, religious experience was normalized. Lay believers felt part of the whole again.

But there is more to say about the Pentecostal sense of the relation between individual and society. Expansion is essential to the Pentecostal movement. The goals of evangelistic campaigns illustrate that ultimately the message is meant for the whole of humanity. Society is viewed as evil, but precisely for that reason it is the arena where Pentecostals must operate. The community of believers, of "brothers and sisters," is a micromodel of society as it should be. The expectation that this goal will be attained is nourished by eschatological, or—better yet—apocalyptic views. In this manner, the relation between the individual and society is defined in a very specific way.

Other Pentecostal preferences regarding the above-mentioned dichotomies have not escaped the critical eye of mainstream Christianity and theology. For example, while the body received attention as something to be healed, even to be used as a mode of expression in dance and song, in matters of sexuality Pentecostals are silent until their fold is rocked by scandal. Likewise, the sacred may have become the normal, but sometimes in a totalitarian way, taking away the very spiritual liberation that it promised. Emotion was welcomed, but as theologians often complain, it is not a good theological counselor. As a consequence, the rationality of Pentecostal theology was said to have remained shallow. Furthermore, the creativity stimulated by the Spirit is often stifled by a reactive fundamentalism and discipline. Prophecy can become subject to censorship. As Stanley Johannesen shows in chapter eight, the church may die. In short, Pentecostal acceptance of religious experience is limited to the area of Pentecostal expansion and does not necessarily become the norm outside it. The ideal is not always realized so that a Pentecostal is, as mentioned above, in a constant struggle to encounter the authentic Pentecostal religious experience.

Is the desire for an authentic religious experience something new or is it the restoration of something that was potentially always present, as Karla Poewe suggests when she talks about a "First Century Christian schema" (1989: 369)? Taking into account the process of secularization and the tidal movements of church history, I am inclined to see normalization as a restoration of a deeply rooted century-old habitus.

In the case of the Third World, a sense of wholeness seems to have been present all along. It would be stereotypical and erroneous, however, to say it was characteristic of a non-Western worldview. Nevertheless, a striking example of Third World wholeness is Roberto DaMatta's characterization of Brazilian society. In his words, it "lavishly presents combinations and connections that are, at first sight, completely out of place or even impossible" (1988: 125). One might say that, in coming to the Third World, Pentecostalism met part of its own roots. It is not surprising, therefore, that Western Pentecostal expansion should have been brought about, in part at least, by non-Western evangelists.

NORMALIZATION: THE SOCIAL SCIENCES
OF RELIGION

Not only have religious experiences been accepted as normal by Pentecostals, they have also been accepted as normal by social scientists. Ever since Marx, Durkheim, and Weber, patriarchs of the sociology of religion, defined the field a fundamental question has been how religion, scientifically an apparent illusion and deviation, could continue to exist. The fact that religion represented the opposite of science and was even defined as pertaining to a reality not open to scientific verification made the scientific study of religion an ambiguous job. In a way, one of the parties in the dispute was simultaneously the presiding judge. Science as a product of a certain era was biased because that same era had reduced religion's relevance and could not have done so without the rise of science.

This had far-reaching consequences for the scientific study of religion. The fact that religious views were thought to be illusory did not help the process of explaining religion. Since religion itself could not be interrogated as a witness, the tendency was to explain religion by way of nonreligious factors. The emphasis was on function, rather than on religious experience. In so far as the social functions of religion were teleologically taken as a satisfactory explanation, it was not even necessary to refer to religious beliefs or experiences. The fact that many of these functions were shared by totally different religions as well as by nonreligious institutions meant the explanation was not sufficiently specific. The nature of religion, in contrast to other institutions, was not always recognized. An exception should be made for Weber, who devoted attention to motivation and signification, and thus to the specificity of religion.

In this context, the expression "the normalization of religious experience" can also be read as pertaining to the restoration of the relevance of religious contents to the social sciences' treatment of religion (see here also Poewe, chapter eleven of this volume). An unequivocal expression of this tendency comes from Jan van Baal, the nester of the anthropological study of religion in the Netherlands who, in a short book in Dutch called *Mysterie also Openbaring* (1990; Mystery as Revelation), made the methodological suggestion that the religious be taken as normal and not as deviation. Rubem Alves, a Brazilian, gave another example when he ended his short introductory book on the sociology of religion, *What Is Religion?* (1984), with the statement, "it is more beautiful to risk on the side of hope than to have certainty on the side of a cold and senseless universe" (90).

The present Western religious situation could stimulate an approach to the study of religion in which religion itself is taken into account, and not just its role in society. Some publications on the future of religion have confirmed that religion is surviving in modern Western culture and that secularization is not the only process of religious change currently taking place (Hammond 1985; Luckmann 1990; Stark and Bainbridge 1985). Though this is not a sufficient reason to rehabilitate religious contents in the social-science approach to religion, it means the presupposition that religion would ultimately disappear has become less self-evident. This opens up possibilities for an approach that takes religion itself more seriously.

Efforts have recently been made to show how the study of religion should incorporate the idea of wholeness. This is not only relevant to Pentecostalism, but also to the social-science approach to the study of religion. Examples include van Baal's book *Man's Quest for Partnership* (1981) and James W. Fernandez's article "The Argument of Images and the Experience of Returning to the Whole" (1986b: 159–87). In both cases, religion is said to restore an experience of unity and of belonging to nature and to society in face of the human condition of feeling apart. Here, too, the problem is how to deal with a fundamental dichotomy. This question is answered in the context of a *scientific* discussion on religion. Yet, the emphasis on religious experience could also be interpreted as a fundamental *religious* insight.

Other authors have written on related topics. Though restricted to certain moments, Victor Turner's concept of "Communitas" did include the social aspect of the experience of wholeness. Ralph W. Hood observed that in the study of mysticism the relationship to the sacred cannot be ignored (1985: 285). He stressed the experiential basis of religious institutions and dogmas (287), yet he cautioned against the risk of methodological theism because it may close the researcher's eyes to the social context of mysticism (289).

With regard to Western dualist thinking, it is interesting to note Meredith B. McGuire's suggestion that religious healing be linked to the emotional *experience* of illness and shaped through symbolic interpretation, so that the human body be reintegrated into the social sciences of religion (1985, 1990). Mark Johnson urged us to put "the body back into the mind" (1987: xiv; see also Connerton 1989). Daniel Moerman held that the Cartesian understanding of body and mind as separated elements hampered the understanding of healing processes in which symbols play a central role (1979). In gender studies, a rehabilitation of the body was defended by Michèle Barrett (1988). An interesting parallel in theology is Walter J. Hollenweger's *Erfahrungen der Leibhaftigkeit* (1979a; Experiences of Embodiment).

In a much wider and more methodological sense, several authors propagate a move beyond the unilateral interpretation of dichotomy and an integration of opposite poles into one model (e.g., Bourdieu 1978; Giddens 1984; Ortner 1984, 1989; Sahlins 1985). This move might be called a practice, or praxis, approach (Ortner 1984). Attention is devoted to the integration, through praxis, of liberty and determination, actor and structure, event and structure, the social and the symbolic, matter and idea. In this approach, power relations are emphasized: How is the behavior of an actor influenced by that of other actors and by the social and symbolic structure of his context? To what degree does the actor transform other people's behavior as well as the structures he lives by? Power refers not only to the influence one actor has on another, but also to the control over or access to resources—social, symbolic, material, or supernatural. The approach is essentially holistic and parallels the interest in wholeness mentioned above. It allows for interdisciplinary work. The emphasis is on contextualized, historical processes. The role of the researcher as a subject is not hidden, but is open to reflection (Parkin 1982). Whatever is said about the researched as human beings should be applicable to researchers as human beings, even though each has a distinct role and need not share convictions. Moreover, in our example, the Western cultural context is common to researchers and Pentecostal believers alike. I can conclude this section and integrate the preceding one by observing that there is a parallel tendency of normalizing religious experiences in religion and in the social sciences. In both cases it is a reaction to the unilateral emphasis on one extreme of a duality. The exact form this normalization assumed is different in Pentecostalism and the social sciences. Yet, strikingly, in both cases rehabilitation of the individual, the body, the sacred, and emotion is at stake. Just as Pentecostalism can be seen as criticism of a one-sided use of at least some of the dualist poles, the recent proposals for a rehabilitation of the actor, the body, religious beliefs, and emotion in the social sciences of religion are a consequence of a similar objection to schemata that have become sterile. In both cases, religious experience is being normalized. Possibly, the tenacity of religion, of which the Pentecostal expansion is one example, has urged social scientists to rehabilitate religion in their explanations.

RELIGIOUS EXPERIENCE

Let us now turn to the term "religious experience." In line with the above-mentioned emphasis on praxis, *religion* can be understood as the actualization, within a social and cultural context, of representations and practices referring to God, gods, and spirits, or any other form of transcendence. This process is social and cultural in nature, actualizing not only religious representations and practices, but in an indirect way nonreligious symbolic and social structures as well.

The emphasis on praxis is in keeping with the theme of Pentecostal religious experience, especially because the holistic dimension of the praxis approach presents a framework for the study of the experience of wholeness. Because of its focus on the actor and the reproduction of culture, understood as *re*-production, a praxis approach devotes attention to experience, including religious experience. The anthropological tendency to opt for a holistic view can contribute to the understanding of religious experience and of its normalization.

Experience should be understood to include interpretation. Viewed from praxis theory, experience is always framed by culture. "Culture" here has a double meaning. Anthropologically speaking, it means that experience can be linked to the general concept of culture, in the singular, as the universal human capacity to produce and manipulate symbols, their meanings, and the patterns in which symbols, with their meanings, are brought together. This universal dimension allows for interpretation. It also facilitates global communication, as is now witnessed by the expansion of Pentecostalism.

Experience is also shaped by the culture in which it occurs. Culture should then be understood in a more restricted way as pertaining to the actualization, at a certain time and place, of a particular way of life, with its own pattern of symbols and meanings. In that sense, one talks not only about culture but also cultures. Experience can, therefore, never exist without a cultural framework, and contextualized religious experience can never be isolated from total experience.

So far I have used the general category of symbol. Poewe (1989: 370) suggested that in the case of charismatic Christianity it is worthwhile to distinguish, following Edmond Leach (1976), between metaphor and metonym. Perhaps because metonym was somewhat ignored in the study of religious phenomena, Poewe brought out its prevalence. She saw in the spread of charismatic Christianity a shift "away from a symbolic-rich to a sign-rich religiosity," which was correlated with "increased emphases on metonym rather than metaphor, on experience rather than cognition, on imagination rather than emotion, and on knowing how models of knowledge rather than propositional models of knowledge" (1989: 361). These distinctions are parallelled by the one between the researcher and the researched: "While academia seems preoccupied with text and genre, and the rarified world of metaphor, many at the grass roots level have returned to experience, 'life,' and a language empowered by metonyms" (375).

Since the theme of this essay is religious experience, and I have chosen to focus on wholeness, the distinction between metonym and metaphor is relevant. I am interested in the comparison of Pentecostalism and the social sciences' study of religion, which is another reason why Poewe's contrast between academia and the grass roots level is pertinent. Finally, my decision to include interpretation in the definition of experience leads to a slightly different view of the role of metaphor, since metaphor, as an instrument of interpretation, is as much an ingredient of experience as metonym. These general remarks will be elaborated upon in the rest of this section.

The first thing that should be clarified is that metonym and metaphor both refer to wholeness. Metonym, though itself a part, refers directly to the whole. My understanding of metonym, which differs somewhat from that of Poewe (1989, 1993b), is that a partial experience, within a sector of one undivided domain, can be generalized. Metaphor also returns the subject to the whole, but in a more indirect way. A metaphor pertains to two domains. What is clear in one domain helps the actor interpret the inchoate (Fernandez 1986b: 176) in another domain. Precisely because metaphor establishes a relation between two domains, individuals who see themselves as solitary within the plurality of their experience recover the sensation of relatedness through metaphor. Since it pertains to two domains, metaphor is less direct and less concrete than metonym. Nevertheless, the movement from the inchoate to understanding creates the sensation of wholeness, uniting the two domains, even more so if they hitherto seemed unconnected.

As Fernandez (1986a: 45) pointed out, the mere association of the two domains is based on the memory of earlier experiences with the two domains merged into one. Metaphors are not reinvented all the time, though the initial and surprising experience of discovering a relation between two unconnected domains is echoed when the metaphor is used anew. Retaking the metaphor, the speaker has to know in advance that the two domains are related. Only new or rarely used metaphors succeed in generating an authentic surprise. Metaphor and metonym both pertain to parts and wholes, the only difference being that in the case of metonym the parts are of the same nature, and in the case of metaphor they represent domains that are essentially different in nature and therefore initially unconnected. Metaphor and metonym are therefore closer than the distinction seems to imply. Like degrees of latitude and longitude, they belong together and help us draw the map of the symbolic world. Like degrees of latitude and longitude, they cannot be found in reality, but are useful concepts to describe reality.

If the two are closer than the distinction seems to suggest, this has consequences for the parallel between academics and metaphoric cognition, on the one hand, and believers and metonymic experience on the other. In view of the fact that the researcher's job is signification and that of the observer maintenance of distance, it seems understandable that academics often speak in terms of metaphor and even take symbol and metaphor as synonymous. Since the founding of the social sciences of religion, the supernatural and the natural—here including the social— have been viewed as two domains, one puzzling, the other more evident. This encouraged the reduction of religion to nonreligious factors.

Those who would refute a simplistic reductionist interpretation of religion do so with the argument that the religious domain can speak for itself. The relation between the religious and the social is not denied, but it is no longer a one-way street. Perhaps the social can be explained in terms of the religious. In that case, it is not religion, but the social domain that is the unknown. In other words, if the domains in a metaphoric comparison are not only distinguished but are also closely related, and if metaphor and metonym are closer than the distinction seems to suggest, the contrast between the researcher and the researched becomes less striking.

Baal's (1990) methodological suggestion would support this view. According to him, when we take the religious as normal and not as a deviation, researchers occupy a position much closer to that of believers, and the contrast is less definite. Researchers then discover the importance of metonym. In adopting such a stance, anthropologists simply do as they always have; they not only observe but participate as well. The recent emphasis on context and praxis, and on the importance of interaction between the researcher and the researched in the formation of knowledge, points in the same direction.

Even if a participatory approach is adopted, the researcher cannot depart from metaphoric thinking without giving up the academic profession. The idea is to keep moving between these two positions, the believers' and the academics' avoiding one-sidedness. A similar observation should be made with regard to the believer. Especially in the Pentecostal movement, experience—often dramatic and total, clearly within one single "twenty four hours a day" reality—is more important than reflection and signification. Metonym is then more important indeed. Healing, prophecy, dreams, and visions refer to God's presence in one single reality. They express the sensation of wholeness. The dualism between natural and supernatural disappears. The religious experience refers to one domain, not two. Yet the Pentecostal believer, particularly when reflecting on and testifying to his experience, cannot avoid signification and metaphor, as Poewe would agree (see introduction and chapter eleven of this volume). He will use metaphorical expressions like "It was as if . . ." The biblical report on the Pentecostal paradigmatic experience speaks of "tongues *as if* of fire." Jesus made ample use of metaphor when speaking in parables.

Moreover, if Baal and Fernandez are right in suggesting that the fundamental human condition includes a tension between being part and being apart, then metonym and metaphor have their own times and places, depending on the degree of participation. Since the Pentecostal experience of wholeness has to be reconquered again and again from pluralism and apartness, Pentecostals do not escape the basic metaphoric experience of two separated domains. Metaphor therefore retains its relevance to the Pentecostal case.

This brings us back to experience and praxis, pertaining to scholars and believers alike (A. Cohen 1985; Johnson 1987; Watts and Williams 1988). The processual nature of assigning meaning implies that scholars can consider adopting metonymic positions close to those of the believers. Believers, however, interpret while observing and can therefore also appeal to metaphor in order to testify to their experiences. The overpowering nature of this experience is too total to be solely expressed by metonymy. It needs metaphor as a complement to understanding.

It therefore seems in keeping with the tendency of the return to wholeness in Pentecostalism as well as in the social science study of religion that distinctions like those between metonym and metaphor should be seen in context and as relative, that is, in relation. Here, too, the problem is how to deal with dualism and dichotomy.

A MODEL OF RELIGIOUS PRAXIS

In order to facilitate the discussion of the case of Pentecostal expansion, I will now tentatively present a heuristic model based on the general suggestions made so far. The purpose of this model is to summarize my findings on the normalization of religious experience in Pentecostalism *and* in the social-science approach to this experience and religion in general. As heuristic instrument, it should help the operationalization of my abstract general questions. In academic activity, praxis similarly means actualization and reproduction (often re-production) of schemata and structures; in presenting the model I am actualizing other versions of that same model (Droogers 1990a, 1990b; Droogers and Siebers 1991). The model has been developed for the general study of the relation between religion and power, and might be tested on cases other than Pentecostalism.

In view of the preceding sections, what should the criteria be for the elaboration of this model? First of all, it should deal in a fair way with the basic dichotomies of individual versus structure, body versus mind, sacred versus profane, and emotion versus reason. It should reflect the rehabilitation of the actor, the body, the sacred, and the emotion. The rehabilitation of the sacred is of importance to the social-science explanation of religion and this should be reflected in the model. Particularly in dealing with healing, prophecy, dreams, and visions, this should be the case. The use of metaphor and metonym should be accounted for, even though almost by definition the model itself is metaphoric. By including metaphor and metonym, the emphasis should be on praxis as a way of dealing with wholeness. The approach is essentially holistic. The model should integrate the universal and the contextual dimensions. It should allow for cross-cultural application and comparison and clarify the dynamism of the contextual actualization and reproduction process. Power relations should have an explicit place in the model. Furthermore, the model should be applicable to the researched as well as the researcher. The researched person is not only an object (of structural influence, power, and scientific study) but also a subject (who acts). Likewise, the researcher is not only the subject of his research and the agent who interacts with the people he studies. He too is an object of structural influences, power relations, and research procedures. Remembering this increases our ability to evaluate the researcher's findings.

As a consequence, the model of religious praxis contains the following elements:

	External Secular	Internal Religious
Symbolic	External Symbolic Structure	Internal Symbolic Structure
ACTOR		
Social	External Social Structure	Internal Social Structure
NATURE		

The core of the model is the actor, individual as well as social, uniting body and mind. Within a specific context, he actualizes and reproduces the symbolic and social structures of his culture and society. A distinction can be made between internal and external symbolic and social structures. Nature is also part of this context. The actor lives in a holistic and dialectical relationship with social and symbolic structures and with nature: he is influenced by them and he transforms them. The actor contextualizes his humanness within space and event, creating a specific pattern of symbolic and social structures, oriented all the while by existing structures. A similar contextualization applies to the researcher when he tries to make sense out of seemingly inchoate experiences.

The internal symbolic structures contain the religious presuppositions and practices with regard to God, gods, and spirits. The actor feels a dialectical power relation with these entities. He may feel overpowered or empowered. The actor's position is expressed and interpreted through the use of symbolic instruments: metaphors and metonyms.

The internal symbolic structure of a religion positions itself with regard to the total symbolic structure of the culture in question. If the criterion for the distinction between church and sect is the degree to which compromises are accepted with secular values, this refers to a specific example of how a religion can position itself. In general the position of a religion is somewhere between a hostile and a tolerant attitude toward the external symbolic structure.

There are two kinds of social structures. There are those belonging to the religious group of the actor. They can be more or less hierarchical, leaving differing amounts of room for the lay believers. There are also the social structures of society, external to the religious group, but including other religious groups. As an individual, the actor has a dialectical relation with these two social structures. In both, power is again an important aspect.

Nature has always been important to religions. People felt part of nature but also excluded by it. Natural symbols, like fire and water, have been widely used. Nature as creation has stimulated believers' responsibility to nature as well as their sometimes ruthless exploitation of it. Environmental awareness is not new in religions. Nature makes itself felt when it fails to contribute to the actor's physical well-being and then stimulates the pursuit of religious interpretations.

The model is universal in that it fits general human characteristics but it can be illustrated via one concrete situation. It then becomes clear how social and symbolic structures are related in specific cases. Especially the religious dimension can be accounted for. Within this relation, power plays a central role. When applied to concrete situations, the model facilitates comparison as well as the study of cross-cultural transformation.

Most important for our study, the model applies to people who are being researched as well as the researcher. It may be used to make the researcher's role and presuppositions more explicit.

THE PENTECOSTAL CASE

Following the elements of the model, I will now apply the model to the case of Pentecostalism in its current expansion. A general, perhaps overly superficial, description will be given. It is possible to add details when applying the model to very specific and localized forms of Pentecostalism.

The emphasis on the actor is particularly fitting in the case of Pentecostalism. As a movement for the rehabilitation of lay experience, it focuses on individuals. Healing, prophecy, dreams, and visions, expressions of the physical experience of wholeness, are actor-centered bodily experiences. As individuals, Pentecostals are confident actors, not afraid to occupy their own position within their society. Though often socially marginal, they perceive themselves as a spiritual elite. They thus reshape the actualization of symbolic and social structures within that society, making their own selection and interpretation. Even though Pentecostals sometimes seem to withdraw from society, they also feel a special responsibility with regard to their society, seeking to transform it. Thus, they create their own version of the dialectical relation between the actor and his society or culture. The dynamism of this relation, ideally nourished by the Spirit's presence, demands an emphasis on praxis in the social science appraisal of Pentecostalism.

In the case of Pentecostalism, the relation with a trinitarian God is experienced as powerful, especially because of the emphasis on what the Holy Spirit does. Its role in creation and on Pentecost is continued in the life of the believer. Therefore, to the Pentecostal the belief in the work of God through Jesus and the Holy Spirit is the basis of a living relationship. The feeling of an overpowering and/or empowering presence of the Spirit is especially clear in the dramatic experiences of healing, glossolalia, prophecy, dreams, and visions that, therefore, become paradigmatic and are revived in every testimony given about them. The believer not only experiences this divine power but affirms that he shares in it and applies it in his relationship with other people. Because of the totality of this experience, it is primarily expressed through metonymy, with the partial experience of the single subject standing for the immeasurable totality of God's omnipresence. In reflecting on this experience, and testifying to it, the believer also appeals to metaphor, if only because it is difficult to directly express the totally different experience of God's presence.

The Pentecostals' praxis is a way of integrating religion and daily life. This leads to a desecularization of healing (McGuire 1985: 269), giving religious meaning to illness, thus going beyond the dualism of body and mind. "Illness is not a simple biophysical fact but—through symbolic interpretation—is shaped into human experience" (McGuire 1985: 272; see also Beck 1978). Through a "reconstructive play of tropes" (Fernandez 1986a: 194) the unitary character of experience is restored.

The external symbolic structure is met by the Pentecostal with distrust. The exclusive claims of the internal symbolic structure reduce the potential value of the external symbolic structure. Yet, as a member of society a Pentecostal believer cannot help but adapt to the essentials of that structure.

The internal social structure is thoroughly influenced by the central religious experience. Since this experience is, in principle, open to everyone, there is an antihierarchical tendency. The ministry of all believers is emphasized. Yet the prestige an extraordinarily gifted charismatic person may obtain makes for differentiation. Besides, the success of the Pentecostal form of religion and its subsequent institutionalization stimulate differentiation within the group between the leaders and the led. This change is symbolically legitimized. In this manner, the symbolic and social structures of a group are transformed in the course of time. With regard to gender, differentiation is almost always evident from the very beginning, through a literal interpretation of the biblical text. Women are often in the majority, but this does not mean they generally act as leaders.

The external social context has received a great deal of attention in the literature on the expansion of Pentecostalism, often at the expense of the religious factors (Droogers 1991). In explanations based on the compensatory function of religion, the lower-class position of many Pentecostals has been taken as a starting point. Where Pentecostal expansion accompanied urbanization, this explanation has been formulated in terms of the social vacuum migrants encountered in the cities. The church acted as a problem solver and presented new values appropriate to the urban situation. Reference has thus also been made to the Pentecostal aptness to adapt people to the process of modernization, creating hard-working responsible citizens prepared to climb the social ladder. Others have stressed how Pentecostal churches presented a modern variety of the rural semifeudal social structure, the urban pastor taking the place of the rural landowner. In all these explanations the power dimension occupies a central place. Pentecostalism is viewed as a means for lower-class people to find their way in society, as a strategy to participate in a complicated power process.

As has been observed, to the Pentecostals themselves, the external social structure often has the double connotation of evil and challenge. The influence of society on the believers is considered negative, including the influence of competing religious organizations. Yet the "evil world" is where new believers are recruited and where a new moral attitude is preached. This can take the form of political activity as long as it remains within the parameters of the church's attitude toward society. The personal relation with God, in obedience to His commandments, determines the nature of political activity. A literal reading of Romans 13 generally leads to respect for authorities and governments. While Pentecostalism is often seen as a form of popular religion and therefore has very little prestige in the eyes of wider society, Pentecostals themselves feel a certain pride and even superiority toward the rest of society. Experiences with healing and other charismatic gifts nourish this feeling of superiority. Real human destiny, they feel, does not depend on society's norms and views. This attitude is only possible because the personal relation with God gives the believers the certainty of being on the right track. Religious power, nourished by the experience of wholeness, is the basis for social behavior.

While nature is not explicitly valued in religious terms, it makes itself felt in the lives of Pentecostals. Where the growth of Pentecostalism is explained on the basis of problems with which people were confronted, nature becomes relevant. If and when illness is the cause of these problems, nature's role is obvious. Especially in Latin America, local growth has been linked to natural disasters like floods, droughts, and earthquakes.

My application of the model to the case of Pentecostalism has been very general. Yet, thinking of a particular church in a specific region, this general picture can gain in descriptive value. The model can be used for the description of differences within a church; for example, following the differentiation according to gender, or corresponding to the difference between leaders and ordinary members. If the transformation of a form of Pentecostalism, brought from one culture to another, is the subject of study, the model can help draw the comparison. If the comparison includes charismatic renewal in "mainstream" churches, Catholic and Protestant alike, the model can also be useful. Different versions of Pentecostalism, as exemplified in specific churches, can be compared using the model. The model can also facilitate a comparison between Pentecostal churches and mainstream Protestant churches. Even the different forms that the experience of wholeness may assume can be examined through the model.

When a case is studied, the unique and holistic combination of symbolic structure, internal and external social structures, and nature can become clear: how important healing is, whether glossolalia occupies an important place, how prophecy is valued, whether and how people interpret dreams and visions. A one-sided reduction to social factors can be avoided.

The model applies to scholars of religion as well. It can be used to obtain a more explicit frame of reference for their ideas, their presuppositions, their paradigms. Even if the actor's symbolic structure is not religious, it is relevant to the way Pentecostalism is appreciated. And even if the scholar is not a member of a religious group, the substitution of the term academic for religious, wherever it occurs, can produce interesting results.

One implication of the model remains to be shown. Following the emphasis on praxis, the model allows us to distinguish different modes of religious construction (Droogers 1990b; Droogers and Siebers 1991:

13–16). Thus, the first pair of modes refers to the internal symbolic structure and the believer's relation with God, gods, and spirits. In the revelatory mode of religious construction, the emphasis is on divine revelation, in the case of Pentecostalism, on the Spirit's workings. Especially in healing, prophecy, dreams, and visions, this occurs. The opposite is the explorative mode, where the emphasis is on the believer's activity in seeking the help of God, gods, or spirits. In the case of Pentecostalism, God empowers the believer to act.

A religious group's position with regard to the external symbolic structure can be anywhere between the extremes of a hostile and a tolerant mode of religious construction. The Pentecostal case is situated much closer to the hostile than the tolerant extreme of the continuum.

The internal social structure can also be described by means of a continuum between extremes. Depending on the power relations within the religious social field, a hierarchical mode, emphasizing the clergy's role, can be distinguished from an inclusive mode, with the laity dominant. Pentecostalism is basically an example of the inclusive mode of religious construction, but as we saw, tendencies in the direction of a hierarchical mode are present.

With regard to external social relations, a transformative mode of religious construction aimed at changing society can be distinguished from a respective mode, directed at legitimation. In the case of Pentecostalism the emphasis is clearly on the transformative mode, though the respect for authorities seems closer to a reflective mode.

Finally, the model suggests a continuum with regard to the attitude of the religious group toward nature. There are several possibilities, but perhaps the most pertinent is the one between a passive respectful and an active explorative mode of religious construction. In the case of Pentecostalism there seems to have been little reflection on nature.

CONCLUSION

The model of religious praxis developed in this chapter helps us become aware of several problems inherent in the study of religion. These problems are centered on the extent to which researchers and the people they research regard religious experiences as normal aspects of a wholesome human life. Starting with the assumption that religious experiences are normal aspects of both religious practice and social-science research frees us of tendencies to think dualistically and to explain religion away.

Chapter 2

Charismatic Churches in South Africa
A Critique of Criticisms and Problems of Bias

Irving Hexham and Karla Poewe

ABSTRACT

The charismatic movement of South Africa and the emergence of independent churches are local expressions of a global culture. Researching charismatic Christianity from a local-global dynamic requires that scholars criticize traditional methods of ethnographic fieldwork and representation and imagine new ones. Students are encouraged to become participant-observers of international networks, reconsider ideals of parallel invention and diffusion, discern transnational and transethnic issues and identities, study history, and research the diversity and creativity that occur within one and the same tradition.

INTRODUCTION

In the previous chapter André Droogers proposed a model that encouraged uniting opposites so that researchers and Pentecostal or charismatic Christians might proceed with their respective tasks of interpreting the world. Unfortunately, this is not easily done in the fractured environment of apartheid South Africa. Here, not only have Pentecostals and charismatics carved out their own symbolic and social worlds, but so too have adherents of other denominations and movements.[1] Furthermore, the stance of mainline Christians and Christian researchers is usually one of severe, indeed, exaggerated criticism of Pentecostals and charismatics.[2] Sociologists, for example, who combine their sociology with the religious presuppositions and practices of another denomination might not only criticize, but misrepresent, charismatic Christian thought and practices. Alternatively, theologians who operate from within the distinctive internal symbolic and social structures of another denomination combine their theology with sociological presuppositions and practices (what Droogers calls external symbolic and social structures) and likewise criticize and misrepresent South African charismatic Christians. Since these highly politicized criticisms have become an accepted part of the Western academic and public environment within which our research and publishing efforts take place, it is necessary that we address them.

In South Africa criticisms directed at charismatic Christians, especially those belonging to African or white-founded independent churches, are particularly severe. This is so because the critics assume that they themselves hold the correct political view so that those not sharing it are automatically classified as reactionaries or enemies.[3] Frequently, this judgment is reinforced by the claim that those with different internal symbolic and social structures to those of the critic are under foreign control, usually, that of the CIA or the American Christian Right. Assessments of the new independent churches by South African scholars, therefore, are always judged from political perspectives.

In this chapter we want to look at some of the popular and scholarly criticisms of charismatic independent churches. The focus will be on the methods and presuppositions of the critics. It is hoped that our criticism of their criticism will improve future research of this sensitive topic in a troubled part of the world.

CHARISMATICS AND THEIR CRITICS IN SOUTH AFRICA

Popular Reactions to Charismatics

As the chapters in this volume on Latin America, Korea, and Japan show, charismatic Christianity is controversial wherever it exits. This is particularly true of South Africa (Gifford 1989). Many members of mainline denominations, evangelicals, and traditional Pentecostals are upset about the charismatic movement and are only too willing to tell horror stories about its excesses, be they theological, financial, or sexual in nature, or simply a matter of disappointed hopes for healing and acceptance.[4]

Charismatic Christianity certainly produces a good number of disillusioned individuals (Barron 1987; McConnell 1988; Horn 1989). Indeed, researching these would be a useful separate project. Whenever the most severe horror stories were checked out, however, they turned out to be predictably exaggerated and frequently false. The exaggeration is predictable because in South Africa it tends to be focused on politics, in the

United States and Canada on financial and sexual corruption, and in Korea on shamanization.

For example, during our research in South Africa in 1987, we were told by a well-known Christian leader that Tim Salmon, of the Pietermaritzburg Christian Center, had helped a right-wing candidate defeat Graham Macintosh, a well-known evangelical Christian M.P., in the 1987 general election. When Salmon was interviewed by us he denied this and explained that as a Christian he felt it was his responsibility to encourage his congregation to think intelligently about the election. Therefore, he arranged a meeting in his church where both candidates were given the opportunity to speak. Later, we met Macintosh, who confirmed Salmon's account of the incident. The story that was circulated, however, focused only on the right-wing candidate because critics regarded his invitation to be politically incorrect. What is not understood by the general public is the fact that politicians of all positions have a tendency to lobby megachurches for support. We observed this not only in South Africa, but also in the United States and Canada. While this lobbying was often disliked and sometimes resented by the church leadership, it was tolerated.

On another occasion, in 1989, we met an evangelical Anglican minister and his wife in Stellenbosch. As soon as they discovered our research topic they told us that we ought to "investigate" the Rhema Church in Johannesburg because they "knew" that Rhemaites were distributing a particularly nasty right-wing, racist magazine.

When we told them that we had studied Rhema and had seen no evidence of their claim they assured us that we were wrong because they had "been told" by an "outstanding Anglican preacher that Rhema was a hotbed of reaction." They also argued that even if what we said was true during our visit in 1987, things had changed since then. Our trip to Johannesburg in 1989, however, did not support their claim. We did find, however, that American right-wing Christian literature was dumped in several churches across South Africa, and that many South African Christians found this practice deeply embarrassing and irritating.

Academic Criticism

Our research of charismatic independent churches was conducted between May and August of 1987 and 1989 in South Africa. This research, which consisted primarily of participant observation and intensive life history interviews, was followed by survey-type questionnaires in 1987, 1989, and 1990. The latter were returned by mail. We maintained contact with South African charismatic Christians by telephone and through meetings at international conferences in 1991 and 1992. This gives us a longitudinal perspective that revealed numerous changes in various churches and the national and international networks to which they were linked.

During 1987 our work was concentrated in Natal, especially Durban and Stanger, and in the Transvaal, especially Pretoria and Johannesburg. During 1989 we covered the Cape, especially Stellenbosch and Cape Town, and returned to look at developments in Johannesburg, Pretoria, and Durban. Furthermore, we looked at independent churches in black and "colored" Townships, including Soweto, Kwamashu, Mitchel's Plain outside of Cape Town, and a "colored" township outside of Bloomfontein. What impressed us was the complexity and diversity of the charismatic phenomenon in South Africa. Methodologically speaking, we saw ourselves doing fieldwork not in a specific village, church, or city, as is usually done (for example, Jules-Rosette 1975; Schwartz, chapter seven of this volume), but among charismatic Christians wherever they were found.

It is our experience of the creativity and diversity of the charismatic phenomenon that made us particularly aware of the short-comings of Morran and Schlemmer's 1984 study, *Faith for the Fearful?* This work and similar ones fail precisely because they lack time depth and spatial reach. Furthermore, Morran and Schlemmer researched only one independent church, the Durban Christian Center (DCC), and this at one short moment of its history.[5] Yet they make sweeping generalizations about all new charismatic Christians. While the Morran and Schlemmer study claims to be based on a survey, other studies are based primarily on newspaper reports and other existing literature. In other words, instead of doing original field research people quote one another. Particularly missing are intensive life-history interviews that reveal not only how charismatic Christians think and what they think about (Poewe 1989, chapter eleven of volume), but also the complexity of national and transnational links, influences, and processes of decision making.

Faith for the Fearful?

Let us look more closely at Morran and Schlemmer's book, which is the most popular academic work on the topic. *Faith for the Fearful?* made a big impact in South Africa during the mid-1980s by confirming the worst fears of mainline Christians about the charismatic movement.[6] Seemingly based on solid sociological evidence, it claimed to show that white charismatics who joined new independent churches were reactionary neurotics, fearful, powerless, politically homeless, and insecure (170, 179).[7] These findings were widely reported in the press (*Natal Mercury*, November 17, 1984; *Sunday Tribune*, November 18, 1984, among others).

Unlike earlier criticisms of new charismatic churches, this book did not look like the work of a disgruntled theologian (for example, Verryn 1983) or rival church leader concerned about the loss of members of his congregation to another church (see *Daily News*, March 25, 1982; *Sunday Express*, July 17, 1983; *Sunday Tribune*, July 31, 1983). Instead, Morran and Schlemmer's criticisms seemed to rest on valid sociological data and, therefore, could not be easily dismissed. Readers ought to have been alerted to potential problems, however, by skimming the book's preface and conclusion. There the authors make three revealing statements: They admit that their study was commissioned by the Roman Catholic organization Diakonia, which wanted to know why new churches grow and why, in their opinion, new charismatics did not share the Diakonia "interest in issues of social justice" (i); they state that Diakonia was concerned about "controversial teaching" and its "effects on social change in South Africa" (1); and they assert that they, and Diakonia, were concerned to alert established church clergy to "incorrect" or "heretical" doctrines of these new churches, presumably to warn off prospective followers (187). Together these three statements constitute clear presuppositions and a strong bias against the newly founded charismatic churches.

It is Morran and Schlemmer's claim that these new churches attract people of a "particular personality type, i.e., those who tend to be anxious, neurotic, or 'hysterical'" and who perceive their immediate and wider environment "as dangerous and threatening" (170). Consequently, they argue, new churches enhance "the authoritarian tendencies or traits of their members," making them "more politically conservative" than Christians in "established" churches (171) and supportive "of the status quo" (179).

Is the Morran and Schlemmer depiction accurate and based on sound sociological evidence? Morran and Schlemmer base their findings on a sample of twenty charismatics from established churches and thirty charismatics from the new churches. And, as stated above, all new church charismatics come from one church, the DCC. Established charismatics come from unnamed mainline churches in Durban.

Are new church charismatics fearful and insecure? And do they behave as if they perceived their environment to be dangerous and threatening? To answer these questions we shall briefly look at data from our questionnaires. More importantly, we then want to show the limitations of numbers by looking at some of the 120 life histories that we collected.

If insecurity is related to class and income, then charismatics offer a complex picture. Class and income composition vary from church to church and from city to city. For example, the DCC seemed to have a relatively soft middle class consisting primarily of white English-speaking South Africans, Indians, and some "coloreds." We shall use fifty randomly selected questionnaires for each of three churches to give a sense of the diversity.[8] Thus, sixty-nine percent of charismatics from the DCC identified themselves as being middle class, twenty-eight percent working class, and only three percent upper class. Many respondents hesitated giving their income. The highest family income mentioned was R 60,000, relatively low given the incomes elsewhere in this country. Twenty-two per cent described themselves as enjoying an above-average standard of living, forty-four percent average, twenty-two percent below average, and twelve percent far below average. One might argue that those with average to far-below-average incomes (a total of seventy-eight percent) are "insecure" and "fearful." Such is not the case, however, as we shall see shortly.

Before discussing Morran and Schlemmer's conclusions, let us mention figures for two other churches. Comparative figures for a new charismatic church in Stellenbosch were as follows: forty-two per cent identified themselves as middle class and thirty-two percent as working class, but a whopping twenty-six percent identified themselves as upper class. The last figure is probably conservative. Of the respondents, thirty-two percent were in the sciences, engineering, and mathematics, and said that they enjoyed an above-average standard of living. About twenty-five percent of the incomes exceeded R 100,000 per annum. The standard of living for the other two classes paralleled more or less their class affiliations. The ethnic composition of these respondents was thirty-two percent "colored," fifty-three percent white English speakers, and fifteen percent Afrikaners. It was primarily "coloreds" and Afrikaners who described themselves as working class.

Comparative figures for a new charismatic church in Johannesburg are different again. Seventy percent identified themselves as middle class, seventeen percent as working class, and thirteen percent as upper class. The percentage of people who said that they earned more than R 100,000 per annum was thirteen percent, half that of Stellenbosch but, of course, more than new church charismatics of Durban. Replies to the question on standard of living paralleled more or less their class affiliation. Furthermore, in this as in the Stellenbosch church, the middle class enjoyed fairly stable jobs, either professional or technical.

In agreement with Morran and Schlemmer, the middle class is well represented in many but not all of these new independent churches.[9] But people who classify themselves as being middle class are widely different from one another in terms of income, type of job held, and job security. For example, people who identified themselves as middle class in Durban had much lower incomes and much less secure jobs than people of that class in Johannesburg, Pretoria, Cape Town, or Stellenbosch. It looks, therefore, as if Morran and Schlemmer's observations that these people might be fearful and insecure could fit at least some people in the DCC. They are wrong only, one might argue, when they generalize beyond this church.

When one now takes into account a different set of data, namely, our intensive life histories, the picture changes significantly. People who on survey questionnaires look "insecure" and "neurotic" are optimistic and creative when one studies their life histories. Indeed, survey questionnaires, no matter how good they are, simply cannot capture the creativity, hope, and courage of individual charismatic Christians. Seemingly "fearful" middle- and working-class individuals at the DCC are often imbued with an entrepreneurial spirit. In this and other independent churches, we found many individuals who started small business ventures with blacks, "coloreds," and Indians. For example, blacks and whites or "coloreds" and whites started a restaurant, a panel-beating shop, boutiques, and other small businesses. One charismatic Christian, a "colored," started a trust to finance, especially, small black business ventures. Blacks, whites, "coloreds," and Indians, in various combinations, started multiracial ministries, church complexes, musical bands, and various other organizations that encouraged interracial social life, including dinners at one another's houses. At the time of the necklace violence in 1985 and 1986, blacks and whites went on fasts together and created works of art, including song lyrics, in an effort to envision a new South Africa. Some of these lyrics were heard across the world.

In short, participant observation and life-history interviews gave us a much more intimate picture of the charismatic Christian life. We observed people who were optimistic and trusting enough to imagine and risk new economic ventures and new social arrangements. Risk-taking of this sort is not associated with "fearful," "insecure," and "anxious" people (Drucker 1985: 13).

But are these new church charismatics "powerless," "politically homeless," and politically "more conservative" than mainliners? For the sake of brevity I shall mention a few figures. It is not the figures that are important, however, but the nature of their interpretation.

Respondents of the DCC, for example, might fit Morran and Schlemmer's depiction of them as "powerless" and "politically homeless." Fifty per cent gave no party preference, twenty-five percent said they were Progressive, nineteen percent National, and six percent Conservative. (In 1990 Progressives shifted their affiliation to the short-lived left-liberal Democratic Party.) Thirty-six per cent of respondents described their political views as confused while fifty-eight percent saw their views as liberal and moderate. Stellenbosch respondents, in line with the general political climate of the Cape, described themselves as primarily affiliated with the liberal Progressive Party (seventy-nine percent), eighty-four percent saw their political views as being moderately to extremely liberal, while most were somewhere in the middle between moderate and extreme. In 1989 one of the churches in Johannesburg surprised us by the high percentage of their affiliation with, and sympathy for, the Democratic Party. These people too described their political views as being moderate to liberal. When we looked at election returns for the respective regions, by the way, new church charismatics consistently came out somewhat more liberal than the general population of their districts.

But why are charismatic Christians less than enthusiastic about politics, and why in Durban, for example, did so many give no party preference? Why did thirty-six percent see themselves as politically confused?

According to mainline Christians, especially their spokespersons, South Africans cannot afford to be politically confused, homeless, and uncommitted. One has to make a choice, it is said, and the only good choice is affiliation with the African National Congress (ANC). At worst one must be against the status quo, which, before F. W. de Klerk became president of South Africa, meant the National Party.

New church charismatics have problems with this ultimatum. Everyone we interviewed was firmly against apartheid and racism, but they were equally strongly against violence and corruption. Much like that of Latin American charismatics (see Stoll 1990; Martin, chapter three of this volume), therefore, the South African charismatic stance was a "walkout." Their aim was precisely to create a space where they could imagine, indeed, live out a new South Africa independently of rigid ideological alternatives. In the long term these rigid political ideologies will, at any rate, prove themselves to have fallen short. Even before disclosures of National Party and ANC atrocities surfaced, even before the fall of the Berlin wall revealed the utter horror, corruption, and bankruptcy of Communism, new church charismatics had the integrity and courage to insist upon their own space. From the perspective of outsiders, therefore, it is not difficult to interpret the political stance of new church charismatics as courageous and that of the followers of either major party as coopted. But whatever one's interpretation, the initiative, entrepreneurship, cross-ethnic, cross-racial, and cross-national networking and assistance, all of which were commonplace among new church charismatics, were entirely praiseworthy. One should remember that these activities took place in a devastatingly adverse environment. Above all charismatic activities had to do with power, not powerlessness, and with a clear sense of home (Welbourn and Ogot 1966).

What has not been researched adequately is the role played by renewal movements, renewed churches, and charismatic independent churches, in providing the space where people dare to imagine the new and alternative. We have many excellent studies on millenarian movements of which the charismatic movement is, broadly speaking, a part (Wallace 1966; Burridge 1971; MacGaffey 1986, among others). But even these studies deal primarily with non-Western peoples. What we need are equally competent studies that look as much at white or multiracial contemporary Western peoples as non-Western ones.[10] Even David Chidester's *Religions of South Africa* (1992) does not include white-founded integrated charismatic churches.

GLOBAL ASPECTS OF SOUTH AFRICAN NEW CHURCH CHARISMATICS: DIFFUSION, INDEPENDENT INVENTION, AND PARALLELISM

Charismatic Christianity

Before looking closely at the simultaneous processes of spontaneous, parallel inventions as well as the worldwide diffusion of charismatic ideas, practices, and new church complexes, we must remind ourselves what is covered by the term "charismatic Christianity." The overarching category, charismatic Christianity, refers to an experiential form of Christianity that emphasizes the Holy Spirit of the Trinity, the gifts of the Holy Spirit, and, generally, a "Spirit-inspired" human creativity, vision, spontaneity, and sense of freedom.

The description, charismatic Christianity, is used to include independent churches, the Pentecostal and charismatic movements, and global charismatic networks and lay ministries. In South Africa, independent churches are African Initiated Churches (AICs). These are the African churches that originated from the people and were not "initiated by Europeans or Americans or other outsiders" (Makhubu 1988: 2; see also Poewe 1988). AICs include Zionists, Ethiopians, and Pentecostals (Sundkler 1961, 1974; Makhubu 1988). Most of these churches were started in the late 1800s or early 1900s. They grew rapidly and split often, but remained dynamic.

South African charismatic Christianity also includes what have been called "new church charismatics" (Morran and Schlemmer 1984), neo-Pentecostal churches, or new independent churches (NICs). These churches grew out of the charismatic movement of the 1960s, either through splits from mainline churches or independently from informal prayer and bible-study groups. Like the AICs, founders of these churches were motivated to act following very specific individual religious experiences, which occurred in very specific and personally meaningful contexts and yet were of a pattern. It is as if very elementary ideas (see Bastian 1860), or what Wilhelm P. Schmidt (1913) called *Uroffenbarungen* (primitive revelations), occurred over and over again in diverse folk contexts where they were then recorded orally, on audio or video tapes, or in popular books, and then disseminated (Koepping 1983).

NICs vary greatly in terms of central themes or doctrines, composition of people, political leanings, and so on. They are usually racially and ethnically integrated or strive to be. Given the variation in core values and political predilections, NICs fall into different streams, networks, and/or affiliations. In line with the importance of an experiential religion, these churches are rooted in specific local contexts. At the same time, and in line with the emphasis on vision and creativity, these churches are always also transnational, international, or global.

Like Pentecostalism and the AICs years ago (Synan 1971; Poewe 1988), so the NICs stand accused of being American creations; financed, controlled, and dominated by the American Christian Right (Ruether 1989: 61–63; Ruether quotes Gifford 1988). Since financial independence through tithing and generous giving, and the international circulation of funds, is discussed elsewhere, we want here to look at the complexity of international networks and relationships in order to dispel the notion that these churches are dominated by America.

The explanations that Paul Gifford (1990), Mary de Haas (1986), and Ove Gustafsson (1987) give for the spread of charismatic Christianity most obviously resemble the old diffusionism of Grafton Elliot Smith and William Perry, who in the 1920s argued that the Egyptians carried sun worship and other cultural elements to the corners of the world (Stocking 1987: 288). Only today it is not the material and spiritual culture of the Egyptians but the right-wing Christianity and "prosperity gospel" of Americans that are said to be exported globally. Furthermore, while Egyptian culture was an instrument of ennoblement, American culture is seen as an instrument of subversion (Gifford 1988: 13–24, 27–31).

Our data certainly show that the diffusion of ideas, especially once these were transformed into successful church complexes and ministries, was a major characteristic of a movement that is thoroughly at home in a high-tech world. Evangelists and prophets from different countries talk frequently at international conferences and urban megachurches across the world. And if they do not travel personally, their audio and video tapes do. Furthermore, many large independent churches publish and distribute testimonies and biographies of various founders of independent churches and ministries (Steele 1986; Michell 1985; Garlock 1981; Boyd 1991, among many others). This diffusion of success stories, however, does not explain how and why the ideas that underpin them are taken up, or why similar ideas occur simultaneously in various parts of the world. Furthermore, the rapid circulation of ideas makes it largely impossible, indeed irrelevant, to determine where anyone idea emerged first.

We turn now to first look at the big picture; namely, the fact that we are not only witnessing a re-Christianization of the world but also a re-Islamicization and a re-Judaicization (Kepel 1991), and we remind the reader that the charismatic renewal occurred in Zulu Anglican churches two decades before its latest manifestation in the United States (Hayes 1990). Finally, and most important, we describe the different streams of charismatic Christianity in South Africa and their differential linkages and linkage emphases to different parts of the world.

The Big Picture

It is our view and that of Gilles Kepel (1991), among others, that the "re-religionization" of the world has something to do with the global breakdown of modernity, most obviously since the 1970s. The five world religions, Judaism, Islam, Buddhism, Hinduism, and Christianity, have inspired folk or urban popular movements that seem to criticize a widespread sense of inner disintegration, anomie, dislocation, and, most important, the absence of an overall perspective. These movements substantiate the view of Adolf Bastian, a nineteenth century German anthropologist who conducted what can only be called global research, that folk religions arise everywhere from the deep yearnings of people (Bastian 1860; Koepping 1983).

There is a sense, especially in a country such as South Africa, that the necessary change is so fundamental that no amount of social engineering, the baby of the Enlightenment, would help. What is required is nothing short of a major cultural reorientation, a new vision of the world that incorporates as equals, or otherwise addresses, such issues as ethnic minorities, women, gays, handicapped people, African contributions to world culture, the poor, and so on. All interviewed founders of independent churches had visions to change their city, South Africa, and finally the world. All started their ministries following specific religious experiences in specific local contexts guided, in the first instance, by specific local Christians.

In South Africa the drama of this cultural reorientation is played out in four major, ever changing streams of what once was the charismatic movement. In the late 1980s these consisted of the Faith, or Word-Based churches, the Vineyard churches, the restoration movement, and the neo-Pentecostal churches (Morphew 1989). The restoration movement forged links primarily to Britain, but increasingly to Asia, East Germany, and Eastern Europe. Some founders of the Faith-Based churches were first inspired, directly or through readings, by Kenneth Hagin, Kenneth Copeland, and Bob Mumford of the United States. The Vineyard churches cultivated some links to the Californian John Wimber, who himself was first inspired by Third World students (Wimber and Springer 1986). The neo-Pentecostal churches were linked almost indiscriminately to similar churches across the world. Finally, in 1991 and in response to local political pressures, a new stream was formed, the Pentecostal/Charismatic Fellowship of Churches in South Africa. It was headed by Ray McCauley, who founded the largest Word-Based church in South Africa. His involvement with this fellowship signaled considerable rethinking and deeper commitment to political change in South Africa.

In short, a multisource diffusion of parallel developments encompasses Europe, Africa, America, and Asia. These parallel developments are grounded in core ideas and elementary religious experiences that are told to a pattern within the discourse of Christian testimonies (Lawless 1988:12–13; Poewe 1989: 370–73). They are then taped, filmed, or published and disseminated.

The Charismatic Movement among Black Anglicans

Earlier we argued that the NICs, whose founders were white, black, so-called "colored," or Indian, have been largely ignored in the academic literature. Stephen Hayes (1990: xi) argues that the charismatic renewal movement among black South African Anglicans has especially been ignored. Even John de Gruchy, an internationally respected observer and author of religious developments in South Africa, could not find a publisher for his work on the history of charismatic renewal movements in South Africa (personal communication 1989; also in Hayes 1990: xi).

To make up for this inadequacy Hayes and Richard Shorten (1987a, 1987b) researched and published accounts of the Iviyo lofakazi bakaKristu (Legion of Christ's Witnesses). Iviyo is a "charismatic renewal movement within the (Anglican) church of the Province of Southern Africa" (Hayes 1990: ix). Because this movement started earlier than the American charismatic renewal and speaks, for that reason, against the claim of American domination, it is important that we review it.

The Legion of Christ's Witnesses, not to be confused with the Catholic Legios of Kenya discussed in chapter seven, is an African initiated charismatic renewal movement that appeared in Natal and Zululand, South Africa, in the 1940s, twenty years before a similar movement originated in the United States at Van Nuys, California

(Hayes 1990: 9). Its name makes clear its intent to be evangelistic, and indeed this movement spread beyond its place of origin. Why has this charismatic movement been ignored? Primarily, argues Hayes, because it is preserved in oral history and because Americans have the resources to publish developments in their country independently and before those of other countries (see Hollenweger, chapter nine of this volume).

Like more recent renewal movements Iviyo was started by individuals responding to local concerns. Its founders, Alpheus Zulu (later Bishop of Zululand) and Philip Mbatha, were concerned with "the lack of power in the life of the church" and with "the failure of the church" to affect people's lives (Hayes 1990: 1). Consequently, they "studied scriptures and prayed together about this problem" (1). The movement spread beyond Zululand when they prayed with a youth leader and her young charges in the early 1950s. Soon gifts of the Holy Spirit began to appear, especially, the gifts of tongues, prophesying, and healing, the very gifts, it should be mentioned, that have always been part of African religion (Iliffe 1987; Oosthuizen 1988).

Though the data is inadequate, it is clear that this renewal movement among black South Africans attracted people of all walks of life, including clergy, teachers, doctors and nurses, clerks, chiefs, government officials and politicians, and many others who did not fall into Western professions (Hayes 1990: 5). Likewise, this movement soon forged links with similar movements among South African Roman Catholics, the Christian Businessmen's Fellowship, Derek Crumpton's Christian Interdenominational Fellowship (CIF), and the Scandinavian Baptist mission. Members of Iviyo also made contacts with an Argentinean Pentecostal evangelist and other visitors to South Africa (12, 14, 15).

The absence of American influence at the inception of Iviyo is notable. Since Derek Crumpton modelled CIF after the "Fountain Trust in Britain" (12), his contact with the movement did not lead to any American influence either. Crumpton, furthermore, told Hayes that he witnessed white lay representatives from other parishes experience the baptism in the Holy Spirit under Iviyo preaching (16). To us this is not surprising, since we witnessed similar white responses to black preaching and prophesying on numerous occasions during our research. In short, if there was any influence, it was from black to white, not the other way around, and certainly not from America.

South African Streams and Global Links

It is quite clear that the emergence of renewal movements requires neither white nor American ideas. Indeed, Christian revivals started more than once among black South Africans (Hayes 1990; Poewe 1988;

Sundkler 1961). Contrary to Gifford, therefore, it can hardly be said that South African revivals were "directed from the USA" by the Christian Right (1990: 382).

But, it may be argued, while black revivals were not directed from the United States, the latest white renewal and the subsequent formation of independent churches certainly were. To dispel this assertion, we direct our attention to white founded, integrated independent churches that grew out of the charismatic renewal movement in the late 1970s. Where appropriate, however, we say something about the numerous black, "colored," and Indian founded churches and ministries and their national and international links.

To understand the diversity of influences we shall first look briefly at three founders of independent churches and ministries within the Faith-Based churches. Then we describe the links and influences of three founders within the restoration movement.

The founder who is most accused of being a South African clone of an American evangelist, in this case of Kenneth Hagin, is Ray McCauley. McCauley founded Rhema, an independent twelve thousand member church in Johannesburg. To assess the importance of American influence on McCauley or Rhema, we define international links in terms of McCauley's visits abroad, the visits of American and other evangelists and prophets to Rhema, and the distribution of videos, tapes, and television.[11] There is not enough space to describe the very personal experiences and contexts that persuaded these founders to realize their visions in the first place. Rather, we look at the global links that founders forged and favored thereafter.

Until 1989, McCauley ministered regularly in five countries, usually four in any one year. These countries included Germany, Australia, England, Norway, and the United States. His German connection at this time was solely through Reinhard Bonnke, a German evangelist who once lived and worked in South Africa. In 1989, McCauley's American base began to expand from the Hagin Ministries to others. At this time, influential visitors to Rhema were primarily from the United States. While Rhema's bookstores had many tapes of American evangelists, it had many more of local speakers. As well, already in 1988 Rhema exported tapes to Europe, South America, Australia, New Zealand, Hong Kong, and South and Central Africa. In other words, even at this time Rhema was influenced by European countries and Australia about as much as by America. Likewise, McCauley influenced ministries in these countries. The friendship with German Reinhard Bonnke, by the way, was first formed in South Africa.

From 1990 on, the linkage patterns shift to a greater emphasis on Europe, including for the first time an East European country.[12] Thus, in

1990 McCauley ministered as usual in Germany, Norway, Britain, and the United States, but he added a new link in Germany, he expanded links in Britain, and he added Portugal and Hungary. The last two countries were visited on the invitation of Reinhard Bonnke. Visitors to Rhema included about fourteen from the United States, four from Europe (Germany, Norway, Sweden, and Wales), and one from Zimbabwe. Rhema tape exports increased.

McCauley's visits abroad increased and expanded further in 1991 and 1992 to include Czechoslovakia, Zimbabwe, and Zaire. His links to Australia multiplied as well, the number of American conferences attended decreased, and he visited Europe several times. During 1991, he also took on a new importance in South Africa itself. He became President of the Pentecostal\ Charismatic Fellowship of Churches in South Africa and was part of the politically important Rustenburg Committee, which included Frank Chikane, President of the South African Council of Churches. Prominent visitors to Rhema included six Americans, four Europeans, and one Zimbabwean. That year, too, he started a television program that he exported in 1992 to Bophuthatswana and the United Kingdom.

The linkage patterns of Ed Roebert, founder of Hatfield, an independent church in Pretoria, and Nicky van der Westhuizen, who runs an independent evangelistic ministry, are significantly different from that of McCauley. Both founders cultivated primarily links to other churches and ministries within South Africa. Van der Westhuizen had contacts with Paul Lutchman, an Indian evangelist from Chattsworth, Michael Kolisang, a black evangelist from Lesotho, and several other black evangelists, one of whom was a former member of the ANC. Both van der Westhuizen and Roebert had regular contacts with Fred Roberts of the DCC, Tim Salmon of the Maritzburg Christian Center, Ray McCauley of Rhema, and, less so, Theo Wolmarans, founder of Christian City in Johannesburg. The latter modeled his program at Christian City after Paul Yonggi Cho (discussed in chapter five this volume). All were influenced by Reinhard Bonnke, through whom Westhuizen made his black contacts. Bonnke's early ministry was primarily to black South Africans as well as the rest of the African continent.

In 1989, Ed Roebert headed the International Fellowship of Christian Churches (IFCC), with which more than two hundred independent South African churches were affiliated. Roebert did not want any American influence in the IFCC (Roebert 1987, 1989), although Benny Hinn, a popular American evangelist and friend of McCauley, was a member. Roebert had contact with Reinhard Bonnke of Germany and the prophet Roger Teale of Britain, but he had no direct links with the United States.

Van der Westhuizen's only American link was the evangelist Morris Cerulla. Both van der Westhuizen and Roebert have, however, read American books on the charismatic movement, including John Sherrill's *They Speak with Other Tongues* (1965) and Dennis Bennett's *Nine o'Clock in the Morning* (1970). They have also read material about the Lutheran Harald Bredesen, who was baptized in the Spirit at a Pentecostal summer camp in 1946, and was encouraged by the South African David du Plessis. Du Plessis in turn was encouraged by Africans in Basutoland. While his parents had contact with John G. Lake of Zion City, Illinois, and William J. Seymour of the Azusa Street revival, Los Angeles, California, David du Plessis was baptized in the Spirit at a meeting held by an English evangelist. These popular testimonies and stories were circulated during the charismatic movement and were listened to, or read, for the purpose of legitimating spiritual experiences, especially tongues, voices, and visions. Both van der Westhuizen and Roebert entered the charismatic movement through the influence of local ministers from the Apostolic Faith Mission and a Methodist church, respectively.

The influences on Dudley Daniel, founder of the New Covenant Ministries, Chris Wienans, co-founder of the young Glenridge church, and Derek Morphew, founder of Cape Fellowship Ministries, are significantly different from the above. Loosely affiliated with the restoration movement in Britain, all three have ties primarily to Europe, Australia, India, China, Hong Kong, Taipei, Singapore, and increasingly East Germany and eastern Europe. The three cultivate close ties to one another and to Derek Crumpton and Johan Filmalter, founder of an Afrikanaer independent church, both of South Africa. Morphew in turn cultivates friendships with Roger Petersen and Clive Dutlow, of the Mitchel's Plain Fellowship and the Koinonia Foundation. Petersen and Dutlow, a research scientist at Cape Town University, are so-called "coloreds," and along with Morphew, enjoy close links with Joseph Kobo, a black evangelist who heads Light from Africa Ministries (LIFA), and David Mniki, a black missions man who studied under David Bosch, professor of theology, at the University of South Africa (UNISA).

The various evangelists and church founders who are associated with Cape Fellowship Ministries are on the whole well educated. Morphew has a Ph.D. in religious studies from the University of Cape Town (UCT). Peter Twycross, who runs an integrated independent church in Stellenbosch, has an M.A. in theology from Oxford. Several others have B.Th.'s from UNISA or Rhodes University.

Finally, it should be mentioned that other South African founders, evangelists, and prophets cultivated links with Yonggi Cho of South Korea. Dudley Daniel, who headed New Covenant Ministries, has since moved to Australia, as have two other prominent founders of independent churches in his network. They now run Coastlands International Christian Center and New Covenant Ministries in that country. It is their interests in the Far East that in turn affect related churches in South Africa, just as their South African experiences affect churches in Australia and the Far East.

CONCLUSION

The intent of this chapter was to dispel some serious prejudices against the charismatic movement and the various independent churches, be they AICs or NICs. To do so we criticized not only badly flawed sociological works, or theological ones purporting to be sociological, we also presented alternative data and hinted at a new way of conducting fieldwork. Survey-type questionnaires were incapable of showing what was most unique about charismatic Christians, namely, their daring visions, creativity, patterns of thought, and their energy, courage, and trust to actualize these visions. Consequently, much of what was written here came from numerous life-history interviews. Furthermore, our awareness of the great variation in matters Christian, economic, or political came from a slight modification of a standard anthropological method. Instead of being participant observers in one church or one community, we became participant observers of charismatic Christianity at large. In other words, we became participant observers of a phenomenon, or of an international community, whose members defined themselves in terms of a first-century Christian schema rather than territorial space, skin color, or ethnicity. In fact, not only did we cover a substantial number of churches in different regions and among different racial and ethnic groups of South Africa, we also looked at major independent churches in western Canada, the southeastern United States, Britain, and Germany. It is this international perspective that brought home the lesson that North American and European churches are as deeply affected by African, Asian, and Latin American churches as vice versa. But this would make another book.

For future students of this phenomenon, however, several lessons are clear. More work needs to be done on renewal movements among peoples who are still part of primarily oral cultures (Ong 1982). Likewise, serious research has yet to be done on white-founded independent churches.[13] Because they are white and often middle class, these churches are either ignored or dismissed as something embarrassing and incorrect. White charismatic Christians practicing an oral and experiential religion are taken to be somehow akin to what Karl-Heinz Kohl (1987: 10) called *kulturelle Überläufer* (cultural deserters), because they are said to have sold out to the American Christian Right, to American capitalism, or because they are looked upon as having gone embarrassingly native. As Margaret Mead was able to probe with equal thoroughness the sexual customs of Samoans and Americans (see Marcus and Fischer 1986: 160), we have been able to probe equally white and nonwhite charismatics. This volume corrects at least somewhat a grave imbalance in our research methods, theories, and findings.

Finally, the noticeable recurrence of elementary ideas and religious experiences, and the adoption of both indigenous and foreign religious discourses to make sense of them, should encourage us to reexamine earlier ideas about diffusion, independent invention, and parallelism. As Klaus-Peter Koepping (1983) says about Bastian, his ideas and those of Wilhelm P. Schmidt (1923) and Leo Frobenius (1933) are relevant to contemporary anthropology (see also Brandewie 1990). They are particularly relevant to the study of charismatic Christianity.

NOTES

1. See the introduction to this volume.
2. I might add the reverse is also the case. It is, however, another story.
3. For a similar view in a more mellow political environment see Coleman 1991. Coleman discusses the *Word of Life* movement (a Swedish version of the prosperity gospel) with its international economic and high-tech links that, for this very reason, is seen as threatening by the Swedish "liberal" establishment.
4. We have been urged by colleagues to be more critical and expose charismatic Christian heresy, sexual scandals, and political conservatism. Where relevant Poewe has done so in several footnotes to the introduction. It must be mentioned here, however, that many criticisms are inadequate. At best, they are ideologically motivated and intolerant. More seriously, they lack any theoretical backing, especially regarding oral theology, folk language, and rhetoric. Charismatic Christians, like Puritans, Pietists, Methodists, and other revivalists before them, deliberately work in the vernacular of the people. It was Pietists, Methodists, and Puritans, after all, who first translated the Bible from Latin into vernacular languages: English, German, Russian, and so on. Pietists, for example, deliberately interpreted biblical texts by way of an existential or experiential hermeneutic. Using common language and commonplace experiences laid these people open to charges of heresy and excess. What they said sounded too syncretistic. Furthermore, to convey the immediacy and power of a "living Christianity" (as Pietists called it) they used especially those figures of speech that would make the abstract concrete, like metonym, personification, and synecdoche. They favored allegory above

analysis and were adept at creating lyrics and ditties. Their language and music was considered distasteful by many of their contemporaries (see Reichel 1969). Furthermore, Pietists then, as charismatics now, had a tendency of suspending disbelief in matters of spiritual experiences. They could not resist believing that such experiences could be authentic. This created, and creates, grave difficulties. For example, the Pietist August Hermann Francke became involved with various women who were called "German prophetesses"—a term of derision. These women were part of a wave of "ecstatic spiritual experiences" that swept through the center of Germany in the seventeenth century (Wallmann 1990: 67). Francke's identification with these prophetesses (he defended some of them against all kinds of accusations) nearly ruined his reputation. For an excellent criticism of Pentecostalism between 1900 and 1950 see Fleisch 1983. It becomes obvious that one must ask why the excesses were more extreme in India, Latin America, and the United States than, say, in England and Germany of the same period (see Fleisch 1983: 19, 75–78, 105–10). From the beginning, Pentecostalism in Germany and probably also England was more intellectual (78–80). Furthermore, the criticism that various Christians made of Pentecostalism in Berlin before 1910 could have been made about charismatics now (109–16). And yet, I am left with the question, did the containment of Pentecostal predilections for experiences and unbecoming displays help Germany?

5. Others criticize especially the "prosperity gospel." For a balanced view see Horn 1989.

6. Anglican archbishop Hurley, Michael Cassidy, founder of Africa Enterprise, and Professor David Bosch, professor of theology at the University of South Africa (UNISA), argued that to "understand" South Africa we must read the Morran and Schlemmer book. The book was used as a basis for an interdenominational conference on charismatic churches organized by Diakonia, November 1984. It was also cited by various church bodies. See, for example, *Report of the General Synod of the Presbyterian Church of Southern Africa* 1986: 39.

7. It is perhaps one of those ironies that the individual who was actually concerned about fear and wrote about it was a black, Elijah Maswanganyi. In the preface to Maswanganyi's *How You Can Be Free From Fear* Gerald Rowlands of *Global Ministries Australia* wrote, "Elijah's background was one of fear and superstition."

8. In all we surveyed six churches. Some of these figures and findings will appear in a separate book on which Poewe is working. Life-history interviews came from people belonging to eleven different new charismatic churches.

9. Nicky van der Westhuizen's followers, for example, are primarily working class of all races.

10. Two exceptions which come to mind immediately are Ross and Hampel 1992 and Kepel 1991.

11. We cannot include the many international telephone conversations and prayers among founders, evangelists, apostles, and prophets. It is, however, common practice for these individuals to pick up the phone and call if, for

example, McCauley had a "word" or "prophecy" for someone across the big pond—or vice versa. Furthermore, at times of important decisions someone in Vancouver, Canada, may be called, for example, by the vice-president of UCT to pray for him. There are international prayer chains that reach into the highest church, business, and government offices of many countries. A New Zealand prophetess and a British prophet, for example, were instrumental in decisions about some major changes of leadership at the DCC.

12. While it is not politically correct, it must be said that American charismatic Christians visited South Africa and invited South Africans to their country at a time when academic liberals and others shunned South Africa and South Africans owing to economic and other sanctions. We must let later generations judge which was the nobler position, to support sanctions or to continue open relationships in an otherwise deadening situation. In the meantime, it is quite clear that many South African professionals appreciated the openness to the world that Americans granted them. The change of visitation pattern had to do with both the end of sanctions and the fall of the Berlin Wall. The practical effect, of course, was that McCauley, like others, sought contacts anywhere in the world and not only with the United States.

13. Hundreds of books and articles exist about white and other Pentecostals and charismatics that are written from theological, mission, or generally popular and Christian perspectives. Very little solid anthropological work exists, although one should mention the work of Thomas J. Csordas (1990) on Catholic Pentecostals; Luther Gerlach and Virginia Hine (1970) on black Pentecostals; and Stephen Glazier (1980), on Pentecostalism in the Caribbean. There are considerably more works written by sociologists (McGuire 1988; Poloma 1989; among others). Grant Wacker (1990) a religious studies professor at the University of North Carolina, has written several pieces on Pentecostalism.

II

Regional Overviews and Variations

Chapter 3

Evangelical and Charismatic Christianity in Latin America

David Martin

ABSTRACT

Although social scientists have tended to dismiss the phenomenon as reactionary or insignificant, Pentecostalism is growing in Latin America. Indeed, the general expansion of Pentecostalism and other forms of charismatic Christianity in various parts of the world would imply that what is happening in Latin America is part of a very broad geological shift in religious identifications. Pentecostalism is a walkout from all that belongs to the status quo, especially the corruptions of the political arena, in order to create a space where local people run their own show.

INTRODUCTION

By common agreement, South America is the Catholic continent, and Brazil is the world's most populous and extensive Catholic country. The recent emergence of a huge evangelical population is unpublicized as well as widely disbelieved, even by persons living a couple of blocks away from areas riddled with storefront chapels. Even those who know about the phenomenon sometimes show signs of having contracted the Western European habit of supposing that what goes on in the psyche, if such exists, is a private matter of no social consequence, unless it should surface in discernible and unambiguous political form.

For many Western intellectuals, the political and the economic spheres are the primary realities from which impulses are transmitted to other spheres. Those other spheres are, in the strictest sense of the word, reactionary, and the sphere of religion is more reactionary than most. Thus even if the expansion of evangelicals is noticed as some kind of fact, it remains a curious blip on the accepted picture of genuine and efficient events, to which it is improper to attribute much by way of significance. Supposing some significance is allowed, then it is subsumed under imperialist cultural diffusion or else under wider categories like "fundamentalism," which is regarded as a kind of historical blind alley and construed as "reactionary" in the more familiar political sense of the word. What is rarely allowed is that such a phenomenon can be independently generated in Latin America, whatever its North American affiliations, that it is of massive significance as an index of disintegration and a form of popular reorientation, and that as time goes on it will be consequential for lives and for culture, and also maybe for politics and economies.

I make these preliminary comments because our models and paradigms really do restrict what we allow ourselves to see, let alone take into account by way of estimates of the likely future. These particular wheels can be allowed to turn as fast or as slow as they please because they are not connected to what (in misleading mechanical metaphor) we call the engines of history. To indicate the operation of such models, I went through a fair selection of what are called the "country" articles in the *Encyclopedia Britannica* charting the historical disappearance of references to religion and the point at which authors treated the political order as the prime reality.

Even in Catholic countries, religious events tended to slide into invisibility once the church had been separated from the state, and that was true even where religion had manifestly impinged on the political sphere. If even the Catholic Church can slide out of subject indices, imagine how difficult it is for evangelical conversions to slide into them. Clearly the encyclopedists and sociologists are alike seized by an evolutionary model whereby religion goes into retirement, and is only residually associated with "events."

THE EXTENT AND CHARACTER OF THE MOVEMENT

When we chart this phenomenon what do we find? First of all, both David Stoll and myself, as the two persons conducting overall surveys of this scene, have concluded that more than forty million persons are currently in the evangelical constituency, comprising one-in-ten or so of the population of Latin America (see Stoll 1990a; Martin 1990). The evangelical proportion has tripled in a generation; and, moreover, the evangelical population is now seventy-to-eighty percent Pentecostal, where once it belonged to such denominations as the Baptists and Presbyterians.

Our figures differ internally: mine are higher for Nicaragua, Colombia, and Guatemala; Stoll's are higher for Chile. But there seems little doubt that Guatemala has the highest proportion of Protestants in Central America. It is at least twenty-percent Protestant and may well be nearer thirty-three-percent Protestant. In South America the highest proportions of Protestants are to be found in Chile and Brazil: somewhere between fifteen and twenty-one percent. The Andean republics fall mostly in the middle range, but well down, with Protestant constituencies of three-to-five percent among the Quechua. Over the last decade Ecuador has been the scene of large-scale conversions. Uruguay, Venezuela, and Paraguay have constituencies around two percent, probably the lowest in Latin America. The two most important omissions here are Mexico and Argentina. Mexico has a fairly long history of Protestant activity, and experienced considerable Protestant expansion in the 1960s, but the really rapid expansion has probably been over the past decade, giving rise to estimates of five percent of the population. Between 1982 and 1989, the Assemblies of God alone grew from about 100,000 to 570,000. Argentina is a special case in that Protestantism came with the great European migrations, just as it came with European and especially German migrations to Brazil. Conversions were not extensive. But there seems to be an upswing of recent years. Between 1982 and 1989 the Assemblies of God expanded from under 50,000 to nearly 330,000. Stoll quotes figures placing the number of Protestants in Argentina at 1.63 percent in 1960 and 4.69 percent in 1985. So we can probably place Argentina and Mexico on a par with the Andean Republics as exhibiting an observable ascending curve.

Without anticipating the kind of comments to come later, some very general points are worth making. Venezuela and Uruguay are highly developed with high levels of general secularization. They seem resistant to religion as such. But otherwise there does not seem to be much of a relationship, negative or positive, with broad levels of development. Nor does there seem to be much of a relationship with the kind of regime, except in Cuba, from which Protestants emigrated in large numbers. Protestants continued to be active and to expand their numbers in Nicaragua during the Sandinista period.

Nor is the phenomenon confined to Hispanic America. It is very evident, for example, in Haiti and Jamaica. For that matter, it exists all over Africa, south of the Sahara, and along much of the western Pacific rim, above all in Korea, and also in mainland China. What is manifestly happening in Latin America is part of a very broad geological shift in religious identifications.

Clearly a large majority of Latin Americans remain Catholic. Often their faith is highly syncretistic, existing in all kinds of combinations with African spiritism and the fragments of indigenous faiths. It has, of course, run counter to nationalism and political radicalism from time to time, and has also run in harness with both. This has left a long-term geography of Catholic strength and weakness that ranges from strong in southwest Mexico and Colombia to weak in Guatemala. Some aspects of Catholicism, like priestly celibacy, have never seemed to take a strong hold, and, moreover, in many parts of the continent the priesthood is itself largely foreign in origin. If Protestant pastors are sometimes foreign in origin, so too are priests, and so indeed are protagonists of liberation theology.

Perhaps the most important point about the Catholic church at the moment is that it is divided. On the right is Opus Dei, said to be favored by the Pope, on the left the Jesuits, said by some to be subversive. The ordinary Catholic encounters the local cells of liberation theologians, and lay catechists; or the Catholicism of the traditional parish; or various national cults with possible right-wing and nationalist resonance, like the cult of the Virgin of Maipu favored by General Ugarte Pinochet. He may even be attracted to a charismatic Catholicism looking very like evangelical Protestantism. Although it is true, as Enrique Dussel (1986) has argued, that a "new moment" exists in the relations between the Catholic church and the left, the church is nevertheless inwardly confused. And it is at this juncture that it meets its first and most potent religious competitor. The fragmentary competition of spirit leaders, mediums, and exorcists could be tolerated, even perhaps in Brazil, where spiritism is widespread and organized, but this new competition gives no syncretistic quarter to Catholicism and only occasionally to spiritism. It hacks apart the nexus of social and religious relationships in the process of creating its own separate space. What was once a loose state-wide monopoly, with several tolerated black markets, is now open to competition across the whole continent.

Out-and-out competition is certainly novel in Latin America. In that limited sense, Protestantism is "foreign." Indeed, in that sense Protestantism is not only foreign but North American, since only in North America has a completely voluntary and competitive religiosity been universally established. What has seeped across the Rio Grande del Norte is not only a religiosity characteristic of Anglo-Saxon cultures, but an instalment of the North American system of competitive and voluntary religious bodies. Where once was a monopoly is now an open market of several hundred religious groups. That is momentous, but it is not necessary to assume that the root source is solely or even mainly cultural diffusion from North America. It is more likely that Latin America is itself undergoing the kind of differentiation of social spheres that releases—or expels—religion from a one-to-one unity of faith and culture.

How far then is it necessary to regard the evangelical and the Pentecostal expansion as foreign? It receives money from outside just as it receives personnel, but so does the Catholic church. And the amounts, so far as one can judge, are not large, even if you suppose that you can achieve mass conversions by financial investment. On this issue I am disposed to quote Stoll because he is a secular liberal intellectual alert for North American economic manipulation. He concludes that "nowhere in Latin America does the flow of dollars seem very large compared to the dimensions of the movement" (1990b: 46). He refers to the fact that the headquarters of the Assemblies of God, in Springfield, Missouri, spends $20.5 million a year in Latin America and the Caribbean, and concludes that sum is hardly calculated to generate more than ten million members and adherents. The resources of Pentecostals are not primarily dollars or even itinerant television evangelists, but vast numbers of Latin American pastors, some full-time, many part-time and unpaid. The real resource is local commitment in structures so fissiparous that there is no question of some control from abroad.

The indigenous character of evangelicalism and, above all, of Pentecostalism can be underlined in several different ways. It is notable, for example, that an evangelical movement has recently emerged among blacks in Cuba, led by young black pastors, and such a development is not readily dismissed as due to North American influence. In the Mexican city of Guadalajara, a complete subsociety has emerged comprising many thousands, called "Light of the World," and led by a charismatic Mexican. In Bolivia by far the greater number among some 390 non-Catholic groups were founded by Bolivian pastors. Again, in Colombia more than half of the pastors and evangelical leaders are Colombian. In Chile the indigenous character of Pentecostalism is indisputable since the largest body, the Methodist Pentecostal Church, broke away from North American tutelage in 1909 and has prospered greatly since mid-century under entirely local leadership.

This is not to suggest that there is no connection between Protestantism in Latin America and North America. The United States irradiates an image of power and prosperity; there is much American money behind the electronic church and other modern modes of communication; there are thousands of missionaries, more particularly in the smallish faith missions; and evangelical relief work draws heavily on North American generosity. But this does not alter the fact that the main thrust is local, powered by commitment, and thoroughly Latin American, down to the elements of authoritarianism and patronage. If pastors brook no internal dissidence and act as brokers in the web of patronage, that indicates an affinity to and an assimilation of local culture.

There are many elements of affinity between Pentecostalism and traditions already existing in Latin America. Pentecostalism expels evil spirits, engages in miraculous healing, offers ecstatic release, insists on ascetic discipline, and arouses millenarian expectation. Brazil, in particular, has harbored millenarian movements and Afro-Brazilian movements for spiritual health and healing. A religion of the Holy Spirit need not be so strange. It unifies the cosmos of the spirits, makes the therapy universally and freely available, and offers at the same time a new initiative in the creation of religious fraternity and mutual support.

A WORD ABOUT THE HISTORY OF THE MOVEMENT

Having established the extent of the phenomenon, and having underlined its voluntaristic, competitive, and indigenous character, it is useful to look back historically to the original genesis of the movement in Latin America and to its genealogy in similar movements of Anglo-Saxon Christianity.

If we leave aside the arrival of Protestants in Latin America by migration, the genesis of Protestantism occurred as church and state fell apart in the mid-to-late nineteenth century. As radicals made the expropriation or legal constriction of the Catholic church part of their program, Protestant missionaries, mostly Americans anxious to disestablish the church, emerged in the liberal column. They set up academies for useful knowledge outside clerical control, and sought to promote welfare. For many Latin Americans the Anglo-Saxon world was in the van of progress, and though they did not want serious incursions of Anglo-Saxon religion, they saw it as having something to do with that progress and so a useful if minor auxiliary in their own battles. Methodist schools, for example, were influential in the early political modernization of Peru. The most striking association of Protestantism with radicalism occurred in the early stages of the 1910 Mexican revolution, before the revolution turned against religion as such. Of course, in the course of the twentieth century, the image of the United States ceased for the most part to be so bright and beckoning, and the estimate of Protestantism suffered accordingly, at least among the cultural elites.

It is probably true to say that commentators were inclined to view this early Protestantism as an inconsequential overflow from the United States, useful in the interim but destined to be subsumed or by-passed by popular radical movements operating directly on the political plane. A sympathetic observer, Jean Pierre Bastian (1979), gives an account of Methodism in early twentieth- century Mexico that is capable of being tuned to such an approach. Methodism abolished the hierarchy of mediation and established layman and lay preacher as the main actor on the religious stage. It promoted schools and libraries and encouraged both mutual aid and self-help among people who were migrating from the old social world to the new. Significantly, the Methodist chapels around Mexico City followed the track of the railway lines built by the British.

And this kind of interpretation was bolstered by a wider view that not only regarded evangelical Protestantism in Latin America as a temporary and insignificant overflow but saw its role in Anglo-American society as destined for subsumption in direct and secular political action. What was evangelical Christianity but one carrier for changes of a large scope and a vehicle for groups without a future, such as grocers and artisans? Self-help moderated by mutual aid, a suspicion of the state modified by a disposition toward welfare, a respect for education allied to a lack of high culture, a fear of intellectuality, a practicality uninformed by a structural theory of society, these contradictions showed evangelical Christianity to be an adjunct of Anglo-Saxon liberalism, and as "a movement" to be a temporary excursus confined to the limits of the Anglo-Saxon world. It seemed unlikely to renew its vitality, to make culture not politics the site of social change, or to move outside its confines to other worlds, like Latin America.

This, however, is precisely what has happened since the late 1950s and is happening now at a remarkable pace. What was earlier delineated implies a massive displacement of paradigms, parallel to the impact of the events of 1989, in which the regimes of eastern Europe fell to pieces, or to the events of the last decades, in which Islam is the unignorable factor in politics from Morocco to Jakarta, or to the shifts in Catholicism, whereby social protest has been spearheaded by priests in many Third World countries.

What we see emerging over the past two or three decades is genealogically a potent extension of the old evangelical movement in a form that fuses the traditions of poor whites and poor blacks and adapts itself with extraordinary ease to the forms of exorcism and healing found in the Third World. The genealogical connection with evangelicalism is established both by many similarities and by direct historical links between Methodism and Pentecostalism in late nineteenth-century America. Indeed, the Methodist Pentecostal church in Chile illustrates the links. But in any case evangelicalism is polymorphous in its very nature, recognizable by family resemblances, not by observable and centralized hierarchies. That means that there is a case for looking at these converts to Pentecostalism with the classical problematic in mind. That, indeed, is what I have done. I have taken the set of questions raised by Methodism in the great period of transition in England and Wales and asked the questions once again in Latin America and the Caribbean.

THE EXAMPLE OF YUCATAN

The point can be illustrated from a research trip made to the Yucatan. The Yucatan is a periphery of Mexico with specific ethnic and historical traditions. It is of interest because whereas the older Protestantism seeped across the Mexican-American border, and is visible today in the solid Baptist churches of Chihuahua and Ensenada, the new wave has taken off in Tabasco, Chiapas, Campeche, and Quintana Roo. If evangelicals make up five percent in Mexico as a whole, they may make up some fifteen percent in southeastern Mexico. That fifteen percent is itself variable, because in rural areas the conversions occur by social segments rather than families. A kin group joins an evangelical church, or a neighborhood or even a whole village joins an evangelical church.

The example used to illustrate the relevance of the original set of issues in England is of the Presbyterian church as it operates in Xochenpiche, close to Chichen Itza, and as it operates in Merida, the local city and center. Xochenpiche is a completely evangelical village in which the Catholic church stands roofless and locked. Instead one finds a neat chapel in pastel shades that has strayed out of Llanelly, in south Wales, apart from the surrounding palm trees. So what was once a key feature of the English periphery has mysteriously reappeared on the Mexican periphery. Near the chapel is a dispensary, since conversion and medicine of one kind or another quite frequently go together. The anthropologist who took me around gave me to understand that the villagers received assistance in the way of agricultural know-how and implements. The village also has a large Bible school, where evangelicals gather for local rallies.

In Merida itself the church was closely connected with Hope Hospital, a small institution staffed by qualified doctors. The pastor spoke of the expansion of his congregation and of the fact that it now included local professional people. In a small Bible school attached to the hospital, groups of adolescent girls, armed with guitars and sweet voices, were ready to go out singing and preaching in the villages. The pastor's own armory included the Bible in Mayan, which he had given much effort and time to help translate. What we have here then is a set of embryonic institutions of social welfare and of mutual assistance linked to education and literacy, most of them in the long run likely to facilitate social mobility and wider geographical horizons. These institutions are not engaged in raising political consciousness, though that is not excluded in circumstances where local people feel the pressure of expropriation. The political area has not proved particularly responsive, and, in any case, these are not people for whom conventional political activity is central.

They are engaged in binding themselves together as a raft that promises redemption and will certainly provide them with strategies of survival.

What has been said of these Presbyterians in Mexico may also be said of the Pentecostals, except that the dynamism is much greater. Pentecostals revive therapeutic gifts of the spirit in ecstatic speech, prolonged prayer, spiritual healing, and expulsion of demons, and are less likely than Presbyterians to stress literacy. Moreover, they offer easier access for lay people to the pastorate, emphasizing spiritual quality, not educational ability. It is with this wider range of promises and services, and this reduced set of formal and professional demands, that the Pentecostals have swept through large sectors of Latin American society. And if the promises and services prove unsatisfactory then one tries an existing alternative or simply creates one.

How does one characterize the Pentecostal phenomenon? In short order, one characterizes it as a re-formation, social and personal. It is a walkout, so far as that can be achieved, from all that belongs to the status quo, especially the corruptions of the political arena, natural and local, in order to create a space where small people run their own show.

SOME COMPARISONS

So far I have provided a broad characterization of evangelical expansion in Latin America. I have indicated an accelerated growth relative to population since the mid-century that is most marked in Chile and Brazil and in Central America, especially Guatemala, Costa Rica, and El Salvador. Obviously, a more localized scrutiny is required, and equally obvious, it is impossible to survey each of more than two dozen societies from the tip of the southern cone to places like Puerto Rico, well nigh in the mid-Atlantic. A selective strategy has to be adopted as follows: first a comparative analysis of Brazil and Chile, then some comments on Guatemala, and finally a look at Ecuador. That completed, I conclude by looking at the economic, political, and cultural consequences of these dramatic changes.

Chile and Brazil are similar in having a long history of indigenous Protestantism, originally propagated by the "historical" Protestants (Baptists, Presbyterians, etc.) and today focused in two Pentecostal bodies, the Methodist Pentecostal Church of Chile and the Brazilian Assemblies of God. The two countries are otherwise very different. In Chile evangelicals are to be found overwhelmingly among the poor. They are marginal people with limited education, engaged in insecure employment and living either in the rural areas or on the peripheries of the larger cities. In Brazil, however, there are, and always have been, fair-sized enclaves of middle-class evangelicals and churches whose appeal is designed expressly for that socioeconomic class.

Chile has a rational and sober culture, at least on the surface, whereas Brazilian culture is uproarious, volcanic, and eclectic, with major African and native American elements. This means that in Chile evangelicals simultaneously continue—and break with—a submerged layer of folk religiosity based on local supernatural agencies, whereas in Brazil they encounter very sharp and intense competition from all the luxuriant forms of spiritism. Indeed, in Brazil a dynamic group has emerged called the Universal Church of the Kingdom of God, which combines an appeal to people in the tourist trade with a controversial campaign to exorcise the deities of Afro-Brazilian spiritism. The Universal Church exhibits features almost entirely traceable to African sources. Brazil also differs in the ethnic variety among its migrants, so that one major Pentecostal body, the Congregation of Christ, took off originally among Italians.

There is a political difference that might follow from the class difference, but more probably follows from the sheer fluidity of Brazilian society. In both societies evangelicals have tended to belong to the politically voiceless, and their pastors, for the most part, have acquiesced to the demands of military government or even offered qualified support. In Chile, however, the majority of evangelical voters have been, for some while, in the center and even center-left. In Brazil we do not know much about evangelical voting, but we do know that evangelicals are themselves part of the political process. They have more than thirty deputies nationally and are very active in regional politics. Non-evangelical candidates openly compete for their votes. As for the evangelical deputies, most are on the center or center-right, but an enquiry by one of the trade-unions, did not find them voting in a way inimical to the interests of the poor.

Clearly, there is also controversy about the political role of evangelicals in Guatemala. In the earlier stages of evangelical expansion, for example, after the overthrow of the Arbenz reformist government in 1954, they were sometimes suspected of subversion. In recent years, however, they have been regarded as representing a merely symbolic protest that substitutes moral reformation for structural change. The most controversial figure in all this has been General Efrain Rios Montt, brother of a Catholic bishop. Rios became converted to a charismatic group called "Verbo," based in California, and in 1982 became president in a coup. He conducted a ferocious and successful campaign against guerrillas based on the slogan "Rifles and Beans," but was eventually deposed as a result of his attempts to control corruption and random violence. However, this episode seems not to have affected evangelical expansion or political credibility, and in 1990 another evangelical, Jorge Serrano Elias, was elected president on the condition that he did not use his position to promote his faith.

Those who have analyzed evangelical expansion in Guatemala have attributed its dynamism partly to a special appeal for the large and depressed native population, and partly to the political and natural disasters overtaking the country. The evangelical churches offer relief and healing, and they also act as apolitical shelters in time of vengeance and civil strife. Stoll (1990) comments that even Catholics have started to adopt evangelical modes of speech, and that many prominent business-men join charismatic groups, where they behave like evangelicals and indeed endeavor to reform some of their practices while still remaining Catholics.

The situation in Ecuador is significant for several reasons. It connects with the Guatemalan situation in that evangelicalism has made an appeal to the Quechua analogous to its appeal to the Maya. A great deal of missionary work has been pursued among the myriad smaller tribes of Latin America by groups like the New Tribes Mission and the Wycliffe Bible Translators, but in Guatemala, and in such Andean countries as Ecuador, the work has been among major non-Hispanic ethnic groups numbering many millions.

Ecuador was for a long time highly resistant to evangelical missions, but following on land reforms promoted by a Catholic bishop the Quechua lent a more favorable ear to the evangelical message. What then followed illustrates the ambiguities of the process, and the extent to which analysis has to deploy a bifocal lens. Broadly, there are those who see the evangelical incursion as leading to cultural disintegration, and those who see it as a revitalization. The critics note the concentration of tribal groups, their confusion by a multitude of sectarian appeals, and their opening up to the blandishments of modern culture, including the desire of national governments to absorb them into the wider commu-nity. Others see significant continuities with folk culture and the rescue of native tongues. They stress the new discipline and confidence of the non-Hispanic peoples facing the outside world and the increasing avail-ability of educational and medical facilities. Tod Swanson (unpublished paper, n.d.), for example, in his account of large-scale conversion in Ecuador, sees evangelical religion as a way to renew the ancient "power" of the Quechua, a people nearly decimated by the effects of alcoholism, and now recovered by a total rejection of alcohol in favor of an evangeli-cal singing fiesta. Whereas the alcohol allowed "power" and money to be evacuated through white mediation (of which Catholicism was a part) the new evangelical fiesta reinstated its own local power and allied itself to more distant powers in the shape of the U.S.-based organization called World Vision. This organization was accused of handouts likely to create "rice" Christians. The Quechua of Ecuador now have five-to-eight thousand evangelical churches and are divided into predominantly evangelical and predominantly Catholic regions, each courted for political support. Apolitical or not, evangelical populations, once established, find themselves drawn into the patronage politics and polarizations of Latin America.

The above suggests what the political consequence may be. On the one hand there is the process of differentiation separating the new religious claims from the search for hegemonic power through political parties tied to a faith. Once fragmented, Humpty-Dumpty cannot be put together again. After all, evangelicals are themselves divided. They tend to be apolitical and they have their constituencies among people hitherto outside the political arena. On the other hand, they are drawn willy-nilly into the patronage politics of Latin America as yet another clientele, represented by cautiously conservative pastors. Though they come from people mostly excluded from the public forum, their very presence announces a latent power. In the same way, black evangelical churches in the United States constituted a free space occupied by people capable of mobilization in later times. How that mobilization comes about depends not on some inherent political stance, except for anti-Marxism, as it does on local context. And that may mean, as in Chile, voting with center or center-left, in company with others of similar social status and experience. In terms of entry into local and national politics, as in Brazil, it may mean a center or center-right contribution, and as events have shown, one not necessarily immune to corruption. One way or another the political stance is not of the old *integrista* variety nor is it the Marxist attempt to mobilize whole societies behind a single project. Evangelicals belong, after all, to a social modus vivendi that is both participatory and fissile.

The economic contribution of evangelicals may be consonant with that position. They emerge, after all, as the exemplars of religious laissez faire and competition, and they run their churches as entrepreneurs seeking a market. In so doing they gain skills and capacities capable of redeployment in secular avocations, and they inculcate a discipline and priorities of consumption that could lead to modest advancement, at least in circumstances where inflation is under control. Even where inflation is not under control, their combination of hard work and mutual aid probably gives them an edge in the search for survival. They are located at the social margin, where respectability and self-control and frugality assist survival and where aspirations can lead to small business ventures—or modest educational improvement. They could also be creating a new personality, with a novel sense of self and of responsibility, capable of being converted into initiative. All this, one has to say, is latent and implied rather than realized and documented.

CONCLUSION: PENTECOSTALISM AS A WALKOUT

These shifts, with their probable political and economic implications, are at base cultural. If culture matters then the shift to evangelical Protestantism is indeed revolutionary. It marks above all a walkout from the structure and from the culture as at present constituted, and, as such, from the Catholic church. It is a walkout from the local fiesta, with its web of entangling relationships. It is a walkout from the male personality, with its violence and familial irresponsibility. As such it is movement for moral reclamation taking off from the need of the women, and profoundly appealing to their need for stability. It creates a new man and new woman based on a discourse of nurture and nutriment.

A crucial part of what this walkout may involve is insightfully indicated in research in Brazil carried out by John Burdick, of Syracuse University. He begins by utilizing the distinction between local cults based on residence and prior identity, and "cults of affliction" (Burdick 1990). Catholic cults, including the base communities, belong to the former, Pentecostalism and Umbanda, a popular spirit cult of Brazil, to the latter. All recruit a preponderance of working-class women, and the stories of these women, as told to Burdick, underline the specific advantage enjoyed by Pentecostalism. Clearly, the arrival of families in the city led to increased household tension, especially over the threat to male prestige caused by unemployment, the drain on resources needed for children's education brought about by male expenditure, and the general loss of parental control. Now, in the case of the base communities, such matters are rarely discussed, though in theory they could be, partly because they are linked directly to the neighborhood and all that implies in terms of repute and gossip, and partly because the priest is not exactly experienced in such matters. As for recourse to the Virgin, this remains potent, but it is focussed on the woman in her loneliness and isolation. Meanwhile, the traditional and efficacious recourse to prayer specialists and "blessers" is downgraded and weakened in contemporary Catholicism. What the Pentecostal believers offer is an opportunity for "troubles" and afflictions to be talked over outside the local circles of neighborhood gossip, as well as a psychological transition so intense in this fervor that men and women alike are re-formed, in themselves and in their roles. The man does, as a matter of fact, recover his fatherly prestige, but only as someone who acts in a fatherly and responsible way. The woman now has a framework within which to influence her errant husband, and both can recover the confidence to influence their children. Pentecostalism, unlike contemporary Catholicism, helps forward this domestic reconciliation by locating the evil outside the self, in the demonic powers, and it claims to have the spiritual resources to counter these powers. All this is only possible if the therapeutic power of the Spirit and the Pentecostal community is separated from the space for gossip provided by the neighborhood and religious practices based on the neighborhood. It is another way in which a walkout is important.

Evangelical Protestantism in Latin America creates an enclave of a people seeking emotional release, personal empowerment, mutual support, and self-government. It announces that these people are there, occupying their own free space apart from the hierarchical mediation, social and religious, of the wider society. They do not want to offer an overt challenge and have a sense that violence only breeds violence. But they are going to give vent, to sing and to play, and thereby gain a sense of power and personal rebirth.

Chapter 4

The Empire Strikes Back
Korean Pentecostal Mission to Japan

Mark R. Mullins

ABSTRACT

Korean Pentecostalism, or, more generally, charismatic Christianity, took off through local leaders and their creative ability to Koreanize, even shamanize, Christianity. Since especially the 1970s Korean megachurches, using high-tech and international boards of directors, have begun to missionize the rest of the world. Paul Yonggi Cho, especially, is seen as an expert on church growth. Consequently, he is a favorite conference speaker not only in Japan, as discussed in this chapter, but also in the United States, Britain, Germany, and Latin America. His church and prayer mountain in Korea is a center of pilgrimage for postmodern Christians throughout the world.

INTRODUCTION

It is widely recognized that Pentecostal churches and movements represent the most dynamic and growing forms of Christianity in the world today. This is certainly the case in East Asia. Pentecostalism in South Korea and Japan is rooted in the missionary movements of North American churches that began shortly after the "Spirit came in power" to Topeka and Azusa.[1] Since the transplantation of these churches, however, numerous indigenous appropriations of Pentecostal faith have led to the development of new churches that are independent of Western control and domination.

The arrival of Pentecostalism in Korea and Japan must be seen as a part of the larger missionary movement of Protestant Christianity. Although the story of Christianity in East Asia dates back to the sixteenth century when Roman Catholic missionaries accompanied the colonial expansion of the Portuguese and Spanish, Protestant missionaries began arriving and establishing churches in the later half of the nineteenth century. Although the size of the missionary force sent to Japan has always exceeded that sent to Korea, churches in Japan have experienced only modest growth and their membership has never exceeded one percent of the population.[2] Christianity in Korea, on the other hand, has spread rapidly since the 1950s, and recent estimates indicate that twenty-five percent of South Koreans are Christian. While Pentecostalism is a part of this success story in Korea, it should be remembered that in the mid-1980s more than fifty percent of Korean Protestants were Presbyterian and that the Methodists represented the second largest denomination.

In this chapter I briefly describe the development of Korean Pentecostalism and consider how Western Pentecostalism has been transformed through its encounter with indigenous folk religion and shamanism. The second section of this chapter considers the missionary expansion of Korean Pentecostalism and reports preliminary findings of field research conducted in Korean mission churches located in Tokyo, Osaka, and Kyoto, Japan.

This is clearly a case study of the "Empire Striking Back." Korea was colonized by Japan and was a part of the Japanese Empire from 1910 to 1945. During this period the Japanese language became the medium of instruction in public schools and Koreans were forced to adopt Japanese names and worship at Shinto Shrines (the state religion of Japan after the Meiji Restoration).[3] Since the end of World War II, Christianity has been closely related to the development of Korean national identity. This is rooted in the colonial period, when many Korean Christians were involved in movements for independence and resisted (to the point of martyrdom) Japanese government orders that all Koreans, including church members and pupils in Christian schools, participate in Shinto Shrine ceremonies. It is not an overstatement to say that Christianity is positively related to Korean cultural identity largely due to the ruthless policies of the Japanese colonial government. Today many Korean Christians regard themselves as the "new Israel," with a special mission to Christianize Asia, including their former colonizer.

THE PLANTING OF WESTERN PENTECOSTALISM

Although Pentecostal-type experiences accompanied the early Protestant revivals of 1903, 1906, and 1907, a Pentecostal church was not officially established in Korea until after the first missionary, Mary C. Rumsey, arrived in 1928.[4] Rumsey had experienced the baptism of the Spirit in the 1907 Los Angeles revival and brought this experience, speaking in tongues and divine healing, with her to Korea. With the language assistance of a former Salvation Army secretary, Rumsey managed to organize the first Pentecostal church in Korea. Other churches were also established, but very little progress was made under the heavy hand of Japan's colonial rule. When the first missionary of the Assemblies of God in the United States arrived in 1952 to organize and consolidate the existing Pentecostal churches, there were only eight congregations with five hundred members. This modest group became the core of the Korean Assemblies of God, formally organized in 1953.

Over the next two decades missionaries representing various North American Pentecostal traditions arrived in succession and established new churches, such as the Church of God (Cleveland, Tennessee), the United Pentecostal Church (Jesus Only), and the International Four Square Gospel. By 1980 the combined membership of the various imported and indigenous Pentecostal churches was well over four hundred thousand. Two important indigenous forms of Pentecostalism emerged during this period and deserve particular attention.

THE YOIDO FULL GOSPEL CHURCH

The most significant development in Korean Pentecostalism during this period was the organization of the Full Gospel Central Church by Paul Yonggi Cho. Cho was educated in the Assemblies of God Bible College in Seoul and ordained as an Assemblies of God minister several years after beginning his evangelistic work. Although Cho was deeply influenced by the Assemblies of God and maintains close ties with Pentecostalism worldwide, the Full Gospel Central Church (now called the Yoido Full Gospel Church) is essentially an independent and indigenous church and represents the most influential stream of Korean Pentecostalism.[5]

Beginning as a tent church with just five members in 1958, the Yoido Full Gospel Church has experienced rapid growth over the past three decades and now claims a membership of 620,000 members, making it not only the largest Pentecostal church in Asia but the largest in the world.[6] After collapsing from overwork and stress in 1964, Cho learned the importance of training and delegating responsibilities to others. Under his charismatic leadership there are now 633 pastors, 400 elders, and 50,000 deacons or deaconesses shepherding this burgeoning flock. The church operates a Sunday School program with an enrollment of more than 26,000, a ten-week training course for home-cell leaders, a sixteen-week training course for church officers and lay leaders, and a three-year Bible Institute for training pastors. The Bible Institute already has close to 300 graduates and a current enrollment of 294.

Yoido Full Gospel Church is now a finely tuned organization with its membership divided into 50,000 home-cell groups in 406 subdistricts throughout Seoul. These cell groups are centered on Bible study and prayer and constitute the major means of pastoral care and evangelism.[7] It is probably most accurate to view Yoido Full Gospel Church as a distinct denomination since it includes nine satellite churches, affiliated churches, educational institutions, and has sent more than 250 missionaries overseas.[8]

On a given Sunday several hundred thousand members will worship in one of the seven services at the main sanctuary (seating twenty-five thousand), by closed circuit television in one of the nine overflow chapels (seating another twenty-five thousand), or by video in one of the nine satellite churches. More than one hundred buses transport members to services from throughout Seoul and outlying areas. Thousands of Sunday School children and teachers can be found meeting in small groups throughout the halls and rooms of either the ten-story Christian education center or thirteen-story world mission center. Foreign members and international guests are given special care and provided with a headset and instructions to select a channel with the appropriate simultaneous interpretation (one can choose between English, Chinese, German, and French). Sunday services are also broadcast throughout Korea from twelve radio stations and four television stations.

Church growth is clearly the major concern of Cho and the Yoido Full Gospel Church. In 1976 Cho established Church Growth International (CGI) to sponsor conferences and seminars that would promote church growth worldwide. According to a recent Yoido Church publication, 1.3 million pastors and church leaders from forty countries have participated in CGI seminars. Peter Wagner, of Fuller Theological Seminary's School of World Mission, and Robert Schuller, of Garden Grove Crystal Cathedral, both serve on the CGI board of directors and on occasion participate in conferences. Their presence undoubtedly lends respectability and legitimacy to CGI, enabling many evangelicals outside of Pentecostal churches to participate in its activities.

SUNG RAK BAPTIST CHURCH AND BEREA ACADEMY

Another important Pentecostal influence in present day Korea is associated with Sung Rak Baptist Church in Seoul and the founding pastor, Ki Dong Kim.[9] Although he is a Baptist minister, Kim's own conversion was accompanied by healing, baptism in the spirit, speaking in tongues, and prophetic visions. In 1961, at the age of twenty-one, Kim began his ministry as a lay evangelist with a primary emphasis upon healing and exorcism. Eight years later Kim founded Sung Rak Baptist Church with a small flock of seven members. Although officially a Baptist church, it has been "Pentecostal" in nature from its inception. All-night prayer meetings, revival meetings, exorcisms, healing, and speaking in tongues are the regular fare at this Baptist Church. Jae Bum Lee writes that "Ki Dong Kim's ministry is well known as a ministry of exorcism in Korea. He has led nine hundred exorcism meetings since 1961. During the same time he has reportedly raised seven people from the dead. . . . he healed 120,000 people who were crippled, blind, deaf, cancerous, and demon possessed. Kim states that he has cast out demons from four hundred thousand people and that fifty-nine of those were completely crippled people" (1986: 285).

By the mid 1980s Sung Rak Baptist Church had grown to a membership of nearly twenty-five thousand and had a pastoral staff of seventy-three. Similar to the organizational structure of Yoido Church, Sung Rak also provides pastoral care and outreach through thirteen hundred home-cell groups. Although not nearly as large as Yoido Church, Lee maintains that Sung Rak Baptist Church is the "fastest growing super church in Korea today" (1986: 279).

The influence of this stream of Pentecostalism extends far beyond the walls of Sung Rak Baptist Church. Believing that all Christians can be miracle workers and exorcists, Kim began Berea Academy in 1978 to train and cultivate these gifts in lay people. Very quickly, however, the student body of Berea Academy came to include discouraged pastors from various denominations as well as seminarians training for the ministry. The curriculum of study is based upon Kim's practical experience with exorcism and his biblical exposition of demonology. By 1985 graduates of this training program had reached 1,119 (J. Lee 1986: 286). Graduates of Berea Academy have gone on to start similar schools. Hahn Man-Young, for example, a professor of music at Seoul National University, has systematized the theology (demonology) of Ki Dong Kim and established Grace Academy and a new church in Seoul. Similarly, Tai-Ka Lee, a disciple of both Ki Dong Kim and Hahn Man-Young, started another academy in Masan and is reported to have a thriving church of more than ten thousand members. The pattern of church growth through schism is clearly not confined to Korean Presbyterians and their thirty-two denominations.

THE SHAMANIZATION OF KOREAN CHRISTIANITY

All-night prayer meetings, exorcisms, prayer mountains, and healing services did not just appear in Korean churches by accident. Although Pentecostal church leaders would deny the influence of "pagan religion," most scholars agree that shamanism has been the central force shaping the development of Korean Pentecostalism.[10] In both Korea and Japan, shamanistic folk religion constitutes the native culture to which organized religions have been forced to adapt.[11] Byong-Suh Kim explains that "shamanism is the belief system of this-worldly blessings—material wealth, good health, and other personal and familial well-being" (1985: 70). In traditional Korean society the shaman (*mudang*) served as a link between ordinary people and the spirit world, which was populated by numerous gods, ancestors, and spirits. Through rituals and offerings shamans can control the spirit world, transforming malevolent spirits into protective spirits, perform healing and exorcisms, and bring about concrete benefits for individuals in this world. Whether regarded as "syncretism" or "contextualization," it is undeniable that this shamanistic orientation has permeated Korean churches. This point has been expressed most forcefully in David Kwang-Sun Suh's *The Korean Minjung in Christ* (1991): "Korean Protestantism has almost been reduced to a Christianized *mudang* religion. That is, the form and language of the worship service are Christian, but the content and structure of what Korean Christians adhere to are basically *mudang* religion. Although missionaries rejected shamanism and thought that it had been destroyed, Korean Christianity has become almost completely shamanized" (116). The influence of shamanism is apparent in the theology of Pentecostal leaders as well as in the practices associated with prayer mountains.

Paul Yonggi Cho's theology might best be viewed as a synthesis of Korean shamanism, Robert Shuller's "positive thinking," and the pragmatism of the church-growth school of missiology associated with Fuller Theological Seminary's School of World Mission. The shamanistic orientation of Cho's theology is clear in his exegesis of John 3:2. "Beloved, I wish that thou mayest prosper and be in health, even as thy soul prospereth." This passage is the foundation for what Cho refers to as the Threefold Blessing of Salvation: "Thy soul prospereth" means that by believing in Jesus Christ we live an abundant life spiritually and "thou mayest prosper" means that we are blessed with material things through a life in which all things work together for good; "thou mayest be in health" means that believers who have received salvation are blessed to be delivered from the pain of sickness because Jesus paid the price of healing at Calvary (from the Yoido Full Gospel Church Doctrine and Creed).

According to Son Bong-Ho, professor of philosophy at Seoul National University, this "triple meter faith" (as it is popularly referred to) leads to an "excessive emphasis on earthly blessings" (1983: 338). If one does not experience healing or personal prosperity, then there must be some unconfessed sin or lack of commitment to religious duties. More active participation in religious services, trips to prayer mountain centers, or speaking in tongues will surely bring about the desired results. As James Huntley Grayson has observed: "Attendance at church and fervent prayer are believed to create a condition in which the person will be blessed" (1989: 205).[12]

In addition to the emphasis upon this-worldly blessing in Cho's theology, the spirit world of shamanism can be seen clearly in the demonology of Ki Dong Kim and Berea Academy. Kim teaches that this world is Hades and individuals who die without Christ become evil spirits that wander about in this world and possess people. Suffering and various kinds of illness are caused by these unclean spirits, who enter a person and use their energy. Exorcism, then, necessarily becomes a central concern of this church. Healing involves calling the spirit of the dead person by name and casting it out in the name of Jesus Christ.

Kim's etiology of illness is essentially that of traditional Korean shamanism. Kwang-il Kim explains that one of the primary causes of sickness according to early shamanistic diagnosis is "a wandering spirit, the spirit of an ancestor, any dead person, or any evil spirit" (1988: 133). Traditionally, the shaman discovers the identity of the ancestor or spirit responsible for causing the illness or disease through trance or divination. In the case of Christian shamans or exorcists, this seems to occur primarily through dialogue with the possessed person.

Prayer mountain centers (kido-won) established by churches all over Korea are another concrete expression of shamanistic Christianity. According to Yohan Lee's study (1985: 10), there were only 2 Christian prayer mountain centers established in Korea before 1945; by 1982 the number had increased to 289. Yoido Full Gospel Church established Osanri Prayer Mountain Sanctuary in 1973 under the leadership of Cho's mother-in-law, Choi Jashil. Today the Osanri center consists of a main sanctuary seating ten thousand, two smaller sanctuaries seating five thousand each, three hundred private prayer grottoes, and Western-style dormitories accommodating three thousand people. Free shuttle-bus service from Yoido Church to the Osanri center is provided daily on an hourly basis. Although not nearly as large a complex as Yoido's Osanri center, Sung Rak Baptist Church also maintains three prayer mountain centers. Religious activities in these centers include mass prayer meetings as well as private disciplines of prayer and fasting. Koreans and foreign visitors stream to these mountain centers seeking baptism by the Holy Spirit, personal healing, answers to prayers for health, wealth, fertility, and success in this life. These centers also cultivate the charismatic gifts. Yohan Lee, for example, reports that "To practice speaking in tongues, some prayer mountain centers push the participants in the prayer meeting to repeat 'Halleluja' seven hundred times or nine hundred times" (1985: 51). In addition to prayer mountain centers related to specific churches or denominations, there are many independent centers with pastors who specialize in healing particular illnesses or diseases.

Dawn prayer meetings, all-night prayer meetings, fasting, regular trips to prayer mountain centers are dominated by this-worldly, individualistic concerns. Lee's survey of prayer mountain centers concluded that "participants are strongly motivated to individualistic interests and do not pray for others" and "possibly half are strongly motivated by magical implications" (1985: 154–57), that is, seeking this-worldly blessing. The high level of religiosity visible among Korean Christians takes on somewhat different meaning when this shamanistic background is understood.

THE EXPANSION OF KOREAN PENTECOSTALISM TO JAPAN

Since the late 1970s, Paul Yonggi Cho's Full Gospel Church mission from Korea represents the most visible, dynamic, and influential form of Pentecostalism in Japan. This is particularly significant in light of the long and difficult history of Korea-Japan relations. Cho probably expressed the feelings of most Korean missionaries to Japan when he wrote: "You must realize how hard it was for me to go to Japan. After knowing about the millions of people massacred by the Japanese before 1945, I had a great hatred toward the Japanese people. However, God healed my heart when I confessed my sin. I now travel to Japan every month" (1984: 102–3).

This mission to Japan began in 1976 with the organization of a church in Osaka. Two years later another church was established in Tokyo and, subsequently, numerous branch churches and home-cell groups have been organized. By 1989 the Japan Full Gospel Mission consisted of twenty missionaries, nine churches, and claimed over five thousand members.[13]

In addition to church development, Cho began television evangelism in 1978 and currently broadcasts a half-hour *Invitation to Happiness* program each week on seven different stations across Japan.[14] This program is hosted by a striking woman, Midori Okubo, a former college professor who came in contact with Cho more than a decade ago.[15] Faithful viewers are brought together each year for an annual conference featuring Cho as the main speaker. In addition, each year approximately 10 pastors and 190 lay people travel to Seoul for a one-week pilgrimage to Yoido Full Gospel Church. The week begins with three days of prayer and fasting at Yoido's Osanri Prayer Mountain and concludes with three days at Yoido Church (including participation in an all-night prayer meeting on Friday).

In 1986 Cho replaced the annual conference for viewers with a larger gathering related to his church-growth seminars. In a recent year, five hundred pastors participated in the seminars and three thousand individuals (including lay persons) attended the general meetings. Although dominated by Pentecostal church leaders, Cho has tried to broaden the range of participants to include leaders of evangelical churches by bringing in such speakers as Peter Wagner of Fuller Theological Seminary.[16]

The development of the Full Gospel Church in Japan has not been without problems. A major schism occurred in 1990 in the Tokyo Church when the senior pastor rejected Cho's authority and established an independent church.[17] More than half of the members remained loyal to Cho and reorganized in a new location. In spite of the schism, the independent Tokyo church still has six evangelists (in addition to the senior pastor) leading a congregation of over two hundred home-cell groups and approximately fifteen hundred members.[18] In a country where most churches rarely have one hundred members after decades of evangelism, the growth and size of Full Gospel congregations in this short period of time is truly remarkable.

Along with television evangelism and church planting, Cho has placed considerable emphasis upon training people for pastoral work and mission in Japan. In 1985 Cho established a Tokyo campus of the Asian Church Growth Institute (ACGI) and, two years later, another branch in Osaka. Students attend regular classes or register for a correspondence course, using taped lectures. ACGI is essentially a three-year course and involves a six-month internship in Korea during the final year of the program. In 1990 there were approximately two hundred students studying in the Tokyo program and thirty in Osaka.

The growth of Full Gospel churches in Japan over the past decade is undoubtedly related to the fact that these ethnic churches provide a home away from home for many Korean immigrants working in Japan. The degree of success in incorporating Japanese into these ethnic organizations varies from church to church. In most Full Gospel Churches the Japanese membership is below twenty percent (many of these members are spouses in interethnic marriages). I have been informed, however, that there are some exceptions. The church in Fukuoka (southern Japan), for example, is predominantly Japanese. What is clear, in any case, is that these churches are making an effort to transcend ethnic boundaries. This is hardly the only factor related to their growth. Following the model of Yoido Church in Seoul, all of these churches have organized multiple services on Sunday and scores of home-cell groups. The Tokyo church, for example, has six worship services on Sunday. Two are conducted in Japanese and four in Korean (with simultaneous translation provided for three of these). The branch church in Kyoto, started in 1989, has already organized forty home-cell groups, and approximately half of its one hundred members are Japanese.

On a much smaller scale Berea and Grace Academy have also made their way into Japan through pastors, traveling evangelists, healers, literature, and tapes. One evening I attended a special healing service at a Gospel Church in Yokohama City that featured Kei-Fa Kim, a "shamanness" from Hallelujah Kitoin, one of the prayer mountain healing centers in Korea.19The service began with a video tape showing the success of her healing ministry in Korea, which attracts thousands. The video was rather graphic, showing her perform surgery by hand and fingernails on patients suffering from various infections, skin diseases, growths, and tumors. The video and lively hymn singing created a climate of expectation.[20] Kim appeared in a white dress and was introduced by the pastor. Her preaching was punctuated with stand-up testimonies by individuals and families who had benefited from her healing touch over the past several years. At great expense, they had gone to her prayer mountain healing center and spent days (in some cases even weeks) in search of healing.

In one testimonial, a man indicated that he had made three such trips to Korea for relief from back trouble (taking a gift of more than seven thousand dollars on his last trip). After several days at the Hallelujah Kitoin (prayer center) he still had not been healed. The shamanness indicated that lack of faith and spiritual problems at home were preventing the cure. He called Japan to check on the situation at home and learned that his daughter had just performed *mizuko kuyo* (a special memorial service for an aborted fetus) in front of the family *butsudan* (Buddhist altar). After hearing this, the Korean healer informed him that he must have his family shut the doors to the room containing the Buddhist altar to control the evil spirits. They apparently followed these instructions and he gained the faith required for healing and returned to Japan.[21] Although not nearly as visible as Cho's brand of Pentecostalism, Berea and Grace Academy are slowly making their way into independent and charismatic churches in Japan through a network of traveling evangelists and faith healers. Because of this Korean Pentecostal influence, it is not uncommon to find fasting and all-night prayer services being practiced in many of these Japanese churches.

JAPANESE NEW RELIGIONS AND
THE FUTURE OF PENTECOSTALISM

Since the late 1970s Japan has been undergoing what sociologists and journalists refer to as a "religion boom," or a "revival of magic and occultism." A number of new religious movements with a common emphasis upon experience, spirits, and exorcism have been an important dimension of this so-called revival. In view of Japan's economic prosperity and highly educated population, this kind of revival was the last thing Japanese scholars anticipated. Having imbibed a good dose of Weberian sociology, they expected the social significance of religion to continue to decline with the inexorable process of rationalization. In any case, the future of Pentecostal Christianity in Japan must be considered in light of this postmodern revival of folk religiosity (see Mullins 1992).

According to Japanese sociologists, an important feature of Japanese folk religion is the dominance of "magical" rituals oriented to "this-worldly benefits" (*gense riyaku*). Ichiro Hori explains that "the magico-religious needs and emotional associations of the Japanese people are important factors of receptibility in the process of borrowing or selecting of foreign religions in Japan" (1968: 14). Protestant Christianity in Japan, for the most part, has been isolated in an intellectual middle-class ghetto, and has been highly critical of what might be referred to as mass religiosity.[22] Pentecostal forms of Christianity, on the other hand, share a great deal in common with the new religions flourishing in contemporary Japan. Both emphasize religious experience and this-worldly benefits. One Japanese Pentecostal leader, for example, explained that evangelicals have long taught the message of salvation from "sin," but failed to teach the biblical message of healing and economic blessings from God. This emphasis upon the material blessing from God is something emphasized by Cho and is an important part of the Gospel.

The experience orientation of many religious "seekers" today simply does not predispose them toward participation in most Japanese Christian churches, which tend to be "clergy-centered institutions" (Dale 1975: 157) whose atmosphere is characterized by intellectualism and predictability. Pentecostal churches, particularly those recently imported from Korea, are characterized by active participation by the majority of members. In contrast to the "client orientation" and dependency upon educated professionals in most denominations, these groups tend to be "member oriented" and have effectively employed lay leaders in recruitment activities. This is not to deny the high status of "charismatic" pastors in Pentecostal churches. Lay members frequently "idolize" the powerful miracle-worker pastor. The point here is that Pentecostal churches tend to "empower" members through gifts of the spirit and education programs. Whereas established religions and churches tend to monopolize "spiritual power" in the hands of an elite clergy, Pentecostal churches and new religions provide opportunities for rapid spiritual mobility among average members. Charismatic or shamanistic powers are not restricted to the founder or pastor. Winston Davis refers to this tendency as the "democratization of magic" (1980: 302) in the new religions. With only a few days of training, all members can achieve power over the spirit world and perform acts of healing and exorcism.

In his recent study of Japan's new religions, Hayashi Minoru argues that "the Christian movement in Japan, which largely represents a Westernized, non-growing, and weakened form of Christianity, can become biblically dynamic and culturally relevant if it becomes more willing to learn critically from the growth dynamics of the new religions" (1988: 14). A critical factor in the acceptance and growth of a religion in Japan, he explains, is the "spiritual power" of a religious leader (not his academic qualifications). This power enables the leader to meet the practical needs of Japanese people. In this context, Hayashi advocates "power evangelism" and suggests that Christianity—if it is to make progress in Japan—needs to recover the "signs and wonders" of the New Testament. Apparently, only a Christian "shamanism" can compete with the shamanism of the new religions (14).

In many ways Pentecostal churches from Korea resemble the approach advanced by Hayashi. Shamanistic leaders perform signs and wonders on a daily basis and assure the faithful of God's blessing upon the living (and sometimes the dead). It is undeniable that these churches are growing faster than Western-oriented churches and often serve a social class largely untouched by other Protestant denominations. A Christianity that emphasizes personal salvation, healing, blessing, and success might yield greater "numerical growth" in the present social climate. Most churches, however, do not understand Christian mission narrowly in terms of numerical growth and will view these Pentecostal expressions as a truncated version of the Gospel that has eliminated personal and public discipleship. The message of many Pentecostal leaders is often indistinguishable from that of the modern shamans of many new religions who advocate new and old ways of controlling the spirit world and its powers for personal protection, happiness, and success in this world.

While Pentecostal movements represent a dynamic stream of Christianity in Asia that deserves serious attention, their significance should not be overestimated. The 1990 *Japan Christian Yearbook* indicates that the total number of Christians (Protestant and Catholic) in Japan is 1,074,676.

Probably no more than ten percent of that number belong to Pentecostal churches or charismatic congregations within the Roman Catholic Church or other Protestant denominations.[23] In 1984 Paul Yonggi Cho wrote: "God has now given me a promise that ten million Japanese are going to be saved in the decade of the eighties" (119). While Full Gospel Churches in Japan have recorded significant progress over the past decade, the results are far short of Cho's optimistic forecast. In spite of their many efforts, the membership in these churches consists largely of recent Korean immigrants or spouses of interethnic marriages. Cho is busy training evangelists in Japan and they will likely contribute significantly to the expansion of Full Gospel Pentecostalism in the years ahead. Observers should be cautioned from holding their breath until even the first million are recorded on Cho's colorful charts and graphs.

Pentecostal Christianity undoubtedly "fits" the current social climate better than the intellectual expressions of Christianity associated with Western churches. This fact alone, however, hardly assures church growth in the Japanese context. Daniel J. Adams helpfully points out that church growth in Korea is related to a unique historical experience and is not readily transferred to other situations: "The differences between Yoido Full Gospel Church and churches in other countries is not so much the presence or absence of the Holy Spirit as it is the process of indigenization and the unique blending together of syncretism, nationalism, and utopianism in Korea" (1991: 43).[24]

Unlike Korea, Christianity in Japan is still regarded by many as a "stranger in the Land" (R. Lee 1967) and incompatible with Japanese cultural identity. Furthermore, many Japanese still regard Koreans as an inferior race and are unlikely to seek religious solace in churches dominated by religious leaders from a former colony.

NOTES

1. Azusa refers to the Azusa Street revival in Los Angeles, California, between 1906 and 1909. The revival was led by the black American Pentecostal leader William Joseph Seymour (1870–1922). Seymour was a student of the Holiness preacher Charles Fox Parham (1873–1929) who led the Topeka revival in Topeka, Kansas, in 1901. This year marks the beginning of the Pentecostal movement in the United States.
2. Except, of course, during the sixteenth century, when the number of Roman Catholics "numbered about 300,000 out of a total population of nearly 20 million" (Swyngedouw 1988: 379). See Grayson 1985: 136–40 for an interesting comparison of Protestant mission efforts in Korea and Japan.
3. See Kang 1987 for a helpful study of this period.

4. For historical background on Korean Pentecostalism I have relied on J. Lee 1986: 169–97 and Yoo 1988.
5. Another significant Pentecostal-type new religious movement called Chondo-gwan (the "Olive Tree Movement") was founded by Park Tae-son in 1957. This movement places a similar emphasis upon divine healing and tongues, but is regarded as heretical by Protestant denominations (most Korean Christians place this movement in the same category as the Unification Association). Before beginning his independent ministry through revival meetings in 1955, the founder was a member and elder of the Presbyterian Church. Through the "Zion Foundation," Park built Christian towns with housing projects, factories, and schools, and by 1964 the Chondo-gwan had approximately two million members and three hundred congregations. For helpful background on the early development of this movement see Moos 1967 and Earhart 1974. According to a recent assessment this Christian syncretic movement is now in serious decline "and may pass away before the end of the century" (Grayson 1989: 245).
6. Information and current statistics regarding Yoido Full Gospel Church were gathered by the author on a field trip to Seoul in September 1990. Reported statistics should not be taken at face value. There are always inactive members and many "floating Christians" whose membership is reported by more than one church. Even with these qualifications, I would imagine that there are several hundred thousand members active in one of the programs of Yoido Church. Regarding membership composition, I am only aware of one sociological survey of the church conducted by Choi in 1978. According to Choi's 1986 study, the majority of the Full Gospel Church members have less than a high school education and women outnumber men by more than two to one. He summed up the results of this survey with the following generalization: "The educational level, occupation and living conditions of the members of Full Gospel Church show that it is a church of the middle and lower classes" (1986: 122). Choi's findings are based upon three hundred responses (twenty-eight percent men and seventy-two percent women) to his questionnaire distributed in eight large parishes. For fuller treatment of Yoido Church see the work of Adams 1991, J. Lee 1986, and Yoo 1986.
7. See Cho 1983 for a discussion of the role of home-cell groups in pastoral care and church growth.
8. In fact, Yoido Church was a major force in the founding of Jesus Assemblies of God of Korea in 1985, an association of Pentecostal churches that do not belong to Christ Assemblies of God or the General Assemblies of God.
9. For information regarding this stream of Korean Pentecostalism I am indebted to Professor Hideo Hida of Meiji Gakuin University, Tokyo, who has been studying various Korean movements for the past several years, and the dissertation by Jae Bum Lee (1986: 279–86).
10. See, for example, Grayson 1989: 205; Suh 1991: 114–16; B. Kim 1985: 70; Adams 1991: 41; and Yoo 1986: 70–74.
11. James Huntley Grayson maintains that shamanism "became the substratum of all Korean religious experience and has shaped the development of all

religions and philosophies which have been transmitted to Korea, including Buddhism, Confucianism, and Roman Catholic and Protestant Christianity" (1989: 271). Ichiro Hori (1968: 2) and Hitoshi Miyake (1972: 122) similarly argue that folk religion has been the comparatively stable "substructure" of Japanese religion.

12. Son, extremely critical of Korean church life, goes so far as to say that "many give in order to receive more, based on the shamanistic practice of bribing the demons" (1983: 339).

13. The growth of the Tokyo Full Gospel Church and its branch churches is described in a recent book by the senior pastor, Kang Hun Rhee, *Nihon issenman kyurei wa kano da* (1989; The Salvation of Ten Million Japanese Souls Is Possible).

14. At the present time, the monthly cost of this program is over ninety thousand dollars per month. Support from eight hundred prayer partners and many Pentecostal churches in Japan funds approximately two-thirds of the budget. The balance is provided by Yoido Church in Seoul. It is probably worth mentioning here that American Pentecostal television empires also expanded into Japan during this same period. Jim Bakker and Jimmy Swaggart, for example, both broadcast in Japan for several years. The scandals associated with their ministries meant an end to both of their broadcasts in that country.

15. I am indebted to Ms. Yoshimi Morikawa, staff person for the *Invitation to Happiness* program, and Midori Okubo for information on Cho's television ministry (personal interviews, March 22, 1991). In addition to hosting and directing this television ministry, Okubo is also pastor of The Lord Jesus Christ Church, Osaka, an independent Pentecostal church with five hundred members. Although organizationally independent, this church has been greatly influenced by the theology and missionary approach of Yoido Full Gospel Church. Okubo is a firm believer in the division of labor and the role of home-cell groups in pastoral care and evangelism. The forty cell groups linked to her congregation are led by six theological students and seven lay regional directors. Viewers of Cho's *Invitation to Happiness* are also being organized for special monthly meetings in various regions in Japan. Okubo sends student evangelists to minister to these groups and hopes that they will provide the core for new church development in the years ahead.

16. In addition to Cho's television ministry, Korean Pentecostalism is spread through Japanese translations of his books and a monthly newsletter. His book *The Fourth Dimension* (1983), for example, has already sold twenty thousand copies. Cho's mother-in-law and founder of Yoido's Osanri Prayer Mountain, Choi Jashil, has also influenced the church in Japan. Two volumes of her miracle stories have been published in Japanese, and until her death she served as president of Far East Theological Institute, a small Bible school located in a church started by one of her disciples in Kobe.

17. According to one informant, Cho views himself as the commander in chief of an army (pastors and evangelists working within Korea) and a navy (foreign missionaries). His authority and the chain of command proceeding from Yoido Full Gospel Church (in Seoul) are irrevocable.

18. This is the estimated membership following the schism. On a recent Communion Sunday around thirteen hundred attended one of the six services.

19. The pastor of the Gospel Church in Yokohama City is the director of Japan Grace Academy. He belonged to a Presbyterian Church in Korea before coming to Japan as a missionary many years ago. Because of the slow growth of Christianity in Japan, he returned to Korea greatly discouraged. A time of study at Grace Academy gave him the "power" to continue his missionary work in Japan. Since his return, the church has grown to approximately one hundred members through his ministry of "signs and wonders." The mission work of this pastor is still supported by Korean Presbyterians.

20. During this time, forms were distributed to the audience so that individuals could indicate whether they wished to receive healing at the close of the service. The form required a signature acknowledging that Kim would not be held responsible and explained that "healing" can often take several weeks. In the meantime, one should attend church, pray, and use the medicine Kim provided (olive oil and Holy Water from the Hallelujah Center). Moreover, one should not go to a hospital or see a doctor during this time.

21. Another testimony was given by a father who stood at the front of the sanctuary with his young daughter, whom he had taken to the same Hallelujah Prayer Mountain center for healing. This was after Japanese doctors and hospitals had been unable to cure her unusual illness. The daughter was accompanied by her parents and spent several days at the center in Korea. Her parents were instructed to chant the Apostle's Creed while a special ingredient placed on the child's stomach was lit and burned for several minutes. According to the father's testimony, she was miraculously healed and they returned to Japan.

22. Both Nishiyama (1986: 10) and Kanai (1987: 34) make this point.

23. For lack of space I have not dealt with the "charismatic movement" in the body of this paper. In the case of Japan, the charismatic revival began in the early 1970s under the leadership of more "ecumenically minded" Pentecostal pastors. Since the late 1970s it has been coopted for the most part by Cho's church-growth seminars, crusades, and conferences. While there are a few charismatic pastors and congregations within various Protestant denominations, and a number of charismatic Roman Catholic priests and parishes, the charismatic movement in Japan is largely a network of Pentecostal pastors and churches (see Nagahara 1983).

24. In personal conversations, two Korean theologians indicated that they wished Korean church growth could be "transferred" to Japan since these rapidly growing churches tend to uncritically support oppressive political regimes in Korea. That present patterns of church growth will continue in Korea, however, should not be taken for granted. The charisma of certain pastors is clearly an important factor in the growth of Pentecostal megachurches. As Grayson suggests, "these great congregations may last no longer than one generation, as too often attendance is dependent on the appeal of the minister" (1989: 205).

Chapter 5

Are Pentecostals and Charismatics Fundamentalists?
A Review of American Uses of These Categories

Russell P. Spittler

ABSTRACT

Because it is common in North America to equate Pentecostals and charismatics with fundamentalists, it is useful to distinguish among them. Eight theses are offered to do so. While this chapter, therefore, has more to do with local, and specifically local Pentecostal thinking, it is included in this work on global culture because even social scientists and their students, not to mention journalists and theologians, tend to start their studies of this phenomenon from a North American perspective. It may alleviate confusion when we remember the main point of this chapter, namely, that Pentecostalism and fundamentalism have separate historical roots.

INTRODUCTION

While many people would say that Pentecostals and charismatics are fundamentalists, an informed response to the question as to whether the two are one and the same is not as obvious as may first appear. The term *fundamentalist* is usually a put-down. It is applied to those who are seen to be more to the right of the theological spectrum than oneself. Consequently, one person's fundamentalist could be, and certainly has been, another's liberal. For some undiscerning journalists covering the American television scandals of 1987–1993, such adjectives as *evangelical*, *fundamentalist*, *charismatic*, and *Pentecostal* could be interchanged at will for stylistic variety.

True enough, each of these designations does have considerable elasticity. The words mean different things to different people, or different things to the same people at different times. Since the meanings of these terms overlap, I should say how I am using the words here.

When I use the term *Pentecostal* I usually have in mind today's centrist or established Pentecostals or their forbears, such as those affiliated with the two dozen or so Canadian and American Pentecostal bodies who are members of the umbrella organization known as the Pentecostal Fellowship of North America (PFNA).[1] Consequently, the generalizations made here apply less suitably to other very significant sectors of the highly variegated Pentecostal movement. They might not suit such groups as the independent Pentecostal congregations, urban and rural, that dot the land; or the Jesus' Name Pentecostals (also called "Oneness");[2] or the very considerable number of Asian, black, and Hispanic Pentecostals; to say nothing of millions of other Pentecostals that ring the globe—especially those in the Third World.[3]

When I speak of fundamentalists, I refer principally to persons and groups loosely connected with *The Fundamentals: A Testimony to the Truth*, a series of paperbound booklets published in Chicago by the Testimony Publishing Company and widely distributed to pastors, missionaries, and other church leaders between 1910 and 1915. These I call classical fundamentalists. Also included may be the revived fundamentalism of the 1980s epitomized in Jerry Falwell's Moral Majority. Only in a few obvious instances do I mean by fundamentalism the broad sociological phenomenon of all major world religions whose leaders incite the masses to militant reactions in periods of social and political upheaval.[4] In contrast, by charismatics I refer to mainstream Christians who have adopted certain Pentecostal beliefs and practices but did not leave their own denominations.

Here then are eight theses offered to help distinguish these otherwise similar movements:

1. *Pentecostals, fundamentalists, and charismatics should be distinguished even when they cannot be separated.* Asked if they are fundamentalists, many Pentecostals (maybe even most) would say yes. Fewer charismatics would do so. Some Pentecostals, mainly those trained in evangelical schools or secular universities, would rankle under the epithet. Roman Catholic leaders, even and especially charismatic ones, caution their charges against fundamentalism (see, for example, Hampsch 1988: 3–6 and O'Meara 1990). They use the term narrowly to refer to excessively literal biblical interpretation.

Pentecostals differ from charismatics in several ways. Two examples appear in dates of origin and forms of institutionalization. Pentecostals form a denominational family of Christians whose beginnings date from the 1890s to the 1920s. Their existence can be traced largely to rejection by the mainstream churches who laid claim to novel experiences of the Spirit so central to Pentecostal piety. Tongues-speaking fanatics were not welcomed under the church spires on main street. Such exclusion forced early Pentecostals, or "Apostolics," as they called themselves, to meet on their own. Eventually, they found each other and gave birth, however reluctantly, to Pentecostal denominationalism.

Thus, Pentecostals could appear on a list of the varieties of Protestant denominational Christian families side by side with Lutherans, Methodists, Baptists, Presbyterians, and the like. All these are institutionalized: they all have denominational headquarters, publications, federal approval for military chaplains, schools and seminaries, and legally incorporated and denominationally affiliated local churches. Further, these Christian families are generic categories: there are several denominations within each branch. Pentecostals fit right in as one more species—one of the newer ones, of course.

But the same cannot be said for charismatics. The decade of the 1990s finds Pentecostals concluding their first century, charismatics their first generation. In the aggregate, only a small fraction of the globe's charismatics form a separate branch of the church. The word *charismatic* more usually functions as an adjective describing mainline folk who have adopted Pentecostal beliefs, values, and practices. Hence, charismatic Catholics, charismatic Presbyterians, charismatic Lutherans, and so on. In the end, it may be best simply to speak of a charismatic lifestyle that can be found all over the Christian map.

The new charismatics stem chiefly from the 1960s, with clearly visible roots in the 1950s. By then a half-century of ecumenical friendliness and other globe-shrinking cultural forces made intolerance a fashionable vice. In that way the absorbency of the mainline churches was enhanced, and a churchly environment developed that allowed the newer charismatics to stay at home. Charismatics, who could be described as Pentecostals in mainstream garb, can be found today in virtually every sector of Christendom—including the Roman Catholic and Eastern Orthodox traditions.

A new variety of institutionalization that emerged among charismatics is the "service agency"—an officially approved office within a (usually mainstream) denomination, staffed by charismatics, with the double aim of coordinating the interests of the charismatics and preserving good relations with the denomination. These charismatic service agencies provide literature, send ministry teams to interested local churches, and offer consulting and mediational services.[5]

Among charismatics where Roman Catholic influence flourished, intentional charismatic communities emerged. This is hardly surprising, given the hundreds of monasteries and other types of communities that grew within this tradition, where community is a particularly strong value. In Pecos, New Mexico, an expressly charismatic Benedictine monastery was established in 1969. The Word of God Community in Ann Arbor, Michigan, is not a cloistered monastery at all, but a linkage of a wide variety of mini-communities. These range from extended families to such subunits as a household of a dozen voluntary, nonclerical male celibates. Such communities are not readily found among Pentecostals.

Where independent charismatic local churches or clustered fellowships exist, their roots can often be found in collapsed efforts at wholesale Pentecostalization of mainline congregations. Other local independent charismatic churches arose from the mixed results of local appearances of televangelists or from entrepreneurial and domineering loose cannons on the margins of establishmentarian Pentecostal clergy. These days, new charismatic denominations are forming apace. Often they are nonexclusive organizations of clergy whose members can hold ordination elsewhere.

Because charismatics are nearly always something else—charismatic Episcopalians, charismatic Greek Orthodox, or whatever—it is difficult to speak in any uniform way about a single charismatic tradition.[6] Such adjectival charismatics take on the theological and ecclesiastical colors of their own churches, much like the paintings of Jesus in the history of art yield figures that mirror the traits of cultural origin. In a few cases, denominational charismatics do indeed reflect fundamentalist notions. As often as not, inclinations like these arise from the perceived aridity of earlier training under liberal auspices.[7]

Because charismatics are more easily known by the ecclesiastical company they keep, the more difficult task lies in accurately differentiating Pentecostals from fundamentalists—both of whom are more institutionalized than charismatics. Pentecostals share with charismatics affirmation of spiritual gifts, especially speaking in tongues, healing, and prophecy. And the religious services of both are likely to be characterized by lively singing, manifest spiritual gifts, personal testimony, prayer for healing, and nonliturgical informality. But the two groups may have quite divergent theological views, eschatological expectations, worldviews, and attitudes toward social action.

Pentecostals and fundamentalists, on the other hand, are arch enemies when it comes to such matters as speaking in tongues and the legitimacy of expecting physical healing in today's world. But their approaches to the Bible, precritical and uncomplicated, are virtually identical. If the word *fundamentalism* gets defined only by biblical style, Pentecostals can be labeled fundamentalists without question. What divides the two movements, however, outweighs their similarities—at least in the eyes of each other.

As stated above, fundamentalism took its name, if indirectly, from the publication of *The Fundamentals*. This series of twelve booklets was distributed with the "Compliments of Two Christian Laymen," as the title page relates. A third of the three million copies distributed, according to an editorial statement appearing in the final volume, went to persons outside the United States (*The Fundamentals*, vol. 12, p. 4). The exact word *fundamentalist*, it seems, originated as a descriptor for conservative Christians in the Northern Baptist Convention in 1920.[8]

With this thesis charismatics can be left aside. The remaining interpretive theses will nuance the differences between fundamentalists and Pentecostals in North America.[9]

2. *Pentecostalism, fundamentalism, and neo-orthodoxy—roughly in that historical sequence—can be viewed as unrelated reactions to the state of affairs in religion and culture at the close of the nineteenth century.* The movements arose separately, and each manifested a different response to such currents as the rise of scientism, religious liberalism, biblical criticism, and the social gospel, along with the perceived (by some) triple threat of Darwin, Marx, and Freud. Cultural developments, such as urbanization and immigration, also contributed to the turmoil.

Fundamentalism reacted in an intellectual style. Essays in *The Fundamentals* took on a mildly apologetic tone, and they were focused on issues that imperiled the truth of the Bible. The approach was argumentative, logical, rational. The implicit assumptions included a definition of inspiration requiring a flawless biblical text that yielded an internally consistent theology. The Bible presented inerrant factual truth wherever it made any statements on any topics. Even incidental biblical references to nature or history were taken to be factually true. At worst, there might remain "apparent discrepancies." In short, fundamentalists asserted that the cure for religious drift and modernism was found in a convincing reassertion of the fundamental doctrines of Christianity.

European Neo-Orthodoxy is best represented by Karl Barth's commentary on Romans, *Der Römerbrief*, which was first published in 1918. He shared with fundamentalists the same intellectual methodology. Despite Barth's passion for paradox, which of course betrayed a different epistemology, he agreed with American fundamentalists that the sickness of the church was theological atrophy.

Contrary to North American fundamentalism, Barth's context gave him no reason to distrust the emerging canons of biblical criticism. Nevertheless, like fundamentalists, he too argued for the recovery of classic Christian beliefs. Fundamentalists and Neo-Orthodox Christians proposed an essentially cognitive rescue of the church from its lassitude.

In contrast to fundamentalists and neo-orthodox Christians, Pentecostalism profoundly distrusted the intellectual enterprise. The Pentecostal critique focused not so much on diluted theology as upon withered piety. The fault lay not in wrong thinking so much as in collapsed feeling. Not the decline of orthodoxy but the decay of devotion lay at the root of the problem. It was not merely that the church was liberal, but that it was lifeless. What was needed was not a new argument for heads but a new experience for hearts.

Fundamentalists and neo-orthodox Christians mount arguments, though the former does it in terms of creeds, the latter in terms of paradox. Pentecostals give testimonies. The one goes for theological precision, the other for experiential joy. There is a profound difference between the cognitive fundamentalist and the experiential Pentecostal.

Lest these distinctions are too simplistic, I hasten to add that fundamentalists also give testimonies to experience, while Pentecostals devise theologies. But one could usually tell which was which by the characteristic personal testimony of the Pentecostal versus the rationalistic argument of the fundamentalist. At least as early as the 1940s and as late as the 1960s, Pentecostal bible schools used fundamentalist textbooks in doctrine and biblical interpretation: the reverse would be exceedingly difficult to document. Furthermore, the Pentecostal movement has not yet produced an engaged polemic theologian comparable to, say, the ex-Princeton Presbyterian J. Gresham Machen. Pentecostal heroes turn out to be evangelists like Aimee Semple McPherson or Jimmy Swaggart. Alternatively, they are spiritual ecumenists like Donald Gee or David du Plessis and, more recently, Cecil M. Robeck, Jr.

3. *Far from being fundamentalist insiders, Pentecostals became one of the targets of fundamentalism.* Since the Pentecostal movement was still in its formative years when *The Fundamentals* were first published, none of the ninety or so essays included directly focused upon Pentecostalism. This is true even though specific articles of *The Fundamentals* critiqued Christian Science, Mormonism, the Millennial Dawn movement (Jehovah's Witnesses), and even Socialism.

George Marsden speaks of "the Fundamentalist coalition" that linked several anterior currents (1990a: 346). These included revivalist preaching from Charles Finney to Dwight Moody, dispensational premillennialism popularized in *The Scofield Reference Bible*, the Keswickian "Victorious Life" movement originating in Britain, conservative Princeton Presbyterianism, and Baptist independence.[10] Clearly, North American Pentecostalism was not part of this coalition—even though it flourished around the same time, was profoundly influenced by it, and drew adherents from the same sources.

To the contrary, in 1919 the World's Christian Fundamentals Association was formed. While many Pentecostals would have liked to join, by 1928 this fundamentalist organization had formed a sufficiently strong opinion about the Pentecostal movement to adopt the following resolution:

> WHEREAS, the present wave of Modern Pentecostalism, often referred to as the "tongues movement," and the present wave of fanatical and unscriptural healing which is sweeping over the country today, has become a menace in many churches and a real injury to the sane testimony of Fundamentalist Christians,
>
> > BE IT RESOLVED, That this convention go on record as unreservedly opposed to Modern Pentecostalism, including the speaking in unknown tongues, and the fanatical healing known as general healing in the atonement, and the perpetuation of the miraculous sign-healing of Jesus and His apostles, wherein they claim the only reason the church cannot perform these miracles is because of unbelief.[11]

This action evoked an editorial in the *Pentecostal Evangel* for August 18, 1928. "Although we Pentecostal people have to be without the camp," wrote editor Stanley H. Frodsham, "we cannot afford to be bitter against those who do not see as we do." "Plaintively," the editor regrets that "this action disfellowshipped a great company of us who believe in all the fundamentals of the faith as much as they themselves do."[12]

The Pentecostals were onlookers, not principals, in the famed Scopes trial in Tennessee during July 1925. The proceedings of the "monkey trial," as it came to be called, resulted in the conviction of John Scopes for teaching evolution in his biology classes—contrary to Tennessee law. (The decision was overturned later by a higher court.) The episode caught public fancy and popularized the fundamentalist-modernist controversy in the mid-1920s. Earlier, within the church world, ire had arisen over Harry Emerson Fosdick's famous sermon titled "Shall the Fundamentalists Win?"[13] The leading liberal minister in New York City smoothly argued against undue fundamentalist influence on denominational missions treasuries and their threat to organizational stability. Fosdick did not have Pentecostals in mind.

Pentecostals of the period affirmed all the core beliefs of the fundamentalists—the virgin birth of Christ, His substitutionary atonement, the verbal inspiration of the Scriptures, the bodily resurrection, ascension, and impending return of Christ. But they believed more, the "distinctive testimony" to the baptism in the Holy Spirit and consequent charismatic gifts. These claims, the fundamentalists could not accept.

The assessment of Edith Blumhofer, most recent historian of the Assemblies of God, applies to other Pentecostal denominations as well: "the question of whether they were fundamentalists did not preoccupy early Assemblies of God leaders; they simply assumed they were" (1989: II, 15). Yet Pentecostals were unwelcome pariahs to the fundamentalists.

This post–World War I rejection of the Pentecostals by the fundamentalists contrasts markedly with their inclusion by the new evangelicals during and after World War II. In the early 1940s, when the older fundamentalism sagged and soured, the "new evangelicals" accepted the Pentecostals. An implicit truce was declared on distinctive doctrinal commitments—a compromise on both sides. But these were war years—the National Association of Evangelicals was formed in 1941–1943—and there flourished a national mood to unite for common ends.

In sum, while early Pentecostals shared most beliefs of the fundamentalists, neither were offered nor sought affiliation with the fundamentalist antimodernist organizations. Pentecostalism and fundamentalism, by the mid-1920s, were discrete and often hostile movements. G. Campbell Morgan, one of the contributors to *The Fundamentals*, is reported to have spoken of the Pentecostal movement as "the last vomit of Satan."[14]

4. *While fundamentalism was a historical movement in twentieth century Christianity, it came to be seen as a religious or political ideology and was associated with militant conservatism.* George Marsden defines a fundamentalist as an evangelical who is angry about something (1991b: 1). Militancy is the key posture. Since the late 1970s, the term has been applied to hard-right thinkers and activists even beyond Christian limits: Islamic fundamentalism is no longer a metaphor (Hiro 1989; Choueiri 1990).

The fundamentalism of the 1920s has gentrified and diversified. While segments of the older separatist fundamentalism can still be found, a newer fundamentalism became associated with such persons as Jerry Falwell. In this variety, prominent in the 1980s, social critique was matched by political activism. Earlier there surfaced a retooled fundamentalism, the so-called "new-evangelicalism," a product of World War II. It linked such entities as the Billy Graham Evangelistic Association, the National Association of Evangelicals, *Christianity Today*, and Fuller Seminary. Where fundamentalism thrived in the 1920s, the new fundamentalism and the Evangelicals thrived in the late 1970s.

What is interesting to observe is that Pentecostalism too followed these directions. Some classical Pentecostals, at least on the North American scene, resemble fundamentalists. They are militant conservatives with added beliefs about the Holy Spirit and spiritual gifts. Other Pentecostals resemble "evangelicals." As such they hold regular appointments on the faculties of prominent evangelical schools in the United States and Canada. There emerged both a fundamentalist and an evangelical style of doing theology within the established Pentecostal movement: these styles consist of divergent, sometimes contradictory, presuppositions and methodologies (Spittler 1991: 291–318). Both styles are discernible within the classical Pentecostal denominations. If this diversity has not been disruptive, it is because the Pentecostal movement values spirituality above theology.

5. *The ideological definition of classical Christian fundamentalism refers to an unbending literalism in biblical interpretation coupled with a theory of inspiration close to dictation.* This extended use of the word detaches it from its historical roots. *Fundamentalism* as a synonym for excessive biblical literalism draws criticism from many quarters. HarperCollins in 1991 published a book by John Shelly Spong, an Episcopal bishop, titled *Rescuing the Bible from Fundamentalism: A Bishop Rethinks the Meaning of Scripture*. Karl Keating has such a definition in mind when he examines Roman Catholicism in *Catholicism and Fundamentalism: The Attack on "Romanism" by "Bible Christians"* (1988). So does James Barr in his notable books *Fundamentalism* (1978) and *Beyond Fundamentalism* (1984). Even a charismatic Catholic periodical can suggest a negative response to the query, "Can a Catholic Be a Fundamentalist?" (see Hampsch 1988).

Does this ideological nuance of fundamentalism accurately describe North American Pentecostalism? For the most part, it does. But the term would not suit those members of the Pentecostal tradition who have adopted an informed exegetical style characteristic of the center-to-left evangelicalism that can be found at such schools as Wheaton, Regent, Fuller, and to some extent Dallas, Trinity, and Gordon Conwell, as well as within many of the biblical faculties of classical Pentecostal colleges.

Classical Pentecostalism varies widely. Among its card-carrying teachers are those whose method of biblical interpretation is like that of ideological fundamentalists. Others accept redaction criticism and other modern approaches to the study of scripture.

6. *Within the North American context, where Pentecostalism has probably been most influenced by fundamentalism, an excessive use of biblical literalism has yielded some curious theological deviations.* A conspicuous early example appears in the emergence, around 1915, of the so-called Jesus Name variety of Pentecostalism. At a California camp meeting a brother announced a revelation that God's true name was Jesus, that the doctrine of the trinity was a later development, and was, therefore, not supported in Scripture.

Followers of this teaching walked out of the Assemblies of God at its 1916 general council. The church, which was formally organized only two years earlier, lost a third of its congregation. For the same reason, the Assemblies of God was forced to produce a defensive doctrinal statement despite pristine vows against ever falling into such credal decadence.

What led to the Jesus Name belief was the exegetical fact that at every place in the book of Acts where persons were baptized it is said they were baptized "in the name of Jesus." That was taken literally, despite the fact that the biblical sense of the term *name* exceeds by far the meaning of "signature," or the vocative a mother uses to call her child—referring rather to the sphere of authority in which an act is performed. Similar literalist hermeneutics can be said to lie at the root of a more recent teaching found in Pentecostal circles—the idea that Jesus was Himself born again in hell.[15]

The production of odd and sometimes bizarre theologies within Pentecostalism receives stimulation from its frequent isolation and detachment from the historic tradition of the church. As George Santayana said, whoever does not know history is condemned to repeat it.

7. *Between World War II and the Vietnam War, say between the 1940s and the 1970s, there occurred the evangelicalization of Pentecostalism. In the following quarter century the reverse process can be discerned: the Pentecostalization of evangelicalism.* Pentecostalism aligned itself with the new evangelicalism, not with the new fundamentalism. Particularly through the effort of Thomas Zimmerman, the evangelical regularization of the classical Pentecostals occurred. (Zimmerman's papers, at his direction, were divided between the archives of the denomination he served for a quarter century and the archive at the Billy Graham Center at Wheaton College in the city sometimes labeled "the Evangelical Vatican.")

North American Pentecostalism sustains the fundamentalist urge. The "Statement of *Fundamental* Truths" of the Assemblies of God, created in 1916 just after the five-year distribution of *The Fundamentals*, may well echo that influence. Because of the conspicuous fundamentalist influence on doctrinal formulations emerging from North American Pentecostalism, one must look to other continents and cultures to see what shape a purer Pentecostal theology might take apart from fundamentalist influence.

Largely through the itinerant ministry of David du Plessis, the roving global ambassador of Pentecostal understandings of the Holy Spirit, Pentecostal beliefs and practices were increasingly absorbed into mainstream churches, and not merely by their charismatics. Much of the mainstream evangelical tradition, for example, surrendered the cessationist viewpoint that insisted that spiritual gifts disappeared from the life of the church following the death of the apostles in the first century. Today, church-page advertisements describe freely workshops and seminars on spiritual gifts in churches that no one would confuse with Pentecostalism.

8. *While North American Pentecostals are fundamentalistic in beliefs, mores, and biblical style, they are and have always been clearly distinguishable from the classical fundamentalists who formed organizations for theological Protest.* Pentecostals can become militant more easily over their differences with fundamentalists than over their agreements with them. Fundamentalist Presbyterians and Baptists were accustomed to intradenominational wars. Not until the emergence of the charismatic movement in the 1960s did that phenomenon appear within the Pentecostal-charismatic tradition.

It is not so much that Pentecostals had markedly different basic Christian beliefs from fundamentalists. Rather, their agendas varied. Fundamentalists sought to rectify theological deviation. Pentecostals urged enhancement of personal religious experience. Fundamentalists connected directly with the Christian intellectual tradition. Many early Pentecostals, with restorationist inklings, wrote off two millennia of Christian history.

A few of the first Pentecostals were seminary trained former mainstreamers. But most early Pentecostals favored a less trained ministry and thought themselves sufficiently prepared for ministry provided they were baptized in the Holy Spirit. A text from 1 John 2:27 was often quoted: "the anointing which you received from him abides in you, and you have no need that any one should teach you."

Fundamentalists aimed at raising the banner for classic orthodoxy. Pentecostals, originally quite restorationist, offered an eschatologically justified, power-added experiential enhancement for Christian life and witness. Individual Pentecostals might so delight in their experience of the Pentecostal baptism that they would sever their earlier church connections. By contrast, fundamentalist movements corporately opposed modernist drifts within their denominations. While Pentecostals at first had no denominations, when they got them, there was no modernism to oppose.

Comparisons may be no less invidious than averages. Still, on the whole, classical Pentecostals can and should be distinguished from the classical fundamentalists. On balance, the Pentecostals turn out to be more restorationist, less aware of the course of Christian tradition, less polemic, collectively less antimodernist, more oriented toward personal charismatic experience, less politically involved, as much or more so-cially involved (increasingly so in recent decades), more ecumenical and less separatist, considerably less rationalistic and more inclined toward religious emotion, increasingly less dispensational, and perennially less theologically sophisticated.

It serves precision therefore to say the Pentecostals, while not part of the classical fundamentalist protest of the 1920s and 1930s, nonetheless decidedly think and act like fundamentalists. Pentecostals are fundamentalistic, even if they were not classical fundamentalists. The lowercased adjective fits better than the capitalized noun. The situation changes significantly with the emergence of the charismatic movement in the 1960s, a period that also witnessed the academic maturation of the classical Pentecostal tradition.[16]

NOTES

I have benefitted much from comments on earlier drafts of this essay given me by Edith Blumhofer (Wheaton College, Illinois), Grant Wacker (University of North Carolina), and, at the first reading, by participants in the conference "Global Culture: Pentecostal/Charismatic Movements Worldwide," organized by Karla Poewe and held at the University of Calgary, May 9–11, 1991. Not they, but I, take blame for the surviving infelicities.

1. The five largest denominations in the PFNA, with national inclusive membership in 1989 (in thousands), are these: the Pentecostal Holiness Church (119.10), the Pentecostal Assemblies of Canada (192.7), the International Church of the Foursquare Gospel (203.1), the Church of God (Cleveland, Tennessee, 582.2), and the Assemblies of God (2,137.9). Statistics from Jacquet and Jones 1991: 258–68. Kilian McDonnell invented the term "classical Pentecostalism" to distinguish this cluster from both Protestant and Roman Catholic charismatics (1970: 35).

2. The largest of these in North America is the United Pentecostal Church.

3. Basic histories of Pentecostalism include Anderson 1979 and Synan 1971. Because of the highly oral character of much of Pentecostal spirituality, it is essential to take into account the perspectives presented by Grant Wacker in "The Functions of Faith in Primitive Pentecostalism" (1984: 353–75). Indispensable are the entries and bibliographies in the *Dictionary of Pentecostal and Charismatic Movements* (1988), edited by Stanley M. Burgess, Gary B. McGee, and Patrick H. Alexander. For a comprehensive bibliography (around seven thousand items) see Jones 1983. For global statistics see D. Barrett 1990: 26–27.

4. These global movements, along with the classical Christian, Roman Catholic, and Jewish varieties, are the subject of a five-year study sponsored by the

American Academy of Arts and Sciences. The first of six projected volumes opens with an informative and comprehensive survey by Nancy T. Ammerman entitled "North American Protestant Fundamentalism," which ranges from the prophecy conferences of the last century to reconstructionism (Ammerman 1990: 1–65.

5. A few such agencies, whose addresses may need updating, appear in *Theology News and Notes* (Fuller Seminary Alumni Publication, 30 [March 1983]: 29, 34). For reasons of fractured historical contiguity, the group aiding the smaller Wesleyan churches enjoys no official connections with the parent denominations.

6. Thomas F. Zimmerman, leader of the Assemblies of God from 1959 to 1985, told of a person who introduced herself to him as a "charismatic Christian Scientist"—a combination difficult to imagine from either side.

7. An example appears in the personal story and expository style of Episcopal Canon Dennis J. Bennett, often credited with founding the charismatic movement. He could not accept comfortably his University of Chicago theological training. See Bennett 1970, esp. pp. 9–12, 18.

8. For a brief account of the first use of the term by Curtis Lee Laws, a Baptist editor, see Marsden 1980: 159. "It should be stressed," cautions Grant Wacker in an important note, "that originally it [the word *fundamentalism*] did not have the connotations of militancy and narrowness that it now has. Indeed, Laws said that he chose the word precisely because it did not have the reactionary implications associated with words such as conservative, premillennialist, or Landmarker" (1985: 111 n.1).

9. Both fundamentalism and Pentecostalism, on the usual historical assessments, originated within North America. Quite different cultural forces have shaped Pentecostalism in places such as Latin America, Africa, Europe, and Asia. But even Canadian and American fundamentalism can be nuanced. The formation, in 1990, of the Canadian Evangelical Theological Association, which does not use the term "inerrancy," reflects a stance differing from the American outlook. According to Frame (1991), Professor John Stackhouse of the University of Manitoba argues that fundamentalism did not as deeply affect the Canadian church scene as it did in the United States (see Frame 1991: 43, 45).

10. See also Marsden 1988: 948–54, where each of the feeder sources is described.

11. "Report of the Tenth Annual Convention of the World's Christian Fundamentalist Association" 1928: 9. It has not been widely noticed that this resolution failed to get a unanimous vote—unlike all others considered at the time (for patriotism, prohibition, anti-evolution and anti-atheism legislation, and union among the globe's fundamentalists; but against "compromise" and the Federal Council of Churches of Christ in America). The motion to oppose the modern Pentecostal movement, the conference report explains, "was adopted according to the ruling of the chair by a majority of four votes." This lack of unanimity occurred, the report explains, because "there were many who agreed with the President [W. B. Riley] that it was not a matter that the World's Christian Fundamentals Association should touch at all, since it

is outside of the nine points of our profession, and since the fanatical advocates of tongues and of healing are not opponents of the doctrine of the inspiration of the *Bible*, or the deity of Christ, or any other of our declarations." Even though "fanatics may profess to be fundamentalists, true fundamentalists are not fanatics" (6). While W. B. Riley's influence let the Pentecostals by four votes miss organizational inclusion with the fundamentalists, the persuasive support of Harold John Ockenga fifteen years later admitted Pentecostals at the formation of the National Association of Evangelicals and launched the evangelicalization of Pentecostalism. On Riley's career see Trollinger 1991.

12. Frodsham 1928. Wayne Warner, director of the denominational archives of the Assemblies of God, located this reference for me.
13. Fosdick 1922. On Fosdick, see Miller 1985.
14. Quoted (without primary documentation) in Synan 1971: 144.
15. McConnell 1988; Matta 1984. For another theological faux pas, see Bennett 1991 and Frame 1991.
16. For definitional pursuits beyond Pentecostal/fundamentalist distinctions see, Balmer 1989: ix–xii; Brereton 1990: 165–70; Marty and Appleby 1991: 814–42; Choueiri 1990: 9–12. Donald W. Dayton and Robert K. Johnston conclude their edited review of *The Variety of American Evangelicalism* (1991) with some queries about dispensing with the term "evangelical," along with more choreography of the finessing adjective.

III

Cases:
Turning Orality into Literary Narrative—
The Making of Pentecostal
and Holy Spirit History

Chapter 6

Conflicting Visions of the Past
The Prophetic Use of History in the Early American Pentecostal-Charismatic Movements

Charles Nienkirchen

ABSTRACT

The process of translating oral into literary culture brings to the surface some fascinating rifts and differences. In this chapter American Pentecostals are distinguished from charismatics on the basis of their respective mythological interpretations of church history. Pentecostals, who were concerned to restore the supernatural powers of their first-century apostolic predecessors, tended to collapse history into an apostolic age then and its full restoration now. It made for ahistoricism, exclusivism, and sectarianism. By contrast, charismatics, who were concerned to keep the movement within mainstream Christendom, created an unbroken charismatic lineage to the first century. The latter historical approach accords well with the notion of global culture as based on an ever renewable and ongoing major tradition.

INTRODUCTION

Twentieth-century American Pentecostals and charismatics stand in a lengthy succession of individuals and movements dotting the landscape of Western Christianity that have attempted to legitimize their existence through the use of a prophetically crafted historical apologetic. Not initially concerned with writing history in a fashion credible to modern social scientists, first-generation Pentecostals and their charismatic grandchildren substituted spiritual inspiration for a rigorous critical analysis of the past. Claiming to be endowed with spiritual insight into the divine agenda for the church over the centuries, early

Pentecostals and charismatics selectively extracted from the annals of Christian history those themes essential to constructing a Pentecostal and charismatic myth capable of sustaining their identity among the historic family of Christian churches, alongside which they were forced to define themselves.

The motivation of early Pentecostal and charismatic historical writing and reflection was one of triumphalism; that is, a concern to demonstrate spiritual superiority to pre-existent Christian traditions that had ostensibly lapsed from the supernaturally authenticated Christianity in the first century. Pentecostal and charismatic prophets spawned idyllic visions of a primal Christian past that was being recovered by their respective movements with divine approval and empowerment. Those who articulated the founding Pentecostal and charismatic myths interpreted church history as a divine drama in which the lengthy interlude between the first and twentieth centuries, though not understood as devoid of significant acts of divine intervention at various times, was nonetheless a prelude to the emergence of the Pentecostal and charismatic movements. Confident that they were the last act in the divine drama, Pentecostals and charismatics interpreted themselves as the major ecclesiastical plot of the twentieth century, which was destined to conclude with the falling of the curtain on the stage of world history.[1]

The twentieth-century American Pentecostal and charismatic movements stand as modern heirs of the ecclesiological perceptions implicit in restorationist and renewal movements. Though espousing a spirituality that is similar in many respects, the two movements in their first generation defined their relationship to established Christianity in markedly different fashions. The resultant conflict between restorationist and renewal motifs made charismatics the reluctant mid-century children of their wary early century Pentecostal parents, in addition to generating considerable tension among the children themselves.

THE RESTORATIONIST CONTEXT OF
THE CLASSICAL PENTECOSTAL MOVEMENT

At a conference held at Abilene Christian University in 1985 on the theme "The Restoration Ideal in American History," David E. Harrell, Jr., concluded that restorationism or some variation of it "may be the most vital single assumption underlying the development of American Protestantism."[2] During the eighteenth and nineteenth centuries such divergent groups as Baptists, evangelical Episcopalians, Churches of Christ, various Holiness denominations, and Mormons were equally fascinated with the restorationist ideal.[3] In his typological analysis of nineteenth and twentieth-century American restitutionists, Samuel S. Hill, Jr., observed that the "full-blown and bold American instinct to restore, renew and rectify developed . . . from the second quarter of the nineteenth-century forward, most particularly between 1825 and 1850, [and] between 1890 and 1915" (1976: 68). Recent efforts to examine the roots of Pentecostalism have also elucidated nineteenth-century restorationism as a key element in the defining context of the movement.[4]

During the late nineteenth century many American evangelicals saw themselves as standing near the climax of human history. They anticipated a return to New Testament beginnings in which there would be restored to the church supernatural powers similar to those possessed by its apostolic predecessor. Against the prevalent cultural depiction of the second half of the nineteenth century as an "age of progress," popularized in the minds of the masses of western Europe and America, these evangelical reformers appealed to the early church as a paradigm for the renewal and purification of the present church with all its ills. Restorationism was a handmaid of premillenarian expectations that God would soon directly intervene in world history and bring it to its long awaited consummation—the establishment of the literal thousand-year reign of Christ upon the earth. A premillennial view of the endtimes with its innate pessimism about the deteriorating condition of the world contributed directly to the intensification of restorationist yearnings.[5]

By supplementing a doctrinal synthesis forged from pre-existent nineteenth-century theological motifs with a postconversion Spirit-baptism according to Acts 2 authenticated by tongue speaking, Pentecostals dramatically carried the restorationist banner into the twentieth century. They professed to continue on in the quest to recover the "full" apostolic gospel where others had stopped short. As a whole, the movement was pregnant with an eschatological expectation imbibed from late nineteenth century evangelical movements.

Early twentieth-century Pentecostal sources testify uniformly to the confident conviction of Pentecostal pioneers that they were providentially raised up as heralds of a "restored" apostolic faith that had been lost since the days of the early church. Historical precedent meant little to them. They exalted the book of Acts over decadent centuries of church history as the divine norm for individual and collective church experience, which was being revived by them in the twentieth century.[6]

Pentecostal patriarch Charles F. Parham (1873–1929) epitomized the Pentecostal restorationist spirit. He had been successively a Congregationalist, Methodist, and Holiness preacher. Prior to his Pentecostal experience in 1901, he had concluded after a tour of several centers of revived Holiness and healing spirituality in the eastern United States that the pinnacle of the apostolic gospel had not yet been attained: "I returned home fully convinced that while many had obtained real experience in sanctification and the anointing that abideth, there still remained a great outpouring of power for the Christians who were to close this age.[7]

Out of his spiritual odyssey, Parham gave birth to the "Apostolic Faith" movement, the opening tenet of whose doctrinal statement announced "the restoration of the faith once delivered unto the saints."[8] Significantly, the first history of the Pentecostal movement, authored by Bennett F. Lawrence, a charter member of the Assemblies of God, was entitled *The Apostolic Faith Restored* (1916). In contrast to the established denominations that valued "precedent," "habit," and "custom," Lawrence, with a model display of first-generation Pentecostal ahistoricism, claimed that the movement had only one ancestor—the primitive church (12). Frank Bartleman (1871–1936), an early Pentecostal evangelist and the primary recorder of Pentecostal beginnings at the Azusa Street Mission in Los Angeles, lamented the alleged "fall of the church" after the first-century. Since that time the church had purportedly operated "abnormally" with only "a measure of the Spirit" until the occurrence of the 1906 "Pentecost" in Los Angeles (1980: 76). Frank J. Ewart (1876–1947), an eyewitness at Azusa Street who later emerged as a prominent spokesperson for the Oneness Pentecostal movement, and A. J. Tomlinson (1865–1943), elected as the first general overseer of the Church of God (Cleveland, Tennessee), offered similar disparaging assessments of Christian tradition (Ewart 1947: 87; Tomlinson 1910: 1).

Pentecostal restorationist rhetoric continued unabated into the movement's second decade. John W. "Daddy" Welch (1858–1939), an early general superintendent of the Assemblies of God, recounted his experience of the Pentecostal baptism with tongues under the rubric "The Power of Apostolic Days for You in the Twentieth-Century" (1919: 2–3). Aimee Semple McPherson (1890–1944), the Los Angeles-based founder of the International Church of the Foursquare Gospel, triumphalistically titled her widely read collection of autobiographical experiences, sermons, and writings, *This is That* (1923), reminiscent of the apostle's own dictum on the Day of Pentecost. *The Bridal Call*, which she began publishing in 1917, was replete with articles by herself and others that construed events at her Angelus Temple and Lighthouse for Foursquare Evangelism Bible College as the reincarnation of the book of Acts.[9] Her meteoric career as a healing evangelist was advertised grandiosely as unprecedented since the first-century Pentecost (McPherson 1926: 24).

Despite the pretensions of early Pentecostals to being the direct successors to the apostolic church (though removed by an interregnum of eighteen hundred years), the evidence indicates that they were not completely at ease with an identity that had apostolic roots but no subsequent genealogy. Conscious of being dismissed by other churches as schismatics, attempts were made by some leaders to establish a sense of legitimate historical continuity between the movement and its first-century prototype.[10] For them, the gap between the biblical Upper Room and their twentieth-century movement was simply too large to be ignored.

Wondering whether or not the "basis for [the] distinctive testimony" of Pentecostals should be an experience of a Spirit-baptism patterned after Acts 2, Daniel W. Kerr (1856–1927), founder of two Assemblies of God Bible Institutes, acknowledged that "orthodox churches" could agree with Pentecostals "on many points." Nevertheless, Pentecostals needed to separate themselves from older denominational churches that could not embrace the restoration of "signs and wonders and divers miracles and gifts of the Holy Ghost." A stalwart Pentecostal separatist (having himself previously left another Holiness organization), Kerr wrote in 1922:

> During the past few years God has enabled us to discover and recover this wonderful truth concerning the Baptism in the Spirit as it was given at the beginning. Thus we have all that the others got, and we have got this too. We see all they see, but they don't see what we see.
>
> That is why we cannot work together with those who oppose or reject this Pentecostal truth. They might invite us to come and labor with them, but you know it would not work. Some have tried and failed. You cannot mix Pentecost with denominationalism. (4)

Relying on a form of dispensational holy history, derived from the letters to the seven churches in Revelation, that saw the successive ages of church history as predicted in a series of letters to first-century Asian churches, Kerr posited the "fall of the church" as extending from the close of the first-century to the outset of the sixteenth, when a divinely initiated "restoration period" began in Europe with Martin Luther. John Wesley (England), Johann Blumhardt (Germany), and Dorothea Trüdel (Switzerland) were credited with discovering the previously neglected truths of holiness, healing, and premillennialism that anticipated the Pentecostal reclamation of Spirit-baptism with tongues (Kerr 1926: 4). William I. Evans (1887–1954), principal of the Assemblies of God Central Bible Institute (later Central Bible College) in Springfield, Missouri, alluded to the same restoration process, begun with Luther, by which spiritual truth had been redeemed "from under the rubbish-heap of religious accumulation" en route to the "normal" Christianity of the Pentecostal movement (Evans 1946: 2). Parham and McPherson cited Luther, Methodists, and Quakers as Pentecostal forerunners (see Parham 1985: 29, 32; McPherson 1927c: 23, 1927b: 28).[11] Lilian B. Yeomans (1861–1942), a Bible teacher on the faculty of McPherson's Lighthouse for International Foursquare Evangelism (L.I.F.E.) Bible College, identified numerous persons, including the nineteenth-century preachers Alexander Dowie and A. B. Simpson, as part of the "revival of a faith for healing" that had been building gradually since the Protestant Reformation and had reached a crescendo in her time (1926: 111–16). Others embraced the Irvingites as predecessors.[12] Bartleman went further to construct an historical apology for Pentecostal tongue-speaking wholly dependent on the writings of non-Pentecostal historians and biblical commentators.[13]

If Pentecostals legitimized themselves with a mythological interpretation of church history, they energized themselves by eschatological speculation, more specifically, the advocacy of a dispensational premillennialism, with its collateral doctrine of the "Latter Rain."[14] The premillennial version of the endtimes, not unique to Pentecostals, was inherited from the broadly based Holiness movement of the nineteenth-century. Among the premillennial mentors of first-generation Pentecostals were A. J. Gordon, the Baptist pastor of Clarendon Street Church in Boston (1869–1895), A. B. Simpson (1843–1919), founder of the Christian and Missionary Alliance (in 1887), and W. E. Blackstone (1841–1935), a prominent American Zionist who authored the popular premillennial manifesto, *Jesus is Coming* (1908).[15] From the early days of Azusa Street onwards, the premillennial doctrine of Christ's second coming was propounded by Pentecostals.[16] Though averse to credalism of any kind, the "Statement of Fundamental Truths," composed in 1916 by members of the Assemblies of God movement, nonetheless devoted four of sixteen articles to eschatology, one of which espoused the premillennial view of the Second Advent.[17]

The "latter rain" corollary was drawn from biblical passages such as Deuteronomy 11:14, Joel 2:23, and James 5:7, which became the basis for the early Pentecostal theologizing of church history. The "early rain" was identified with the first Day of Pentecost, and the "latter rain," separated from the former by the long intervening "drought" of church history, was equated with the Pentecostal movement. The Holiness movements of the nineteenth-century were tokenly acknowledged as "preliminary showers" to the Pentecostal "latter rain" in the twentieth century, which would even exceed the outpouring of apostolic days in both its supernatural intensity and scope (see Taylor 1985: 21; and Welch 1916). Pentecostal apologists went so far as to reproduce rainfall charts for Palestine during the second half of the nineteenth century as meteorological support for their prophetic proclamations.[18] That their movement was indeed the long prophesied "latter rain" immediately preceding the final apocalypse seemed confirmed by larger-scale events, such as the birth and growth of Zionism (the first congress in 1897), the San Francisco earthquake (1906) and the apparent apostasy of denominational churches.[19] In the final analysis, however, it was the restoration of tongue speaking that constituted the sine qua non for the divine clock entering its final hour.[20]

In their overall demeanor, first-generation Pentecostals, by virtue of their restorationist ecclesiology and claim to have recovered the "full" apostolic gospel, became exclusive and sectarian. They quickly took on an adamantly antidenominational posture, denouncing even those Holiness organizations with whom they had a natural affinity in the harshest of language. Thus Azusa Street spawned a new family of Pentecostal denominations that carved out their own ecclesiastical identity in the first half of the twentieth century in isolation from older evangelical and established churches that spurned them. Ironically, when tongue speaking and other related phenomena inundated Protestant, Catholic, and Orthodox traditions later in the century, Pentecostals (now designated by scholars as "classical") gave these new charismatics reluctant approval. By then what was once preached as "new wine" was adequately contained in "old wineskins."

THE CHARISMATIC MOVEMENT AND THE SEARCH FOR HISTORICAL CONTINUITY

Whereas early Pentecostals were at best minimally concerned with the issue of historical legitimacy, the "new Pentecostals" who emerged in the 1960s and 1970s devoted their academic skills to constructing an historical apologetic that would bring added credibility to the charismatic movement and justify its attempt to affiliate with the mainstream of Christendom. Consequently, they developed revisionist interpretations of what they deemed past "renewal" movements, which were accompanied by glossolalia, prophetic utterances, healing, and other related supernatural phenomena, and which traditional ecclesiastical historians had pejoratively judged as schismatic and heretical in character.

The bedrock theological premise of charismatic historiography was that the book of Acts was not indicative of a transitional phase in church history, but rather served as a normative blueprint for the church in all ages.[21] Though mostly forgotten, the apostolic pattern was spasmodically recovered during various periods in the church's past. Furthermore, charismatic scholars opposed any hermeneutical tendency to view the historical narrative of Acts as of lesser doctrinal importance than the explicitly didactic portions of the New Testament. To the contrary, the former was regarded as the interpretive backdrop for the latter.[22] The pneumatic narratives of Lukan writings were set forth as a liturgical guide concerning how the Spirit was to be received in post-apostolic times.

Like their Pentecostal prophet forebears and many restorationist groups before them, Protestant charismatics subscribed to the "fall of the church" thesis, which explained the gradual disappearance of charisms of the Holy Spirit during the postapostolic era in terms of the spiritual decline and the growing institutionalization/sacramentalization of the church. J. Rodman Williams, a charismatic historical theologian of Presbyterian extraction and founding president of Melodyland School of Theology in Anaheim, California, eruditely critiqued the church of the Middle Ages and the Protestant Reformation as mired in "structural rigidity" and largely ignorant of "the extraordinary and unique event of the coming of the Holy Spirit," as well as being oblivious to the importance of the charismata (1972: 33, 37–39). Williams looked instead to the "enthusiasts" of the Radical Reformation and their successors, the Puritans, Quakers, Pietists, Wesleyans, Holiness groups in America and classical Pentecostals, as the avant garde of the "extraordinary spiritual renewal," which he saw as "beginning to occur across Christendom" (53–55).

Charismatics, though they were convinced they had ancestors, did not necessarily agree on who they were. Williams's list was an abbreviation of the one earlier constructed by the British Anglican Michael Harper (1965, expanded 1971) to include Irenaeus, Justin Martyr, Montanists, Hueguenots, Jansenists, and Irvingites. Martin Luther, Francis Xavier, Thomas Walsh, and the Curé d'Ars all found a place in charismatic genealogy (1971: 17–22). Roman Catholic and Eastern Orthodox charismatics who were unaffected by post-Reformation Protestant restorationism investigated their respective traditions with a much expanded definition of "charismatic" and assembled a veritable potpourri of monks, mystics, heretics, saints, and religious orders from all ages as their authentic forerunners.[23] As René Laurentin, a French Catholic charismatic, astutely observed, charismatic historiography entered the domain of what had been traditionally studied as the history of "revivals" and "enthusiasm" (and, I would add, "heresy"). Laurentin suggested a more all-encompassing category of study, the history of "pneumatics," but admitted that the difference in terminology mattered little since it was "pretty much the same movements passing in review" (1977: 132–35).

The concerted attempt of neo-Pentecostal popular writers and scholars to construct an unbroken "charismatic" lineage that tied them to the first-century singled out the second-century Montanists and nineteenth-century Irvingites for special attention, the former because of their proximity to the apostolic church, the latter because of their proximity to neo-Pentecostals. The Episcopal clergy-person (with charismatic sympathies) Morton Kelsey wrote that there were "Pentecostal writers who look back to Montanus with some of the same historical reverence a Presbyterian offers up to Augustine" (1981: 34). The concern of charismatics, in the case of both movements, was to rehabilitate them from heterodox sects into bona fide renewal movements. Discussing the question of whether Montanism was a Jewish-Christian heresy, J. Massyngberde Ford, a charismatic Scripture scholar at the University of Notre Dame, stated her preference for the original designation of Montanism as the "New Prophecy" since it did "not seem to have been a heresy in its beginnings" (1966: 145). The Lutheran charismatic William Olson interpreted Montanism in a similar vein. He reconstructed the movement as a reactionary force against the drift toward hierarchical consolidation in the second-century church. As such, it was a "thorn in the side" to a Church, which was establishing a "format of faith in creeds and doctrines, and cautiously curtailing the freedom of revelatory truth maintained by lay renewal movements" (1974: 62). The conflict with Montanists was interpreted in the light of the age-old dialectical tension between structure and freedom in the Church.

For charismatics, history also had pedagogical value. Another Lutheran charismatic author, Larry Christenson, posited that the charismatic movement offered a new point of reference for a revised understanding of the Scottish preacher Edward Irving and the Catholic Apostolic Church in the nineteenth century. In his brief but intriguing book *A Message to the Charismatic Movement* (1972) Christenson used Irvingite teaching and practice as a context for appraising charismatic spirituality. Drawing an analogy between Irvingites and Pentecostals/charismatics and the relationship between John the Baptist and Christ, Christenson lauded the Catholic Apostolic Church as the biblical "seed" that fell into the ground and died in order that it might bring forth much fruit, that is, the charismatic movement (see pp. 15, 17, 108–12). The oddities and excesses of the Irvingites, long enumerated by noncharismatic scholars, were mostly ignored. A prophetic view of the past called for a certain amount of sanitization of charismatic ancestors.

Reading church history through the lenses of their respective ecclesiastical traditions, first-generation charismatics differed somewhat in the identification of their forerunners. Many of them did agree, however, that renewal was not to be achieved at the expense of their church affiliation. The resurgence of supernatural charisms and an ecumenical vision of the Church were closely linked (McDonnell 1976). Published accounts of "charismatically" renewed Protestant and Catholic parishes, including a charismatic Benedictine abbey, a Franciscan university, and a Protestant charismatic university established by a Pentecostal turned Methodist, buttressed the claim that the charismatic movement could enrich the overall spiritual life of the church and be a source of greater unity, not further fragmentation.[24]

For Catholic charismatics it was axiomatic that the true church always renews itself, hence their vigorous efforts to locate their movement within the mainstream of the Catholic Church. They owed their spiritual debt to classical Pentecostals but eschewed the cultural baggage and sectarian image of the Pentecostal movement.[25] For them the use of the term "Pentecostal" distracted from the focus of the total renewal of the Church, hence their insistence on promoting a "Catholic charismatic Renewal" as opposed to a "Catholic Pentecostal movement" (see McDonnell 1973; see especially Ranaghan 1973b: 12–20). The dangers of Pentecostal separatism and divisiveness were underscored repeatedly in early Catholic charismatic literature (e.g., see O'Connor 1971: 239–62; Ranaghan 1973: 47–50; and Gelpi 1971: 4–42). Leaders of the renewal refused to heed the exhortation of David Wilkerson, a prominent, self-styled Pentecostal "prophet," to leave the Catholic Church because of impending persecution, dismissing instead his "independent spirit" as "one of the least healthy elements that traditional Pentecostalism [had] contributed to Christianity.[26] Protestant counterparts were criticized as less effective because of their failure to discard Pentecostal elitist tendencies and embrace a vision for the complete renewal of their churches.[27] Moreover, the movement was written ex post facto by its apologists into the script of Vatican II as the fulfillment of Pope John XXIII's prayer for "a new Pentecost" in the Church.[28] Pope John's successor, Pope Paul VI, was also made out to be strongly sympathetic to the charismatic cause (see O'Connor 1978).

For all of their stated unified commitment to the inclusive renewal of the Church, however, strained relations surfaced among Catholic charismatics over the issue of alleged sectarianism. The covenant-community stream of the movement, associated with the Word of God community, in Ann Arbor, Michigan, was accused of developing rigid para-ecclesial structures more akin to the separatist ecclesiology of the sixteenth-century Anabaptists and modern Protestant fundamentalists than to the inclusivist organizational style and sacramental theological tradition of the contemporary Catholic church, with its respect for non-Pentecostal traditions of spirituality.[29] Though refuting the charge that they were headed in a sectarian direction, by pointing to a precedent for their communities in fourth-century ascetic movements, covenant-community leaders had earlier admitted that their call for the formation of intentional communities as a means of renewing the Church was "vaguely schismatic" (Clark 1971: 33).[30] It was, however, also asserted that this strategy was not the only (and in some instances not the most desirous) option for effecting the renewal of the Church (Martin 1978: 20–22).

The conflict over styles of renewal that erupted among Catholic charismatics was also mirrored in Protestant segments of the movement during the early 1970s. Here it took the form of a "discipleship/ shepherding" controversy in which prominent nondenominational charismatics were pitted against denominational charismatic leaders. Restorationist teaching associated with Christian Growth Ministries in Fort Lauderdale, Florida, posed a formidable challenge to the earlier ecumenical mind-set of Protestant charismatics.[31]

Despite internecine disputes among first-generation charismatics, the Kansas City Conference on the charismatic Renewal in the Christian Churches (1977) was prophetically billed as bringing together the three main streams of North American charismatic renewal in the twentieth century—the classical (denominational) Pentecostals, the neo-Pentecostals, and the Catholic Pentecostals—"to form one mighty river of the Spirit."[32] Denominational and nondenominational charismatics, as well as Messianic Jews, were represented among the organizers of and delegates to the conference. The official agenda of the gathering was ostensibly ecumenical. The conference was reputedly the fruit of "the largest grass-roots ecumenical movement that Christianity [had] known in the last 800 years."[33] As the flowering of first-generation charismatic conciliarism, Kansas City was a watershed in the evolution of the movement, which marked the triumph, at least temporarily, of an inclusive "renewal from within" strategy over an exclusive, restorationist ecclesiology.

In summary, at the practical level, restorationist and renewal ideologies took first-generation Pentecostal and charismatic leaders, all of whom appealed to prophetic interpretations of history, in opposite directions, ecclesiologically speaking. Pentecostal pioneers quickly abandoned any ecumenical intentions, exited the "apostate" established Churches, and translated their restored "full" gospel into the founding of new separatist Pentecostal denominations. By contrast, charismatic leaders in the first two decades of the movement established renewal agencies within their respective denominations, occupied important administrative positions in the World Council of Churches, and initiated a series of Roman Catholic/Pentecostal dialogues.[34] The preeminent internationally active apostle of neo-Pentecostalism, David Du Plessis, though defrocked by the Assemblies of God in 1962 because of his ecumenical activities, especially his involvement with the World Council of Churches and Roman Catholics, nonetheless persisted in disseminating his vision of a charismatically renewed Church within all Christian traditions.[35] The amelioration of official Church attitudes toward the charismatic movement in the 1970s made Du Plessis's vision seem all the more plausible.[36]

In its 1972 statement on the charismatic movement, the Assemblies of God, in recognizing that "the winds of the Spirit [were] blowing freely outside the normally recognized Pentecostal body," sought to avoid "the extremes of an ecumenism that compromises scriptural principles and an exclusivism that excludes true Christians."[37] The adoption of such a stance by the largest white Pentecostal denomination, belated and cautious as it was, nonetheless constituted a significant stride in the direction of effecting a greater harmonization of Pentecostal "restorationist" and charismatic "renewal" consciousness.[38] The Pentecostal and charismatic prophets were moving closer to agreement in their visions of the past and future.

NOTES

1. The prophetic use of history is addressed in an African charismatic context in chapter seven of this volume.
2. As quoted in Hughes 1988: 7.
3. See Hughes 1988: 143–52, 153–70, 179–95, 220–31; and Hughes 1976: 87–103.
4. See Donald W. Dayton's masterful study (1987: 25–28) and that of the Assemblies of God historian Edith L. Blumhofer (1989: I, 18–22).
5. On the upsurge in premillennialist fervor in American evangelicalism during the second half of the nineteenth century, see T. Weber 1983: 43–64. Concerning the earlier outbreak of apocalyptic millenarianism at the beginning of the century, see Sandeen 1974: 104–18.
6. See the vigorous defence of the normality of Spirit baptism with tongues according to Acts 2 in George F. Taylor's *The Spirit and the Bride* (1907; reprinted, with two other documents, as *Three Early Pentecostal Tracts*, 1985: 46), perhaps the first book-length exposition of Pentecostal theology. Taylor (1881–1934) was a Pentecostal Holiness Church leader.
7. As quoted in Parham 1930: 48.
8. For Parham's career as the pre-eminent White leader of American Pentecostalism, see Goff 1988. The 1906 statement of faith of his Apostolic Faith Movement appears in Hollenweger 1988a: 513; see also *The Apostolic Faith*, September 1906: 2.
9. See McPherson 1925: 10, 13, 26, 27; 1927a: 16; and 1929: 7–8, 30.
10. I am indebted for the observation of this ambivalence in Pentecostal thought to Grant Wacker (1986: 84–87).
11. Gladwyn N. Nichols (1926: 22) listed Franciscans, Huegenots, Waldenses, Luther, and Wesley as forerunners of the Pentecostal movement.

12. An editorial, "Whose Faith Follow," in *Pentecostal Evangel*, 8 July 1922: 1–3, outlined lessons to be learned from the errors of the Irvingites.

13. For evidence of Bartleman's restorationism, see Bartleman 1980: 43–44, 62, 89; for his historical defence of tongue speaking, see 1980: 77–78.

14. Note the preponderance of eschatological/restorationist themes in the titles of early Pentecostal periodicals: *Apostolic Banner, Apostolic Herald, Apostolic Faith, Latter Rain Evangel, New Acts, Pentecost, Pentecostal Evangel, Pentecostal Wonders, Upper Room, Meat in Due Season, Christian Harvester*. Full bibliographic information on these periodicals is available in Jones 1983.

15. See Gordon 1889. More specifically on the development of early Pentecostal premillennialism, see Goff 1983. More generally, on the indebtedness of early Pentecostals to nineteenth-century premillenarians, see Dayton 1987: 143–67.

16. See A. W. Orwig's (1916) recounting of the essential doctrines he observed being preached ardently at Azusa Street, among which he included the "premillennial coming of Christ" (quoted in Sheppard 1984: 7). See also "The Millennium" 1906: 3; and Seymour 1907: 2.

17. For the full text of the statement, see Hollenweger 1988a: 514–16.

18. For example, see the "Chart Showing Rainfall in Palestine from 1861 to 1907," which appears at the conclusion of Myland 1910.

19. See especially Bartleman's reference to the San Francisco earthquake and his castigation of Holiness people for their "spirit of prejudice," "pharisaism," and "pride" (1980: 48). The antagonism between Pentecostals and Holiness groups was so strong that the first time a major group of Pentecostals was hosted by a Wesleyan-holiness institution (Asbury Seminary) was in 1988. See Dieter 1990.

20. See the comments to this effect by the Pentecostal evangelist Elizabeth Sisson (1843–1934), in *A Sign People* (n.d. [ca. 1918]): 9, 12.

21. See the works of the Baptist charismatic theologian Howard M. Ervin (professor at Oral Roberts University): *These Are Not Drunken As Ye Suppose* (1968: 226); *And Forbid Not to Speak With Tongues* (1971: 22–28); and *This Which Ye See and Hear* (1972: 13).

22. For the use of an integrated hermeneutic that sees doctrinal value in Acts, see the Catholic charismatic Stephen B. Clark's *Baptized in the Spirit* (1970: 50–58). A more general charismatic holistic hermeneutical paradigm is set forth in Montague 1979: 77–95, and esp. 90–94.

23. As examples, see the Catholic writers J. Massyngberde Ford (1970: 9–17); Judith Tydings (1977); see also Synan (1975: 169–91) and the Orthodox perspective of Athanasios F. S. Emmert (1976: 28–42). More generally, on the spread of the charismatic movement in the Orthodox Church in the United States, see Walker 1984: 163–71, and esp. 163–65.

24. Among the foremost showcase charismatic parishes in the early 1970s were the Church of the Redeemer, Houston, Texas; St. Luke's Episcopal Church, Seattle, Washington; St. Paul's Episcopal Church, Darien, Connecticut; St. Patrick's Catholic Church, Providence, Rhode Island, and Trinity Lutheran Church, San Pedro, California. For uncritical descriptions of their development, see Pulkingham 1972, 1973; Bennett 1970; Slosser 1979; J. Randall 1973;

Jorstad 1974: 51–62. For the stories of Pecos Benedictine Abbey in Pecos, New Mexico, and the Franciscan University in Steubenville, Ohio, see Geraets 1977: 20–23; and Jahr 1976: 261–65; Manney 1985: 10–14. Regarding Oral Roberts's charismatic university see Chappell 1988: 759–60. The Catholic charismatic Kevin Ranaghan described the ecumenical atmosphere of Oral Roberts University in "The Liturgical Renewal at Oral Roberts University" (1973a: 122–36).

25. For the acknowledged Pentecostal origins of the Catholic charismatic movement see Ranaghan and Ranaghan 1969: 6; and Ranaghan 1971: 114–25.

26. I refer here to Ralph Martin's response to David Wilkerson's "vision" delivered at the 1973 International Lutheran Charismatic Conference, Minneapolis, Minnesota (1974a: 11–12).

27. See Byrne 1971: 22–23 on the "elitism" of Protestant charismatics; on the Catholic charismatic movement as an example to Protestant charismatics to avoid sectarianism and seek the renewal of their denominations, see Martin 1974b: 11, 15.

28. See O'Connor 1971: 287–89. The charismatic Belgian Cardinal, Léon Joseph Suenens, one of the architects of Vatican II, authored a book entitled *A New Pentecost?* (1974) that included the prayer of Pope John XXIII on its title page. Regarding the allusion to Vatican II as creating an environment conducive to charismatic renewal, see Ranaghan and Ranaghan 1969: 251–52; Roh 1972: 5–6. For the charismatic Renewal as one of God's answers to Pope John's prayer, see Ford 1976a: 3.

29. See J. Massyngberde Ford's thesis that there were actually two "types" of Catholic charismatic renewal, "type I" (epitomized in the covenant communities of Ann Arbor, Michigan and South Bend, Indiana), which was inspired by the Radical Reformation, and "type II" (exemplified by the Pecos Benedictine Community in New Mexico), which was consistent with historic Catholic models of renewal (1976b: 40–62, 65–85.

30. See Steven B. Clark (a coordinator of the Word of God community) 1978: 14–20.

31. A documentary survey of the controversy is given in Harper 1979: 139–44. For a nonpartisan account of the controversy, see Plowman 1975: 52, 53–54; and Synan 1976: 46. The restorationist premises of the "discipleship/ shepherding" doctrines associated with Christian Growth Ministries in Fort Lauderdale, Florida, are set forth in Prince 1976: 37–58. For a sharp criticism of the "nondenominational" form of renewal as "shallow and one-dimensional," see Christenson 1976: 10.

32. See Synan 1984: 126–30; see also the unofficial narrative of the conference by David Manuel, *Like A Mighty River* (1977).

33. Blattner 1981: 193–200; see also "Charismatic Unity in Kansas City" 1977: 36, 37. For the nondenominational, restorationist endorsement of the conference see the entire October 1977 (vol. 9) issue of *New Wine* magazine, published by Christian Growth Ministries, Ft. Lauderdale, Florida.

34. See Sandidge 1985: 41–60, for the history of the dialogues that began in 1972 in Zurich-Horgen, Switzerland. On the structure and substance of the dialogues, see also McDonnell 1974: 4–6; Meeking 1974: 106–9.

35. On Du Plessis's ecumenical wanderings and vision, see his autobiography, *The Spirit Bade Me Go* (1970); Spittler 1988: 250–54; Du Plessis 1973: 223–50, 1975: 91–103; Robeck 1987: 1–4.
36. For an analysis of the change in the responses of established churches toward the charismatic movement through the 1960s and 1970s, see Connelly 1985: 184–92.
37. The full text of the document is included in McDonnell 1980: 319–20.
38. In 1977 the Pentecostal Holiness Church followed suit, issuing a statement on the charismatic movement with marked similarities to that of the Assemblies of God. The full text of that document is included in "Minutes of the Eighteenth General Conference of the Pentecostal Holiness Church," Oklahoma City, Oklahoma, August 3–10, 1977: 68.

Chapter 7

Christianity and the Construction of Global History
The Example of Legio Maria

Nancy Schwartz

ABSTRACT

Legio Maria is an independent Catholic church that combines a Latin mass with charismatic activities. Legio emphasis on the Holy Spirit led to an open, incorporative identity and church history. What we see here is a first effort to transform oral into written culture. As we, who are part of a written culture, quote written texts from respected authors to boost the authority of what we say, so those who are part of an oral culture quote oral texts from the author of the whole universe to boost the authority of what they say. Access to this supreme author, for Legio, the Holy Spirit, is achieved through metonymic and typological patterns of thought. As later chapters show, metonyms convince; typological exegeses establish connections to a history of salvation. Typologies enhance the globality of Legio's created history because local events are seen as types of national and international events from any period of time, including that of the Bible. Thus their founder, Baba Messias, is a type of Melchizedek, a type of Elijah, a type of Mau Mau General, a type of Christ.

INTRODUCTION

Legios are like Catholics. There is no difference in the mass, except that (in Legio) the holy mass is in Latin. . . . Other masses have gone local (Alexius Owuoth, Roman Catholic truck-driver, son of Rusabela Ohinga, a Legio church mother. September 18, 1984).[1]

Legio Maria of African Church Mission is the largest independent Catholic church in sub-Saharan Africa. Membership estimates over the years have ranged from 20,000 to more than 1,000,000.[2] A conservative recent estimate puts Legio membership at 248,000 (Barrett and Padwick 1989: 66). Legio has creatively combined a Catholicism that is conservative and retains the Latin mass and Roman Catholic ritual forms with charismatic activities. The charismatic experiences of healing, exorcism, prophecy, glossolalia, glossographia, dream interpretation, and visions have been some of the most notable attractions in drawing members to Legio, along with Legio's tolerance, unlike the Roman Catholic Church, for practices like polygyny and the levirate.[3] Another important factor in Legio's success, which emerged from my Kenyan fieldwork in 1982–1985, is the view of members that the Holy Spirit is author and authority.[4] Under the Spirit's inspiration Legios have created their own church history and sense of identity that is open and incorporative. Perhaps some African independent churches have been "places to feel at home" where home is writ small. Imaging African independent churches as "counter-societies," "parallel societies," "encapsulating," "withdrawals from the 'real world,'" "withdrawals from the global society," "withdrawals to smaller communities" might still apply for some.[5] Such images are not apt for Legio. Staunch belief in possession by the Holy Spirit need not have "introversionist" consequences, directing a church and its members "away from the world" (B. Wilson, quoted in Rollman 1991: 4).

Legios described Legio as a "reformed" Catholic church, and therefore potentially a universal church.[6] For Legios, one of their important reforms was offering members alternate ways to engage in a "worldwide communion." One of these ways was history. This was a history that proceeded from the Holy Spirit and its agents. Legios would affirm:

> Chuny Mtakatifu ema owacho . . . (It is the Holy Spirit who said . . .)
> Roho ema ofule . . . (It is the Spirit who disclosed it . . .)
> Malaika opuonjo ji . . . (The Angels taught people . . .)
> Teko onyisowa . . . (The Power has shown us . . .)
> Dhano adhanya ok onyal . . . (An ordinary person couldn't . . .)
> Roho ema olor, owacho niya . . . (It is the Spirit which descended, saying that . . .)

According to Legios, the Holy Spirit led them to make connections between the Legio, which "started to be heard" as an organized movement in Kenya in the early 1960s, and a variety of personages, places, and events in African, European, American, and Asian political-religious history. Legios built a church that was responsive to "local needs," but they did not want to be isolated, to have "gone local." The preposition that has always been a part of the full name of the church contained a proposition that was important to them: Legio was *of* Africa, but not just *for* Africa. Even before "Mission" was officially added to its name, the Legio church constitution stated that one object of Legio was outreach and missionization, to "maintain the apostolic ways or lines of worship through the African communion churches of East Africa, and at the same time maintain the faith of world Maria Legio within the spiritual order of the leader of Maria Legio of Africa."[7] Legios would point out with pride that the language of their mass remained a universal language, that their charismatic activities met universal needs for healing and for wholeness, and that their historical focus reached beyond the narrow line Roman Catholics would trace from Israel-Palestine to Rome.[8]

Legios saw their church as going further in charismatic belief and action than the various charismatic groups that remained within the Roman Catholic church in Kenya and other parts of Africa.[9] Legios claimed to have influenced some Kenyan Roman Catholic charismatics, and to have prompted the rise of some small independent Catholic churches in Tanzania and Kenya that seem to be schisms from Legio or Legio inspired (Schwartz 1989a: 54–55, 517–20). They asserted they had an influence on some smaller Kenyan churches that followed Anglican prayer books and Pentecostal practices but which had some symbols and rituals in common with Legio, like the African Roho Musalaba Church, among many others (Schwartz 1989a: 522–23). They also contended they had influenced larger churches like the Kenyan Holy Ghost Coptic Church, also known as the Holy Ghost Hermetic Church (520–21). However, Legios were more interested in the question of influence than the actualities of building formal interactions on the institutional level.

While their leader, the Baba Messias Ondeto, had often preached tolerance for other denominations and encouraged members and clergy to interact as individuals with those from other denominations, the "ecumenical spirit" of Legio had its limits (OAIC 1982: 28). As a church, Legio had participated in interdenominational gatherings, but it did not have extensive dealings with African organizations of independent churches or with other ecumenical bodies. This stance seems to derive from the church's concern to maintain its independence and avoid foreign control, a concern shared by other religious groups in Africa.[10] In limiting its institutional links, Legio was showing it wanted to be open on its own terms. Its caution was not closure, and seemed to show an appreciation of the problems of postcolonialism in Africa.

LEGIO AND ITS LUO BACKGROUND:
GEOGRAPHIC SPREAD

Legio began among Kenya Luo (Joluo) in the western part of Kenya and Tanzania. A number of observers have put emphasis on these origins, noted that membership has been predominantly Luo, and highlighted an image of circumscription and "tribalism." Harold Turner, for example, has maintained that the leaders are quick to declare its intertribal nature, but in fact it is very largely confined to the Nilotic Luo in western Kenya who are unpopular with the surrounding Bantu peoples (1979: 177).

Some members, such as Nathaniel Ogana, who were pessimistic about the pace of Legio missionization, gave an assessment similar to Turner's: "sani e piny Kikuyu, WaKamba, 'Lango,' moja achiel achiel kuomgi osechako biro e Lejio Maria, bang' neno kaka Lejio ogolo masiche kuom ji. To bende jomoko kuomgi pok oyie, gichung' thenge." (Now in the land of the Kikuyu, Kamba, Nandi, Kipsigis, and Maasai, one, one, one among them have begun to come to Legio Maria after seeing how Legio took away people's troubles. Then again, some among them don't yet believe, and they stand aside.)[11] However, images of a church confined to one ethnic group and a specific locus do not address the full situation of Legio.

As many scholars of Kenya Luo have recognized, Luo have long had an orientation toward movement, pluralism, and flexibility, along with an orientation against closure. This outlook marks the several thousand years of history preceding their migration into Kenya, on which there is an ever increasing scholarship. It was part of the "plural society" Luos helped make in the western part of Kenya before Western colonialism. It marks their "indigenous" spirit possession and religion, which has been quite osmotic. It is part of a pragmatic patrilineality, which has not been monolithic for either men or women.[12] It has been part of their later labor migration, which is the highest rate for any ethnic group in Kenya.[13] For most Luos, commitment to an ethnic identity as Luo is still strong, but ties to the Luo community have never excluded other linkages. Association, assimilation, incorporation, and change have been accepted and expected as a "traditional" part of Luo culture for centuries. This continuing legacy has influenced Legio.[14]

Legios have lived as labor migrants in many parts of East Africa and beyond. Within Kenya itself, there have been more Legio dioceses outside of Nyanza Province, the Luo "homeland" in Kenya, than inside Nyanza. Some of the congregations beyond Nyanza, in the various areas where Luo have lived as labor migrants, have had a largely Luo membership, but there were also laity and clergy from other ethnic groups, for example, Kikuyu, Kamba, Luyia, Turkana, Gusii, and Nandi. Legios reported there had been several Europeans who joined Legio as laity. They also had "half-caste" members (people of mixed European-African descent) in Legio, and a few Asian members in the past. Legio has had congregations outside of Kenya. There have been several in Tanzania and Uganda, and a smaller number reportedly in Burundi, Rwanda, Zaire, Zambia, Ethiopia, and possibly Egypt.[15] Legios spoke about one congregation existing in Nigeria. One church member maintained Legio had reached Ghana. David Barrett's statement that Legio was "initially" Luo but became "increasingly multitribal" (1979: 2087) seems to point in the direction in which Legios wanted to move.

Legio was not just a church of an urban proletariat or a rural peasantry. Its members did not live solely in city slums, nor in the poorest rural areas furthest from good roads and development.[16] While many Legios in the towns were "working class," unemployed, underemployed, job seekers, uneducated, or undereducated, there were also members who were more successful. There were members who were literate and members educated beyond the primary level. The age structure of Legio was also diverse, ranging from the very young to the old, including children who had joined Legio independently of either parent. The age range of different congregations has, however, been affected by labor migration.

In Kisumu, the capital of Nyanza Province, James Ongo, a Legio priest to a town congregation who said he had held a position in local government in Uganda, told me he had become interested in Legio while living there in 1970. A vision and then a dream had stopped his drinking, his seduction of women, and given him a distaste for "that country."[17] Returning home directed to be "a Legion, a Legio Maria . . . to go and preach what God is," he had resisted joining Legio. He had seen Legio as lacking dynamism, as a church for the old, for those left behind. He had gained this impression when he visited his rural home. His opinion was challenged and changed by a visit to Nairobi. There he found a more diverse membership:

> When I reached home in . . . [the] location, I saw only old people, women and men who were old. Only those entered the religion, I thought. I thought that I would like to enter in the mission. When I saw them, I refused. After that, I went to Nairobi and attended Legio Maria one day. I saw very many different people. Some have cars, as Benz, as Peugeots, and other cars. I said in my heart, "Today I will enter in this *kanisa* because I thought this religion is

> entered by old people. I saw many different people. I must join
> today." And that is the day I entered. After that, I saw many
> things through the Holy Spirit. So I believed in this church.

In the 1980s, I found the membership of rural Legio congregations more diverse than the twenty-eight-year old Ongo once had. Cosmopolitan Nairobi, Kenya's capital, still had more of the mixture that had attracted him. In Nairobi, I met with Legios who worked for international firms as accountants and secretaries. One prominent Legio was a customs official, another a former engineer. Claris Madaga, a Luyia woman and civil servant living in Nairobi, was an Anglican from a well-off family with a father highly placed in a national "mainline" church organization. She had taken one of her young relatives to Legio for healing, and sought to counter an image of Legio as a church for the marginal and lower-class: "There is a tendency to pull you to Legio Maria Church. You need a strong heart to refuse . . . [Oginga] Odinga has been a Legio man up to now.[18] Others I know of, big people, [government] ministers who call the Legio in to remove medicines and other things, they won't change their church. But they believe that Legios have power. You can't say that Legio is for the lower class. In town, you won't know. They'll wear the rosary beads inside their shirts."

Stephen Ondiek Oluoch, a Legio Archbishop, has been the M.P. for Ugenya from 1983 to the present. Several of his wives are well-known as educated and articulate headmistresses of private secondary schools run by his St. Stephen's Educational Trust. They are also Legios. Since his 1983 election, Ondiek Oluoch has been an assistant minister in the government ministries of cooperative development, water development, and more recently, public works. The government's placement of Ondiek Oluoch in such positions may have been designed to help replace earlier images, some raised in Parliament itself, that Legios were not concerned with the social dimension, with practical and worldly matters.

In rural areas, most Legio men and women I met were subsistence farmers, small-scale traders, former labor migrants, or migrants to be. While the most-successful people in East Alego, where I did most of my work, tended to be Anglicans and Roman Catholics, some Legios were from successful families in the area, relatively wealthy and well-regarded members of their community. In the "Lihudu" neighborhood where I lived in East Alego, Legios supported the largest church building. While Legio's reach for an "interethnic communion" and "classwide" appeal was still further than its grasp, moving in this direction did seem an interest of laity and leaders.[19]

Although all are still within Nyanza Province, Legio is a church with more than one holy site. Its headquarters is at one of them, St. Mary's Basilica, Jerusalem-Amoyo, West Kadem location, Nyatike Division, in South Nyanza District. The Baba Messias Simeo Ondeto, regarded by most Legios as Christ come back to Africa in the form of a Luo, was not partial to centripetality, and spent much of his time away from Jerusalem-Amoyo, traveling around to various congregations in Kenya.[20] He "died" away from the headquarters while visiting a Legio congregation in the Manyatta area of Kisumu town, early in September 1991. There seems to have been no question of burying him at Angoro in Kano location, Kisumu District, where he had spent his youth, and which was home to his Luo parents, thereby localizing Legio on a specific lineage's land. Despite some initial attempts to have a burial at the Jerusalem-Amoyo headquarters, Ondeto was finally laid to rest in a rectangular burial vault ("Limbo") on the Legio holy mountain, Got Kwer-Kalafari (Calvary), the site of Legio's first headquarters some thirty kilometers from Jerusalem-Amoyo, in Suna West location, Migori Division.

BEYOND THE "ROUTINIZATION OF CHARISMA": BILOCATION, THE CONSOLATION OF HISTORY, AND THE HOLY SPIRIT

Legios had been prepared for the death of their leader for a number of years. Toward the end of my fieldwork, some Legios confided that the Baba Messias Ondeto had said, "ool odwaro a" (he was tired and wanted to depart), that "ndalone orumo mar a" (his days for leave-taking were drawing to a close). They reported that church donations to fund the construction of his tomb were being sought, and that work had already begun. Luke Opol, a young Lihudu Legio mass-server, was the only Legio I recall as willing to estimate the date of the departure. On May 20, 1985, he told me he thought that the activities around the "Limbo" indicated that the Baba Messias Ondeto could be on earth four more years, but he might not even finish four (nyalo bedo higni ang'wen...aparo ok onyal tieko higni ang'wen), a prediction not quite on the mark but nonetheless interesting.

Almost twenty years earlier, some Legios were quietly speculating about the Baba Messias Ondeto's departure well before there was any work on a "Limbo" or plans for succession. Shortly before her own "death" and "return to Heaven" in 1966, the ninety-year-old Luo woman Legios held to be the Bikira Maria (Virgin Mary), in consultation with the Baba Messias Ondeto, had selected Timotheo Atila, a man unrelated to either in terms of Luo kinship, as Pope and "second spiritual son." This African Pope was to become the head of Legio "in the absence" of the

Baba Messias Ondeto, the "extraordinary spiritual leader" and "Eternal Father of the Church of Legio Maria of Africa."[21] The 1979 church constitution specified that after Atila's death, "Subsequent ascension to the leadership of Baba Matakatifu-Pope will be determined by the help of God through the Holy Spirit."

The reflections of Jacobo Ndege, a young Legio who worked in Nairobi's "Industrial Area" in a low paying job, on how Legio contrasted with the Roman Catholic church (which he had left), are an example of how Legios saw the Holy Spirit as providing a solution to "the problem of the routinization of charisma." Legios knew that the Baba Messias Ondeto was already speaking "through" Legios at sites where he was not physically present. They knew that Christ, Mary, and angels-saints-prophets were capable of speaking this way because of bilocation, a "miracle" accomplished through the Holy Spirit that those with "open hearts" could see/witness (*neno*) and hear/listen to/understand (*winjo*).[22] Conversion to Legio brought access to charisma. One's own charismatic gifts or the charismatic gifts of others gave Legios a way to engage in dialogue where there had existed an information gap.

Jacobo Ndege had become a Legio in 1978. When I spoke with him at his Kibera house in April 1983, I began by asking about a series of three posters he had on one wall of his house that had interested me on my first visit. They had been printed by the Christian Witness Press, in Kowloon, Hong Kong, were entitled "The Human Heart," and featured Chinese faces, animals, and a representation of Satan. Jacobo Ndege described the posters as illustrating demons being cast out of the human heart. I sensed he might be trying to draw me under their influence, as he made the affirmation that the posters could bring people who looked at them closer to God. Jacobo Ndege brought "bilocation" into his discussion of how the Holy Spirit had brought him closer to God when he left the Roman Catholic Church for Legio:

> "Because I was a believer, a Catholic believer . . . I had nothing to know him [the Baba Messias Ondeto] through something called the Holy Spirit . . . .I had no aim in the Holy Spirit which could speak to me . . . Joseph died, you know this Joseph? Abraham, these angels. I could not even talk to them. But when I joined, I can talk to them. And sometimes, when I pray, I see them coming. . . . Some like Lucia, Catherina, all. . . .
> After receiving this Holy Spirit from him [the Baba Messias Ondeto], I wanted to see him. I was longing, I was very much eager. . . . He comes to me . . . every now and then. And I was asking these people [when I was joining], "How comes, when he's in South Nyanza . . . he's speaking to us here?" He can speak to us here, when we are here now . . . he speaks to us, telling us

everything . . . even if he's in Tanzania, everywhere, whether you
are in the Congo [Zaire], he will speak to everybody in Legio
Maria. . . .
      Maria . . . [also] speaks to us. Bodily, she's not with us. Spiritually
she's with us. She can speak even now.

The prospect that the Black Christ, the "living God" (Nyasaye
mangima) dwelling among them, would leave Africa and go back, as the
Black Mary had, to a Heaven in which such spiritual personages were
"without color," was one that did not seem to deeply trouble most Legios
who spoke to me.[23] For Legios, there was no "myth of eternal return."
Through the Holy Spirit, "eternal return" was a reality. By means of the
Holy Spirit and bilocation, Christ and Mary could continue to communicate with them through dreams, visions, glossographia, and Legio's
often semantic "tongues."[24] In 1985, Nathaniel Ogana, a Legio who was
a retired school watchman with some charismatic abilities and a gift with
words, contemplated Ondeto's expected "death" without gloom. Ogana
placed the event that he knew was coming, the Baba Messias Ondeto's
"return to Heaven," in the context of other exchanges between heaven
and earth. Ogana clearly had the consolation of history to sustain him:
"Nathaniel Ogana Kuom Nyisechegi ok gidag e Polo kucha kuom kinde
mang'eny. Iwilogiga. Koro Baba nodong' kod Wuoro to Chuny Matakatifu
biro biro. (About these Divine Ones, they don't stay up there in Heaven
for a long time. You keep on alternating them. Now Christ will remain
with the Father, but the Holy Spirit will be coming.)
      Most Legios who spoke about the return of their Black Christ and
Black Mary to Heaven added that they did not think either would walk
in bodily form in any other country on earth again. For some Legios, this
was because such events indicated "the end of days was near." Most
Legios, however, did not seem beset by an eschatological crisis. After all,
they remarked, "near" could mean *kiny* (tomorrow) or *higni million apar*
(ten million years) hence. Views that Christ and Mary would not come to
earth again physically seem to their way to preserve pride of place,
primus inter pares, to affirm that a black Christ and black Mary deserved
the veneration of a world that had for too long centered devotion upon
Christ and Mary in their European forms.

HISTORIES, STORIES, MYTHS,
THE POSTMODERN, AND LEGIO

Following the attainment of political independence in 1963, it
soon became obvious that Kenya needed a new past of her own. It
became clear that political independence could have meaning

only if it was accompanied by historical independence. And during the first decade of our independence, creative writers, historians, and political scientists have been engaged in the struggle for historical independence (Ogot 1976: 1).

Previous works by sociologists, missiologists, and historians argue that Legio began in or around 1963. My fieldwork did find Legios agreeing that "to our knowledge" it was in this period that Legio "started to be heard." For Legios, the centrality of such a dating gave Legio's forced rupture with the Roman Catholic church in Kenya the character of being one episode in a shared history, the wider independence struggle. December 12, 1963, was when Kenya finally wrested its Uhuru (freedom/independence) from Britain:

> In 1962, when the Republic of Kenya is ready, we hear that somebody was seen on the hill of Kalafari (in South Nyanza). The people . . . have seen and heard singing over the heaven. . . . They saw . . . angels. They . . . saw them exactly. Those people didn't know what happened. There was running up the hill, on all sides, all sides [different groups] came to meet on the hill. In the morningtime, they went near the hill to see what happened there. They saw somebody calling them, "Just come, just come. I am coming to visit you. . . ." (James Ongo)

> The whole thing was started. It just happened at one time. The Holy Spirit came upon people. The most important thing in this religion is the action of the Holy Spirit. You can see the actions of the Holy Spirit. . . . It started in the 1960s. The first decade was when it started. (Gerfas Waringa)

For Legios, however, history was no simple straight line. Legios looked to plural beginnings that preceded the start of Legio's "active history" in Kenya in the 1960s. As Legios saw it, there had not been one "call" to start Legio. For Legios there had been several calls that had reverberated throughout history. In a metonymic mode of thought characteristic of charismatics elsewhere, they regarded the Legio first heard of (to Western knowledge) in 1963 as part of something larger.[25] It was one instance, and a crucial one, in a series of challenges to oppression, where succor and success had been provided to people by the presence, aid, and activities of the Virgin, her Son, and the Holy Spirit.

Some of these linkages to these events had been promulgated by the Baba Messias Ondeto or the Bikira Maria when they spoke in front of a group of Legios and relayed messages from Heaven, reporting what the Holy Spirit or God the Father had told them to tell Legios. Other linkages were put forth by individual Legios on the basis of "inspired" personal interpretation of various religious books and songs, histories, newspaper reports, religious pictures, movie stills, and other goods and ideas available to them from an array supplied by global, supraregional, and national markets. Some Legios saw connections based on what they claimed were first-hand experiences; for others, experiences known at second-hand provided enough evidence to affirm some linkages. Some Legios spoke about connections learned from the Holy Spirit speaking "through" a Legio in *dhum* (tongue-speech).[26] Different nodes of the network of associations drew more Legios to them than others. Such a history is one in which scholarly standards of proof are rarely of primary importance, in which readings are often free rather than close. Linkages to other personages, movements, and events might be documented only by the standard of the Holy Spirit.

Given all of this, it might seem that what I have called "Legio history" is more properly called "Legio myth." In Sir Edward E. Evans-Pritchard's famous distinction:

> myth and history are in important respects different in character, not just in the degree to which they can be substantiated by appeal to evidence or to the laws of natural science. . . . [Myth] is not concerned so much with a succession of events as with the moral significance of situations . . . where it is firmly placed in historical time, it is also, nevertheless, timeless in that it could have happened at any time, the archetypal not being bound to time or space. Then the very improbabilities . . . in many myths are not to be taken . . . as naivety and credulity, but are of the essence of myth which . . . demands an act of will and imagination. (1964: 179)

In our time *myth* has pejorative connotations. It makes for "otherness." And however different from the rigorous work of Bethwell A. Ogot and other academicians, Legios show a shared concern to assert a "historical independence" and participate in the work of the "first decade." Moreover, Legios wanted, much in the manner of the Western Pentecostals and Roman Catholic charismatics that Charles Nienkirchen describes in chapter six of this volume, to gain "historical legitimation" by building upon apostolic or biblical roots, finding further "historical continuities," and constructing a "charismatic genealogy" with "wide-ranging" and sometimes different collections of "predecessors" and "forerunners."[27] Their concerns deserve the respect accorded these other efforts.

Legio narratives might be called "postmodern history" rather than "mythic history." Diversely defined, the postmodern attitude does not set history apart, "consigning story to the realm of tale, legend, myth, fiction, literature" (Trinh 1989: 120). It views ours as "the epoch of the near and far, of the side-by-side, of the dispersed" (Foucault 1986: 22); it partakes of "pastiche," meaning "a mixture of styles, or pluralism" (Marks 1991: 195); it "regards the whole universe and the whole of history . . . as consisting of signs . . . available to explore the meaning of life" (Poewe 1989: 367).

A HISTORY OF NAMES:
"YOU GAVE HIM THE NAME JESUS"

Legios usually set the Bikira Maria and Baba Messias Ondeto into separate histories before the start of Legio. Aspects of the latter's biography, as given by Legios, contained more elements that approach a conventional history, and is the one I will treat here.[28] The accounts of Legios are like the biographies given by non-Legios in placing the Baba Messias Ondeto in Kano location in Kenya in the early 1900s.[29] Legios, however, affirmed that Ondeto was Christ come back from Heaven to earth. He had come with the Virgin Mary, at her behest, and with the support of God the Father. They had to come back because of the ways in which the world "was crooked," because "all the different peoples" on earth were on "the path to Hell." They were particularly troubled about the fate of "all their black children." One Legio song has the two coming down to earth on a rainbow. Because it was slippery, the Virgin Mary and her Son took trajectories that put them in different places, and different historical depths. The Virgin Mary landed in Lake Victoria Nyanza, emerging to become the powerful old woman of some Luo oral literature narratives.[30] Christ arrived on land and took on the appearance of a young Luo boy who was found by a poor man of the Watombori, Ombimbo Misumbaor, or, in some accounts, by the old man's wife, Margaret Aduwo.[31] He was fostered by them at Angoro, a village not far from the Nyanza-Rift Valley provincial border. Watombori are a Luoised group of Bantu.

While still a boy, he performed several miracles in the home of his foster parents. When grown, or in some accounts when he was as young as twelve, he left Angoro. He went to work at a variety of jobs elsewhere in Kano, other parts of Kisumu District, the Rift Valley Province, South Nyanza District, and Tanzania. These jobs were variously described as a "herdsboy" for Kalenjin and other Africans, a sisal (or sugarcane-estate) worker, a house servant (*boi*) for Europeans or wealthy Africans, and a watchman. He would not take much food or money for his work. He gave the money he obtained to others. He would disappear from one job at the times that people were sleeping. He would reappear at another place, taking up yet another of the low-paying jobs the colonial economy made available to migrant men. Descriptions like these, built from events in which the Baba Messias Ondeto comes into Kano and is raised by Watombori near a border, goes to work in areas outside of the Luo community, and becomes a hard and mobile worker under the harsh conditions of a colonial remittance economy, may be seen as a point for an "interethnic communion."[32] The person of Ondeto himself is described as a laboring "everyman."

The Baba Messias Ondeto sought to downplay his childhood in Kano and make himself "a son of Man" who was a son of the nation:

"Baba Messias Ondeto An awuod Kano gi tiende. To kipenja niya, 'Ijakanye, JaKano?' To KANU, KANU mar kanye." (I myself am a true son of Kano by the meaning of the term. And if you ask me, "Where are you from, man of Kano?" Well, its KANU [the national party], KANU is where I am from.)[33]

Attempts by Legios and non-Legios to root the Baba Messias Ondeto to the particularities of a Luo genealogy were rejected by the majority of church members. When one of the son's of Ombimbo tried to give a detailed family history at the Baba Messias Ondeto's funeral by placing the Baba Messias as the third born in a family of four brothers and one sister, he was shouted down by Legios who objected with, "Huyu hajui . . . Messiah hakualiza. Yeye ni Mungu." (He does not know. The Messiah was never born. He is God.)[34]

Though I had met with some Legios who spoke of Ondeto's birth in Africa from the womb of Margaret Aduwo rather than arguing for fosterage, this was presented as a second and parallel event, as a general birth to Africa. When I went with J. S. Warambo Owino, a Legio who was also a young journalist, to speak to Benjamin Adundo, an old Legio near the Luo landmark of Kit Mikayi (Stone of the First Wife), even this general line of argument on the Baba Messias Ondeto's birth in Africa provoked a debate. The more worldly young journalist seemed to feel that talk of Ondeto as Ombimbo's and Aduwo's son would not be interpreted by me correctly. He took the side of those who spoke for fosterage. When Adundo stated, "When Jesus was born to a Jewish family, just as Messia was born to Africa. He came into Ombimbo's house. He was the son of Ombimbo," Owino replied, "There's not much right there. He wasn't born to Ombimbo."

Some Legios, who like Benjamin Adundo described Ondeto as having an African birth, were concerned to preserve claims to the Baba Messias Ondeto having recapitulated a non-ordinary birth. None of these Legios, or any other Legio I spoke to, ever described Margaret Aduwo herself as being the Bikira Maria.[35] However, I did hear of Joseph-like descriptions where Ombimbo was depicted as an "old man" when he became father to Ondeto. In 1983, James Ongo, presenting himself as a Legio very much in search of "history," addressed the fosterage-birth issue and labor migration theme. He gave Ombimbo a Joseph-like aspect and provided a striking description of Ondeto:

> There was a child who went into a village of a man called Ombimbo. Ombimbo took him in as a lost child. Ombimbo was an old man . . . So many people knew him as Ombimbo's son because he was there and people saw him. Ombimbo didn't know where the child came from . . . he [Baba] walked up to Kitale and other *shambas* [farms] of the Rift Valley. He tried to preach for each and everybody in the village, in the market. . . .
> And up to now, I can't believe that Messia is a man from Kano. I myself went in that place because I liked to know the history of him. . . . He went there as a young boy.
> Those people [who say otherwise] don't know where he came from. . . . He is like the wind that flows from side to side.[36]

The name Ondeto, a Luo name, gave the "Son of God" a special connection to the Luos among whom he had come. Some Legios said that the name Ondeto was a polite reference to skin rashes their Baba Messias had suffered as a foster child in a poor man's home, and then scratched (*ndeto*). Etymological interpretations could move to a more synthetic level. They might stress another meaning of the verb *ndeto*, that the name Ondeto bespoke a person who sought to incorporate, to be inclusive, to "chew on" (*ndeto*) and think about all religions: "Albertus Ombong Owacho ni ne en Ondeto wuod Ombimbo, ma nondeto tiende dinde duto." (He says that he was called Ondeto, the son of Ombimbo, who chewed on the meanings of all religions.)

Legios did more than talk about the etymology of the name Ondeto. Discussed more often was their point that the name Ondeto, and other "praise names" bestowed on the Baba Messias during his time in Africa (or through knowledge of activity in India and elsewhere, gained via the Holy Spirit), were just as legitimate as names bestowed upon Christ by Western religion. Not all these names elicited the same degree of commentary. As with many Legios, James Ongo was not very forthcoming with details about what the Baba Messias-Christ had done when he lived in India under the name Melchizedek.[37] In a country where multiethnic relations could become subsumed under three rubrics, Asian, European, and African, a presence in India, where there was a Roman Catholic minority on the island of Goa, may have been what was important.[38] When James Ongo spoke about the name Jesus, there was more force. The

tone of his voice and penetrating glance during this discussion, one of our
early ones, contained a challenge to contradict him, which I did not do.
I expect if I had, we might not have had many later discussions. He was
as terse then as he was ever to be. Quietly he insisted that Jesus was the
Europeanized name of Christ: "You [Europeans] gave Him the name
Jesus."

Petronalla Otambo, an old Legio woman who lived in Uganda but
now lives near Siaya Town with her husband, was determined to correct
me about the name Jesus. She had been too distrustful to speak directly
before. I had stayed several times with her daughter-in-law, Elizabeth
Odawa, who was somewhere between being a Legio and an Anglican
like her own parents. When Petronalla Otambo knew me, I was not yet
connected to a Legio priest, congregation, or living with a Legio family
in the area. I had denied to her having had any dreams from the Baba
Messias or Bikira Maria when she made this inquiry soon after our first
meeting. I had to report to her that I had failed to meet the Baba Messias
Ondeto when he was nearby. Unlike her other children, her eldest son,
Aloys Obura, had left Legio to return to the Roman Catholic Church.
When Obura, a post-expulsion returnee to Uganda, came home on a visit
and took me to his parent's house, Petronalla Otambo finally agreed to
answer a few questions. Her parting shot was her statement about the
names of the Son of God. Closed to me as an investigator, she presented
one of the most open-minded views on religion I was to hear. Just before
breaking off the discussion, she told me: "Jesus has appeared in the world
at different times, with different names. At places he's Melchizedek,
Mohammed, and Buddha."

A HISTORY OF ACTS:LEGIO, MAU MAU, THE DINI YA MSAMBWA, AND MOVEMENTS AROUND THE WORLD

In addition to a history of names, Legios looked to connections
through a history of acts. The Baba Messias Ondeto himself gave speeches
about participating, under the name of Lt. Colonel or Sgt. Major Onyango,
in the Mau Mau (also known as the Kenya Land Freedom Army, or
KLFA) struggle for independence from British rule. Some Legios used a
photograph of a younger Baba Messias Ondeto, standing near trees, to
support claims that he dwelled in forests long before Mau Mau. He
continued to do so, they said, as he supported the forest dwelling
guerrillas of Mau Mau. Some Legios held that the Baba Messias Ondeto
had entered inside the Mau Mau as Spirit, becoming one with them, and
giving them strength.[39] Other Legios went further and maintained that
the Holy Spirit had shown them that the Baba Messias Ondeto had
carried the name of, and indeed somehow been, the martyred leader of

Mau Mau, Dedan Kimathi. Barack Obilo, a young man in his early twenties who had been in Legio about two years, expressed evident enthusiasm about this pre-Legio identity of the Baba Messias Ondeto. He lived at Obunga village, where the poorest and smallest of Kisumu's three Legio churches was located. We met briefly at the Kisumu bus station at a shop run by another young Legio who was a more devout Legio and generally more knowledgeable about Legio than Obilo. Obilo became animated as he spoke about the Kimathi-Ondeto identification. This pre-Legio activity seemed an important part of what had attracted him to Legio: "Obiro e piny Afrika. Pok ochako Legion. Nyinge Dedan Kimathi, Milimashon!" (He came to the continent of Africa. He had not yet begun our Legion. His name—Dedan Kimathi, Field-Marshall!).

The ability of the Baba Messias Ondeto to "shape-shift," the mythos of Dedan Kimathi as a "shape-shifter,"[40] and Kimathi's use of speech rich in parables and biblical references,[41] made an Ondeto-Dedan Kimathi transformation possible, if puzzling, for some Legios. There were some Legios who affirmed a Kimathi-Ondeto linkage with less excitement than Legios like Barack Obilo. Arthur Obul, a fourteen-year-old Legio primary school student in Alego who did not yet have any charismatic gifts, had faith and puzzlement in his voice when he tried to deal with what the Holy Spirit had disclosed to other Legios:

> We're just hearing rumors. Just that he was an army man
> around Mt. Kenya. So they struggled for Independence. It started
> in 1952, I think, with Jomo Kenyatta, Achieng' Oneko, and others.
> Nowadays, Kikuyus are crying that he was their blessing, but
> they didn't know. So nowadays, so at first, they didn't know it
> was Messia. So now when they see the dominion, they say, "I
> wish I knew." So they have to maintain the blessing.
> But it is a mystery how he came from the Kikuyus to the Luo.
> Because when he was there, he was a big man, and when he came
> to the Luo, he was a small man. And Ombimbo got him when he
> was a small man [a boy]. And when he was a Kikuyu, he was a
> big man, and an army man.

Gilbertus Olweny, a Lihudu Legio in his sixties, and his wife, Helena Oyie, who was also a Legio but less active than Olweny, argued in my presence about the Kimathi identity. It was clear that for some Legios the Kimathi-Ondeto linkage could mitigate, but not eradicate, ambivalent feelings toward the Kikuyu, Kenya's largest ethnic group, who had frequently been seen as rivals of the Luo. Helena Oyie gave voice to the often stated Legio position supporting nonviolence. His Peaceful Baba Matakatifu (Holy Father) was one of Ondeto's titles. In her view His

Peaceful Baba Matakatifu could not have been someone who committed the violent acts she associated with the Kikuyu at that time ("thievery") and during Mau Mau. Olweny, however, argued that the often repro-duced photo of Kimathi handcuffed and in police custody, which he possessed, showed Kimathi bore a physical resemblance to the Baba Messias Ondeto.[42] Without espousing violence per se, he insisted that an ordinary person could not have done the deeds credited to Dedan Kimathi, but as the following dialogue shows, Helena Oyie disagreed:

> GILBERTUS OLWENY: Messias nowuotho e piny Lango, e piny Kikuyu. Messias nochako e thim e piny Kikuyu. Ka nowuotho gi Kikuyu nodakie e thim. . . . Utegi nowang' kendgi. Ng'ama nowang'o ok ne. Ineno picha? En chal Messias. Ji wacho ni Dedan Kimathi en Messias. (Messias walked in the country of the Nandi, Kipsigis, and Maasai [as a labor migrant], and in the country of the Kikuyu. Messias started [his activities] in the forest in the country of the Kikuyu. When he traveled with the Kikuyu, he lived in the forest. . . . These houses burnt by themselves. . . . The person who burnt them couldn't be seen.[43] You see the picture [on the wall]? It is like Messias. People say that Dedan Kimathi is Messias.)

> HELENA OYIE: Iriaso nang'o? Kikuyu en janek. (Why are you telling lies? The Kikuyu is a killer.)

> GILBERTUS OLWENY: Riek Kikuyu ok onyal oloyo Msungu. Oriwore gi rieko mar Baba. Gimomiyo Kikuyu oloyo Jarachar. . . . Kikuyu onge rieko manyalo yawo dhoot Msungu. Kuom teko mar Baba Messias oyaw jela mar Langata. En jela maduong'. Messias nokwayo kifungu. Nodhi e kido mar Sarjent. Askari nowacho ni, "Iwuok kanye?" To aye, "Imiya kifungu." Aye, oyaw. Mabuse nowuok, duto e jela. (Kikuyu cleverness cannot be superior to that of the European. It joined with the wisdom and cleverness of Baba. That's the reason the Kikuyu overcame the white man. . . . The Kikuyu lacks the cleverness to break open the door of a European. Through the power of the Baba Messias the Langata detention center was opened wide. It was a large prison. Messias asked for the key. He went taking on the appearance of a Sergeant. The guard said, "Where have you come from?" He said, "Give me the key." Then, he opened it up. The prisoners walked out, all in the jail.)[44]

The relationship of Mau Mau to the Kenyan nation has been a contested one, its continuing significance a matter of sometimes divisive debates, both popular and academic. In evocative language, Tabitha

Kanogo, joining the debate on the side of those who have found Mau Mau "tribal in membership," questioned efforts to widen its scope and "accord the movement a place to feel at home" in the literature on national resistance movements (1977: 243).[45] Others have persisted in pointing to Mau Mau endeavors to become more interethnic.[46] This camp has attempted to argue that Mau Mau "attracted particular attention on a global scale" (Okoth 1985: 108), and has tried to draw more attention to international aspects of Mau Mau.[47] Resonant for Legios would be references to Kimathi's travels through Africa and to Palestine, and his letters seeking support from Egypt, India, and other countries.[48] Also resonant for Legios would be Kimathi's criticism of the motives of foreign missionaries. Images of Mau Mau as an "anti-Christian cult," promulgated by some missionaries and other Europeans from the time of Mau Mau, probably drew more Legios to Mau Mau than from it, for Legios were people whose Christianity had been questioned.[49]

It is understandable that some Legios, confronted by images of Legio as a "place to feel at home only for the Luo," of a church (and people) not engaged enough with wider Kenyan society, would be sympathetic with more "radical" readings of Mau Mau and Kimathi. Most Legios who made an Ondeto-Kimathi-Mau Mau equation, however, took a more moderate path. They did not want to make a choice between "Kenyatta or Kimathi."[50] They did not discuss which was the more "narrow nationalism" against imperialism and colonialism—the "reformist," "constitutionalist," and "parliamentary" methods of KAU/KANU, or the "politically directed violence" of Mau Mau.[51] They would not oppose KAU to Mau Mau, Mau Mau to KANU, and never mentioned parallels others have suggested between Mau Mau and the proscribed political party led by Oginga Odinga, the KPU (Furedi 1989: 211; Mueller 1984: 423; Cohen and Atieno Odhiambo 1989: 128–30; D. Barrett 1973: 131; Odinga 1967: 72–74). Both Jomo Kenyatta and Dedan Kimathi were pronounced nationalist Uhuru leaders linked to Legio positively. While a once effulgent image of Kenyatta lost a good portion of its light for elements of Mau Mau over time, the first president of Kenya had a different role in Legio discourse.

In a long discussion on Legio history, Nathaniel Ogana, a Legio in his late sixties, and a raconteur par excellence, gave me a richly detailed version of the Mau Mau period. Ogana incorporated Kikuyu, Luyia, and Luo nationalist men, understanding Europeans, and Kikuyu women into his narration of the years leading to independence. He legitimated the activities of both those engaged in legal struggles and of the guerrillas in the forest as vital and complementary projects. Though Ogana held there was a "leader of the battle of the blacks" who gave Kenyatta orders to leave the forest for negotiations with the English, Kenyatta himself was depicted as a person of consequence, someone who loomed up, or shone forth (*thinyore*). The word *thinyore* has religious significance for Legios; using it was a clear mark of praise.[52] Whether the leader telling Kenyatta what to do was Ondeto, Kimathi, or Ondeto-Kimathi was left unstated. Leaving possibilities open seemed part of Ogana's effort to read Legio history as open and plural.

A shortened version of our conversation can still show the expansive character of Legio thought:

> Bang'e koro Mau Mau ochakore e higa mar '52. Messias opango joge—Mboya, Argwenge, gi owadgi miluong'oni Muliro gi Oginga Odinga, "Bas koro iloso Uhuru." Bura ne jogo dhiga Ulaya. Koro negiwachoni, "Wadwaro lochwa kendewa. . . ."
>
> Bas ng'ama nodwaro Uhuru nogono Kenyatta nothinyore. Bas Wasungu makoni notamore. Koro Kenyatta kod Tom Mboya gi Odinga gi Muliro nodok Ulaya. Bas JoUlaya madongo nowacho Kenyatta giri ni, "Dhi wachni jowa manie kuro giduogo Ulaya ka. . . ." Kuomogi moko oyie to moko odag. . . . Negiwacho, "Jomafuwo, bim kod onyugo nyalo kwayo ng'ato?" Koro eka Mau Mau nochakore. . . .
>
> Kendo Joratenge nene ndiko barua ni Wasunge modak e Kenya ka kod Joratenge moko bende, ne gindikogi mondo gikonyogi gi lewni kod chiemo kama gidakie e thim. Kendo mond Kikuyu nonego Wasungu gi risasi mar bunde. Bang'e lweny nodhi nyime. Koro teko mar Nyasaye chako tiyo ka JoAfrika nego Wasungu to bende inegogi ka gidwaro loch. Bang'e jatend lweny mar joratenge nowachoni Kenyatta mondo owuog e thim kendo odhi bura Ulaya.

> (Now Mau Mau began in the year '52. Messias drilled his people, including Mboya, Argwenge, and a [Luyia] brother you call [Masinde] Muliro and Oginga Odinga.[53] "Well, now it is time for you to prepare for independence." A council drawn from those people went to England. They said, "We want our independence ourselves. . . .
>
> "Well, the person who wanted that very independence, Kenyatta, shone forth, made himself visible. The Europeans this side refused. So Kenyatta, Tom Mboya, Odinga, and Muliro returned to Europe. The English leaders told Kenyatta and his people, "Go tell our people who are there that they should return to England here. . . ." Some of them agreed, but some refused . . . . They said, "Those fools, baboons and lice, how can they rule anyone?"[54] Well, then Mau Mau began. . . .
>
> The blacks [in the forest] wrote a letter to the Europeans who lived in Kenya here, and to other blacks as well, they wrote them so that they might help them with food and clothing where they were living in the forest. The Kikuyu women killed Europeans with bullets from pistols. And the war went forward. The power

of God began to work as the Africans killed the Europeans, but Africans were also killed as they looked for self-rule. Then the leader of the battle of the blacks told Kenyatta to leave the forest and go to a council in England.)

When I asked Ogana, "Where was Messias?" he replied:

Messias ne enie thim to kendo en owuok oko gi ji koloko kite mar Musungu. Onyalo dhi gi mtokeni e puotho to okaw rabuon, sukari, muhogo to mo mar tedo chiemo to oteroni joge e thim. . . . Sama nobiro omo chiemo ni joge to joma omo chiemo gin Wasungu lilo. Negilokore duto jomakwar pip. Mano en kaka Messias okelo loch kuom JoAfrika kaka wuon mare nooro mondo obi oti kuom JoAfrika.

(Messias was in the forest, but when he went out with people he changed his appearance to that of a European. He could go with lorries into fields and get potatoes, sugar, cassava, get cooking oil, and take them to his people in the forest. . . . When the time came to fetch food for his people, the people who went out to fetch food were all Europeans. They changed into "red people" everyone of them.[55] That is how Messias brought independence for Africans as his Father had sent him to come and work for Africans.)

By references to both Kimathi and Kenyatta, Legios sought to make a case that Legio had been in the struggle for national independence, continued to support the nation, and so deserved the more positive support Legio had gained vis-à-vis the government after a rocky start in the 1960s. Luke Opol, a Lihudu Legio mass-server in his twenties with some training as a craftsman, developed such an argument in a conversation we had in June 1985 on the Baba Messias Ondeto's first visit to the state house in 1966. This was an event commemorated in photographs still on sale at Legio gatherings. These photographs are placed on the wall above church altars and in Legio homes. As Opol saw it, the Holy Spirit had done its work in 1966. Kenyatta might have had to be reminded, but he had perceived something he had been missing.[56] Kenyatta then acted accordingly, helping Legios because of the help he had received from the Baba Messias during the days of his lengthy trial at Kapenguria and subsequent imprisonment: "Kindeno ne en Dedan Kimathi. Kendo notweye Kapenguria kod Kenyatta. Chieng' nodhi moso Kenyatta nopenje, 'Donge inena? Wan kodi e jela.' Kenyatta nowacho, 'Ndiyo.'" (At that time (during Mau Mau) he was Dedan Kimathi. Also he was jailed at Kapenguria with Kenyatta.[57] The day he (the Baba Messias

Ondeto) went to greet Kenyatta, he asked him, "Didn't you see me? I was with you in jail." And Kenyatta replied, "Yes" (in Swahili.)

When I asked Opol if, at the time Baba Messias Ondeto was at Kapenguria with Kenyatta, he was Dedan Kimathi, he replied, "Ne en pod Dedan Kimathi. Nodwaro Uhuru kod Lemo. Uhuru nolor kod Lemo. Kenya noyudo Uhuru. Bende Lejio nodonjo e piny." (He was still Dedan Kimathi then. He wanted freedom and prayer. Freedom came down with prayer. Kenya got independence. Also Legio entered the land, the world.)

A few Legios also presented a linkage between Legio and Elijah Masinde, leader of the Dini ya Msambwa, or DyM (Religion of the Ancestors).[58] The Dini ya Msambwa has been presented as largely a movement of one section of one ethnic group, the Bukusu group of Luyia, to which Masinde belonged.[59] As with Mau Mau and Legio itself, while its members were mostly from one ethnic group, in this case the Luyia, the DyM had a more multiethnic reach. It had members in both Kenya and Uganda, and Karimojong, Sebei, Teso, Turkana, Pokot, Nandi, Samburu, Kipsigis, Gusii, Luo, and individuals from other African ethnic groups.[60] Its economic basis also seems diverse, with the DyM drawing its membership from African farmers, well off in terms of land and cattle, in addition to squatters and migrant laborers (see Wipper 1977: 224–47). While it had much of its support in western Kenya and eastern Uganda, there were DyM in Mombasa and other parts of Kenya.

In the 1940s and 1950s, Masinde was known as an anticolonial and antimission religious leader and nationalist. Bethwell Ogot and Tiyambe Zeleza have provided a good summary of the DyM as "a movement that sought to reassert African religious autonomy and provide for political protest, and doubled as a nascent trade union. Missionaries, government officials, African chiefs, Indian and European employers, all became the object of Dini ya Musambwa's wrath and violence" (1988: 402).

Gideon S. Were has dated the start of the DyM to 1943, with reference to reports of arson in Bukusu, Western Province, indicating the DyM was "active" then (1972: 89).[61] However, the DyM seem to have been in existence for five or six years previously (Wipper 1977: 126).

The DyM had been involved in several violent anticolonial clashes, including the "Malakisi Riot" of 1948 and the "Kolloa Affray" of 1950.[62] Masinde had broken from the Friends African Mission because they refused to accept his polygyny. He spoke out against Quaker, Roman Catholic, and Church of God missionaries, and those from other Western churches, for "fleecing the poor," for "not practicing what they preached," and for excommunicating Africans for practicing customs found in the Bible, like polygyny.[63] Masinde was jailed for the first time in 1944. In

1945, he was sent to Mathare Mental Hospital for reasons that seem to have been more political than medical.[64] He was released from Mathare in May 1947. From October 1947 to February 1948, Masinde was on the run in Western Province, the Rift Valley, and Uganda from another arrest warrant. Finally captured, he was placed in detention on the coast or northeastern part of Kenya, at Lamu, Marsabit, and then Manda Island. He remained in detention until May 1961, a period of thirteen years. The colonial government had been concerned that no link be "allowed to become established between Mau Mau and the DyM."[65] The DyM was proscribed in 1948. Activity of DyM in western Kenya was restricted by the institution of pass rules in 1949 and the deportations of members of ethnic groups associated with the DyM from neighboring districts. As with Mau Mau, some DyM were sent to "rehabilitation" camps, at Athi River, outside Nairobi, in South Nyanza, and in Rift Valley Province.

Masinde was seen as a prophet who had predicted several events, including Kenyan independence in 1952, which turned out to be the year that the state of emergency began.[66] He was also seen as a "shape-shifter" who had outwitted arrest and later the degradations of jail life by his ability to do things ordinary men could not.[67] For DyM members, Masinde was a man come from Heaven, "sent by God especially for the Africans" (Wipper 1971: 169). Masinde denounced Christianity as "a religion of the imperialists and the missionaries" (Wipper 1971: 160). Masinde was thought to be definitely "against Christianity."[68] As with Mau Mau, DyM religious beliefs and practices were more complex than a simple anti-Christian definition would imply. It used Christian rhetoric and sought biblical validation. Members wore crosses, lined up in a cross formation, and called their sacred site on Mt. Elgon, Sayoni (Zion). There were complexities in the DyM rituals of dress, as well. Some DyM wore turbans. Masinde, on occasion, would wear a monkey-skin cape over shirt and trousers.[69] Masinde was a Black Messiah figure for some DyM followers, a prophet like Mohammed or Moses for others, and a "folk hero" even for many non-DyM.[70]

As a narrative constituting a link for Legios to world and nationalist history, the DyM is more problematic than Mau Mau. Masinde and his movement had never caught the national (or international) imagination to the degree of Mau Mau.[71] Masinde and the DyM had also run afoul of the postcolonial government of Kenya. With the help of Masinde Muliro, Elijah Masinde had been released from detention in May 1961. The colonial government's ban on DyM was revoked by the Kenyatta government on April 21, 1964, and DyM got official registration from the independent government on May 15, 1961. However, the DyM soon suffered from allegations that members had burned down churches of other denominations, that Masinde had abused the Luo and Kikuyu, and that he had delivered a new prophecy that Mzee Jomo Kenyatta would not be in office long. While some ex-Mau Mau came to serve in the government, and a street was named for Kimathi, DyM were less fortunate.[72] By 1968, Masinde's DyM was proscribed by the government of an independent Kenya. Masinde continued to have court battles almost up to his death in 1987, served time in jail in both Kenya and Uganda, and was even taken again to Mathare Mental Hospital for an examination.[73] Most important for Legios, Daniel arap Moi, who succeeded Kenyatta to the presidency, had, as minister for home affairs, linked Msambwa and Legio together in a warning to "splinter sects."[74]

Those Legios who brought up a DyM-Legio linkage did not look to the Masinde of the postcolonial period. They did not discuss DyM practices they considered anathema, such as smoking tobacco, bhang, and opium, and drinking African beer and Nubian gin (*changa'aa*, "kill-me-quick"). They did not broach theological differences that their church had with the DyM. Though Masinde's "shape-shifting" mythos made it possible, no Legio claimed an identity between Masinde and the Baba Messias Ondeto, as some Legios had with the Baba Messias Ondeto and Dedan Kimathi. The Elijah Masinde for whom they admitted admiration was the nationalist of the 1940s and 1950s. The Baba Messias Ondeto was seen as having only inspired Masinde spiritually. Masinde and the Dini ya Msambwa were made into a precursor to Legio. In this way Legios sought to share credit for Masinde's historic nationalism, but maintained a degree of dissociation from his more recent crises.

Dalmas Oyier, Legio teacher and confidant and companion to the Baba Messias Ondeto, spoke about Masinde to a group of young Legios when he visited the Lihudu Legio church with Ondeto in 1985, and again in a conversation with me during that visit. Oyier began by connecting Elijah Masinde to Ham, the black son of Noah cursed to beget a line of slaves for failing to cover-up his father's nakedness when Noah became drunk. Oyier proceeded to link Legio to "Legico" (the Legislative Council) and KANU (the national party), affirming that if violence might have been understandable in the colonial past, Legio still placed itself on the side of legislative process:

> Nyasaye nooro leke ni ji adek. Nyasaye en keche adek:
> Nyasaye Wuon, Nyasaye Wuowi, gi Chuny Matakatifu. Nokelo ni
> lek kuom Kam, Shem, kod Jafeth. Bas nowachonigi ng'ama
> okwongoni kanyo Elgon okaw loch. Higa 1949. Ng'ama okwongo
> kawo buk onwang'o Uhuru mare. Jarateng' okwongoni buk
> mokaw. Koro enie Elija. . . . Koro Musungu ok oneno maber,

omako Elija botweye. Kendo Elija nowachone, "In dhi thuru."
Kendo niya, "Nyasaye biro kuom joratenge. Ochal kodgi. To
ubiro make, ubiro tweyo Nyasaye e jela." Kendo ka nobiro
negimako Nyasaye adiera. Negitweye e jela, Homa Bay, Asego.
Mano loch maradek. Oduogo kuom joratenge. . . . Nyasaye obiro
gi giko moko: Lejico gi Lejio Maria. Gik ariyo, gik adek.

(God sent dreams to three people. God is three persons. God
the Father, God the Son, and the Holy Spirit. He brought a dream
to Ham, Shem, and Japheth. He told them that the first one there
at Mt. Elgon [in Western Province] was going to get the victory.
The year was 1949. The first one to take the book would get his
independence. The black man was the first to get to the book and
take it. Well, that man was Elijah. . . . Now the European did not
feel good about this, he seized Elijah and imprisoned him. Elijah
said to him, "You, go back to your own country."[75] He also said,
"God will come among the blacks. He is like them. But you are
going to seize him, and you are going to imprison God in jail."
When he came, they seized God, truly they did. They imprisoned
him [Baba Messias Ondeto] in jail, Homa Bay, Asego.[76]
    That is the third victory. He returned among the blacks. . . . God
came with some things: the Legislative Council and Legio. Two
things, three things.)

When I asked Oyier the nature of the third thing mention, he
responded, "En KANU." (It's KANU). Oyier finished on this occasion by
telling me I could find out more about Elijah Masinde by reading Malachi
4. In this, the last book of the Old Testament, there was material about an
Elijah who would precede "the Lord's coming." He thus marked Masinde
as a prophetic precursor.
    For Legios, events like the DyM and Mau Mau were signs that "the
Holy Spirit of God is moving in Africa now." They also linked DyM and
Mau Mau to Legio as part of a struggle for "worldwide independence."
Speaking to a large audience in Uranga, Alego, at the opening of a new
church that was attended by the M.P. for Alego, Peter Oloo Aringo,
Ugenya's Archbishop Ondiek Oluoch, and other officials, the Baba
Messias Ondeto directed Legios and others in the audience to look back
to the past in a certain way, to link that past to the present, and to look
outside of Alego. KANU and Legio were again conjoined, and both
linked to other events:

Bende Lejio Maria akelo gi thuon. Kendo achak, akelo
KANU . . . Kapenguria. Suku, Pokot. Na, iluong'a ni Mau Mau.
An an Mau Mau. Wuon thuon magaidi machon. Ma ung'e chon.

An makonyo Kikuyu gi lweny, gi mach kabisa. Eh, to ung'e chon
ni ni Jaluo bende nokonyo Kikuyu. . . . Remba onjo piny. Ok
Alego kende monwang'o rembago. Kano. South Nyanza.
Misungu. African. Congo, Belgiji. Kahawa. Wasomo e pinyni.
Mapod nambwa pod nie e jende ka jende nyaka sani.

(I brought Legio Maria with force. And I initiated, I brought
KANU . . . [the] Kapenguria [trial]. The Suk, the Pokot [and the
DyM Kolloa Affray amongst them]. You call me a Mau Mau. I
myself was a Mau Mau. The father of the heroism of the guerrillas
back then. This you knew long ago. I helped the Kikuyu in the
war, with a whole lot of fire. Eh, and you know back then a Luo
helped the Kikuyu. . . . My blood poured down. It was not just
Alego that found that blood of mine. It was Kano. South Nyanza.
The European. The African. The Belgian Congo. Kahawa [army
barracks]. We pray in this world. And still our numbers are in
each and every jail up to now.)[77]

Legios were encouraged to pray for those still in jail, for those still
living under foreign domination. Examples like Mau Mau and DyM
were presented to make Legios look outward and forward. The Legio
Charles Oruako told me the Vatican had withheld the "Third Secret of
Fatima" from the world in 1960 because it feared the acts "a black
Messias" could accomplish "around the globe." The "message had not
come through," so as another Legio put it, the Black Christ and Black
Mary had "come with their feet." For Legios, this had made a difference.
Boas Opondi, a Legio working in the Nairobi office of a shipping
company, looked out upon events in Africa in such a light:

We are descendants of Esau. In the present age, the descendants
of Jacob have been successful, and dominated us. But it turns out
that our time has come. When the Messia came to Africa, people
were able to get their power back, we got independence in
various lands. . . . The unliberated lands will fall. . . . It is a matter
of time. . . . But meanwhile, we are encouraged to pray hard, to
pray for all those who have lost their lives unnecessarily, for
fighting for their rights, all over the world, it's not confined to
Africa.

For some Legios, the time span in which Legio had been there, in the
world, fighting against religious and political oppression, was long.
Laurende Rateng, a Legio working as an accountant in Nairobi for an
international firm, was one of several Legios who looked to such a time
span. He began in a quiet and leisurely voice, never changed his tone, but

the tempo of activity was rapid: "The Legio Maria emerged in England in 1652. Then they stopped it because it was powerful. During the war between the English and others, only Legios could be asked to kneel and pray. A thunderstorm would come that could kill enemies. So the government stopped it. Again it appeared in 1844 in France. And a teacher was killed because he was trying to teach students about Legio Maria."

I questioned Rateng about what he was referring to in 1844. Rateng, who came from an area of Nyanza where the Seventh Day Adventist Church was strong, went out of the room and came back with Ellen G. White's *The Triumph of God's Love* (1957). He gave me chapter thirteen, "Daybreak in France," to read. I began to read the chapter while he talked. It started with a discussion of Jacques Lefevre D'Etaples, a teacher, papist, and reformer who had brought to light in 1512 "saints not in the Roman calendar." It concluded with mention of the work of later figures from "small countries" who had fought Rome's efforts "to quench the light of the Reformation" (125–39). According to Rateng:

> After 1844, news of the breakaway of Legio Maria from the Catholic Church started in 1952 with Mau Mau. There was a great fight for freedom, for independence, a war, a civil war, not a civil war. People wondered where the power came from. Even the churches started to have their own war. Africans were against the slaying by evil people, the slaying of sisters, monks, fathers. This was very wrong. No one can tell where this power came from. Why it happened.
>
> Then Baba came to light. Many didn't know. He had not taken action himself. People came to know Baba in 1963 when the Holy Spirit revealed himself to people at Got Kwer or Got Oyawore. The Holy Spirit came to instruct people. He talked through them, "This one you have here is the Messia of the Black Nations." So people came to believe that this is the true Messia.

A little later, after discussing several passages from Revelation 1–3 and Revelation 6, and reaching for Arthur Maxwell's *Bible Stories* (1957) to illustrate his points, Rateng turned to a source that he might have thought would be of more interest to me. He had clipped an article from the *New York Times* in 1962. He had misplaced it, but hoped to find it to show me. He told me there had been a picture of a cross split in two, and information about a council (Vatican II?) where bishops and priests had started to rebel within the Roman Catholic Church.

Rateng had at hand a copy of *The Prophecies of Daniel and the Revelation* (1946), by another Seventh Day Adventist, Uriah Smith. He turned to it next, opening the book to an illustration where a robed and crowned figure gazed at a globe facing Africa (304).[78] With the book opened to the picture of a globe turned toward Africa before us, promising again to try to find the old *New York Times* clipping, Rateng asked if I thought it "a coincidence that there was a rebellion in America the same year that Legio Maria started breaking *kong'o* [beer] pots." His bibliographic tour de force had left me almost breathless, his knowledge of world religious history was so much better than mine I could hardly keep up. Not certain whether he was referring to Vatican II or some event in the 1960s in America, I was more or less speechless. I responded with some brief and immediately forgettable reply. His concern with a figure looking at a globe is, however, one I will never forget.

CONCLUSION

There is not space nor time here to deal with all the manifold links Legios have used in making their own history. I have tried to show how Legios have used space and time very broadly. In speaking to me about their sense of history, Legios were trying to have their voices and versions of history enter our discourses about Legio and Africa. Sometimes, in their discussions of this history, Legios turned the tables and questioned me. They asked if I believed that Christ had truly come back into the world "in the black color" with the Virgin Mary. They asked if I believed that they had the "living God" in their midst. Did I believe that Baba Messias Ondeto was Christ? I wanted to be honest and yet not alienate. I fashioned my rejoinder to their terms. I responded that I did not know these things as truths for myself. I had been told it was necessary to have the Holy Spirit to know such things as certainties. I said that the Holy Spirit had not yet fallen upon me. In truth, it still has not done so (though some Legios tried to convince me it had). Yet the spirited accounts of Legios have fallen on me. I now find their history more revealing than a conventional history of churches. Theirs is a history where meaning is what is most important.

If we want to understand what moves people, a history of meanings becomes the most meaningful sort to look at. A history of meanings attends to our species in this postcolonial and postmodern age. Homo sapiens have lived (and died) by such things as meanings, more often they have followed any paper trail. If we let histories like these into our dry academic discourse, let words like those of Legios cited here penetrate our academic world, we may understand what the Holy Spirit does for Legios, even if we do not have, nor want, their religious sensibility. At least we may have more sensitivity. While Western religion may not be "dry of any spiritual claim," both it and Western social science have been arrogantly arid when dealing with Africa. Patrick Nyarombo held out this lesson along with some Legio history:

> Christ told his Apostles, "It is the Father who knows the time." They couldn't know what time or place to expect his return . . . Legio appeared at the time of independence. Perhaps Christ was going to bring independence to Africa. Christ knew the Kingdom of God was going to come to Africa at the time of independence from colonial rule. That is why he made the statement he did in Acts.[79]
> The religion brought by the white man was when the Holy Spirit left them, it was dry of any spiritual claim. Catholics and Protestants fought among themselves and killed sixty-eight million.[80] It was necessary for Africans to receive the Holy Spirit as the Israelites did at Pentecost.

NOTES

My research in Kenya was conducted under the auspices of the Institute of African Studies of the University of Nairobi. I am grateful to the institute and the Office of the President of Kenya for facilitating my research. My fieldwork was funded by the Wenner-Gren Foundation, the Society of Sigma-Xi, and Princeton University. For comments on this work, I am particularly grateful to Chris Wanjala, Atieno Odhiambo, John Padwick, James Fernandez, Hildred Geertz, Parker Shipton, Ivan Karp, Edward Steinhart, Neven P. Lamb, Johannes Fabian, David Sapir, and Cynthia Hoehler Fatton. I would also like to acknowledge the help of the Baba Messias Simeo Ondeto and Dalmas Oyier in supporting my work on Legio, as well as all the Legios in Kenya who aided me in my research.

1. Unless a person's name is commonly known with reference to Legio or the Luo, and has appeared on public documents, in press accounts, or similar records, it should be understood that all names of people cited in this text are pseudonyms. The name 'Lihudu,' the village discussed below, is also fictitious, for the same reasons. Some of the personal names I have chosen are among the less common Christian names. While this may lead to some loss of data, it seems to me that this is preferable to a loss of privacy.

2. The latter figure appeared in an article about Legio in the Nairobi newspaper, the *Daily Nation*, on September 20, 1991. An October 11 article spoke of "millions of . . . followers on East and Central Africa." For further reference to figures on Legio membership, and the vexing problem of determining numbers of followers, see Schwartz 1989a: 430–32, 500.

3. Legio priests tend to support the levirate by reference to Deuteronomy 25:5. Legio's tolerance of polygyny is also shared by others in Kenya. Important sources on these topics include Kenyatta 1965 (1938): 261–62, 266; and Maillu 1988.

4. I arrived in Kenya in September 1982 and departed in late December 1985. Although I still get occasional correspondence from Legios in Kenya, my work is largely drawn from this period of fieldwork. Because Legio began as an organized movement in the early 1960s, I was talking with first and second generation Legios.

   The case of Legio contrasts with the Flemish Roman Catholic charismatics studied by Roelofs, where figures of speech centered more upon God the Father and Jesus than the Holy Spirit (1990: 3–4). In Legio, it is God the Father who receives somewhat less emphasis than Mary, her Son, and the Holy Spirit. Greater emphasis on Mary and her Son seems to be related to the importance of the mother-son bond among the patrilineal-polygynous Luo. For further discussion of the latter, see Schwartz (1989a: 80, 540). For a related discussion of the mother-son emphasis in Jamaa, see De Craemar (1977: 61, 183).

5. See Ranger's very astute comments (1985: 185).

6. In discussions of religion, one man (or woman's) church is another's sect or cult. The latter terms marginalize and are pejorative (Shack 1979: xii; Hexham and Poewe, chapter 2 of this volume). I am using the term church rather than "splinter sect" or "breakaway" deliberately to move away from such readings.

7. "Mission" is given as part of the church's name in the *Kenyan Government Gazette* for November 9, 1979. I was also given a copy of a three-page typed collection of some sermons the Baba Messias Ondeto delivered between August 9, 1967, and May 1, 1968, that was headed "Legio Maria of African Church Mission." I am not certain, however, as to when the sermons were typed in the form in which I saw them. For a discussion of some other African churches that have had success in missionizing abroad, see Poewe (1989: 362–63). Maria Legio was a name used by the church in its 1964 and 1967 church constitutions. For further discussion of the various permutations of Legio's names and some errors in the literature on Legio, see Schwartz (1989a: 488–90).

8. For further discussion on the theme of charismatics and wholeness, see Droogers, chapter one of this volume.

9. For a brief discussion of Legio attitudes to charismatics within the Roman Catholic church, attitudes of Kenyan Roman Catholic charismatics to Legio, and Legio attitudes to the case of Archbishop Milingo, see Schwartz (1989a: 55, 382–83, 521–22, 524). Gerrie ter Haar has a very interesting discussion of the role of the Luyia (Bukusu) Cardinal Maurice Otunga of Kenya in compiling the report that led to Milingo's recall to Rome (1987: 482).

10. Dirven stated that Legio ended its affiliation with the East African United Churches and Orthodox Coptic Communion because "it treasured its independence too much" (1970a: 175–77). Francis Joseph Odhiambo, Archbishop in-charge of the Legio Maria Church in Uganda, in a letter to the

Kenyan periodical the *Weekly Review* (March 29, 1985), stated, "The church receives no kind of financial assistance, administrative or materially from any body in the world." In the *Daily Nation* of October 20, 1985, Archbishop Stephen Ondiek Oluoch was quoted as saying, "Kenya was proud of Legio Maria because it was the only church run by Africans without foreign assistance." Fabian has discussed how the Roman Catholic charismatic prayer groups he studied in Zaire insisted they had been in place before the international movement reached Zaire, and saw the international organization as one part of efforts to bring these independently started groups with a prior history "under control" or "even repression" (1991: 19, 23, 39–40).

11. Lango is the name of a Nilotic ethnic group in Uganda. However, Kenya Luo often used the term *Lango* to refer to Nandi, Kipsigis, and Maasai, and called Uganda Lango *Langi*. I am following this translation. It should also be noted that *moja* is Swahili for "one" and *achiel* Luo for "one." The code-switching is emphasizing incorporation, albeit in a small way.

12. For migration history, sources include Crazzolara 1950–1954; Ayany 1964; Ogot 1967; Odingo 1971: 3–4; Atieno Odhiambo 1975: 120; Ochieng' 1975: 51–55, 1979; Cohen 1983: 345, 1988; Burton 1988. Works in which the "plural society" is discussed include Ayany 1964: 34; Ogot 1967: 7–8, 1983: 27; Oloo Aringo 1969: 17; Whiteley 1971: 2; Southall 1971: 381; Hay 1972: 58; Whisson and Lonsdale 1975: 3; "Editorial" 1975 (anon.); Herring 1978: 126–27; Berg-Schlosser 1984: 127, 195). For a discussion of how possession among lakeshore peoples has evolved over several thousand years, see Atieno Odhiambo 1975: 120. For material on how intelligibility of spirit-inspired speech was affected by changing interethnic relations, see H. Owuor Anyumba 1971, 1974: 9; Schwartz 1989a: 209–12. For an interesting account of how spirits have been "indigenized" in the interlacustrine area, see I. Berger 1976: 169. For this "rethinking" of Luo patriliny, sources include Southall 1952: 5–8; Pala Okeyo 1980: 191; Cohen 1981; and Cohen and Atieno Odhiambo 1989. For similar positions on related Nilotic groups, see Deng 1988: 159, 161; Southall 1986; and Burton 1988: 459.

13. This point has been made by Obudho 1974: 161, but see also Middleton 1967: 432; Ali Mazrui 1979: 263; Potash 1978: 381; Goldenberg 1982: 2; and Shipton (1987: 16). It has been estimated that between thirty-three and seventy-nine percent of Luo men have been labor migrants at some point in their lives. While the rate for women is lower, women have been mobile as the "rotating wives" of polygynist labor migrants (Parkin 1978: 33–63) and as traders and migrants themselves (Hay 1976: 99).

14. With Renato Rosaldo, I think we must get beyond "elegiac postures" and "overly romantic visions of bygone harmonious societies" (Rosaldo 1989: 72–73; see also "Editorial" (anon.) 1975). Instead of mourning "the passing of traditional society, we should recognize that cultures can show remarkable resilience" when confronted with "the assaults of imperialism and capitalism" (Rosaldo 1989: 81). As I have already indicated, Luo society was never enclosed by a glass "pleasure dome" (cf. Fernandez 1982: 4, 562, but also 1986a: 206–7). Imperialism is not well-imaged as a billiard ball, and was not

the first force of any strength to strike Luo society. The image of a shattered microcosm does not apply.

15. In Tanzania, Legio seems most numerous in the North Mara and Musoma areas near the border with South Nyanza. I also heard of Legio being in Dar es Salaam, the capital of Tanzania. For a discussion of Legio in Tanzania, see Perrin Jassy 1966, 1973. Kimulu reported members in Egypt (Kimulu 1967: 15). My Legio informants did not speak of church members in Egypt, and I do not know if there still are any Legio congregations in Egypt.

16. The more common view is found in Buijtenhuijs. He notes that Zionist (expressive, or Spirit) churches "tend to recruit their followers from among the uneducated, which includes almost all rural Africans, and from amongst women." Buijtenhuijs seems to prefer the more instrumentally oriented noncharismatic "Ethiopian" churches of the "elite of the dominated society," feeling their members will ally with a political agenda and develop an "efficient political strategy or analysis of the current situation" (1985: 339–41). Atieno Odhiambo, who once took such a view of rural life (1977b: 239–40; Cohen and Atieno Odhiambo 1989: 46) has recently noted, "Political consciousness may be raised in the great crucibles of the cities and work place, but it is also raised simultaneously amidst what is disparagingly referred to as the 'idiocy of rural life'" (Cohen and Atieno Odhiambo 1989: 82). As I will show, the political consciousness of many Legios is acute. This perspicaciousness varies with individuals and their experience, and usually is not tied to education, income, or gender.

17. The political climate in Uganda should be noted as part of the background to the decision of this informant to leave it. The Ugandan government's decision to Ugandanize the national economy in this period led to a large-scale return of Luo to Kenya (Ali Mazrui 1979).

18. Jaramogi Oginga Odinga, who was born in 1911, and served as vice-president of Kenya from 1963 to 1966, has been a prominent and sometimes controversial figure on the Kenyan political scene most of his adult life.

19. For a recognition that some African religious movements are more than "tribal churches" or "tribal surrogates," see Fernandez (1975: 131).

20. The term *Baba* literally means "father" in Swahili. *Messias* is a late Latin term taken from the Greek for Messiah. Legios did not minimize the revelation of Jesus. However, they did see Christ's revelation as continuing, and Jesus as only one of the forms of Christ, the Messiah and Son of God. Legios prayed to the Jesus of Israel-Palestine who sat at "the right hand of his Father in Heaven," but they also believed that the Baba Messias Ondeto was sent by God the Father and the Virgin Mary in a second coming and was right among them. When they sang "Jarwar Obiro Kuomwa" (Our Savior Has Come among Us), they looked back to the "historical Jesus" born in Bethlehem, and at the same time "solemnly swore" that they had the living God-Messiah in their midst, come to earth, born again or fostered among the Luo. Most Legios told me that the Baba Messias Ondeto had not said that he was Christ, but that the Holy Spirit had shown them that this was so through "signs and miracles." A few Legios said they thought that the Baba Messias was an

inspired prophet and messenger (*jaote*) of Christ, but not Christ himself. While they sounded sincere in their minority position within Legio, a few may have been moved by a reading of westerners similar to that of Londa Shembe of the Amanazaretha Church, who told Karla Poewe, "We say [Isaiah] Shembe is a prophet to you westerners because the truth would cause you cultural and mental indigestion. We are simply being polite because it is not important to us that you should know the truth about us" (1989: 377n). That many Legios were emphatic in their dealings with me that the Baba Messias Ondeto was Christ does not derive from any lapse in politeness. It probably has something to do with my own presentation of myself as a someone whose parents were Jewish, but who wanted to "learn from all religions." As a "lapsed Jew," I was a good potential convert for some Legios. This was conversion I successfully resisted in my own mind, but perhaps less successfully in the minds of some Legios. For a discussion of some of these interactions, see Schwartz (1989a: 100–15, 134–37, 153–62, 167–75, 414–17).

21. Following the Baba Messias Ondeto's "death," a series of articles in the *Daily Nation* gave the name of Ondeto's successor as "His Holiness Pope Timothy Joseck Blasio Ahitler" (September 10–13, 16, 20, 1991). The name does not seem to have appeared correctly in the *Daily Nation* until October 3, 1991. *Ahitler* is not, to the best of my knowledge, a Nilotic word or a Luoised form. Its repetition in a series of newspaper accounts is curious, jarring, and unfortunate. The order of succession appears in the 1967 Legio church constitution.

22. *Neno* is a complex word in Dholuo. As a verb, *neno* means to see/behold/look at, but encompasses more than observation. *Neno* also means "to feel, experience, think about, regard." Further meanings are to "meet with, visit." *Neno* also refers to something that is "in sight" and "visible." As a verbal noun, *neno* means "witness" or "testimony." Thus a person without charismatic gifts can observe/look at the same place as someone with charismatic gifts. The two will *see* different things. Similarly, *winjo* refers to more than "hearing" something audible. *Winjo* also means "to comprehend," "understand," and "feel with." Such an understanding of the visual and aural modes makes participant-observation a very limited way of doing ethnography on charismatic groups. For an appreciation of these limits, see Fabian 1983: 139–40.

23. In an early article, James W. Fernandez indicated that affirming a doctrine of a black Christ could have the consequences of indirectly supporting a religious "apartheid" (1965: 75). Legios' views that Christ and Mary had undergone many changes of "color" in history, and still appeared to them in different colors and of varied age in dreams and visions, seems designed to avoid this separatism and localization.

24. In his work on Flemish Roman Catholic charismatics, Roelofs (chapter 10 of this volume) has described a situation in which charismata were seen "as a spiritual opportunity for both clergy and laity." In Legio, there was some "spiritual division of labor." Few priests had the "gift of tongues," and the few who had this "gift" did not give voice to more than a single utterance or

two during masses. Other charismatic gifts were held by both clergy and laity. For further discussion of "tongue-speech" as a charismatic gift of laity and a resource for turning Legio's Catholic hierarchy "sideways," see Schwartz 1989a, 1989b, 1990.

25. For a discussion of metonymic thought and charismatics particularly relevant to Legio, see Poewe 1989, chapter eleven of this volume.

26. Particularly interesting is an affirmation of a December 1984 Dedan Kimathi-Legio linkage (see Schwartz 1989a: 338). For reference to other connections made or supported through *dhum*, see Schwartz 1989a, 1989b, 1990.

27. In making claims of biblical legitimation, Legios cited many passages. A sample from my notes includes Legio references to the following texts: Revelation 1–4, 6, 10:1–11, 21; Acts 1:6; 1 Corinthians 12:1; Matthew 10–11, 12:27–28, 24:3, 6–7; Mark 16:14, 17–18; Luke 11:13, 17:20–26; John 1:10, 3:8–12, 7:37–39, 50, 14:16–18, 15:19–20; Galatians 3:8–10; Philippians 3:17–21; Hebrews 7:11; Malachi 4; Isaiah 2, 41:10–13, 60:19–20; Proverbs 14; Song of Songs 1:6–8, Numbers 6:22–27.

28. This section is influenced by Peter Amuka's 1991 discussion of the elements of history, reincarnation, word-game poetry, dialogism, and open-endedness in Luo naming practices.

29. Various birth dates have been given for Ondeto: circa 1910 (D. Barrett 1971: 31); 1916 (Ogot 1974: 6) and 1926 (*Daily Nation* September 20, 1991). All these sources describe Ondeto as being born in Kano location. Peter J. Dirven has described Ondeto as being born in the Nyabondo mission area, and being baptized, as an adult, on October 12, 1952, in the white farm area of the Matetei Valley (1970a: 122).

30. For further discussion of these narratives, see Schwartz (1989a: 38–41, 445–56, 480–81).

31. A newspaper account, which misspells Ondeto's name as Ondetto, gives the name of the foster parents as Obimbo Misumba and Margaret Aduwo (*Daily Nation*, 20 September 1991). Informants, and some previous accounts, used both Ombimbo and Obimbo, but the former was more common. On a few occasions, I was given the Luo name of Ombimbo's wife as Oduol and Oduor. However, most informants just used the name Margaret. Given the error of Ondetto, and likely error of Obimbo, I am not certain Aduwo is correct.

32. For a poignant discussion of the remittance economy, see Cohen and Atieno Odhiambo 1989: 61–84).

33. This statement comes from an evangile I recorded in Alego on August 26, 1984.

34. This account was reported in the *Daily Nation* (September 20, 1991). This son, Wilson Owino Obimbo, is described as "the cardinal in charge of Kenya" and "also the messiah's elder brother." While the paper translated "yeye ni mungu" as "he is a god," there is no definite article. Moreover, *Mungu* is usually used in Swahili to refer to God, in the sense of a supreme being. I have therefore modified the *Daily Nation* translation.

35. In the *Daily Nation* (September 20, 1991), Wilson Owino is cited as having made the claim, "Mama Margaret who the faithful refer to as Maria became

a staunch and respected Legio Maria follower after her son had founded it. She died in 1966 and was buried at Effessos in South Ugenya, Siaya District." This was not a version of events that I heard from Legios or non-Legios during my work in Kenya.

36. This description seems to relate to two well-known Luo proverbs: "Oh we are like water that flows until it finds it own level." "Oh I am the Wind that also changes, and is everywhere. What doesn't change, what isn't everywhere?" For a discussion of these proverbs and how they relate to views about Luo character, see Amuka 1978: 147–48; Onyango-Ogutu and Roscoe 1974: 9; Amin 1983: 80. For a discussion of how they relate to identity and views about the Spirit, see Schwartz 1989a: 92–93, 266, 269–77, 569, 648, 1989b: 3–4).

37. Melchizedek appears in the Old Testament as a priest who blesses Abraham (Genesis 14:18–20). Legios frequently referred to themselves as "Jokamama, Jokababa, Nyikwar Abraham" (People of Baba, People of Mama [Maria, the Virgin Mary], Grandchildren of Abraham). In addition to their own reading of Psalms 110, which promises "a Messiah-Priest-King" and victory (*Bed gi loch*) to those who follow in the order of Melchizedek, and of Hebrews 5–7, which include a description of Melchizedek as "without father, without mother, without genealogy . . . likened to the Son of God," there may be an influence from other independent churches for Legios' identification with Melchizedek, as interest in Melchizedek occurs in other African independent churches. Succession from Simon Kimbangu to Joseph Diangienda in the large Zairian Eglise de Jesus-Christ sur la terre par le Prophete Simon Kimbangu (Church of Jesus Christ on Earth by the Prophet Kimbangu [EJCSK]) was modeled on "the order of Melchizedek." Simon-Pierre Mpadi, leader of a related development, the Eglise des Noir en Afrique (Church of the Black Race in Africa), named Melchizedek as one of those who appeared to him, along with Elijah, Abraham, Moses, and St. Peter, in an annunciatory vision, bestowing upon him a khaki uniform, book, staff, holy oil, and religious mission (MacGaffey 1983: 181, 195). There is one Kenyan newspaper account that links Mpadi to Legio. The *Daily Nation* (August 1, 1971) reported the following: "In Congo Kishasha, there was a prophet Simon Mpadi who LMC adherents say told that Christ's second coming would be in Africa. He was sentenced to 20 years jail by the Belgians in 1939." While only one ex-Legio ever spoke to me of a Simon Mpadi-Simeo Ondeto linkage, a positive evaluation of Mpadi, and concern to link Mpadi to Legio, is possible. Mpadi was an early and ardent black nationalist, and his church allowed polygyny (MacGaffey 1983: 60, 135, 179, 219).

38. See Ogot 1981: 179; Odinga 1967, regarding the Legio-Indian link.

39. This Legio interpretation of the Baba Messias entering Mau Mau as *Muya* (Holy Spirit, Divine Breath) is consonant with Mau Mau views such as those in *Rwimbo Rwa Kimathi* (Song of Kimathi). As cited by Maina wa Kinyatti, it contains these lines, "We are tormented / Because we are Black / We are not white people / And we are not their kind / But with God in us / We will defeat them [the colonialists]" (1977: 309, 1983: 119; 1990: 81).

40. In their play *The Trial of Dedan Kimathi* (1977) Ngugi wa Thiong'o and Micere Mugo provide several statements about Kikuyu belief that Kimathi was a

"shape-shifter" who "could change himself into a bird, an aeroplane, wind, anything." The informants they spoke to before they wrote their play insisted Kimathi was more than mortal, someone who "will never die" for "as long as women bear children" (20–21, 61–62, introduction). While such statements may appear hyperbolic fictions to a Western reader, as well as some African readers (e.g., Wanjala 1977: 389), "fictions" can be very real for Kenyans. Ngugi wrote an allegorical novel about a truly fictional freedom fighter, *Matigari* (1987), which contained some suggestions Matigari might be "the resurrection of Christ." Four months after publication of the Gikuyu original, the Kenyan government tried to find Matigari to arrest him. When they found out Matigari was a fictional character the book was seized and banned (vii). The word *matigari* means "remainders" and refers to the "survivors of bullets." Ngugi's novel has further relevant background. In 1971, ex-Mau Mau fighters had tried to organize. They first called themselves the Old Mau Mau Company. They then changed the name to the Old Matigari Enterprise. Their stated purpose was to "give more publicity" to the role of Mau Mau in the independence struggle through writing books and making films. Both groups were banned in 1972 (Ng'anga 1977: 380). Legio linkages to Kimathi and Mau Mau therefore belong to a politically charged climate. I think this background may have affected the way some Legios talked (or did not talk) about the Kimathi-Ondeto equation.

41. For some of Kimathi's speeches with these religious referents, see Buijtenhuijs 1982: 120–21; Barnett and Njama 1966: 264.

42. Olweny was the only Legio I saw who had a picture of Kimathi on the wall of his house. However, other Legios used community knowledge of the oft reproduced picture of Kimathi as factual evidence of a Kimathi-Ondeto identification. A leaflet announcing Kimathi's arrest on October 21, 1956, which contained this photo, had an early distribution of one hundred thousand in Central and Rift Valley Provinces, and twenty thousand in other provinces (Abuor 1971: 137).

43. During a general strike in May 1950, a large bonfire was lit on the banks of the Nairobi River. Makhan Singh notes that following this event, "MOTO MOTO (FIRE FIRE) became the slogan everywhere" (quoted in Abuor 1971: 387). For a discussion of arson early in 1952 in Nyeri, Nanyuki, and other areas that were held to be the work of Mau Mau, see Throup 1987: 224.

44. In the first forty-eight hours of "Operation Anvil," a police sweep against those in Nairobi believed to support Mau Mau that began on April 24, 1954, Langata detention center received 8,300 prisoners (Edgerton 1989: 90–91). By the end of 1954, 150,000 people were in detention camps and jails (Ogot and Zeleza 1988: 406). Mau Mau successfully liberated all the prisoners from Lukenya Prison on September 17, 1954.

45. Scholars who share in the "tribal in membership" position include O. W. Furley (1972: 131); William R. Ochieng' (1976: 138–40, 1985: 88–89); Bethwell A. Ogot (1977a: 176–77, 1977b: 282); B. E. Kipkorir (1977: 303, 315–16); E. S. Atieno Odhiambo (1977a: 386); Robert Buijtenhuijs (1982: 135–38, 140); Maia Green (1990: 70). Frank Furedi takes a more moderate stance, arguing that though Mau

Mau was primarily Kikuyu, it was not tribalist (1989: 5–6, 141–42).

46. For this line of argument, sources include Odinga 1967: 112, 119; Abuor 1971: 91, 192–93; Kaggia 1975: 193; Ngugi wa Thiong'o and Micere Mugo 1976: 14, 18, 33, 46; Maina wa Kinyatti 1977: 305, 1983: 95, 110–20; Spencer 1977: 216; Seidenberg 1983: 115–18; Ngugi wa Thiong'o 1983: 12; Okoth 1985: 106–7; Newsinger 1985: 17; Al-Amin Mazrui 1987a: 55, 1987b: 22–25; Furedi 1989: 142–43. For other modifications of the "tribalist" position, see Ogot 1977b: 278–80; Buijtenhuijs 1982: 138–39, 149–57; Kanogo 1987a: 150; 1987b: 78–79.

47. See Abuor 1971: 110–14; Maina wa Kinyatti 1977: 287; Spencer 1977: 209; Seidenberg 1983: 119; Okoth 1985: 107–8; Al-Amin Mazrui 1987a: 55, 57, 1987b: 23–26; Cleary 1990. Bethwell A. Ogot and Tiyambe Zeleza point to vocal but not material support from "Pan-Africanist and other progressive circles" (1988: 406).

48. These are recorded in Maina wa Kinyatti 1987: 10, 16–17. See also "Song of Africa" in Maina wa Kinyatti 1990: 76–77.

49. For Kimathi's criticism of foreign missionaries, see Point 8 of the Kenya Land and Freedom Army Charter (Maina wa Kinyatti 1987: 16–17) and Ngugi wa Thiong'o and Mugo (1976: 47–51). For a discussion and critique of the "anti-Christian cult" imaging of Mau Mau, sources include Mboya 1963: 42; Furley 1972: 106, 112–14; Maina wa Kinyatti 1977: 301–2; Ng'anga 1977: 368; Kipkorir 1977: 316; Buijtenhuijs 1982: 125–27.

50. For a statement of this opposition, see Ngugi wa Thiong'o (1983: 7–8).

51. A clear statement of the Mau-KAU opposition is in Maina wa Kinyatti 1977: 291, 1987: 1–2. KAU was the acronym for the Kenya African Union, the precursor to KANU, the Kenya African National Union. KAU grew out of the Kenya African Study Union, which was formed in 1944. Jomo Kenyatta became its president in 1947 upon his return from Britain. For further discussion of the KAU/KANU-Mau Mau opposition, see Ali Mazrui 1967: 20; Kaggia 1975: 112–13, 182–96; Kipkorir 1976; Ogot 1977a: 169–70, 1981: 89–90, 135–36; Buijtenhuijs 1982: 152; Ngugi wa Thiong'o 1983: 7–8; Newsinger 1985: 12–13, 15–16; Ogot and Zeleza 1988: 407–8; Furedi 1989: 130–31. For a consideration of some connections between Mau Mau and KAU, see Spencer 1977: 209–13.

52. In Dholuo, the first line of the catena prayers contains the word *thinyore* (cometh forth).

53. Tom Mboya, a Luo-Suba born on a sisal estate in Machakos in 1930, was a labor leader at the time of Mau Mau. He went to England to attend Ruskin College in 1955. While in England Mboya tried to give "the other side of the Mau Mau story," and to oppose popular images. Mboya carried this message to America, and to European and other African countries. Although the Roman Catholic Mboya had sometimes clashed with Legios (see Schwartz 1989a: 164–65), he became something of a Luo martyr after he was assassinated in 1969 (see Ogot 1981: 138–40; Abuor 1971: 290–300; Goldsworthy 1982). Chiedo More Gem Argwings-Kodhek (Argwenge) was the first and only African lawyer practicing at the start of the government campaign against Mau Mau. He was a specialist in criminal law and provided legal defense for

Mau Mau (see Abuor 1971: 13, 230–31, 244; Ogot 1981: 22). His slogan, "Heaven on Earth," was also a force mobilizing "his people" to work for Uhuru (Abuor, 1971). Argwings-Kodhek died in a road accident on January 29, 1969. His anticolonialist stance and "horrifying and almost unbelievable" manner of death (Abuor 1971: 13) made him a hero for some Luos. Ogana is certainly alluding to such aspects of Argwenge's biography. Masinde Muliro was a Luyia politician and nationalist. Along with Mboya and Odinga, he was among the first eight Africans to be constitutionally elected to the legislative council (Ogot 1981: 144–45). He is more specifically related to the issue of religious freedom, as he was a member of the same clan as Elijah Masinde, the leader of the Dini ya Msambwa. Muliro led the campaign to free him after his long detention by the colonialists (see Shimanyula 1978: 18).

54. Maina wa Kinyatti reports that when Mbiyu Koinange and Ramogi Achieng' Oneko went to London to explain KAU's concerns on the "land question" to the government, "the Colonial Secretary dismissed them as 'irresponsible Black monkeys'" (1977: 293). Settlers called C. M. G. Argwings-Kodhek "Commander of the Monkeys and Goats" for his legal defense of Mau Mau (Abuor 1971: 13).

55. An infant in Dholuo is called a "red child" (*nyathi makwar*). With reference to Europeans, the term could be one of disparagement, indicating they would never grow to an adult brown or black color as would an African *nyathi makwar*. This red-black color opposition has a wider range, and is also used by the Nilotic Dinka (Lienhardt 1982: 82).

56. See Poewe's discussion in chapter eleven of this volume of Western charismatics, where "the Spirit is said to work through the individual's imagination and senses enabling him or her to perceive what was formerly missed."

57. The trial of Fred Kubai, Achieng' Oneko, Bildad Kaggia, Paul Ngei, and Kungu Karumba for their association with Mau Mau, which took place at Kapenguria, in Rift Valley Province, from November to April 1953, was "one of the longest in Kenya's legal history" (Ogot 1981: 98). However, after the trial Kenyatta was not imprisoned at Kapenguria itself. He was jailed with other nationalists at Lokitaung, which is near the Kenyan border with Sudan and Ethiopia, and then at Lodwar and Maralal.

58. A large number of translations have been offered for the vernacular: "Church Adapted to African Tradition," or "Religion of the Old Customs" (Odinga 1967: 70; J. Wolf 1977: 181); "The Faith of the Spells" (Abuor 1971: 169); "Religion of the Ancestors or Departed Spirits" (Shimanyula 1978: i); "Religion of the Ancestral Customs," "Religion of Ancestral Power" (J. Wolf 1983: 265, 273); "Religion of the Ancestors or Good Spirits" (Dirven 1970a: 164); "Cult of the Ancestor Spirits" (Wipper 1971: 155); "Religion of the Creator Spirit or Supreme Being" (Wipper 1977: 149); "Religion of the Ancestor Spirits" (Wipper 1988: 353). I am not competent to enter into a debate as to the merits the translation for *msambwa*. My translation of *msambwa* therefore remains tentative. I do of course object to Wipper's earlier statement that, "*Dini* is Swahili for sect or cult" (1977: 159). It is a translation that she has moved away

from (1983: 198, 228). I raise the objection because "cult" and "sect" are still common usages in the discussion of African independent churches, and figured in discussions of DyM after 1971 (Were 1977: 61; Shimanyula 1978: i; Turner H. 1979: 56).

59. Jan J. de Wolf described the DyM as "mainly Bukusu." Bukusu are the most northern of the large Luyia ethnic group. While he did state that the DyM had some support in adjoining areas of Uganda and the White Highlands, Wolf contended the DyM, "did not extend into other Luhya (Luyia) sub-tribes" (1983: 265).

60. Sources that point to more diversity include: Kenya National Archives DC/NN/10/1/5, quoted in Were 1967: 1, 5, 1977: 63, 65; Wipper 1971: 161, 163, 1977: 221; Shimanyula 1978: i, 11, 13; Irungu and Shimanyula 1982: 54.

61. For further references to arson of mission churches, government schools, administrative buildings, settler's farms, and personal property linked to the DyM, see Were 1967: 2–3; Wipper 1971: 157, 1977: 194, 1983: 283–89. Robert Buijtenhuijs criticized Wipper for her book on the DyM, counting only sixteen acts of damage to property, including arson, given in an appendix to her work for the years 1943–1955 (see Wipper 1977: 333–46). Buijtenhuijs does not feel this level of arson deserves her term "guerilla warfare" (1985: 327; see also J. Wolf 1983: 267–71). In her work, Wipper actually details more acts of arson that were associated with DyM at the time. In any event, if a few acts were built up by Africans and colonialists to mean something more, the attempts of Buijtenhuijs and Wolf to be technical about the matter fail to appreciate how small acts can become significant symbols to people. For Wipper's own defense of the efficiency of sporadic arson and violence against the colonial administration, see Wipper 1988: 355. For a valuable critique of Buijtenhujs, see Ranger 1986: 4.

62. The "Malakisi Riot" of February 10, 1948, involved approximately one thousand DyM followers who went to the Malakisi police station to obtain the release of three DyM who had been detained on February 7 after a crowd of about the same size had gone to Kibabii Roman Catholic Mission to demand that the missionaries leave. On February 10, J. H. Walker and a group of African police fired on the crowd. At least eleven Africans were killed and sixteen or seventeen wounded (Wipper 1977: 184; Shimanyula 1978: 8–10). The affair "came to symbolize the brutality and insidious character of the colonial regime, its corrupting effect on Africans who gunned down fellow Africans" (Wipper 1977: 298). The "Kolloa Affray" involved a group of three- to five-hundred Pokot followers of DyM, under the leadership of Lucas Pkech (Pkiech), in another bloody clash with the police. It took place on April 24, 1950. Three European officials and an African police corporal were killed, along with Pkech and twenty-eight DyM. An additional fifty DyM were wounded. Seven Pokot were later hanged for causing the deaths of the British officials and the African corporal. Police were brought in from Nairobi and Kisumu to impose order on the area, many DyM were jailed, and heavy fines and compulsory labor imposed (Wipper 1977: 211–18; Shimanyula 1978: 11–17). A government inquiry followed, which also looked into the Malakisi Riot

(Wipper 1977: 205). Occurring "only months away from the outbreak of Mau Mau," the Kolloa Affray became another evocative symbol for both Africans and Europeans (Abuor 1971: 199–200). For further contextualization of Malakisi and Kolloa, see Ogot and Zeleza 1988: 404–5.

63. For a strong statement from an original DyM member on missionary opposition to polygyny being a motive for the start of DyM, see Wipper (1977: 124). For reference to Masinde's specific criticism of the Roman Catholics in the colonial period, see Shimanyula 1978: 4; J. Wolf 1977: 152; and Wipper 1977: 180–81. For a discussion of DyM recruitment of laity and clergy from former Roman Catholics, Friends African Mission, and Salvation Army, see Were 1977: 64. The Church of God in East Africa, formerly the South African Compound Interior Mission, began missionary work in Kenya in 1905–1906. It is related to the Church of God (Anderson), a fundamentalist group that was founded in the United States in 1880 (Rosberg and Nottingham 1970: 17; Wipper 1977: 101. Born around 1910, Masinde's first schooling was at a mission school run by the Church of God at Kima, Bunyore location (Shimanyula 1978: 2). He did not join the Friends African Mission until 1928. The statements attributed to Masinde are cited by Gideon Were from material in the Kenya National Archives DC/NN/10/1/5 (1967: 5). Stoneham's work on Mau Mau also includes a reference to Masinde's "exhaustive study of the Bible" to show that the missions' prohibitions on polygyny was an "arbitrary rule of the Church, unsupported by biblical testimony" (quoted in D. Barrett 1968: 128). See also Wipper 1977: 178–81.

64. For a discussion of the colonial government's attempt to use Mathare Mental Hospital as "a detention camp" for Masinde, see Were 1972: 99–100; Wipper 1977: 126, 256.

65. The archival notation Were (1967: 7) gives for this statement is DC/NN/.2/6. He does not supply a date. Wipper, however, indicates that the report, entitled "Handing Over Reports and Notes," was dated August 1952 (1977: 129). Odinga reported that around 1951, within Mau Mau, "there were plans for coordinating with the *Dini ya Msambwa* sect" (1967: 112). By 1954–1955, the North Nyanza District Court deemed the DyM "a greater potential threat to law and order than Mau Mau, owing to the fact that a large portion of the labor force in the District comes from the North Nyanza reserves" (*African Affairs Department, Annual Report, 1955*: 2, quoted in Shimanyula 1978: 17). Wipper has said that during her fieldwork, DyM followers rejected any suggestion of DyM–Mau Mau links, said they had repudiated efforts to have them join Mau Mau, and had condemned its violence against Africans (1977: 192–93). However, she felt that it was "questionable" whether such statements would have been offered at the time (1977: 192–95).

66. For the prediction about independence, see Were 1972: 94. Other predictions are recounted in Rosberg and Nottingham 1970: 328.

67. For further information on these events, see Wipper 1971: 166–67, 170, 1977: 156, 161; Abuor 1971: 200; Shimanyula 1978: 48.

68. For an expression of this view, see J. Wolf 1977: 119. For a critique of such a view, see Were 1977. Also suggestive is Wipper's discussion (1977: 125) of the

history of names that Masinde thought of using before DyM: Dini ya Israel (Religion of Israel) and Dini ya Umoja (Religion of Togetherness) do not lead as easily to an anti-Christian interpretation as the problematically translated Msambwa.

69. The following sources talk of DyM dress: Shimanyula 1978: 52; Wipper 1977: 144–45; Were 1972: 86. Shimanyula also includes several documentary photographs.

70. For Masinde was a Black Messiah figure, see Shimanyula 1978: ii; Wipper 1971: 169, 1977: 153–54. For Masinde as a prophet, see Wipper 1971: 168–69; see also Were 1977: 66. Wipper gives extensive treatment to Masinde as a folk hero in two of her works: 1971, 1977: 152–69.

71. For some attempts to elevate Masinde's stature, see Abuor 1971: 169–70; Ali Mazrui 1978: 60, 84; Atieno Odhiambo 1984, 1989: 125; Ngugi wa Thiong'o 1983: 30; Maina wa Kinyatti 1990: 3. Gideon Were notes that an anonymous letter a DyM sent to administrative officers in December 1949 stated that the DyM "had received international recognition, and would, therefore go on despite Government attempts to eliminate it" (1972: 93). Were and the other sources I have examined to date do give further details on a DyM concern for an international reach, or on international interest in DyM.

72. For a discussion of the Mau Mau's postcolonial role, see "Moi's Mau Mau" (1984 [anon.]: 26–27). For the DyM's postcolonial history, sources include Ngugi wa Thiong'o 1983 and Furedi 1989: 205–23. For an interesting assessment of what street-naming means for nationalism, see Ochieng' 1977: 135–39.

73. The *Kenya Churches Handbook* described the DyM as the "only proscribed (illegal) religious body in Kenya in 1971" (Barrett: 249). For further details on the acts that caused DyM to run afoul of the independent government, see Shimanyula 1978: 24–43; Wipper 1971: 182–87, 1977: 271–86, 342–46; and the references in Schwartz 1989a: 73, 508.

74. This speech was cited in the *East African Standard*, March 1, 1968. For further discussion of DyM-Legio links in the Kenyan press, see Schwartz 1989a: 506.

75. Shimanyula has dated Masinde's Mt. Elgon revelation as occurring at the end of August 1948 (1978: 10). For an account of the DyM version of Masinde and his book, which is very similar to the Legio version, see Wipper 1971: 168, 171, 1977: 153–54; J. Wolf 1977: 181–82. The statement, "You, go back to your own country," follows directly from those made by Masinde and his followers. Sources for these include: Odinga 1967: 71–72; Wipper 1971: 159, 165, 172–73, 1977: 137–38; Were 1977: 68; Shimanyula 1978: 11; Furedi 1989: 70, 75–76. However, the words express a widespread feeling. Barnett and Njama have noted that a definition of Mau Mau, invented after the name was established, was "Mzungu Arudi Uingeresa, Mwaafrica Apate Uhuru," meaning, "Let the European return to England, and the African obtain his freedom" (1966: 53).

76. Ondeto and several Legios were arrested in April 1964 for activity in Kisii and Kisumu. They were tried and jailed for one month that summer. The court case and surrounding controversy drew press attention for some time (*Sunday Nation*, April 19, 1964; *Daily Nation*, May 2, 1964; *East Africa Standard*,

May 14, 1964; *Sunday Nation,* June 21, 1964; *Reporter,* July 17, 1964). See also Dirven's discussion of "police action" against Legio (1970a: 158–61).

77. The abortive coup of August 1, 1982, was led by junior air force officers. Major General Mahmoud Mohammed, of the army, led its suppression. He was then given the task of reorganizing the air force, which had been disbanded following the attempted coup. A member of the audience alluded to this by intruding the word *Eff* (air force) after the Baba Messias Ondeto's mention of the word *Kahawa.* Kahawa is the site of the army barracks outside of Nairobi. For a summary of the 1982 events, see Stamp 1983. There were attempts to link the coup to Luo that have been judged unsuccessful (Schwartz 1989a: 515; Brittain 1983: iv). Some press accounts implicated a Legio priest in the blessing of some air force men at Odinga's Kisumu residence (*Nairobi Times,* December 23, 1982; *Daily Nation,* December 23, 1982). The *Nairobi Times* gave the priest's name as Odeto. Legios tried to place the Baba Messias Ondeto and Legio on the side of the government and in strong opposition to the coup. His statement here, recorded on September 9, 1984, is only one example of such efforts.

78. Uriah Smith identified the figure as the Archangel Michael-Christ. The picture is captioned, "At That Time Shall Michael Stand Up . . . The patient Savior has long waited for the harvest of the earth. He will soon come as a mighty reaper."

79. This informant had earlier spoken of Acts 1:6–11. He had then moved to a discussion of Revelation 6, saying that Africa had reached the fifth seal. He said Billy Graham had spoken on the same topic. I think that both passages are the context for the statement he gave.

80. In his *Twentieth Century Book of the Dead* (1972), Gil Elliot calculated the number of man-made deaths in this century at 110 million men, women, and children "as a conservative estimate" (211). While Elliot included more than religious wars in his calculations, the Legio informant's figure of 68 million is in line with work like this. See also Leviton 1991.

Chapter 8

Third-Generation Pentecostal Language
Continuity and Change in Collective Perceptions

Stanley Johannesen

ABSTRACT

In accordance with a reflexive methodology, a third-generation white North American Pentecostal church is described from an explicitly historical and ex-Pentecostal perspective. The author looks at what once was his internal symbolic structure with an acute awareness that he does not perceive what Pentecostals perceive. He does not, nor does he want to, employ the symbolic tools that Pentecostals use to access "their reality" any more than he wants to give an empirical description. And yet, a radical, empirical description of gesture and practice skillfully captured by powerful metaphors is precisely what this chapter constitutes. In the process it recapitulates the history of many an independent charismatic church from its vigorous beginning in revivals and rented halls to its sterile end in institutionalization and modern church complexes.

INTRODUCTION

The following essay is a reflection on fieldwork I have been conducting since 1989 in a third- and fourth-generation, white, North American Pentecostal church.[1] The work is still in progress. Parts of the research will not bear fruit for some time yet. Nevertheless, the outlines of an understanding both of this church and of Pentecost itself have taken shape in my mind. This understanding has a strong personal meaning that I should make explicit.

I grew up in a Pentecostal church and went to a Pentecostal Bible school.[2] While still a young man, however, I ceased to be a Pentecostal. Attending a Pentecostal church over the last year and a half has therefore been in some sense a return to a point of origin. Although the world of the Pentecostal church is a familiar one to me, it has not been possible for me to create the feeling we associate in our culture with the idea of roots. I make this confession at the outset because it is possible and even inevitable that my interpretation of this experience and of Pentecost itself will be understood as part of this failure. Pentecostals themselves would not interpret this failure as a failure of ethical imagination, a failure of loyalty to one's people or tradition. They would interpret it as a failure of will, a failure to believe, a failure to make a commitment based on knowledge already received and sufficient. I do not think this is quite the case. As I scrutinize my own failure to "come home" to Pentecost it seems to me to be rather a matter of the inability to activate a perception. I do not see things that the Pentecostal sees.

Pentecostals do not all see things exactly the same way, of course. One of the rich lessons of my fieldwork was that the longer you stay with a group of people the more the existence of fields of resistance, of opposition, of undigested centers of contrariety make themselves felt. Schemes that make sense at one level dissolve into something else at the next. There is nothing simple about a local church. This would seem at first sight to be a seriously damaging qualification of the view that there is a Pentecostal perception. It would seem that the best we can do is an empirical description of the many individual opinions represented in the group and hope to discern some statistically significant patterns that make some sort of Pentecostal profile of attitude and personality. The alternative would seem to be to accept the idea of a reality only mystically apprehended. If I do not see what a Pentecostal sees it must be because I have no access to that reality.

I think neither of these alternatives is necessary or even helpful. A collective perception is not a concentration of opinions, tastes, dispositions, needs, wishes, or something dependant on emotions, moods, private mental states. Nor is it something mystical, generated from a source independent of the social life of the group, something in its essence incommunicable that is known only by its effects. Instead I think of a collective perception as something intrinsic to social life, the core reality without which the social arrangement would make no sense at all, the thing that cannot be denied without profound crisis to the social bond itself. It is therefore not an aggregate of persistent moods—although moods, along with other dispositions, may be part of the perceptual field—but rather something public and enforceable. The perception does not depend on unusual psychological conditions or pressures. It is not a social or mental aberration. Nor is it incommunicable. On the contrary, an important kind of power accrues to people who are specialists in its communication.

Finally, one should be able to derive empirically the collective perception from practices. The test of a perception is that it may be cast in the terms of the native language without reduction to something else, and that the native has no trouble recognizing it when he sees it. When a Pentecostal says something like "That was a real Pentecostal meeting," and when he says it, not as I would say it, as a recognition of a familiar pattern, but rather as offering a kind of proof or evidence of a reality requiring no other sign or speech, he is exercising the perception I mean. Whatever we are both looking at is at that moment, for him, invisible as a thing. It has become a metonym for a totality, a perception that is equivalent to a membership. The criticism of a collective perception is therefore a social criticism, the criticism of a society. It is also the case that such a criticism works both ways. I felt I was beginning to understand the nature of the collective perception of the Pentecostal church when I reached the point of offense, the point of crisis in my own participation in the church, the point of mutual incomprehension and mistrust. The issue arose over the question of prayer, of Pentecostal prayer, what Pentecostals call *praise*. This was easy to miss because to someone reared in such a place this is the thing most familiar, most easily taken for granted. Just as I began to see that this was the meaning of the social experience of the church, the practice that could not be removed without removing the very logic of this form of social existence, it happened that this was also the issue that singled me out, that made me for the first time an object of criticism: not my beliefs, or my way of life, or my intentions or purposes, but my failure to pray. I had stumbled on to what I believe to be the heart of the discourse that is Pentecostalism: quite simply, the social perception to which the only possible response is, "Praise the Lord."

THE PENTECOSTAL AND MODERN PERCEPTION

The premise of this chapter is that Pentecostal language points to a core meaning that has survived considerable historical and social change. The changes in Pentecostal congregations in North America are striking, but concentrating on these changes obscures something fundamental. The modern Pentecostal revival was born in this society at a period coincident with the foundation of modern society. There is a homology between Pentecostal practice and modern life even though they are superficially opposed. The key to this homology is the practice of praise. Rather than being primarily an organic outgrowth of earlier spiritual phenomena, or a restorationist impulse in the conservative or nostalgic sense, it seems to me that Pentecost is best understood as an adaptation to modern society, even a feature of it. Further, I would say it is evidence of the depth of the modern revolution in everyday life. What is characteristic in Pentecost has deepened rather than attenuated as the outlines of modern society develop and harden. Although this study developed in a quite specific environment, a mature, conservative, suburban, classical-Pentecostal congregation, I believe it likely that many of its central conclusions would apply even more obviously to charismatic groups and to non-Western charismatic movements.

The contours of a modern perception include what is in it—the judgments, discriminations, displacements, errors, regularities, surprises, deceits, strategies. They also define what is not in it—the excluded, the absent, the failed, the forgotten, the useless, the lost. Those things that are not there are as important as what is there. The absence determines the meaning of what is present. The meaning of what we see as the contours of a collective perception is a form of compensation for an absence. By emphasizing the idea of perception, moreover, we avoid the mistake of supposing that the material conditions of modern life produce Pentecostalism as a direct reaction, as a defence against itself. Instead we see that Pentecostalism is one of many possible adaptations to modern life, which is a substitution for an absent form of life rather than a successor to an earlier form of life. The practice of praise in a Pentecostal church is both the index of that absence and the homeopathic cure for it. It tells us where the site of the injury is, and it heals by imitating the injury. Like everyday life in the modern world, Pentecost is a language that fills a missing reality with a made-up reality. For that reason I want to begin my argument with an account of the history and the society of the Pentecostal church, those things that in the economy of Pentecostal perception are not the real things at all.

HISTORY OF A PENTECOSTAL CHURCH

Kitchener Gospel Temple, or KGT, as members call it, was founded in 1909 following a split among the ministers in the Ontario district of the Mennonite Brethren in Christ, a Canadian Holiness denomination later called the United Missionary Church.[3] Some of these ministers had spoken in tongues and had introduced the question of tongues as initial evidence of the baptism in the Holy Spirit at a district meeting in Kitchener (then called Berlin) in 1908. The brethren could not agree and parted amicably. The ministers who left included the venerable Solomon Eby, a firebrand Mennonite who had been the founder of the denomination in the 1870s and a revivalist whose influence had been felt as far away as Kansas (see Huffman 1920; Storms 1958; Engbrecht 1985). Others included future leaders of the Pentecostal Assemblies of Canada such as George A. Chambers and A. G. Ward. These men were aware, of course, of the Azusa Street revival in Los Angeles. They also knew of the Pentecostal revival in Winnipeg under the leadership of a Western business man named A. H. Argue, and in Toronto at a mission run by a husband and wife named Hebden. They therefore had a language of explanation for the experiences that were at issue and knew what to call themselves. They quickly formed Pentecostal fellowships not only in Berlin (Kitchener) but also in Markham and Vineland, the other two centers of Mennonite settlement in Ontario. Although this network, with Toronto, was not the first point of entry of the Pentecostal revival in Canada, it was the most developed network and became the nucleus of the national denomination.

George A. Chambers was by all accounts a powerful and dominating figure in this group of Mennonite Holiness Pentecostals. With the symbolic weight of Solomon Eby at his side, Chambers seems to have created the Kitchener church. Other well-know Canadian Pentecostal worthies were pastors for brief periods, notably R. E. Sternall in 1911–1912 and R. E. McAlister in 1916–1917. But Chambers was pastor during two relatively long tenures in 1912–1916 and again in 1921–1925, and extended his influence by the appointment of his protégé, W. L. Draffin, as pastor in 1925–1933. His hand lay on the congregation for a very long time. He continued to live in Kitchener while pursuing an evangelistic career and kept in touch with the church through his son-in-law, Roy Spaetzel—the most powerful lay member of the church throughout most of its history and the official church historian. Chambers seems to have been a symbol of opposition to later developments and had his partisans on the board and in the congregation.[4] The legacy of this vision was firm constitutional control of the church and its pastors by a strong board, conservative fiscal management, and an evangelical style closer to the camp-meeting and prayer-room ethos of the Holiness movement than to the flamboyant style of the Pentecostals. Some of the major struggles in the congregation in the generation after Chambers were, significantly, over the introduction of an electronic organ and over the aggressive popular evangelism (some said entertainments) of one of the ministers and his wife. Those sorts of issues are firmly in the past, however. Few people in the present congregation are aware of its Mennonite origins, and even fewer of its roots in the Holiness movement.

The church has had three distinct periods that correspond to three different buildings, three different names, three cohorts of pastors. The church that Chambers and Eby founded before World War I occupied rented quarters, mostly second floor "halls" in various places in downtown Kitchener, settling finally into a building of their own called the Scott Street Mission. In the late 1920s the congregation built a plain, dignified, and capacious brick meetinghouse with a distinctly Mennonite look and called it the Pentecostal Tabernacle. The pastors of that era, from 1909 through the 1930s, were all born within a short span of time in the 1870s and 1880s. They constituted a definite cohort, in other words, of men who remembered the Pentecostal revival as an event of their adult lives. They were clerics who became Pentecostals as an act of principle at a time when such an act required personal and professional courage. Consequently, they dominated their congregations and remained legendary figures for many. The next group of pastors, who served from the 1940s into the 1960s were all born right about the time of, or just after, the Pentecostal revival, and were therefore the first generation to grow up in it. These were men who took the tradition for granted and thought rather in terms of expansion and institutionalization. This generation was also the one that came under the control of the lay board of the church, who, from the 1940s on, were able to set the agenda of the church and hire pastors who suited this agenda. The culminating achievement of that generation was the move out of the tabernacle, in the early 1960s, into a modern church complex in the suburbs with a parking lot, christian education schools, office space, and so forth. With the move came a change of name to the present one, Kitchener Gospel Temple.

The final cohort of pastors are men born in the late 1930s and early 1940s. They belong, of course, entirely to the Temple era. They had no previous association with the congregation until they became pastors of it and they are products both of the charismatic renewal of the 1950s and 1960s and of professional training in Pentecostal Bible schools. Their ministries are more careerist than were any of their predecessors; they expect to move on eventually, at least in part for reasons of career development. Although these pastors still have to deal with a church board and a mature congregation with a mind of its own, they have a degree of independence that comes from their professional standing, their loyalty to and reliance on a bureaucratic denomination, their superior managerial skills, and their access to a wider Pentecostal culture. They cannot easily be intimidated by the congregation or the board and they are therefore largely indifferent to the local history and traditions of the church.[5]

The total membership of the church has been stable for decades, recruiting just enough from the reproduction of members, and a small but steady stream of young families entering from outside, to offset the deaths and departures of older members. The people who seem to be prominent in the activities of the church are about equally divided between those with credentials as second-, third-, and even fourth-generation members and newcomers who establish credentials by enthusiasm for the activities of the church. There is no sharp division, much less antagonism, between these groups. There is, however, a sort of map of social sectors of the church visible in the seating arrangements of the main services. The newcomers are more likely to sit near the front during services and to be more visibly charismatic in their behavior. They are also likely to be engaged couples, young families, or single mothers with their children. This group is closely tied to the interests of the pastors of KGT. Since they are new they are most dependent on the pastors' ministry and less likely to be party to the folklore and the traditions of the lay leadership of the church. They are likely to support innovations in programs and in styles of worship. They constitute, in fact, a model for proper behavior in a Pentecostal church as that is understood by the pastors.[6] Older people, especially long-term members, sit further back in the church and are often the object of thinly veiled sarcasm from the pulpit about lack of enthusiasm in meetings. Young unmarried people tend to sit to one side and participate little in the general meetings. They have their own places and times of gathering where a more emotional and charismatic tone is given full exercise and where they receive their baptisms in the Holy Spirit with speaking in tongues.

KGT is a wealthy congregation, leading the denomination in missionary contributions as well as sustaining over the years several ambitious building and expansion programs. Although the church is located in the suburbs, its members live throughout the metropolitan area with no special concentration in the vicinity of the church itself. The members represent all ages and income levels. The well-to-do tend to be self-employed entrepreneurs or managers in manufacturing and service industries. The middling folk are self-employed tradesmen, government and social workers, school teachers, and clerical, technical, and sales employees. At the lowest end of the economic scale are pensioners, wage laborers, unemployed, single mothers, and students. I am not aware of any doctors, lawyers, judges, scientists, or politicians who are members, or of any members who are prominent in the civic or social life of the region. University professors and students are somewhat under-represented in this church because there is another large Pentecostal church near the university campuses in Waterloo that attracts most of these people. The Waterloo church has a reputation for being more charismatic in feeling than KGT. There is also good relations with a congregation of the German-speaking branch of the Pentecostal Assemblies of Canada, and with an independent Hispanic Pentecostal group and a Croatian Pentecostal group, both of which use the church facilities from time to time but do not mingle socially with its members. There are a few black families in the church and a few East Indian families. There is no fellowship with the black Pentecostal congregations in the community or with any of the other Pentecostal denominations or independent churches. All in all, KGT has an air of permanence and stability with firm institutional and social boundaries. It will likely go on as it is for a long time.

To enter the world of the fellowship of a Pentecostal church is to enter a world of manifest human warmth. People are eager to receive new members or visitors. They exhibit friendly affection for one another, calling each other brother and sister and expressing sincere and persistent solicitude for one another's health and well-being. The preacher frequently refers to the congregation as the body of Christ—sometimes simply as "The Body"—exhorting them to love one another in even greater measure, to be tolerant of human failings, and to actively assist in relieving the burdens of one another's lives. The organization of their social lives is undertaken with care for the satisfaction of the needs of every person, *persons* being understood as members of an age group of one of the sexes, or members of a family. There is a woman's group, a men's fellowship, a youth group, and Sunday school and other leisure-time activities structured even more finely according to age and social status.

All of this sociability has a periodic and cyclical temporal dimension related in complex ways to the week, the month, and the year.[7] Most groups meet every week. Some people have multiple memberships, and all attend the main services of the church, which are weekly meetings. The week is particularly significant in a religious context, being related to no rhythm of nature but rather itself an artifact of a periodically recurring sacred day. The week may be even more significant in a sectarian context than in other religious contexts because of the natural liturgical and ritual—not to say pagan—implications of the month and the year. The week is the basis for a cycle of services and activities to which are attached expectations of renewal from the cares and pressures of family and working life. The Sunday services particularly dominate the weekly cycle, and the Sunday services are particularly the province of the pastor and the senior church leadership. The month is the periodicity of financial responsibilities of membership, of certain recurring practices such as communion services or missionary Sundays and of special outings and recreations, guest speakers, and so on, within the groups and fellowships.

The year has many implications for the business and administrative side of the church: annual financial reports, business meetings, elections, planning and projecting activities, reconsiderations of purposes and mission, revising of material and spiritual goals. These sorts of recurring activities fall on the leadership of the church. Longer periodicities belong to the more developed bureaucratic culture of denominational bodies. The local church gets on mostly year by year, as this periodicity belongs to customary observances of annual resolutions, birthdays, the natural cycle of the seasons, and so forth, and therefore lies within the limited means of the local institutional memory.

The year is also the domain of the sacred cycle from Christmas to Easter and back again. In a Pentecostal church the sense of this progress through the year is thoroughly suppressed, there being no liturgical or ritual observance of the traditional church calendar. Easter and Christmas are instead annually recurring occasions for the introduction of appropriately seasonal themes in the activities of the church and of the groups that comprise it. Christmas and Easter do not belong to a sacred year. The activities of these seasons bear strongly the impress of a sort of vernacular postmodernism, in which the traditional liturgical and ritual elements are assimilated to the commercial and sentimental themes of the seasons with little regard for the annual religious cycle of which these liturgical and ritual elements were a part.

Finally, the year is the domain of the rhythm of membership itself, a rise and fall in the intensity of participation according to seasons of family and working life, and according to the opportunities of vacation time. Thus camp meetings, revival campaigns, vacation Bible schools, volunteer work parties, Christian workers' conventions, and the like, are annually recurring events and practices both institutional and social that correspond to the loosening and tightening of everyday life in the annual rhythms of the wider society and culture.

The sociability observable in these weekly, monthly, and annual cycles and rhythms, the diffuse friendliness that permeates all of it, raises the question of social bonds and religious life. Consider in this light the family. In KGT, as in evangelical culture generally in North America, the family constitutes a powerful ideology (see Ault 1987). Typically, only those political issues that touch the maintenance of a conservative idea of family life—issues such as divorce, abortion, secular-humanist education, homosexuality, pornography—are systematically addressed from the pulpit and in the activities of groups in the church. These are not topics for open discussion, much less debate or disagreement; they are virtual touchstones of membership, and they are invariably understood as being about the family: the protection of the integrity of the family, and the defence of the family from antifamily forces. A leading metaphor for the people of the church as a whole, and for the nature of their relationships with one another, is the metaphor of the family. The church is frequently called "one family." We should expect that here, if anywhere, we would find the key to a religious bond.

Yet in fact almost all of the activities of the church are segregated by age and sex. Family night is the night when families are separated. What family night is intended to mean is that there is something going on for every member of the family, so that everyone can come at once. Further-

more, although the family ideology is conservative, and therefore assumes that husbands and fathers are heads of households and in charge
of family life, the activities of the church give very little scope to adult
men except in finances, building programs, the main ritual observances
and, under the heading of Men's Fellowship, occasional outings with
other men. All of the elaborated activities of the church beyond its central
management are by and for women, children, and single young people.
Institutional power belongs to the men, but everyday life by and large to
the women. It therefore happens that the idea of "one family," while far
from an empty one, is not elaborated in any way that corresponds to the
structure of the real families in the church. There are no spiritual fathers
or spiritual mothers or spiritual children, or a theology of spiritual or
social reproduction rooted in such an idea. Family is not a specifically
religious form of bonding.

The lack of a bonding principle to cross the boundary between the
structure of the family and the collective life of the church is connected
with and reinforced by the refusal to sanctify or give religious significance to the times and cycles of the calendar. Although the year and the
month have natural bases—in the periodicity of the return of the sun and
moon—they are, in modern everyday life, like the week, culturally
determined. They are also the temporal framework of family life; the
cycles of schooling and work, of vacations and holidays, of paydays and
shopping days. These in turn determine the scheduling of activities in the
church. But since nothing about these cycles, either in their natural
meanings or in their cultural meanings, has religious significance in a
Pentecostal church, they are not carriers of a religious bond into the
society of the church.

The most important times of all are the times that have no fixed
periodic return or duration and that stand altogether outside the natural,
cultural, and religious calendar. These are the times given to Pentecostal
worship and praise, messages in tongues and interpretations, prophecies, spontaneous prayer, and the like. Some of these phenomena have in
fact become rare in older Pentecostal churches, and others are routinized
to some degree as periodic episodes. Nevertheless, they are conceptually
inseparable from ideas of what it is to be Pentecostal. Apart from the
presumption that these are the times in which the supernatural inter-
venes in the surface regularity of events and cycles of events, these times
derive their quality from the contrast with those other times. This, in
some way that is difficult to be precise about because it is never explicitly
formulated, is the appearance of spontaneous prayer, worship, praise,
and so forth, which does not effect a sign of the consecration of a place or
a people as such. These special times are not a confirmation of the value
of ordinary times. They are rather judgments on, exceptions to, break-

throughs from the work-a-day. They are foretastes, harbingers, entrances into an alternative reality. They do not sacralize what was already there; they rather make the world more worldly by contrast, including—and perhaps especially including—the religious world. When a Pentecostal consecrates through Pentecostal prayer he does not consecrate something, rather he consecrates himself *to* something. This is not just a question of the existential element in religion, the private dimension of a religious world. The very idea of the private requires the integrity of the public and the historical. What we have seen in KGT is that the collective historical memory has withered and so has the possibility of a sacralized general economy of time and space. What has replaced it is an economy of prayer that is not private at all but is a compulsion that operates directly on every person at once, in the very same way that the everyday does in the modern world.

THE QUALITY OF PENTECOSTAL PERCEPTION

How do people know their God when they are ready to talk to him? What is the basis of this perception and in what temporal and social medium does it exist? Does this perception operate reflexively to create social bonds among the people who pray to him? The practice of Pentecostal prayer suggests that God is recognized as God by the nature and quality of the affective disposition of people who pray to him.

God is certainly not in any way in the calendar or in the family. Therefore his will in these or any other matters is not perceived in these arrangements themselves. Or consider the perception of God in relation to the Bible, or in the history of Christianity, or in the history of the Pentecostal movement, or of the particular Pentecostal church. There is no question but that the Pentecostal believes the God he prays to is the God of the Old and New Testaments, the God of the Christian dispensation, and the God of the Pentecostal revival. The identity of these Gods with the God prayed to, however, is not established on the basis of these narratives, since there is no acknowledged temporal or social medium that such a tradition might have been transmitted. That is, it would be contrary to Pentecostal piety to say that one believes because one's parents believed, or because belief was entailed in some involuntary membership such as an ethnicity or a nationality. Indeed, such phrases figure in Pentecostal narratives only when describing the mere religion of a condition before conversion to Pentecostalism. On the contrary, the narratives of the Bible and of collective and personal histories are validated by the experience of prayer. The Pentecostal meets God in prayer. He knows this is God because of what he feels, and then he sees this God in the Bible or in history. The same thing is true of the narratives

that constitute the folklore of Pentecostal people: the *memorats* of supernatural intervention—healing, escapes and rescues from either natural
or demonic powers, prophetic foreknowledge of events—and the
chronicats of past and present wonderful successes of God's programs in
the world. Faith in all or any of these narratives and reports as the activity
of God is based on the perception that the God who does these things is
real, and that reality is established in Pentecostal prayer.

Thus the Pentecostal is against religion. This is not only a case of
iconoclastic reaction, anticlericalism, restorationism, millenarianism, or
even gnosticism, all of which have appeared frequently in the histories
of religions and which represent adverse judgments on prevailing religious states of affairs. The possibility of an antireligious religion, of a
piety based on the erasure of a former religious practice or even site of a
religious practice, is extremely common. Protestants deleted sacraments,
relics, the treasury of merits, as acts of piety, not as acts of impiety.
Quakers did away with preaching, and even with religious speech, as a
move to deeper spirituality. In the ancient world, we are reminded, the
complaint of pagans against Christians was that they were atheists. A
character in Flannery O'Connor's novel *Wise Blood* founded a "Church of
Christ Without Christ." What motivates and sustains such iconoclasms,
deletions, erasures, is a perception that the religious practice erased or
deleted has itself become irreligious, that recovering the core experience
of the religion requires this move against dead or dysfunctional elements.

The mark of this type of religious antireligion is the specificity of its
transgressive or transformation movement. Through this specificity we
can identify the bond of the community whose boundary is violated. For
example, in the west the introduction of a cult of relics is a transgression
of the boundary that ties living people to their own ancestors and
transforms these bonds into a transregional cult centered on the dead.
The erasure of a cult of relics is a transgression of this bond between the
living and the dead and its transformation into a universal cult centered
on the living Christ or of Mary.[8] It may be that the boundary between
communities is formed on the practices of perception themselves. My
colleague, Arnold Snyder, is studying the early stages of the Reformation
in St. Gall, in which Protestant insurgents, who assembled for Bible
reading and study, opposed themselves to Catholics, who assembled for
the adoration of the Host. Each side employed identical scatological
language to characterize the others' devotion. "I shit on your creed," the
Catholics would say, "I shit on your mass," the Protestants would say
(Snyder 1991). Thus the boundaries, at this stage, were defined by
loyalties to different perceptual modes rather than to different celestial
patrons. These boundaries were separated by a zone of pollution, iden-

tical for both sides, consisting of the image of excrement. Such perceptual loyalties, transformations, resistances have a logic to them that is rooted in the cumulative narrative of the everyday life of whole populations, their religious and social practices, and their political arrangements, and that can be traced over long periods of time.

In spite of many appearances to the contrary—such as the restorationist motifs of early Pentecostalism, the roots of Pentecostalism in Methodism and the Holiness sects—the Pentecostal revival was not a transformation in collective perception according to the logic of development of social bonds. It neither grew out of a people nor defined one. It was rather an example of modernist separation between perception and social bonds and of the development of a metalanguage of the quotidian to replace the lost language of a real everyday life—to use the terms advanced by Henri Lefebvre (1971). The quotidian is the made-up everyday, a language scrupulous in its attention to the sensory surface of experience and which may even be a technical advance on an older literary realism, but one which is a simulacrum of the everyday and which has abandoned responsibility for the consequences of perception.[9] An antireligion along these lines may have friendliness, as we have seen, but it can have no sustained loyalty, whether to the dead or the living.

The radical transformation in Pentecostal practice lay in the nature of prayer, which, from being an elocutionary practice consisting of petitions and intercessions in the framework of an extensive temporal and social space, became increasingly a mood-centered mantra, defining an extremely constricted temporal and social space within which God is experienced with a power proportional to this constriction. The iconoclasm of Pentecost does away not only with all the dispensable, dead, and dysfunctional bits of religion; it does away with religion, that is to say, with the historical process of orderly transformation in the felt presence of the social bond, the social correlative of the collective perception. Without religion God cannot exist outside of personal experience. The Pentecostal recognizes that God he prays to because he has made him in his prayer. And since he has made his God he owes nothing to the dead or the living. That is, he has not generated in his prayer an opposition to the devastation of the quotidian and a return to religion. Rather, he has joined the attack on religion through the same nonhistorical, nonsocial consciousness that is exhibited in modern everyday life.

There is an undeniably therapeutic function to Pentecostal prayer, and a body of interpretive writing about it—by no means hostile or unsympathetic—that see in Pentecostal practices a psychologically and culturally integrative process that includes hysteria as a means of personal breakthrough and insight.[10] This is no doubt a fruitful line of inquiry and discussion. But it has to do entirely with personal psychology. The Pentecostal breakthrough is an element in a biography, a one-time experience whose repetition would in fact risk its undoing. My own sense of these practices would understand the hysterical element in this speech as conceptually inseparable from being a Pentecostal. V. S. Naipaul has recently, in another connection, used the phrase "philosophical hysteria" to mean an institutionalized refusal to see the damage that has been done to oneself and one's own people by the voluntary acceptance of a compulsion (1991). Speech in a Pentecostal church is not normally a speaking from or to hysterical people. Speech is a compulsion at the level of a permanent and institutionalized philosophical hysteria. Hysteria in one form or another may be the only sane response, after all, to an everyday consisting of compulsion and terror.

This understanding of Pentecostalism is consistent I think with several well-know phenomena, among them the extraordinary ease with which Pentecostalism crosses regional, ethnic, national, and cultural boundaries, including the boundary dividing colonialist societies from their former colonies. There are only two interpretations possible of this unprecedented transformational fluidity: the interpretation of Pentecostals themselves that this is a movement of the Holy Ghost for which there is no parallel in history; and the interpretation I am suggesting, namely, that there is no cultural obstruction to the spread of this form of piety because it has no cultural specificity. The God we make does not bind us to a community, neither our own nor a transgressing one. If we accept that the Holy Ghost is precisely the literary and historical name of God with the least personal specificity, these interpretations are virtually the same thing. Another phenomenon, closely related to the fluidity of the Pentecostal movement, is its equally astounding success in transforming lives. It is precisely because the God of the Pentecostal does not bind to a community that he is able to change radically the course of the individual life. It is well known to students of Pentecostal movements that these breakthroughs can be astounding in their scope and permanence. Once again there are only two interpretations possible: either that the God of the Bible has chosen to bestow on people in the last days, as he promised, an unprecedented gift of spiritual power, or that when a person makes his God in his prayer he makes himself at the same time, free of bonds to human community and therefore peculiarly potent in himself. The Pentecostal prayer, which occupies no space larger than the duration of the mood of the one who prays, can be in its way a revolutionary and liberating act, especially in the context of cultural and political degradation. Without question the finest hours of the Pentecostal movement around the world are in those situations where communal bonds are degraded, if not devastated. And where, one may well ask, in this century is such a degradation of bonds not the case?

PENTECOSTALS AS PEOPLE OF THE DEEP SUBURBS

A frequent assertion with important ideological functions in the Pentecostal church is that they are a uniquely fortunate people. Besides having the good fortune to be saved, they mean also having good fortune in their affluence as compared with people around the world, good fortune in their greater social opportunity, good fortune in the sense of their belief that the political and economic regime in which they live is the best, and good fortune that Christians (in the restrictive sense they employ to denote conservative evangelical Christians) enjoy unique civil liberties and even moral and political influence in North American society. They feel lucky. Sometimes this is expressed as gratitude, but always, either in addition or alternatively, this sense of good fortune is expressed as an obligation: not an obligation to the system of society from which these benefits derive, but to God.

In spite of this feeling of luckiness, it would not be difficult to describe the moral and social situation of these late twentieth century people of the deep suburbs as catastrophic. The phrase "deep suburbs" I take from a book by John D. Dorst, *The Written Suburb: An American Site, an Ethnographic Dilemma* (1989), who means by it a certain fantasized rural landscape that has premium value in late capitalist society.[11] I will use it here in a less geographically and materially specific sense to mean a point of destination at once physical, temporal, personal; a point equally distant from traditional community and from the city. In traditional communities people maintained intercourse with the dead. This was a form of society with an identity in time and place based on the incorporation of the dead in the community, whether the dead aided the living or imposed obligation on them. In the city, on the other hand, people connected with the dead not by remaining in their vicinity but by recycling the cultural capital of the dead through intercourse with strangers. In the deep suburbs, by contrast, there are neither the dead nor strangers, neither rites of filiopiety nor urban sociability. There is instead only the modern family, the organ of the reproduction of desires with no root either in place and blood or in the society of urban practices. It is a feature of the deep suburbs in contemporary discourse that there is no middle ground between the perception of this mode of life as the luckiest in the world and the perception of it as the most dreadful in the world.

The people of the deep suburbs are lucky because from the standpoint of the desires of the rootless living, the deep suburbs are organized as no other society for the gratification of these desires. Furthermore, they are, in their foreshortened generational perspective, in which there are only parents and children, and the dead have disappeared, a machine for the production of new desires in every generation. The (imperfectly) gratified desires of each adult generation become the ground of discontent for the next. It is clear in such a situation that the children and not the parents are the generative force, the originators of such a society. For when the dead are forgotten, and the desires of the living must not only be met but expanded constantly, the tastes of the children can be the only source of change and novelty. So it is that such a society cannot be criticized of reformed in any of the classical ways, that is by struggles over the patronage or custodianship of the dead. The deep suburb is therefore either the fullest realization of the ancient dream of the kingdom of the child, or it is the end of full human community.

The discourse of the deep suburbs is registered with extreme sensitivity in the social and linguistic structures of the Pentecostal church. The Pentecostal prayer, which everywhere registers in the religious dimension the absence of communal bonds and the need for personal breakthrough, is also at home in the deep suburbs, and registers in its own way (that is, nonreflexively, nonironically) the ambivalence of the deep suburbs. On the idealized sentimental and utopian side of this discourse we have friendliness with all of its deeply ramified and ingrained reflexes, the child-centered and child-caring face of the institution of the local church, and above all the pervading sense of luck, of good fortune, of blessedness and a corresponding sense of gratefulness and obligation. We should also say that this is the side of the discourse that is acknowledged, as a set of linguistic and social practices, to be learned, manipulated, improved upon. It goes without saying that the other side of the discourse of the deep suburbs, the recognition of the human devastation of this way of life, is not explicitly recognized in Pentecostal prayer. That is the reason that Pentecostal prayer is praise and not lamentation.

The deep suburbs dictates a somewhat controlled and decorous public expression of praise. Nevertheless, even here, there is no mistaking the visible affects of Pentecostal prayer: the lifting of hands, the swaying, the susurration of random, nonunison but simultaneous prayers of praise, including tongue speech, the lengthy repetitions of brief songs ("choruses") with simple lyrics of praise, the connective tissue of expressions of praise that bridge the gaps between the syntactical units of the service, such as the sermon, the offering, formal prayer, song. These more-or-less routine and voluntary behaviors are, moreover, linked in cadences that from time to time produce more profound manifestations or affecting presence; gifts of the spirit, such as messages in tongues, prophecies, healing, and also general marks of more-or-less involuntary possession with profound physical and vocal symptoms. Profound manifestations are rare in the deep suburbs (although thought to have been less rare in former times) but not for that reason less significant in the discourse of Pentecostals and particularly in that of their leaders. In fact, to the degree that conditions make such occasions rare, the memory of them, or the possibility and desirability of them, serve in this discourse increasingly important ideological purposes, confirming the leader in his position as the one whose responsibility it is to bring around again the desired Pentecostal times.

Chief among these powers and skills is the ability to sustain the ordinary level of Pentecostal praise. This in turn is dependent on knowing the choruses, being able to lead effectively in their singing, being suitably voluble in prayer and in the sustaining of the tissue of ejaculatory and hortatory phrases that accompany all stages of Pentecostal meetings, and above all having to a high degree a quality of theatrical discernment and discretion: piecing together the appropriate elements of a cadence with the proper timing and sequence, gauging the mood and desires of the group from moment to moment, identifying other charismatic players, and so forth. Skill at doing these things is acquired by practice. It is not taught formally, either in local churches or in the training institutes of the denomination, and it would be abhorrent to Pentecostals that it should be. Preaching, pastoral, and administrative skills can be taught in this way, but what is distinctively Pentecostal cannot be. This confirms the charismatic nature of these skills; their appearance in someone is rather more often thought to be a mark of divine selection for the role of leader than the outcome of professional training. It is called "having the anointing of the Spirit," or being "called of God."

What is important to recognize in any discussion of charismatic leadership and charismatic phenomena is the nature of the perceptual loop, or feedback, between the group and its leader. In relation to the charismatic phenomenon the leader cannot present himself as an expert. That is, his authority does not rest on a hidden knowledge or arcane source of power. On the contrary, in principle his power is available to everyone. Furthermore, his authority rests on the collective perception that his powers and skills are conferred by God and not by demons or mere human talent, fleshly ambition, or deceit. The experience of Pentecostal praise is, in other words, at once mystical, ineffable, incommunicable except by personal engagement, and at the same time democratically accessible and open to public proofs of authenticity. Pentecostal people have no difficulty in knowing the real thing from the spurious, the counterfeit, the inept, the lazy, the failed, the misfired. The leader therefore does not create the terms of his own legitimacy; these are already known before they appear.

The linkage between the collective perception of the charismatic and the authority of the charismatic leader may be taken to stand for another linkage of much wider application, namely, between the knowledge of

God and the affective states of people. Just as the leader's charismatic credentials do not lie in his mastery of expert systems but rather in his ability to produce expected charismatic phenomena, so the existence of God is not read from the world or from society but rather from the expected experience of him in praise. Pentecostal praise constitutes the Pentecostal God. The Pentecostal fashions his God directly from his feelings. This religion is biblical insofar as the Bible is read as a book of stories of characters who similarly knew God from the character of their feelings. Exemplary biblical characters are never understood as having the religion of their people. Rather they are understood as having experiences with God the way Pentecostals do.

The principle of the deep suburbs is the realization of desires. Pentecost is a discourse and a perception that corresponds with this in the way that it disposes authority, whether of the charismatic leader or of the Bible. It is not required in this regime that authority deliver all that one's heart desires. Indeed that would work against the regime because it would affirm the independent existence of a source of authority outside of the desires. Authority is a principle projected from within. It is made up out of the tissue of the desires themselves, and therefore is always obeyed, always delightful. The subject of such a regime is always lucky. The space that separates the authority that communicates and the subject that receives the communication is zero.

Pentecostalism is a twentieth-century movement, a product of the linguistic and perceptual revolution of its time. The Pentecostal revival is a measurement of the depth of that revolution, as diagnostic as any modernist movement in painting or literature. Lefebvre locates the shift in Western sensibility in precisely the years of the first Pentecostal awakening, between 1905 and 1910. He describes the shift as a break-down in the referentials that had governed the nineteenth-century world, a series of linkages "cohesive if not logically coherent" that had "a logical or common-sensical unity derived from material perception (euclidean three-dimensional space, clock-time), from the concept of nature, historical memory, the city and the environment or from gener-ally accepted ethics and aesthetics" (1971: 111, 113). Lefebvre then goes on to describe the nature of the change, which, it should be at once apparent, can refer almost without revision to Pentecostal prayer:

> It is not only that the complexity of our senses and of the information they impart has increased; the sense of hearing has acquired a greater aptitude for interpreting visual perceptions and the sense of sight for interpreting auditive ones, so that they signify each other reciprocally. The senses are more highly educated and their theoretical ability has

increased; they are becoming "theoreticians;" by discarding immediacy they produce mediation, and abstraction combines with immediacy to become "concrete." Thus objects, in practice, become signs, and signs objects; and a "second nature" takes the place of the first, the initial layer of perceptible reality. (113)

When we speak therefore of the "roots" of the Pentecostal movement we must also be conscious that while the plant may appear to be made of the same stuff as the roots it is in reality cut off from these roots by a transformation of the surrounding medium. God once occupied a position in the "initial layer of perceptible reality" along with matter, time, and moral causalities. We may still talk about God in this way, but the cognitive security behind this talk has given way and nothing can restore it. Nor can everyone who feels the effect of an earthquake give a philosophical account of it. God in Pentecost is a "second nature," constructed by taking the sign for the object and the object for the sign. The very mottoes of the movement, the "sign" of the baptism, "with signs following," "signs and wonders," suggest this sensitivity to a shift in the nature of knowledge, of proof, of reality. The concreteness of God became, to paraphrase Lefebvre, an effect of immediacy joined with abstraction by the cultivation of the senses. God became real in a new and startling way by the opening up of the field of piety to demonstrations of feats of synaesthesia, which is the faculty of the art of seeing with the ears, hearing with the eyes, touching sound, tasting an apparition, and so forth; once mystical accomplishments that are now the very stuff of the everyday, and which with fair exactitude describe the essence of the Pentecostal prayer.

The construction of God by synaesthetic virtuosity is emotionally satisfying, because, paradoxically, conforming as it does to the pattern of the construction of everyday reality in the modern world, it bears the only authentic marks of reality that are available in everyday life. The power and authority of Pentecostalism lie in its irreligion, its claim that in place of religion it represents reality. The peculiar claim to reality is based on the correspondence between the quotidian flow, the surface realism of the everyday, and the Pentecostal prayer. This correspondence is a homology that constitutes the claim of reality. In a make-believe world only the make-believe is real. Furthermore, if life is to be transformed at the everyday level, so that, for example, people are empowered to quit bad habits and behave themselves, one effective and efficient way to do this is to cut off the substantiality of these undesired constructions of the feelings by a construction made of more powerful feelings.

An extension of the same homology would be the principle of distraction as an effect of loneliness, emptiness, and boredom. Simultaneity without exchange creates on the one hand powerful feelings of impotence and isolation, feelings more powerful than those generated by being alone. To be alone is at least to be self-possessed, but to have experiences identical with others and to be aware of those others having the same experiences without directly communicating with them is to experience an absence of privacy without compensating social bonds. The "message" of the simultaneously broadcast experience is the sameness and interchangeability of persons. For these persons have nothing of interest to exchange with one another, stimulation and interest come from outside. We must suppose that this absence of exchange in a social animal is distressing and that it accounts for the escalating appetite for distraction and novelty and the horror of quiet or rest in the surface of the quotidian flow. Pentecostal prayer as a social rite or spectacle strikingly presents these features. God appears as a communications technology capable of distracting many people at once. What appear to be exchanges among the consumers of these distractions—the testimonies of experiences of God—are often in fact expressions of a type identical with expressions of enthusiasm for television programs, celebrities, sporting events, holidays and vacations, and other packaged and broadcast experiences of modern life: testimonials to the pleasure of a distraction couched in highly general terms and in a degraded language. Thus, in the Pentecostal church one will frequently hear that a service was "a good Pentecostal meeting," or that someone "really met God," or even that such-and-such a manifestation was "awesome," and so forth. What is at stake here is not the possibility of the ineffable or the mystical but the nature of the sociology of the ineffable and the mystical. The mystic in a classically religious context is a specialist in communicating a very definite aspect of a collectively generated and apprehended whole. This is clear because while people may be surprised by what the mystic has to report, they are not surprised by his appearance and have no difficulty recognizing the marks of a communication of the mystical. The mystic, in other words, is a social type among other social types. Pentecostal prayer, on the other hand, is not the communication of specialists. Since Pentecost has rejected religion it has assimilated the function of the mystic to the only realm that is left, the only test of the real that is possible, that of the quotidian. Since the quotidian is not a whole of any kind, but rather a series of distractions under various headings, Pentecostal prayer cannot communicate an aspect of a religious whole, one in which there are other specialties (including ritualism, dogmatism, atheism, and so forth); it cannot be other than a competing source of distraction in a society in which people live in the quotidian.

A further implication of the Pentecostal prayer as a form of the quotidian is that it has recurrence but no accumulation. This lack of the cumulative may be understood at several levels: at the level of speech acts, at the level of social relations, and at the level of what we might call, for want of a better word, the divine. Understood as speech acts, to which it bears at least a superficial resemblance, Pentecostal prayer is very peculiar indeed. Speech acts are typically cumulative: oaths, petitions, vows, consecrations, and the like have consequences such that they establish states of affairs and limit the possibility and the effects of new speech acts and new states of affairs. Being in their nature solemn, acts of this type are not recurrent. They assume that the signifier (that is the speech act itself, the promise, the vow, the threat) is nothing compared with the signified, the bond, the obligation, the surety or sanction, the *other* who is already there and has already an interest. They presuppose an exchange in the real world, acts that can never be repeated, only fulfilled. The Pentecostal prayer massively lacks this element; its essence, on the contrary, is recurrence. It can never be repeated enough. As rhetoric therefore it is more like a mantra than a speech act in the constitutive sense, for Pentecostal prayer is not the foundation of a bond; it is the recurring constitution of a recurring moment.

Here is perhaps the central point of the connection between Pentecostal prayer and the everyday world. The everyday world is not cumulative either. It only recurs. A society that lives in the everyday of the modern world does not consecrate any soil. It celebrates no festival of the city. It has even lost the true everyday, which is a style, a defining mark of a civilization, in favor of a make-believe everyday of desires and their satisfactions. The prayer of simultaneous and recurring desires, without exchange or foundation, is therefore not an escape from modern society in any of the senses usually advanced, whether from the so-called complexities of modern life, or from the humiliations and deprivations of a class society, or from the anomie and rootlessness brought on by mass migration in modern times. Whether any of these escapes actually occur, or whether if they occur escape is quite the word wanted, the Pentecostal prayer does not derive its social meaning from a form of accumulation, however regressive. For escape, and the means of escape, must be an object of accumulated wisdom and accumulated strategies. We should expect, among other things, for it to be the province of the old, the counsel of the experienced sufferer. The recurring and the noncumulative, however, have no use for wisdom. Neither does the Pentecostal prayer. There is no quantity of experience at it that makes it any better, nor is there any quality of it that experience can transfer to inexperience. It can therefore have nothing to do with any program of escape from modern life. The social meaning of the Pentecostal prayer of praise is that it is the spirituality most closely adapted to the everyday life of modern society. It is not surprising that Pentecostal prayer produces floods of relief and happiness. Happiness comes from a reduction of stress, of tension, of terror. Under the conditions imposed by the compulsions of the everyday, Pentecostal prayer brings relief precisely because it does not resist but instead substitutes a compulsion of praise. A spirituality of resistance to everyday life and to its compulsions, which attempted to recover the religious, is increasingly beyond the means of people who live in everyday life, and would in any case put them at risk. Pentecost does not require questioning the technologies of control in modern life. It may even be a feature of a general adaptation to modern life, producing rather more well-adjusted people than otherwise.

CONCLUSION

The content of Pentecostal prayer is praise, worship, adoration, love directed toward God. During the year that I attended the Pentecostal church these issues, in fact, became the center of collective attention. The church had been enormously preoccupied during the early part of that period with the completion of an ambitious building program—the remodelling of the sanctuary, the construction of a gymnasium and other facilities—that had disrupted certain activities and diverted attention to others. During the summer, however, even while the diversionary activity was at its height, a guest speaker from California was brought in for a week of revival meetings. His sermons were on the theme of praise; how to do it and when, the synaesthetic techniques that are effective in praise and that are also the sign of its authenticity, the personal and collective benefits of praise, the biblical foundation for supposing that this is God's demand, and so forth. Since this was in the summer, the attendance was small but consisted disproportionately of those members with charismatic leanings. These people were visibly encouraged to put the stamp of their style on the meetings. It was noticeable from this time on that the practice of praise in public worship became bolder, more prolonged, more encouraged from the pulpit. For the rest of the year, and particularly after the completion of the building project and the return of meetings to the refurbished sanctuary, sermons emphasized the importance of a return to forgotten or neglected Pentecostal practices, and in particular to Pentecostal prayer, culminating in a series of sermons right at the end of the period in question on the theme of worship. A point frequently emphasized in fact was that the successful building program was somehow itself a danger to be countered with new dedication to traditional Pentecostal practices. A new practice was instituted of preceding the Sunday morning service with a period of singing of choruses, particularly of the mood-setting, mantra-like ones that repeat the name of Jesus, that refer to his majesty, that invoke attitudes and gestures of praise and adoration. It was possible to discern within this renewed emphasis a difference and even sometimes the breath of conflict among the three pastors, each of whom encouraged a different form of managing the cadences of praise, from a style of seamless, swaying, end-to-end repetition of choruses, to a hearty revivalistic manner with frequent injunctions to get in the mood of it, to a quietly authoritarian mode of compulsory sequences through hymns to gospel songs to choruses. The end of all these techniques was, however, more or less the same, to induce the desired situation of simultaneous, private, vocal acts of praise arising from everyone in the congregation, the standard attitude being the well-known Pentecostal gesture with eyes closed and hands lifted in adoration.

The opposition that is cultivated in this discourse between what God is not impressed with (the building program and the expansion of services and facilities for the people) and what God is impressed with (what in one of their choruses is called "the sacrifice of praise"), we may now understand as conceptually rooted in the attack on religion and on the temporal, cultural, and social realities that constitute the religious project. God does not inhabit those realities. Or rather they are not realities anyway, but make-believe. Another way of putting this is that God is not prior to the desire for him. The famous four-fold gospel of the Pentecostal revival catches this poignantly if unintentionally: Christ the Savior, Healer, Baptizer in the Holy Spirit, and Coming King are all projections of desire that are future in respect to the desire. None of these projections of desire stands for anything that already or primarily exists to mediate a bond in the real world or among people independent of the desires of each isolated person. None of them constitutes a people or gives them a place before they have a desire. They are the projections of a people whose desires are under the compulsions of modern life. These people are in need of the things signified in the four-fold gospel—namely transcendence, well-being, competence, government—things that are beyond the powers of everyday life to deliver. If they want these things they will be disappointed. Praise, however, in the absence of the satisfaction of these needs, at least produces happiness and love.

The cornerstone of the everyday is love. The Pentecostal loves his God but his God does not love him. There is no temporal or social medium in which his God may be said to have loved him. Since what he loves has not inhabited a past or a place, the Pentecostal lover of God is cut off from every past and place as well. He must not love the house he has built or the houses his ancestors have built. He is an orphan. He cannot even be a Christian, because to be a Christian is to inhabit a Christendom, to consecrate those very places his God does not inhabit.

He is like a child who must create a relationship with an unloving parent by loving for both himself and the parent. What he has is the reality of his own love. The signifier has become the signified. The synaesthetic experience of Pentecostal praise assembles a God that can be loved, a God more real than the world, who makes his children happy in the everyday.

NOTES

1. Besides attending the church as a participant-observer, I have been collecting audio tapes of services and transcribing them into a database with which I hope to test further some of the propositions included here. Other material on which this work is based includes published and unpublished archival material in the possession of the church and interviews and conversations with many of its members. I am grateful to all of them. I wish to thank the Social Sciences and Humanities Research Council of Canada for their generous support of this research.

2. I have written about the Scandinavian Pentecostal church I went to as a child in Johannesen 1989, and about some of the issues raised by research in Pentecostal history in "Remembering and Observing: Modes of Interpreting Pentecostal Experience and Language" (1990).

3. Much of the following information comes from Spaetzel 1974; Shantz 1977.

4. This can be inferred from Spaetzel's history (1974) but is clearer in the letters and minutes of the period in the church archives.

5. Compare this with the more negative status and identity model in B. Wilson 1959.

6. These new charismatics in KGT correspond fairly closely to the process of sectarian formation *within* churches described in Berger 1959.

7. A starting point for discussions of periodicity and duration in the life of an institution is Zerubavel 1981 and 1985.

8. For a lengthy discussion of this process, see Rothkug 1980. I am indebted also to Rothkug for many discussions on these themes both before and during the preparation of this paper.

9. The ethical theory linked to perception that underlies this remark, and much of the argument in this essay, is influenced by two remarkable books: Iris Murdoch, *The Sovereignty of Good* (1970), and Martha C. Nussbaum, *The Fragility of Goodness: Luck and Ethics in Greek Tragedy and Philosophy* (1986). It is not incidental that these are both works by classicists. On the language of modern literature, besides Lefebvre 1971, see Lodge 1977.

10. Hexham and Poewe 1986. I am also indebted to a reading of Poewe's *The Namibian Herero: A History of Their Psychosocial Disintegration and Survival* (1985) for the idea of collective psychologies as a background for understanding the meaning of charismatic movements. Another approach to the issue of therapy and worship, with many insights and the merit of close attention to

language and genres, is Jean-Daniel Plüss, *Therapeutic and Prophetic Narratives in Worship. A Hermeneutic Study of Testimonies and Visions. Their Potential Significance for Christian Worship and Secular Society* (1988). My own approach to these issues distinguishes itself from these, I believe, by a greater emphasis on meaning than on function. Pentecostal praise functions in a variety of ways personally and socially, but its meaning is to be sought in the cultural moment in all of its potential for good and evil. A model study of language in a religious and cultural situation from this point of view is Ann Kibbey's *The Interpretation of Material Shapes in Puritanism: A Study of Rhetoric, Prejudice and Violence* (1986). Since I have been studying Pentecostal language in the deep suburbs my emphasis has been on meaning as deracination, loneliness, incoherence. It would be profitable, following Kibbey, to consider this same material as aggression. Praise also constitutes material shapes in the form of names, catalogs, lists, hortatory cadences that operate autonomously from their authors with meanings these authors would not recognize (see Ferry 1988).

11. More could be done in research at a church like KGT in pursuing issues of layout, display, historical reconstruction and celebration, souvenirs, and tourist and visitor orientations as features of the deep suburban site. Dorst's discussion of veneer and vignette as terms for a postmodern mode of processing both the past and the environment would apply to many of the performances and the material arrangements of life at KGT. I have made an attempt at integrating such observations into my research in "Language and Experience in a Pentecostal Church: An Historical and Critical Perspective" (1991).

Chapter 9

The Pentecostal Elites and the Pentecostal Poor
A Missed Dialogue?

W. J. Hollenweger

ABSTRACT

A reflexive methodology coupled with a genre of writing that deliberately mixes narrative with analysis is used to criticize affluent Pentecostals. These critical tools are peculiarly appropriate because the insulation of elite Pentecostals from a meaningful dialogue with poor ones is not only the result of institutionalization. Rather the exclusion of the poor has to do with the disrespect shown toward oral and narrative patterns of thought. Oral and narrative thought patterns are ruthlessly transformed into written and conceptual ones until language itself becomes a tool of exclusion. To remain true to the spirit of charismatic inclusiveness, privileged Pentecostals and scholars must learn to speak in, and listen to, stories.

INTRODUCTION

This chapter starts with a reminder that Pentecostalism was a religion of the poor that, especially in the West, became a religion of the affluent. Beyond this, the chapter is written around the following questions. What happens when these poor become rich? Do they have enough strength to dig into their past in order to find the language and tools to dialogue with Pentecostals who are poor today? And what happens when these poor, largely of the Third World, disagree with North American and European Pentecostal theology, ethics, and politics? Are we still listening, and do we realize that the Third World poor are the overwhelming majority, while Western Pentecostals and Christians generally seem to be a small and dwindling minority? And what are the topics, methodologies, and places for such an inter-Pentecostal *oikoumene*? What, finally, is the function of the intellectual in this process?

A RELIGION OF THE POOR

It is possible to distinguish five roots of Pentecostalism: black oral, Evangelical, Catholic, critical, and ecumenical. Some of these roots have been described elsewhere (Hollenweger 1988a; Quebedeaux 1983; Synan 1975). Others, for example the critical and ecumenical roots, are now in the process of being discovered. For purposes here, however, the first root is the most important. It is this root, after all, that is responsible for the unprecedented growth of Pentecostalism in the Third World (MacRobert 1988; Nelson 1981; and Dayton 1987).

Excepting early Christianity, Pentecostalism is the only worldwide church that was initiated by a black, namely, William Joseph Seymour (see Synan 1988; Tinney 1978; and Poewe 1988, for a variation of this view). Through Seymour's mediation, black (African and pre-Christian) oral means of communication became part and parcel of Pentecostalism. The oral quality of Pentecostalism consists of the following: orality of liturgy; narrative theology and witness; maximum participation at the levels of reflection, prayer, and decision making, and therefore a reconciliatory form of community; inclusion of dreams and visions into personal and public forms of worship that function as a kind of "oral icon" for the individual and the community; an understanding of the body-mind relationship that is informed by experiences of correspondence between body and mind as, for example, in liturgical dance and prayer for the sick.

These elements made it possible to overcome racial, social, and linguistic barriers. They were responsible for the phenomenal growth of Pentecostalism in the Third World. They resulted, finally, in an ecumenical holistic understanding of Pentecost as a "body of Christ," which embodied all barriers and which was there at the heart of the Pentecostal Mission at Azusa Street.

Neither Azusa nor the more recent affluent missions learned from, or passed on, the lessons of their own experience; namely, that Pentecost is the coming down of the creator to the level of specific and concrete human weakness. And just as the uniqueness of the Bible is not its accommodation to the primitive preconceptions of an Asian herding people, so the uniqueness of the Pentecostal experience is not its accommodation to the modern preconceptions of a North American urban people.[1] Melvin Hodges (1953), therefore, is surely right when he argues that the weakness of Third World mission churches has something to do with the preconceptions of Western missionaries who, by virtue of these preconceptions, treated people like irresponsible children. They mistook the scaffolding for the building. Missionaries, said Hodges (and this is echoed by Mark R. Mullins in chapter four of this volume), were not intended to be a permanent factor. They should have worked themselves out of a job long ago. Missions failed, he argued, because mission work was centered on the idea of a mission station rather than on that of a local church.

The statement by Hodges, a Pentecostal, was meant to criticize mainline mission societies at a time when Pentecostals were poor and could not rival them. In the meantime, Western Pentecostal churches have become rich themselves. And if Stanley Johannesen's depiction in chapter eight of this volume is accurate, Pentecostal practice no longer follows their theory. As if to create a corrective, they continue to plant small Pentecostal mission churches next to established and flourishing indigenous ones. Alternatively, they seek to lure independent churches under the umbrella of their denominational headquarters—just as mainline churches did at the time when Hodges criticized them.

I concur with the view of Legios, described by Nancy Schwartz in chapter seven, who argue that the Holy Spirit was already present in all mission fields before missionaries arrived. The Spirit works through the independent churches, such as the Celestial Church in English-speaking West Africa, through the Kimbanguist Church in French-speaking West Africa, the Zionist churches in South Africa, the charismatic Guru Churches in India, the Shamanized mainline churches in Korea (see Mullins, this volume), Legio Maria in Kenya (Schwartz, this volume), the Jamaa Movement in Zaire (Fabian 1971), and many other Pentecostal-like local churches across the world (Hollenweger 1988a, Burgess, McGee, and Alexander 1988). While many of these churches had contacts with Pentecostal missionaries, they became financially and theologically independent. Not only do they produce their own theologies, liturgies, and ethics, they also export them globally. Furthermore, while it is largely ignored in the literature, North American churches and missionaries are deeply affected by Asian, African, and Latin American practices and beliefs. Poewe's interviews with Paul Yonggi Cho, Benson Idahosa, and Kenneth McAll are but three of many examples (see also McAll 1985).

Nevertheless, in the Third World, tensions arise between indigenous or independent Pentecostal churches and Pentecostal mission headquarters in Europe and North America. Proof of this tension is found in Stanley M. Burgess, Gary B. McGee, and Patrick H. Alexander's *Dictionary of Pentecostal and Charismatic Movements* (1988). In the "Global Statistics" section, Pentecostals proclaim the truly amazing size of the worldwide movement. Within less than a century Pentecostals are in the process of outgrowing all other Protestant churches taken together. A growth from 0 to more than 320 million (if these statistics are to be believed) is unparalleled in Protestant church history. Pentecostals are rightly drawing attention to this extraordinary growth. But, when it comes to the historical and theological sections in the same dictionary, one finds primarily Western material. The rest of the world, which is now the numerical and spiritual center of Pentecostalism, is largely ignored. Had the traditions of this majority within Pentecostalism been included, a picture of a genuine and growing Third World movement would have emerged, along with its theological contradictions, social pains, and political compromises.

The missiological theories and praxis of Pentecostalism before World War II were revolutionary. Pentecostal missionary pioneers learned from their grassroots experiences. With little money and education, they used their natural gifts for listening to the people whom they wanted to evangelize. After World War II, Pentecostal missionary agencies prospered. Unfortunately, they began to practice the very things that they criticized in mainstream missions. They established a network of heavily financed denominational churches around the world, at times in direct competition with flourishing indigenous Pentecostal churches.

A frightening example of a neo-Pentecostal power elite, in this case in Central America, is reported by Heinrich Schäfer (1989, 1990). He calls them the neo-Pentecostal money aristocracy. They meet in exclusive hotels for their prayer meetings and actively support police terror and torture.[2] That means, in certain cases, torturing those of their own faith, the poor Pentecostals. The aim would appear to be freedom for big business and suppression of social protest through an authoritarian state. These self-interests, however, are biblically camouflaged as a fight of good against evil. That "the evil" can also be their brothers and sisters in the faith who happen to be on the other side of the social divide is a particularly cruel irony of this story. Small independent Pentecostal churches have discovered, however, that they are not helpless victims of a cruel world law. They organize themselves, assume a prophetic stance, and accept political mandates.

SOME POOR BECOME RICH

The social upward mobility of Pentecostals in the West (as well as in some Third World countries) is too well-known to need further documentation. Its cause, on one hand, is the work and life-discipline that Pentecostal conversion entails. On the other, it is the fact that these emerging elites operate in a context that is favorable for such social upward mobility. In countries with high unemployment, no opportunity for education, no proper sanitary infrastructure, no medical care, and no political freedom, such upward mobility is difficult. Although it must be said that even here Pentecostals actively create, and work in, the informal sector of the economy (de Soto 1989: 40; Poewe 1992: 163–65).

Paralleling the upward movement of Western Pentecostals is the institutionalization of international Pentecostalism. The European Pentecostal Conference in Stockholm (1939) and the World Pentecostal conferences in Zurich (1944), Paris (1949), and London (1952) started from a genuine need to articulate the identity of Pentecostals. They wrestled with a number of controversial issues in Pentecostalism, including the definition of Spirit-baptism, the organization of the church, and the nature of their relationship to Eastern Europe. Since the Toronto conference (1958), however, World Pentecostal conferences seem to have lost their critical acumen to become, instead, public relations exercises (Hollenweger 1988b; Robeck 1988: 707–10). The disappearance from charismatic conferences of such critical voices as Simon Tugwell, J. M. Ford, Kilian McDonnell, and others, indicates that charismaticism is perhaps going in the same direction.

What holds these conferences together is either a kind of Pentecostal/evangelical standard ideology or a conservative Catholic theology. The early ecumenical enthusiasm has been lost in the charismatic movement as in Pentecostalism. In other words, new religious elites call the tune.

The most important marker of their elite status is the fact that they use the conceptual language of those in power. Even when they defend the oppressed, they couch the needs and aspirations of the poor in elitist (that is, conceptual) language. It is a language that makes it impossible for the poor to articulate their needs and interests themselves. Instead of speaking for themselves, others speak for them. Belying their oral roots, the documents of the Catholic and Pentecostal dialogue are written in conceptual language. If the poor want to be heard directly, they have to translate oral narrative patterns of thought into conceptual ones. We are left with the irony that the very religion that was authentically theirs now serves to alienate them.

Culture and language are not neutral means of communication. Those who decide on the language decide who will participate in the decision-making process. An invitation "to all and sundry" does not change the fact that the language decision excludes many grassroots Pentecostals. So far Pentecostalism has presented itself as a kind of arch evangelical phenomenon. It sees itself as combining evangelicalism with "fire," dedication, mission success, speaking in tongues, and gifts of healing. But that will no longer suffice (Sheppard 1984). Pentecostalism is a denomination sui generis. Its roots in the black oral tradition of American slaves, in the Catholic tradition of Wesley, in the evangelical tradition of the American holiness movement (with its far-reaching political, social, and ecumenical programs), in the critical tradition of both the holiness movement and critical Western theology, in the ecumenical tradition of its beginnings—all this qualifies it as a movement that is not just a subdivision of evangelicalism "on fire." It is inherently an ecumenical movement.

Unfortunately, Pentecostalism was not able to project itself in this way. One reason for this is the fact that of the more than three hundred million Pentecostals, charismatics, and independents only about sixty million are represented in the Pentecostal World Conference (Vanvelderen 1991: 792; Hollenweger 1991: 91–104). These numbers indicate that Pentecostalism has not yet found a mode of cooperation and communication that effectively expresses its global coherence and pluralism.

To find this global communication is one of the main tasks facing researchers of Pentecostal phenomena. The problem is how to articulate a theology that expresses at once unity and diversity in a way which goes beyond Western bureaucratic organizational models and conceptual patterns of thought. Can Pentecostals deal with the emergence of power structures in their midst, with ideological hard-liners, with their own amazing capacity to forget their own history? Can they avoid the religious rat-race with its money-based power structures and worldly conformism?

There is some cause for optimism. The critical root of Pentecostalism has been rediscovered. There is not only Seymour's stand for oral and reconciliatory spirituality; there is also the old tradition of pacifism and the original understanding of the ministry as not belonging exclusively to a full-time and paid pastorate (Beaman 1989). Furthermore, there is the moving testimony of Frank Chikane, a pastor of the very conservative Apostolic Faith Church in South Africa. He is also director of the Institute for Contextual Theology and general secretary of the South African Council of Churches (see Chikane 1988; Horn 1989; de Wet 1989). For Chikane and his friends it is necessary to remain faithful to Pentecostal spirituality and language, not only because they are loyal to their own tradition but also because that is the language of the poor. Here the Pentecostal option becomes automatically a political one. Using oral language, they express their solidarity with their own roots, with the poor and persecuted in their country—a fact that made Chikane in turn a victim of persecution and torture, even by his own church, which had become a church for the white elite.[3]

Moreover, in the United States, Eastern Europe, Holland, and Latin

America we also find an amazing sharpening of conscience amongst Pentecostals.[4] The social-ethical analyses, the criticism of the identification of salvation with the comfortable life of the middle-classes, a rejection of the "Signs and Wonders" apostles who see the kingdom of God in their own luxury (Pratt 1991; MacDonald 1982; Robeck 1982; Farah 1981; Guerlich 1991), a new and discriminating search for critical exegesis and hermeneutics—all this is a "re-take" of early Pentecostalism by means of sophisticated research and scholarship.

Another example is the establishment of the Center for Black and White Christian Partnership in Birmingham, England. Through this center, a way was found to give black Pentecostal worker-pastors access to a university education and accreditation without destroying their oral and Pentecostal spirituality. This is a remarkable achievement by a secular university (Hollenweger 1987; Mazibuko 1987).

It is quite clear that inclusion of the diverse poor implies an ecumenical partnership that is not necessarily identical with membership of the World Council of Churches. There are signs in the United States that some Pentecostals have recognized their inherent ecumenical roots (Robeck 1970, 1987; Alvarez 1987; Palma 1985; Randall 1987; Rusch 1987; Gros 1987), the fact, in other words, that Pentecostalism began as an ecumenical revival movement in most countries. Pentecostals expressed this when they argued that their movement was not based on "man-made doctrines" but on the idea of a "community in the Spirit," that is, on a community that includes (not excludes) those who experience and articulate the Spirit in different ways. Unfortunately, this original vision was abandoned. While ecumenical relationships with the World Council of Churches (see Bittlinger 1981) and the Roman Catholic Church exist in the United States (and not only there), it is as yet a "Koinonia [or fellowship] of the Establishment," that is, the Koinonia of the elites from different churches, and not the "*Koinonia Christou*" (Hollenweger 1979a).[5]

On the academic level, a growing number of scholars, both secular and Christian, are engaged in research of the Pentecostal and charismatic movements. Unfortunately, their research is seldom sponsored by these churches (Pentecostals and charismatics rarely fund research). Even so, scholars exchange knowledge through the Society for Pentecostal Studies in the United States and European Pentecostal research conferences in Europe.

From a Pentecostal perspective, it is surely time to organize a transnational inter-Pentecostal ecumenical debate to discuss, for example, the following issues: the theological status of ancestors, the place of visions and dreams in cognitive theological processes (see Poewe, chapter eleven of this volume), theory and praxis of oral theology on a sophisticated level, and exorcism in the West and in the Third World. Also discussed should be the relationship between alternative medical and spiritual healing, the church as a therapeutic and liberating community, and the consequences of the latter for evangelism (see Schwartz, chapter seven this volume). While these experiences are well known at the grassroots level, they are rarely recognized, not to mention discussed, at a transnational academic level. Furthermore, the language of international conferences reduces them to a straightforward Western understanding—or misunderstanding. What is the alternative? Which Pentecostal and charismatic academic institutions could take up this task? What is the place of Pentecostal elites in this process? And how can scholars shape their research so that the poor of many cultures have a say in this work?

The challenge is formidable. Elites must face the question of how to cope theologically with the bewildering pluralism within the Pentecostal *oikoumene*. So far the theological contributions of Third World Pentecostals have been largely ignored. Apart from human pride and weakness, from which Pentecostals are not exempt, there are, as said, language reasons for ignoring this contribution. To begin with, where documents exist, most are not in English. It might be salutary for an English-speaking conference to realize that, from a global perspective, English is rather a secondary language among Pentecostals. By secondary language I mean that the majority of Third World Pentecostals do not speak English as their first language, and even when they do their English is colloquial. It is not the conceptual English of an international research conference. Pentecostals speak in grassroots languages, in the languages of the people, and that is in many countries not English. English is the language of the elites, foreigners, multinationals, and of those in power. It is also that of the missionaries and international donors.

Furthermore, their documents, where they exist, are difficult to get hold of. More often than not their theologies are not contained in their confessions of faith, if they even have such written documents. Rather, their theologies are contained in their songs (in the vernacular), in prayers, liturgies, and collective biographies. In fact, their oral theology consists in forms that resemble the raw material from which the evangelists wrote their gospels and the authors of the Old Testament composed their stories (see Hexham 1993).

A type of research is required that can deal with these forms of theological documentation. Furthermore, the overt meaning of these documents often obscures the hidden but true meaning. As in biblical research the context is an important ingredient for interpreting the text. An uninformed Western theologian might take the overt meaning for the true meaning. Pentecostals, however, who know (or should know) better, are aware that they have to dig for the hidden but real meaning. Doing so calls for considerable competence in interpreting language and culture. For example, when a Caribbean Pentecostal in Britain says, "Thank God, I am saved," he means something totally different from what a middle-class British charismatic or evangelical means by the same words. In the case of the Caribbean British it means literally "I am saved," not unlike the original biblical meaning of *sozein*. It means, I owe my physical, cultural, and spiritual survival to that God and his community who saved me. Without them I would be lost and perish. A British middle-class charismatic means by these words, "I have gone through a religious crisis experience that gives meaning and direction to my life." That is not necessarily inferior, but it is certainly different.

One way of solving the dilemma for Pentecostal research would be to acknowledge the diversity and unity of spiritualities, theologies, ethics, and liturgies that we find already in the biblical witness. This is at least how I interpret the work of such evangelical scholars as James Dunn and Charles Kraft (Hollenweger 1991; Spittler 1983).

We see the beginnings of such a rethinking, for example, in the article of H. V. Synan in *Dictionary for Pentecostal and Charismatic Movements* (1988). The same dictionary also contains a farewell article to the old theory of verbal inspiration and inerrancy (Arrington 1988: 376–89). Instead one now speaks of the reliability and authority of Scripture. Whether one is prepared to accept the conclusion that not all "inerrant statements" are also reliable and not all "reliable statements" are necessarily inerrant, I do not know. Every marriage partner, however, should know this from experience. Important is that Pentecostalism be delivered from its Babylonian bourgeois captivity.

Further evidence of such rethinking is the discussion on the Virgin Birth by the Catholic author J. M. Ford. She claims, for example, that the New Testament makes no explicit connection between the divinity of Jesus and his virginal conception (1988).

There is also a growing acknowledgement of pluralism within Pentecostalism, as in an article by D. A. Reed on Oneness-Pentecostalism and on black theology (1988). Finally, the black Pentecostal theologian L. Lovett offers a remarkable critique of the "gospel of Prosperity" (1988).

But these important strands rarely appear in the mission reports and public relations addresses of the Pentecostal and charismatic elite. Sometimes they are not aware of them and other times they find them unimportant. Yet, a genuine dialogue between the Pentecostal poor and the Pentecostal and charismatic elite would no doubt be a more telling testimony of the power of the Spirit than all church-growth propaganda.

If the conflict between poor and wealthy Pentecostals is not solved, Pentecostalism will surely disintegrate into numerous discarded new religions.

I have often asked myself why in our meetings the Spirit is so eloquent on "peace of heart," on marriage problems, and on questions of individual ethics, and so silent on racism, oppression, and starvation? I do not think that the Spirit is unaware of these problems and that he does not want to lead us to better solutions than those of the politicians. Could it be that we do not listen or that we do not have the institutions and "places" where he, or she, can express him or herself? Could it be that by using a language that excludes the majority from our deliberations, we unconsciously have passed over "the least of these my brethren?" (Matthew 25:40)

TWO PENTECOSTALISMS OR ONE?

Do we have to be satisfied with the split of Pentecostalism into a silent majority and a vocal minority? Who could build a bridge over these troubled waters? International mission departments that might provide bridges do not. Members of mission departments function as American, Swiss, or British executives who make decisions for thousands of people whom they rarely meet. Furthermore, they make these decisions following their denominational strategy and on the basis of what they think is necessary.

Let me give some examples in story form. A few high-powered mission executives (in a country that I shall not name) once invited me for a frank talk on mission issues. Each executive introduced himself by saying, "My name is X; I represent the mission of such-and-such, a church. My budget is twenty million (or five million)." When I had ended my talk they said, "We know only too well that our so-called projects in the Third World do not help the churches nor the societies there. The educational, medical, and media infrastructures introduced by our societies do not fit the context. In many cases they favor an already privileged elite. We should have programs that cost much less, are nearer to the people, and can be administered by them. But then, what are we going to do with the millions that we have to spend each year?"

In answer I suggested the following: (1) Use part of your millions to tell your constituency the truth. (2) Use part of your millions to find projects that really help people. Do not say to your donors, "Every single penny that you give goes directly to the needy." That is blatant nonsense. Tell them that it is a very costly process to take the money where it is needed. (3) Use part of your money to fund research on Pentecostalisms and independent churches that are different from yours. It might show how differently the Spirit works in a culturally different context. It would also make you more cautious in exporting your own understanding of the Gospel. (4) If you begin to tell your sponsors the truth, you might get less money. Indeed, other agencies might spring up and take some of the millions that were once yours. Nevertheless, it is better to have less money for long term profitable investment than too much money for prestige projects.

The second example is taken from my own country. The Swiss Pentecostal Mission decided to build a training college for craftsmen in South Africa—a good project, one would think. Only they took that decision without consulting their constituency in the field. They did not ask the obvious questions: Who will be the teachers, who will be the students, and what will the students do after their training? So they sent a Pentecostal builder to South Africa. Swissair transported the material. No sooner had construction work begun when the South African constituency revolted and said to the builder: "You have a few days to stop your project and go home. This is our country." So the project manager went home frustrated, hurt by these "ungrateful natives," and confirmed in his heart of their wickedness. Had he (or the mission committee) cleared up obvious questions before starting construction, this failure might have been avoided. Perhaps they would have found out that something else was needed or that another location should have been chosen.

The third example is from Nigeria. The deputy chancellor of a university, an agriculturalist, explained to me why the universities trained agriculturalists. It went like this. They were trained in order to get agriculturally competent high school teachers, in order to get agricultural students at the university, in order to get more high school teachers in agriculture, in order to get more agricultural students at the university, and so on. "And what has all that to do with agriculture in the country?" I asked. "Nothing whatsoever," was his answer.

In the same city is an Anglican church. It is housed in a modern, concrete church building. Unfortunately, this church is so hot inside that the congregation had to install an air-conditioning system. But in Nigeria the electricity supply is unpredictable. To prevent the air-conditioning from breaking down during worship hours, a generator was installed. Not far from this Anglican church is a Celestial Church (an important independent West African Pentecostal church). Their building is constructed according to Nigerian architecture. The huge windows on both sides have no glass, providing a natural air-conditioning system. Believers are dressed in long white gowns in the vestry. They feel cool even if the service lasts twice as long as in the Anglican church. The deputy chancellor and many other intellectuals are members of this church. The fact that the church has no glass windows makes it possible for passers-by to follow the service. It might even persuade them to participate. The Celestial Church receives no subsidies and no experts from abroad. It is an independent church, financially and ideologically. By contrast, the Anglican church can only function with subsidies from abroad. Consequently, Anglican Christians have to buy things and build churches that might please the donors but which are dysfunctional in Nigeria.

These examples show that education, evangelism, radio, TV programs, and agricultural projects were conceived by elites who have money and master the language. They export their money, their language, and their priorities to the mission field. No dialogue takes place. A foreign culture is benignly put over the poor. And that makes them even poorer because it makes them dependent on subsidies, expertise, and manpower from the elites. It destroys the very thing that makes these churches grow, the use of their own cultural, human, and material resources and their own theologies.

One might object: What you say might be true for agricultural and educational projects but not for evangelism, theology, and spirituality. They are the same everywhere. They are part of our old-time religion, which we of the mission committees discovered and therefore have the right to export.

This line of argument is, however, in flat contradiction to the Bible. Leonardo Boff, the famous Brazilian theologian, says in a remarkable book on Charisma and the church: "Christianity is a syncretism par excellence" (1985: 92). One need only look at the Bible. The temple was built by Canaanite craftsmen and planned according to Canaanite plans (except that at the place for the idol the Israelites put the ark of the covenant). The magi found the way to Christ (at least according to Matthew) on the basis of their pagan horoscope. The Bible-reading scribes in Jerusalem wanted to kill the baby Jesus. The "Haustafeln" of Paul take up concepts from his context. In 1 Corinthians 13, a collage of popular religious sayings of the time, the name of Christ does not appear. All the biblical documents are the result of an interaction between the Gospel and the surrounding cultural, political, and religious situation. They also show us, however, that not all cultural contexts are equally suitable. The idols in the temple were not acceptable. Corinthians 13 became a Christian document when it was inserted into 1 Corinthians and was thus reinterpreted in the light of the rest of the epistle. The quotations from the rabbinic literature (in the synoptic gospels) or from the apocalyptic literature are still recognizable as quotations. But equally well one can see the modifications that the biblical authors applied. It means that the Bible shows us a theologically responsible syncretism whose author did not accept nor reject everything. They chose with discrimination and thus are our masters in this business.

Present day churches, including Pentecostal ones, are further examples of syncretism. If we act as religious celebrants at patriotic celebrations (such as Remembrance Day or the swearing-in of the president), or if we accept the thought-patterns of a pagan philosopher, Aristotle, in our Pentecostal theology (called coherence and logic), we have to have reasons for such choices. I do not want to be misunderstood: there might be perfectly legitimate reasons for these forms of syncretism. But that has to be demonstrated and not simply taken for granted. The issue becomes burning if churches from other cultures in which Aristotle is not predominant (for example, in Asia or among the Mexican Indians) begin to articulate their theology, or when they integrate their patriotisms, their ancestors, and their nationalisms (or their revolutionary antipatriotic ideas) into their theologies and liturgies. A major topic for a dialogue among plurivocal Pentecostal elites and poor should be centered on the question of distinguishing between theologically responsible and irresponsible syncretisms?

Such a question cannot be answered in a monocultural situation. That is why Pentecostal mission departments are good places to take up this issue. They can only intelligently answer such questions, however, if they take into consideration the convictions of the diverse poor in the mission-field. For example, American and British Pentecostals can only come to an articulation of their conviction, let us say on the Gulf war, by consulting their constituency *sur* place: the Pentecostals in Egypt, Iraq, Syria, and India.[6] To voice their opinion without consulting their fellow Pentecostals directly is irresponsible syncretism.

Likewise Pentecostals in the West can only come to a responsible conviction, let us say on the question of world trade and the debts of the Third World, by consulting those concerned, that is, the Pentecostals in Brazil, Argentina, West Africa, and India. To back up a policy that is entirely in the interests of the West is not only short-sighted, it is also un-Pentecostal and unspiritual. It is in our interest to ease the pressure on Third World countries because the time is already upon us when the numbers of economic refugees has become too big.

If one says that these are all secondary problems that do not touch the heart of the Gospel, let us now turn to some specific spiritual problems. For the dialogue on these problems could very well be a practice ground for us. At the heart of our biblical interpretation are questions of hermeneutics. At least the better informed Pentecostal theologians can no longer say, "The Bible says," and then quote a verse of Scripture. They have to account for the principle of their selectivity. For example: Why do some Pentecostals take literally the command of Jesus in the Gospel of John to wash each other's feet, and others do not? Why are black (and some white) Pentecostals uneasy about Paul's obvious hesitation to attack the institution of slavery, but are comfortable with his condemnation of homosexuality, especially in light of the fact that others still have already found a Pentecostal association for homosexuals? Why do some Pentecostals take very seriously Paul's regulations about women in the church, while others could not care less about them? Why do many Pentecostals reject infant baptism because it is not in the New Testament, yet they appoint army chaplains, organize Bible schools, celebrate the twenty-fifth of December as Christmas, and have extended youth work, when none of this is in the New Testament either? Finally, why do Pentecostals and charismatics teach so many different doctrines on the baptism of the Spirit but refuse to look at doctrines on ancestors or dreams? (Lederle 1988).

CONCLUSION

Though culturally diverse, on the whole, the Pentecostal poor are oral nonconceptual peoples who are often masters of the story. Their religion resembles more that of the early disciples than the religion taught in our schools and universities. Likewise, despite their cultural diversities, Pentecostal elites are literary conceptual peoples who pride themselves on speaking the language of science and technology. The question is, therefore, can the Pentecostal elites and the Pentecostal poor enter into a genuine dialogue?

It seems to me that Pentecostalism, precisely because it wants to be faithful to the Bible, should take seriously the fact that the Bible is first and foremost (although not exclusively) an oral document. It prefers songs to systems, stories to statements, parables to (our style of) preaching, healing signs to discussions of distinctions. Do we have the ability, the places, the language, the institutions, the finance, to present our theology in oral categories lucidly and critically (just as Christ and the apostles did)? If we were able to do this, we would not only open up a dialogue on life and death with our own constituency among the poor, not to mention the religiously immune rich, we would also become a shining example for the Vatican and the World Council of Churches.

In the meantime, we repeat the mistakes of the other churches. We cut ourselves off from our own poor people in the interests of a stream-lined theology, of an efficient organization and a façade of unity. For this "conformity with the schemata of this world" (Romans 12.2) the price is too high. The price is the sacrifice of the poor. The price is the tears of those mothers who see their teenage girls sell themselves to tourists in San Paolo in order to pay their college fees. The price is the millions of starving people whose own subsistence economies have been destroyed in the interests of a so-called free market and whose language is not taken seriously because it does not fit the schemata of this world (Romans 12:2), the schemes of the koinonia of the elites.

NOTES

1. This concept is based on the writings of Johann Georg Hamann, the eighteenth-century Christian philosopher of Königsberg, East Prussia (see Jorgensen 1968: 169–70.) In the accommodation method of P. Mateo Ricci some of those preconceptions of people (as of the missionary) have to be broken (see Poewe, introduction to this volume).
2. It is important that we remain cautious about this blanket criticism. In Poewe's research in South Africa, some charismatic Christians, especially business and professional people, also met in hotels, and, after hours, in various offices. These people did, however, give generously of their time and money to the church. While many admitted that they had little in common with the poor in their church except, of course, their Christianity, they remained in their churches precisely because they knew their support was needed. None of the people interviewed by Hexham and Poewe supported police terror and torture. They were unanimously opposed to apartheid.
3. For the quality of orality see Ong 1982.
4. For evidence of this "sharpening of conscience" in the United States, see Dempster 1991, 1987; Villafane 1990. For Eastern Europe, see Volf 1987a, 1987b, 1989; Kuzmic 1990. For Holland, see Zegwaart 1988; C. Laan 1991; P. Laan 1988. For Latin America, see E. Wilson 1987.
5. An important root of Pentecostalism is its Catholic root, which was transmitted through John Wesley. Wesley was an Anglo-Catholic clergyman and recommended Catholic devotional literature to his lay-preachers. It was from this root that the Holiness and Pentecostal two-stage spirituality emerged (second grade, perfection, Spirit baptism). For a strict reformation-theology such a concept is unthinkable, hence the fierce opposition of these churches.
6. Most revealing is the argument of early Pentecostals who did not argue for pacifism with the ten commandments but by stating that wars are fought for other reasons than the stated ones, mainly for economic reasons. They explicitly saw a link between capitalism and war (see Dempster 1991, 1987).

IV

Charismatic Christian Thought

Chapter 10

Charismatic Christian Thought
Experience, Metonymy, and Routinization

Gerard Roelofs

ABSTRACT

This study of Flemish Catholic charismatics shows how charismatic Christian experiences are translated into religious narrative. Mental and psychological processes involved in this transformation include surrender, expectation, reading events and behaviors as signs, and talking about experiences in terms of apposite metaphors and metonyms. The chapter expresses the fear that metonymic structuring leads to literalness, intolerance, and fundamentalism. Equating metonymic thought with naive realism, this chapter misses the irony which is picked up in the next, namely, that symbolic, in the sense of metaphorical, interpretations may lead to sterility and routinization, while literal ones may lead to discoveries and breakthroughs.

INTRODUCTION

Christianity is a religion of the word. It is based on a written text (the Bible) that, so its adherents hold, is a revelation of God Himself. Through the ages interpretations of this text have led to numerous religious doctrines. Putting convictions into words—be it in written or oral form—starts a process in which not only belief turns into language, but at the same time language also turns into belief. That is to say, religious experiences are not merely reflected, but also constructed by the form, content, and context of the utterances in which believers express them. Hence the importance of a linguistic study of religion that does not limit itself to a philological concern with texts, but which widens its scope to include the processes through which these texts are produced.

Within cultural anthropology this insight has inspired scholars to advocate a sociolinguistic approach to religion (Samarin 1976), a hermeneutics of creativity in ritual language (Csordas 1987), and an interpretation of religion in the direction of a theory of religious praxis (Fabian 1985). The study of charismatic Christian movements can also gain by concentrating on the concerns that underlie these approaches. Charismatics would not be who they are if they did not express themselves in their particular religious language. It is not sufficient—as seems to be the rule in studies of Pentecostal and charismatic movements—to restrict oneself to striking phenomena like glossolalia and prophecy. The way in which participants talk about their religious experiences has also to be taken into consideration.

From this perspective, I will address the relation between charismatic Christian experience and its articulation in religious narrative. This chapter is divided in three sections. The first section deals with the characteristics of charismatic experience. These will lead us to the issue of a metonymical, rather than metaphorical, structure of charismatic Christian thought, recently proposed by Poewe (1989), which I discuss in the second section. In the third section, attention will be directed to the routinization processes with which religious movements are sooner or later confronted.

The ethnographic case that will be used is that of the Flemish Catholic charismatic renewal.[1] In Belgium, the first prayer meeting of Roman Catholic charismatics was held in December 1971. In the course of 1972 more groups were formed (Sandidge 1976: 51–69). The rise of the renewal in Belgium coincided with the movement's spread from North America to other continents, which took place in the early 1970s.

EXPERIENCE

Self-surrender

During the discussions I had with Roman Catholic charismatics, the central topic of conversation that emerged repeatedly was their "personal relationship with the Lord." The essential feature that seemed to characterize this relation to God resembled the position that William James considered as indispensable for conversion, namely that of "self-surrender" (1985: 211). According to James, "passivity, not activity; relaxation, not intentness, should be now the rule" (121).

A striking expression of this state of mind was uttered by a religious sister who told me that during a charismatic retreat some years ago she gradually reached a point at which she could say, "I dispose of myself. . . . Look Lord, here it is, it is all Yours, I hand it over, this is just how it is, it is all Your work, here You have me" (Cecile 1987).

This stance of submission resulted for her in a thankfulness toward God "for everything ... whatever it has been." Someone else told me, "To choose in favor of the Lord, that means giving up your own will and letting yourself be led by Him" (Bock 1987).

Here, people decide to choose radically for God and take Him as the central point of reference in their lives. They draw the conclusion that it is necessary to follow God's will and to no longer go their own way. The belief that all things come from God leads to a relative indifference about what happens. Charismatics feel strengthened by the certainty that God has their lives (and the lives of their fellows) in His hands. Both ups and downs are interpreted from this viewpoint. It ensures that, in the final analysis, the downs can be transformed into ups.

All this offers a new perspective on life. The reinterpretation of the past, which forms an integral point of conversion, produces new starting points and prospects for the present and future. Converts reorder their lives and reconsider their relation with their fellow human beings. For charismatics, this personal renewal by way of consciously accepting God as their Superior triggers the healing potential of Christianity.

Praise and Thanksgiving

One of my interlocutors once defined being charismatic as follows: "We are passively active, we let ourselves do" (Hauman 1987). As this pronouncement indicates, charismatic activity is a derived activity. According to those who are concerned, it does not originate from the individual's own will or initiative, but it is said to be received from God: it is something given.

From an issue of *Jezus Leeft!* (Jesus Lives!) the monthly periodical of the Flemish Catholic charismatic renewal, we learn that charismatics consider praise of God as the basis on which their relationship with God rests: "Through and from praise we receive all good from God" (December 1987: 8). Indeed, it is hard to imagine a charismatic event in which prayers of praise and thanksgiving do not occur. These are the *conditio sine qua non* of charismatic religious experience.

One could therefore say that charismatics are involved in an exchange relationship with God in which they are asking for a religious experience. Having had such an experience—which I, following Samarin (1972a: 183, n. 4), define as going through an event to which a religious meaning is attributed—charismatics are overwhelmed by feelings of joyful gratitude and love of God that need to be expressed. The vivid and spontaneous way in which they express these emotions underlies the labeling of charismatics as "religious enthusiasts." Although at first sight this enthusiasm seems to contradict the passive attitude of self-surrender, which I took as the central characteristic of charismatic experience in the preceding paragraph, a closer look reveals that the two are interwoven.

By their enthusiasm charismatics create a context in which they are able to have a religious experience. Awareness of their submissive position toward God is not only a precondition for this enthusiasm, but it is also continually reexperienced in the religious events that it evokes. The latter element is the prerequisite to keep the process going. As long as participants are convinced that they are receiving responses from God, they can keep their spirits high and will continue to look for points of orientation outside themselves.

Expectant Belief

Charismatic Christians do not confine their religious activities to particular times and places that are considered to be exclusively reserved for coming in touch with the sacred. They are continually living in an "expectant atmosphere" (Samarin 1972a: 54) that prepares them for happenings to which they can attribute religious meaning. As I have shown above, this works in two directions: charismatics are not only ready to pray to God at any time and place (Roman Catholics may hereby address themselves to the Virgin Mary and the saints with the request to intercede for them), they are also permanently open to be confronted with tokens of God's existence.

Charismatics are consequently well known for recounting numerous instances of divine intervention in their lives. Strong cases in point are to be found in testimonies. Following the Pentecostals, charismatics have revitalized the testimony, which has, with time, disappeared into the background of Christianity as a means of evangelization.[2] They have given it a prominent place in their religious praxis. While testifying, charismatics tell the story of their religious experience. The topic may be the way in which a conversion came about (conversion testimony), or a special experience within an already established relationship with God (nonconversion testimony).[3] Testimonies are first hand accounts of how participants themselves experience religion. They are worth considering, since they can shed light on the thought patterns of Christian charismatics.

Signs of God

In testimonies of the conversion type, people tend to divide their lives in a number of parts that succeed each other schematically and that, all together, represent the autobiography of their conversion (see here Poewe 1989: 371–74). First of all, they describe a period that is characterized by all kinds of personal difficulties and uncertainties, mostly culminating in a stage of social, relational, physical, or spiritual crisis (see also Hexham and Poewe 1986: 10, 106–10). Next comes a phase in which they search for a way out of the crisis. Help is sought in diverging directions, among which Eastern religions, spiritism, *paragnosy,* and psychotherapy are often mentioned. During this confusing time in which things do not get better but, on the contrary, tend to get worse, the persons involved get acquainted with the charismatic renewal, mostly through a friend or relative inviting them to come along to a prayer group "just to have a look." From this time on, the situation is said to improve. A period starts in which "the Lord came into my life." This can happen gradually or drastically, but very often the converts can pinpoint the exact date and place when they "encountered Jesus." From that moment on—also described in terms like "Jesus touched me with His endless love," or "the word of God became alive"—the converts feel the need "to yield myself to Christ," "to stay in Jesus," and "to share the joy of Christ with others."

A feature emerging from the testimonies I analyzed is that most people did not pay any attention at all to the Holy Spirit's involvement in the process of their conversion.[4] This is quite remarkable, since the testimonies were given within a movement that takes its very name after the Spirit's gifts. People made clear that during and after the time of their conversion they were experiencing the presence of God. Surprisingly, they were not reflecting on how this contact came about, nor were they wondering how it was possible: it just happened and seemed to be the most common affair in the world.

This was even the case in testimonies in which prophecies, visions, and inner prompting were the catalysts in the conversion process. In the majority of cases, these were not referred to in terms of charismata or workings of the Spirit. Especially here, of course, one would expect the Holy Spirit to enter the narrative. At best, the converts gave voice to an astonishment that with God happened to them personally. Furthermore, the figures of speech that were used to express these experiences, and of which I cited a few above, were predominantly centered on God and Jesus, but not on the Holy Spirit.

The findings also emerged in nearly the same degree from testimonies of the nonconversion type.[5] They seem to support W. J. Hollenweger's thesis that charismatics, like Pentecostals, have so far not developed a pneumatology that fits the experience of Pentecost: they are strong on experiences of the Spirit, on pneumapraxis, but weak on the interpretation of these interpretations (Hollenweger, chapter nine of this volume). Or does one have to conclude that even the assumption of a "first order" interpretation of the Spirit among charismatics is not as self-evident as might be expected? Is the role of the Holy Spirit taken for granted or is it simply ignored?

Of course, it would require a great deal of intensive research at the grassroots level to answer this question. The results will probably not be very coherent, since here we are operating in a field that James defined as "personal religion" (1985: 48). In contrast to the branch of "institutional religion"—under which James arranged elements like theology and ecclesiastical organization—this is the branch of religion where "the inner dispositions of man himself . . . form the center of interest, his conscience, his desserts, his helplessness, his incompleteness" (48). Here, "the individual transacts the business (of religion) by himself alone" (48).

The extent to which individual charismatics interpret their religious experiences in terms of the working of the Holy Spirit will depend mainly on their familiarity with charismata, that is to say, whether they believe to have received one or more of these themselves or attribute these to others, and how deeply they have delved theoretically into the subject matter. In this respect, it is noteworthy that during fieldwork among Roman Catholic charismatics in Antwerp I found that there was much diversity of opinion with regard to the "fulfillment with the Holy Spirit." Experiences varied from immediate to gradual to no awareness of it at all. Fulfillments were said to be accompanied by manifestations of charismata or just by salutary effects.[6]

Furthermore, I would suggest that individual reactions of participants are also related to the "pneumatological depth" of their prayer group. In this connection it is relevant to remember that, at least in Belgium, the meeting of the prayer group has still "the meaningful badge of identification for Catholic Charismatic Renewal participants." This, at least, was Ralph Lane's conclusion with regard to the first years of the Catholic charismatic renewal in the United States (1976: 164). These prayer groups operated independently from each other. Each group had its own atmosphere and style.[7] For example, the second largest group in Antwerp, Rabboeni, consistently started its meetings with prayers and songs directed to the Holy Spirit, wherein His coming and assistance were asked for.[8] Moreover, prophecies and Words (biblical passages) were received weekly. All this in contrast to the Rabboeni-Leerlingen (Disciples of Rabboeni), who began their meetings with prayers of praise and thanksgiving without explicitly asking for the Spirit's coming, and among whom the charismata just mentioned hardly came up.[9] The former group seemed to create a more "Spirit-minded" context in which charismata flourished better than in the latter.[10] It could be inferred that the degree in which participants were confronted with the significance of the Holy Spirit for their religiosity also depended on the institutional setting wherein they found themselves.[11]

Whatever specific ideas individual charismatics may hold about the position of the Spirit within the Holy Trinity, they are convinced that a personal encounter with God is possible.[12] From this encounter they tend to derive a personal message that sheds light on the direction of their life. Charismatics claim to hear His voice directly—through inner prompting, or mediated by others—in prophecies and teachings. They read His word in the Bible. They see His revelations in dreams and visions. They experience His leading hand in all kinds of occurrences: in miracles, like conversions and healing, and in everyday happenings, like the sunrise and the end of a quarrel.

In other words, charismatics experience God through signs: "The body, world, and universe, in this sense, constitute a language of signs" (Poewe 1989: 366). According to charismatics, these signs refer to God: to His existence and to His involvement with human affairs. As Poewe has said, "these signs are *metonymic*" (1989: 367).

METONYMY

Metonymy versus Metaphor

Metonymy (literally, "behind the name;" *meta*, behind, *onuma*, name) is a trope or shift in meaning that is accomplished by using "an adjunct to stand for the whole" (Soskice 1985: 57). Both terms, the absent one and the one used instead, "occupy a common domain but do not share common features" (Sapir 1977: 20). This is in contrast to metaphor, which literally means "transfer:" *meta* "trans" *pherein* "to carry" (Soskice 1985: 1). "Metaphor is that figure of speech whereby we speak about one thing in terms which are seen to be suggestive of another" (Soskice 1985: 15). Here, we are concerned with "the relationship of two terms from separate domains that share overlapping features" (Sapir 1977: 20).

But tropes are functionally different. Janet Martin Soskice states that, unlike metaphor, whose purpose is "both to cast up and organize a network of associations," "instances of metonymy . . . point one directly to the absent term" (1985: 57). A metonymy "is essentially an oblique and less prosaic way of making a direct reference" (57). Soskice concludes that with metonymy, "meaning is largely subsumed by the reference it makes. With metaphor, this is far from always the case" (58).

A metonymy directs one's attention straight to the non-uttered term. A metaphor, on the contrary, involves "the pregnant . . . interplay of two disparate terms" (Sapir 1977: 32), which may compel "a new referential access" (Soskice 1985: 58). It follows that the metonymy's creative potential is less than that of the metaphor. The use of a metonymy presupposes

that the absent term that the speaker replaces by another one is for him
or her less "abstract and inchoate" (Fernandez 1977: 106) than it is in the
case of a metaphor. Actually, the speaker has to be quite familiar with it.
If not, he or she would use a metaphorical statement instead of a
metonymical one in an effort to make the subject graspable.[13]

What has all this to do with the religious experience of charismatics?
To answer this question, it is important to realize that language offers a
fruitful entry into the domain of religious experience. Language is more
than a vehicle to transport or "translate" the essence of religion. It must
be seen as an essential component of religion (Samarin 1972b; 1976).
Form and content of religious communication are sense-giving elements
in the construction of religion. Thus, the modes of communication within
charismatic Christianity are not without significance. These constitute
the religious language in which charismatics articulate their spirituality
and thereby reinforce their social and religious identity.

Soskice suggests that we take religious language "in the narrow
sense, as talk about God" (1985: 64). But if we define it more broadly, as
language in which people articulate religious experience and reflect on
it, we are able to deal with talk and meta-talk about those events to which
believers attribute religious meaning. This includes not only participants' talk about the supernatural, but also talk about worldly affairs and
human beings. From an anthropological point of view, I propose this
broader definition of religious language.

Metonymical and Metaphorical Talk about Religious Experience

Let me restrict the definition of religious language in the first
instance to its narrow meaning. It could then be advanced—as was put
forward at the end of the previous section—that the way in which
charismatics talk about God is characterized by a metonymical structure.
The metonymies of charismatics refer unequivocally to God. (For example: "An inner voice prompted me to . . . .")

Speaking about God, charismatics tend to make use of substitutive
terms that can be considered to occupy one and the same "domain," that
is to say, the whole of conceptions that speakers have about Him. The
success of a metonymy as a trope "depends on how fully this idea of
wholeness can be conveyed" (Sapir 1977: 20), that is, in our case, how well
the terms in use can trigger the preconceived images of God. No new
insights or ideas about God are added to the ones already in the speakers'
minds.

This means that metonymical talk about God can only be detected
among speakers who hold explicit ideas about Him: who He is and what
He can establish in their lives. Such an attitude of confidence originates
either from a strong conviction of faith or from a position of uncertainty.

In the former instance, people are so sure about God that they do not need the help of their fantasy in an effort to make their religious experiences understandable. In the latter, people are anxious to avoid the slightest provocation that could jeopardize their essentially unstable belief. In both cases, the best strategy is to avoid metaphorical predications and stick to metonymical ones. In a little while, I shall return to the source from which charismatics derive their ideas about God.

All this is not to suggest that it would be impossible to detect the use of metaphors in the religious language of charismatic Christians. Thomas J. Csordas has explored the role of metaphor in the creativity of charismatic ritual language (1987). The author not only specifies the conditions and processes of that creativity but also what is created in particular. He shows that the creative movement is "a self-sustaining dialectical process: motives generate metaphors, metaphors move people, people are reoriented by motives, motives generate new metaphors, and so on" (459). Within the discourse itself, new meanings are created. In the everyday lives of participants, "the performance of metaphors can create collective identities for groups and personal identities for individuals" (463). So here we see that the use of metaphors fulfills important functions in the domain of social action.

Charismatic Interpretations of Metonymy and Metaphor

The essential and interesting point about tropes is that they "operate on the meaning (the 'signified') rather than the form (the 'signifier') of words" (Sapir 1977: 3). It follows that, when dealing with tropes, interpretation comes into play. Since tropes are about (re)producing meaning, they always must be viewed in relation to the referential accesses they create.

For the reasons mentioned earlier, metaphors pose major problems regarding interpretation. Metonymies, on the other hand, point directly and unequivocally to the absent terms. They "function as oblique reference and as such they, if any of the tropes, fit the bill for being primarily ornamental ways of naming" (Soskice 1985: 57). The use of a metonymy reflects and upholds a stance that is characterized by a clear view on the subject matter that the trope is supposed to refer to.

From where then do charismatics, when metonymically speaking about God, take their self-confidence? I would suggest that the answer to this question has to be found in the experiential character of charismatic Christianity itself. Experiencing God brings forth the certitude that He exists. At the same time, it reveals the ways in which the contact comes about. This offers the foundation for the strong religious convictions from which the charismatic way of thinking and consequent modes of expression originate.

The charismatic model of thought is furthermore inspired and reinforced by a "surrender to . . . the First Century Christian Schema" (Poewe 1989: 364). This schema is said to be found in the texts of the New Testament, starting with the description of Pentecost in the Acts of the Apostles. Here, charismatics find the "authentic model" of a Christian community after the resurrection of the Messia. It offers them a blueprint for strong experiences of God. Many of them testify that they recognize themselves in these texts. For these people, what happened among the first Christians does not belong to a different and past culture. It is "everyday reality."[14] Since the charismatic way of thinking is rooted in what is known and found to its cost, it is more likely to stimulate literal interpretations of religious language than symbolical ones.

If indeed charismatic thinking is based on such a closed worldview, would not it have consequences for the way in which charismatics deal with metaphors? Of course. First, it should be noted that every metaphor contains metonymical features. According to James W. Fernandez: "The utterance of metaphor itself . . . is attended by a set of associations which 'belong' to it by reason of contiguities in previous experience. The assertion of metaphor thus provokes a metonymous chain of elements or experiences associated with it as part to whole, cause to effect, or other contiguity in time or space (1977: 126).

Thus, any interpretation of a metaphor is based upon the selection of certain associations out of the possible ones that the metaphorical image may evoke. To put it in Fernandez's words, "the metaphor does not simply excite associations but imposes a schema upon them. . . . The associations . . . are conceptually mediated by the metaphor" (1977: 127).

This confronts us with the possibility that charismatics interpret statements that to outsiders would appear to be metaphors, literally. (For example: "We are children of God the Father.") For charismatics these would then be direct statements. As Andras Sandor has argued: "whether certain predications are to be taken directly or metaphorically depends on the beliefs of those who make them" (1986: 103).

It appears, then, that inherent in the charismatic Christian model of thought is a tendency that stresses the literal reference of language to God and to the world. This is so because it is a model of certainty. While many people in the secularized world of today "are unsure (of God) both at the experiential and the expressive levels" (McFaque 1983: 1), for charismatics these do not pose special problems. They understand their experience of the world to be permeated by divine power. Therefore, they are convinced that their religious language mirrors concrete things.

These observations shed a different light on Csordas's depiction of the circulation of metaphors through charismatic ritual language. Instead of evoking continual transformations of these metaphors, this circulation would more likely run the risk of turning soon into a circularity of fixed and literal interpretations. The condition of creativity lies in the human potential to create new meanings through time. Metaphorical extension in itself is no guarantee for creativity. The decisive question is whether a model of thought is open for continual interpretative innovation or "doomed to sterility and eventual exhaustion" (Fabian 1979: 181). In the case of the charismatic Christian model of thought, the latter option seems to be quite realistic.

ROUTINIZATION

Oral versus Literary Spirituality

The tendency toward literalness, to which the argument has led us thus far, was repeatedly brought home to me with regard to biblical hermeneutics. During my fieldwork in Belgium, a continual point of frustration for Roman Catholic charismatics appeared to be the symbolical interpretation of the Bible within dominant church practice. Uneasiness with this theological approach was expressed in particular in cases of miracles and healing. These, according to my interlocutors, are not only to be found and taken literally in the Bible, but also in everyday life.[15] They regarded the dominant symbolical interpretation of the Bible as being the very reason why Christianity has become meaningless and without significance for so many people's daily lives.[16] In their view, Christianity has turned into a forum for intellectual debating that does not affect most people.[17]

Enthusiastic charismatic spirituality, on the contrary, results from a stance in which experiencing God is central instead of dealing with Him intellectually. Its medium of expression is that of "oral liturgy" and "narrative theology and witness" (Hollenweger, chapter ten of this volume). These, according to Hollenweger, can be traced back to the black roots of Pentecostalism (1974: 22). This oral spirituality can be said to challenge the theology of the historical churches "by dismantling the privileges of abstract, rational and propositional systems" (26). An enthusiastic and oral spirituality is not compatible with a rigid doctrinal system that prescribes liturgy in words and deeds.

However, vitality in itself does not offer protection against routine and dogma. It can just as well result in "frozen thinking" (Hollenweger 1974: 26) as in the case of a "literary" theology. In the previous section this point was already put forward with regard to the charismatic interpretation of religious language. Any serious analysis of charismatic Christian movements will therefore have to face the possibility that routinization processes may also occur here. If omitted, unrealistic and uncritical images of this religion will be created. Having said this, I turn to the issue of routinization in terms of what Max Weber called "die Veralltäglichung des Charisma" (1964: 182).

Routinization of Charisma

According to Weber, who introduced the concept of "charisma" into sociology, "routinization" of charisma involves the return of a process that originated "out of the everyday" (*Ausseralltäglich*) to a more everyday existence (*Veralltäglichung des Charisma*). This takes place at both the ideational and the organizational level. If, on the basis of a charismatic leader's ideas, a charismatic movement develops, the original ideas will gradually undergo a process of transformation under the pressure of the needs and desires of the followers. After the death of the original leader, when the question of his succession is acute, a similar process occurs at the level of organization (M. Hill 1973: 170).

By means of the concept of "latency," Michael Hill understands Weber's idea of routinization as the "embodiment of (originally personal charismatic features) in a latent form in an institutional setting, such that they are always available as a source from which new obligations may be articulated" (1973: 168). Precondition hereby is that the transfer of charismatic power is not being restricted to the original group of followers, that is, it involves "a process of *depersonalization* and objectifying of the charismatic endowment" (174). In the process of routinization, the originally personal charisma, in this manner, "retains a degree of latency which may emerge as extra-institutional challenge or intra-institutional leverage: in either case, it is a source of innovation" (179).

With regard to Christianity, Hill notes that Jesus Christ sent his disciples out by a divine commission, whereby "the apostolate was taken to be a charismatic gift *before* it came to be seen as an institution" (1973: 174). Since the transmission of charisma was not restricted to the original group of disciples, routinization did not take place. From his view on routinization, Hill finds himself in a "much better position to analyze some of the most crucial 'breakthroughs' in the history of Christianity (173).

I think an analysis of the Catholic charismatic renewal may also benefit from Hill's application of Weber's concept. Assuming that Christianity started within established Judaism as a charismatic renewal movement with Jesus Christ as charismatic leader, and that the installation of the early church was "a classic example of the transfer of power from a charismatic leader to his followers" (Hill 1973: 173), then it could be argued that the legitimacy of the Catholic charismatic renewal goes back to the very charismatic roots of Christianity itself.

The Catholic charismatic renewal's view on charisma, one could say, is based on the principle that the transmission of the original charisma of Christ involves a process of depersonalization. This can be derived from the charismatic argument that the Holy Spirit was neither exclusively meant for Christ, nor for His first disciples, but for every Christian until the return of Christ.[18] In this view, Jesus' baptism in the Spirit, which is considered to have taken place simultaneously with his water-baptism by John the Baptist, is seen as the origin of the church: "The church is the historical continuation of Jesus' Spirit-experience" (Maes 1983: 2). All Christians are expected to follow in Jesus' footsteps. Fulfilled with the Spirit, they will preach the Word of God and keep Jesus' experience alive by "doing the things Jesus did."

The routinization process can next be seen as the ideological and institutional development within the Roman Catholic church since Jesus' transmission of His charisma to the apostles. This process led to the dominant church model in which the gifts of the Holy Spirit were attached to clerical offices within an hierarchical, bureaucratic institution.[19] By making an appeal to the "Spirit-experience origin" of Christianity, Catholic charismatics are, in Hill's terms, using the latent form of the original charisma of Christ as an intra-institutional source of new ideas and obligations. They stress the "original" potential of the charismata as a spiritual opportunity for both clergy and laity.

Routinization within the Catholic Charismatic Renewal

From the very start of the movement it has been the explicit goal of the Catholic charismatic renewal to stay within the Roman Catholic church and to renew it from inside. By this, the Catholic charismatic renewal itself created the conditions for the hierarchy's interference.

Catholic charismatics have always been loyal to church authorities and anxious not to alienate them. This is, for example, evident from the great importance they attach to statements on the Catholic charismatic renewal made by the Pope and the national bishops' committees.[20] In Belgium the appointment of priests, who were supposed to function as contacts between the bishops and the prayer groups, never posed any problems for the latter. Actually, the first initiatives to coordinate the various charismatic activities in Flanders came from the charismatic side itself. In concurrence with the increasing involvement of Cardinal Léon Joseph Suenens an institutional framework evolved in which Catholic charismatic activities were supervised. Within this framework, the broad ideological lines of the Flemish Renewal developed and spread.[21] However, it remains to be seen to what degree these are observed at the grassroots.

Attitudes of prayer groups toward authority vary. Groups that encourage strong control of members' activities will select authoritative leaders. These will promote highly routinized patterns of behavior. Groups that resist leadership's claims will stress the importance of members' spontaneous participation. They are likely to be more open to changes and initiatives from anyone.

But apart from institutional circumstances like these, which influence the potential introduction of more formalized roles and ideational definitions, more factors are involved with regard to the development of routinized patterns of thinking and behavior within charismatic Christianity. An additional catalyst worth mentioning is the national and international dissemination of religious propaganda. Not only books and magazines but to a growing extent cassettes and video-tapes are used as means of evangelization. In order to reach as many people as possible, the message has to be kept simple. At the same time, prototypes of ideal behavior are provided. Selected examples of exemplary religious talk and ways of behavior are shown to an international public. It may encourage worldwide imitation of religious praxis at the cost of individual and culture-specific expressions.

CONCLUSION

In this chapter, I have dealt with three aspects of charismatic Christian religiosity: experience, metonymy, and routinization. It was put forward that the charismatic stance of self-surrender to God requires and stimulates a continuing need for confirmations of divine power. Charismatics experience these through signs that they take to refer directly to God. Hence, they express themselves in a religious language that is characterized by a metonymical structure. Since, for charismatics, their language mirrors concrete and familiar things, they need no additional referential accesses in the form of metaphors. They tend to take their religious language literally. It follows that this language is open for routinization and semantic exhaustion. This point will be reached when, within the charismatic discourse, no further new meanings are created.

The Catholic charismatic renewal, which formed the ethnographic case in this paper, is international in scope. It figures in an increasing worldwide circulation of religious praxis. According to Poewe, "the more global a religion becomes the more it will give expression to *known things*" (1989: 364).

So far, "known things" were related to individuals' religious experiences. It was the strong experiences that referred metonymically to God. To these "known things" we can add internationally distributed religious images. These have a much wider reach, moving beyond the particular speech community of prayer groups. Cultivated examples of religious behavior are imposed with the authoritative impact of modern means of communication. Individual colorations of religious experience are likely to give way more and more to stereotypical expressions.

This might generate a worldwide development within the field of religion in the direction of a metonymical way of thinking that is based on the assumption that religious language reflects God and the world "as they are." Where this trend toward literalness gets the upper hand, instances of fundamentalism and intolerance may come to the foreground, because "to remain within the bounds of the established observational language and its logic restricts discussion to what is already 'known' and 'understood'" (Overing 1987: 73).

NOTES

I am grateful to Birgit Meyer and Sjaak van der Geest for their comments on an earlier version of this chapter.

1. Empirical data has been gathered during field research among Roman Catholic charismatics in Antwerp, Belgium, from March until June 1987.

2. In line with this development, the entry "Testimony" is missing in the *Geloofsboek* (De Bisschoppen 1987; Book of Faith), published by the bishops of Belgium. Interestingly, this work was written in compliance with the call for a "new evangelization" by Pope John Paul II during his visit to Belgium in May 1985.

3. Conversion, in the case of charismatic Catholics, is not to be understood in the strict meaning of the word; that is, as a person's change to a (new) religion. Here, it refers to a change of attitude within the same religion (Christianity). On this subject, see McGuire 1982: 49ff.

4. I analyzed twenty-one testimonies of the conversion type. These belonged to the forty-seven testimonies that appeared in issues of *Jezus Leeft!* during the period November 1986 until August 1990. In six cases out of twenty-one converts mentioned the Holy Spirit by name.

5. The Holy Spirit was mentioned here in five cases out of twenty-six. For that matter, eight testimonies dealt with physical healing. In the conversion type, this was the case in five testimonies out of twenty-one.

6. This diversity of opinion is possible since Roman Catholic charismatics have not accepted the doctrine of the "initial evidence." This doctrine sees speaking

in tongues as "the initial sign" of the baptism of the Holy Spirit. It has been accepted by many Pentecostal and charismatic groups (Hollenweger, chapter nine of this volume). On this doctrine, see Hollenweger (1988a: 330).

7. Christopher O'Donnell warns that "almost any assertion about . . . the Charismatic Renewal . . . may be rejected by some group, community, or even country as being no real representation of their situation" (1983: 51).

8. At the time of my field research this group gathered weekly. It was visited by approximately 40 to 60 participants.

9. In 1987 this was the largest group in Antwerp. Gathering weekly, attendance varied between 130 and 160 participants.

10. More factors are in play, of course. Important are, for example, the stress that is being laid on "teachings" and "sharings" during prayer groups' meetings, and opportunities to attend introductory seminars, the so-called "seven weeks," in which neophytes are introduced into charismatic Christianity.

11. This discussion shows that James's distinction between personal and institutional religion is not absolute. Religious ideas and attitudes cannot be "nakedly considered," as James wants it (1985: 49). These ideas and attitudes are involved in a dialectics with the institutional context in which they are developed and put into practice.

12. As to the position of the Spirit within the Holy Trinity, one more influential factor could be added. Those who restrict their involvement to a weekly participation in one prayer group are likely to develop a relatively narrow spiritual viewpoint that will not easily surpass the spiritual level of that particular group. Those who spread their wings in more than one direction (visit various groups, charismatic seminars, special days of prayer, etc.,) will be in a better position to acquire a more pronounced opinion about the charismatic dimension of their belief. As to the factor of having a personal encounter with God, perhaps the main force of attraction of the charismatic renewal lies in the context it offers for such an experience. The reevaluation of the Holy Spirit may in itself be of less importance for adherents than is generally accepted.

13. The speaker need not be aware that he or she speaks in metaphorical or metonymical terms. To evaluate the nature of a certain predication, the listener will have to be acquainted with the speaker's ideas.

14. It should be noted that charismatics stick to a specific interpretation of the first-century Christian community. According to James D. G. Dunn, "There is clearly no single model of Christian community which emerges from the *New Testament* as *the* New Testament church" (1984: 17).

15. With regard to the role of the so-called "words of knowledge" within charismatic faith healing, see Roelofs (1990).

16. This argument is strongly put forward by MacNutt 1974.

17. This viewpoint is sharply formulated by Hollenweger in "The Pentecostals say: 'An experience is better than an argument'" (1974: 80).

18. Two biblical sources that are put forward to support this opinion are John 14:25–26 and Acts 1:8.

19. During Vatican II, held in the early 1960s, this concept came under attack by an intervention of the Belgian Cardinal Léon Joseph Suenens (1974). Suenens

became acquainted with the charismatic renewal in March 1972 during a lecture tour in the United States (Sandidge 1976: 58). Since then he has kept an interest in the movement. In 1973 he implemented supervisory activities with regard to the Flemish Catholic charismatic renewal. In 1975 Pope Paul VI invited him to supervise the Catholic charismatic renewal worldwide. He directed the preparation of the "Malines Documents," which are concerned with the theological and pastoral implications of the Catholic charismatic renewal.

20. Kilian McDonnell evaluates reports on charismatic Christian movements by commissions within the historic churches between 1960 and 1975 (1976: chapter 3). The statement by the bishops of Belgium appeared in 1979.

21. This framework consists of "diocesan teams" in which delegates of prayer groups and the bishops' contacts are represented. These teams deliver representatives to the "interdiocesan team." Its chairman (Daniel Maes) is the Flemish Renewal's contact of the bishop's committee of Belgium.

Chapter 11

Rethinking the Relationship of Anthropology to Science and Religion

Karla Poewe

ABSTRACT

Edward Evans-Pritchard (1965) once argued that believers and nonbelievers approach the study of religion differently. The latter tend to formulate diverse sociological, psychological, existential, and biological theories to explain an illusion or misrecognition. By contrast, believers tend to explain how people conceive of, and relate to, reality. Since the question of illusion versus reality is especially important to scientists, charismatic Christians who are scientists are looked to for help in answering it. From them we learn that charismatic Christianity sanctions the use of the receptive imagination, revelation, metonym, and a globality that postulates a specific relationship with God but, beyond that, is entirely open—occasionally to the point of heresy.

INTRODUCTION

> Scholars speak as if they know that the hymns were composed by Isaiah Shembe. Whereas some of them were *revealed* to him. . . . In fact, Isaiah Shembe described exactly how each song *happened* (Shembe, 1987).

> Folk religions arise everywhere from the deep yearnings of people (Bastian 1860).

In my research of the charismatic movement that swept across the United States and other parts of the world in the 1960s, and which affected both mainline and sectarian churches and created literally thousands of new independent churches (Quebedeaux 1983), I was startled by the fact that I came across a number of scientists. Whether in South Africa, Canada, the United States, Britain, or Germany, countries that became part of my global research project, I found scientists—from physicians to astrophysicists to psychologists—who participated in this controversial, experiential Christian movement. It did not take long to figure out that these believers exemplified the very thing with which Evans-Pritchard ended his book; namely, religion was, to them, a special conception of, and relation to, reality. All else, social ties, services, and structure, were subsumed under the primacy of their specific sense of reality.

Given this research, I became aware that there are several things about charismatic Christianity specifically, and religion generally, that have been almost, if not entirely, ignored by anthropologists or have been regarded as of minor importance to the discipline. Thus Brian Morris reduces Rudolf Otto's conception of holiness to "a theory of religious instinct" and argues that "it has little to offer anthropologists and could be left aside as purely of interest to theologians" (1987: 142).

The things that are usually ignored, but stood out in my research, included the scientists' sense of "holiness" and more. Vital were: the relation of charismatic Christianity to reality and its specific epistemology and ontology; its meeting point with science; its relation to the receptive imagination and the senses; its relation to revelation; its revitalization through popular theologies; and its relation to people anywhere in the world, irrespective of class, "race," ethnic group, or nation—in short, its globality.

Extrapolating from numerous life-history interviews, what these scientists seemed to be saying was that within the context of "holiness," often created by iconic leaders, aspects of one reality are revealed to them through the receptive imagination, with its heightened sense perceptions and metonymic pattern of thought. By metonymic pattern of thought, what is meant is the habit of seeing a simple happening as an aspect of a whole that caused it, even when the whole itself is but tacitly known. In this sense metonymic thought is revelation and metonym a vehicle that makes known personally a reality that is otherwise invisible and independent.[2] While all interviewed scientists followed the accepted procedural rules of their profession, at points of discovery, and in their style of and commitment to service, they recognized that science and religion were one. Furthermore, they were one precisely because these scientists held to the fundamentals of a triune God and the story of Christ's promise that following his death and resurrection he would leave behind his "Spirit" to comfort and inspire his followers.[3]

HISTORY OF THOUGHT

Let me make this point from a history of anthropology perspective. Evans-Pritchard (1965) and Stocking (1987: 190–94) sketch with great insight and sensitivity Tylor's (1871) theory of religion and its impact on the discipline. Tylor was a monogenist and, like Adolf Bastian, a defender of what came to be called the psychic unity of humankind. In this position, he was simultaneously part of his time and a defender of "the savage." He was also very much a Victorian anthropologist in his belief in science and adherence to classical evolutionism. Consequently, he was interested in the origin, development, and eventual disappearance of religion, except perhaps as a "survival." What is important here, however, is the fact that, in final analysis, Tylor saw religion as science gone wrong, as an error or illusion (Stocking 1987: 192; Evans-Pritchard 1965: 25, 121).

Thereafter, the history of an anthropology of religion took two major courses. On one hand, some anthropologists (usually nonbelievers), returned to religion those aspects that Tylor had stripped away, namely, its emotional (V. Turner 1967),[4] psychological (Radin 1957; Malinowski 1935; Freud 1938; Jung 1938; Csordas 1990), ecstatic (Lewis 1971), symbolic and mythological (Geertz 1973; Lévi-Strauss 1978; H. Turner 1974), rhetorical and metaphorical (Bourdieu 1977, Csordas 1987), as well as its millenarian and transformative (Wallace 1966; Burridge 1969) aspects. Religion was fleshed out in all ways except one; for most of these scholars it remained an illusion or misapprehension.

On the other hand, and as Evans-Pritchard observed, some anthropologists, a small minority who insisted that faith and science go together, argued that even a return of the above-mentioned aspects could not explain the vital relationship between religion and reality. As said, people who dealt with the latter were dismissed as too theological or philosophical, or had their belief held against them (Morris 1987: 102, 142, 143). It was implied that believers were incapable of grasping reality while nonbelievers were, or, if they were not, as in the special case of postmodernists, they knew enough to relativize it. This was said despite the fact that believers tend to be epistemological and/or ontological realists, for whom reality exists independently of the observer, while nonbelievers, although we expect it of postmodernists, tend to be epistemological and/or ontological relativists, for whom religion, sometimes all reality, is definitely an illusion. As Gellner points out, postmodernists have repudiated "objectivity as such" (1992: 35).

Among those who insisted on the unity of science and faith (which need not be Christian) were especially German philosophers of anthropological thought going back to Johann Arndt (1555–1621), Philipp Jakob

Spener (1635–1705), August Hermann Francke (1663–1727), Johann Georg Hamann (1730–1788), Johann Kaspar Lavater (1741–1801), Johann Gottfried Herder (1744–1803), Wilhelm von Humboldt (1767–1835), Adolf Bastian (1826–1905), Theodor Lipps (1851–1914), Leo Frobenius (1873–1939), Wilhelm Schmidt (1868–1954), and Bruno Gutmann (1876–1966), among others.[5] It is helpful to repeat the passage of Wilhelm Schmidt with which Evans-Pritchard was in agreement: "If religion is essentially of the inner life, it follows that it can be truly grasped only from within. But beyond a doubt, this can be better done by one in whose inward consciousness an experience of religion plays a part. There is but too much danger that the other [the nonbeliever] will talk of religion as a blind man might of colors, or one totally devoid of ear, of a beautiful musical composition (1965: 121, quoted from Schmidt 1931: 6).[6]

It is appropriate that I point out here, because it is important for the ongoing argument of this article, that for these German thinkers oral and written literature, empathy, reciprocal illumination, mirroring, experience, and global and local aspects of ideas (*Gedanken*) were central parts of any empirical research in psychology, culture, and ethnology (Bastian 1860).[7] In short these thinkers insisted that faith was the real link between science and religion. But what did they mean by faith? Faith seemed to be an attitude that fostered trust in intuition, insight, inspiration, and revelation, manners of perception that were often at the core of proleptic experiences. By proleptic experience is meant that profound moment when the scientist experienced the existence of "God" with such "persuasive power" that, from that moment forward, "God's" existence was assumed. None of these faculties and experiences were to displace reason. Rather, they were assigned an equal place beside reason. Likewise, all of these thinkers admired British empiricism and did empirical research. Consequently, we get a stream of Enlightenment, Victorian, and early modern thought that combined, for example, religion, faith, Puritanism, Pietism, and now charismatic Christianity with empiricism (Unger 1968: 123, 126).

We are now ready to return again to the point with which Evans-Pritchard ended; namely, short of personal confessions of belief by researchers, can the believer-nonbeliever problem be at least broached, if not overcome, by studying scientists, including social scientists, who are charismatic Christians? Can the latter's popular theologies, experiences, and imagination teach something about the relationship of social science to religion that would otherwise be missed? Further, does this study of scientists who are charismatic Christians advance the project of doing anthropology in a world of eclectic cultures, high-tech, and rapid travel? Is it not curious that scientists who have tired of ethnic, political, and national identities should return to Islam, Judaism, and Christianity, thus defining their identities in terms of a major and, importantly, transnational, transdenominational, in short, global tradition? (Kepel 1991; Branover 1982).

With but few exceptions, most notably Barbara Myerhoff's video *In Her Own Time* (1985), works about religion take for granted that the reflexive attitude of the researcher is independent of, and privileged above, that of the researched. But can we afford to explain religious practices, as Thomas J. Csordas does, for example, in terms of a paradigm that ignores the ontology and epistemology of those who practice it, especially when those who practice it are themselves scientists? Can we consider an explanation of a religious practice adequate when it disregards the fundamental assumption on which religious practitioners know their religion to be based? Can we consider our explanation of their religion adequate when we call their basic assumption a "misrecognition" (Csordas 1990: 23; Bourdieu 1977: 82, quoted in Csordas 1987: 463), the result of an inadequate "level of awareness" which is, however, adequate for us the researchers?

Given these questions, the purpose of the chapter can be narrowed further. It attempts to look at the ontology-cum-epistemology, indeed, the patterns of thought and philosophical underpinnings of self-aware charismatic Christians who are scientists. This study is not just about any charismatic Christian (here, for example, see Stoll 1990a; Martin 1990; Quebedeaux 1983; Hollenweger 1988a; Csordas 1990; Poewe 1989). Rather, it is about charismatic Christians who are successful scientists because it cannot be said of them that their "level of awareness" is beneath that of the author. Nor can their religious practices and processes of thought be dismissed as "misrecognition" simply to preserve the privileged status of the author. Consequently, as in the eighteenth century (Hart 1990: 13, 14; Langham 1981), the study of religion (but here a late twentieth century expression of it) pushes anthropologists to face methodological, theoretical, and value issues of the ethnographic revolution in which we find ourselves. Although Gellner professes himself to be a "humble adherent" of "Enlightenment Rationalist Fundamentalism" and would not agree with the seemingly sympathetic reading that is here given scientists who are charismatic Christians, his *Postmodernism, Reason and Religion* (1992) is written in the spirit of the much needed dialogue between believer and nonbeliever scholars, especially since the nonbelievers themselves are now in very different camps vis-à-vis science.

IMPLICATION FOR METHODOLOGY

My study of charismatic scientists features two methodological innovations or potential innovations. First, it attempts to address Evans-

Pritchard's believer-nonbeliever problem by studying scientists who are charismatic Christians. All scientists who were interviewed were successful, something I was able to verify by visiting both their offices and homes and by learning of their reputation from the wider community as well as, in some instances, by their publications. Given the academic suspicion of Christianity (including my own at the beginning of this research), their success, intellectual openness, and service orientation must be mentioned.

The second methodological innovation has to do with the fact that I took a global-local perspective. Rather than doing fieldwork in one culture and/or society, as I have done several times in the past, I chose to study a major tradition, but one that traveled the globe and took on specific local coloring, so to speak, in different local and regional situations. In the process, I became aware that many people preferred to define their identity and social life primarily in terms of this major tradition, rather than ethnicity, nationality, and/or class. Their transnational and transethnic orientation affected decision-making, travel, and migration. Major decisions frequently involved people from entirely different parts of the world. Furthermore, because I could gain considerable familiarity with the tradition at home, it meant that my field trips to different parts of the world could be shortened to two or six months and could focus on differences or similarities as the situation warranted.

Initial interest in charismatic Christians stemmed from my fieldwork in three African countries. While I studied charismatic Christians in African Initiated Churches (AICs) as well as white-founded but integrated churches generally, in this chapter I draw generalizations from the thirty-seven life-history and twenty casual interviews with scientists who, at the time of the interviews, were charismatic Christians in Canada, South Africa, the United States, Germany, and Britain. Interviews were done in charismatic independent churches between 1987 and 1991. Because these interviews highlight interesting anthropological problems, they are given special attention in this chapter.

Charismatic Christians are defined especially in terms of the emphasis they place on the "Holy Spirit." The significance of this emphasis on the "Holy Spirit" (rather than Christ) is that the "Spirit" symbolizes a conception of a world or social system that crosscuts national, ethnic, and racial barriers, ignores barriers of communication and language, crosscuts professionals and laborers, the rich the poor, and diverse denominations (Richardson 1967). Many nondenominational, multiethnic churches are in the inner cities and made the news during and after the Los Angeles fires (May 1992). They were mentioned on CNN, the "MacNeil/Lehrer News Hour," and "Washington Week in Review." The charismatic tapestry of which I speak is a transnational and transethnic network of individuals among whom are circulated ideas, knowledge, funds, and decisions. For anthropologists it implies focussing our research on global cultures where formerly we concentrated on distinct local ones.

RELIGION AND REALITY: EPISTEMOLOGIES, GENRES, AND ICONIC LEADERS AS SANCTIONERS OF "TACIT KNOWLEDGE" OR "REVELATION"

What is fascinating about people involved in charismatic Christianity is that they are able to overcome what Gerardus van der Leeuw regarded as an almost insurmountable problem, namely, the absence of a "path from the revelation in Christ to art and science" (1963: 4). Scientists who are charismatic Christians found a path by taking literally the biblical story that upon his death and resurrection Christ would leave his followers with the "Holy Spirit," who is precisely revealed through art, science, dreams, visions, and so on. The significance for anthropologists of the use of this self-defining story by scientists who have become charismatic Christians is that it represents a shift in "reflexive attitude" (Watson 1991) or in "sensibility" (Bebbington 1989). It is a shift from a realist epistemology (usually associated with empiricism but also Christian fundamentalism) to, one might say, its "twin," a revelationist epistemology (associated with postcritical philosophy and charismatic Christianity). As said, similar movements, which also involve scientists, are underfoot in Judaism and Islam (Kepel 1991).

Contrary to postmodernism, which tends to be relativist in both its ontology and epistemology, the ontology of charismatic Christians is realist while their epistemology is both realist and revelationist. Charismatic Christians share with empiricists the assumption that reality exists independently of the observer. But contrary to empiricists, the reality of charismatic Christians does not only refer to a priori facts or discrete objects in space or time. Rather, as we shall see, their reality is something "tacitly known" that "is expected to reveal itself indeterminately in the future" (Polanyi 1964: 10).[8] The reality of the charismatic Christian scientist is the opposite of that of the empiricist; it is the unseen that is tacitly known and therefore will inevitably reveal itself through a happening some time in the future.

For charismatic Christians revelation, therefore, contains truth and this truth is the window to the bigger reality of which it is a part. Unlike postmodernists, however, the "partiality" of the truth or the partial knowledge of reality is not the consequence of the surprise recognition that ethnographic truths are made "possible by powerful *lies* of exclusion and rhetoric" (Clifford 1986: 7). Rather, revelatory truth is constrained metonymically by its connectedness to that bigger reality of which it is a part. It is not just anything, nor is it but arbitrarily associated with reality (as is metaphor); it is part of the truth and reality to which it is connected.

But that unseen reality reveals itself to the human being through his intellect, intuition, senses, feeling, and mood. Revelation is, in this sense, personal knowledge that, if it is to remain honest, must honor its experiential roots. It is synesthetic and, in the secular sense, intuitive, and for that reason alone its truth comes in numerous modalities and is expressed in many genres: dance, music, parables, poetry, science, historical accounts, realist writing, among others. It is, however, knowledge with a foundation in reality. It is not, what Paul Rabinow says postmodernism is, "knowledge without foundations; a knowledge that essentially amounts to edifying conversations" (1986: 236; see also Gellner 1992: 38–39). We shall see later that even scientists tell stories, but they are stories that have their fixed point in reality. Here, however, we need only note the peculiar dialectic between relativism and absolute truth. The relativism of charismatic Christians who believe in objective truth, rather than hermeneutic truth (Gellner 1992: 35), lies in this: what is revealed to them, at any one time, through multiple modalities or genres are parts of the truth about one reality.[9]

In sum, empiricists and charismatic Christians (whether scientists or not) approach reality from opposite directions. The empiricist tries to get at one truth (or one reading) by bringing all necessary detail into one accurately corresponding description or explanation (Watson 1991; Friedrich 1992). By contrast, the charismatic Christian scientist begins with the assumption of one truth or reality. She knows and trusts that she will discover new facts or the "mechanisms or systems which account for already known facts" in the future (Polanyi 1964: 28). In other words, facts are constituted by hidden truths that are expected to reveal themselves. They are not constituted, as postmodernists would have it, by individual writers or peoples. While Graham Watson argues for the latter constitution of facts, so that a fact "is not a thing encountered, having an existence prior to and independent of the writer's discourse" (1991: 79), in the charismatic Christian's sense, a prior and independent existence is precisely what a constituted fact has. Facts are so constituted by reality as to be capable of being revealed to us through a process of encounter and relationship. (This is a point, by the way, which Olivier de Sardan [1992] missed in his excellent criticism of the exoticization of occultism).

One reflective scientist described such an encounter this way. He talked about having experienced a Latin American evangelist, one particularly appealing to intellectuals, as "concrete revelation of the holy or of Christ as the holy one of God." The particular evangelist was a man visibly broken by cancer, which he survived. Thus when he gave his testimony, he told a story contextualized or framed by his visibly broken body but renewed spirit. It opened in the listening scientist an area of sensory perception that was hitherto unused. He mentioned that it affected not only what and how he saw, but also his sense of touch (his body was overpowered by warmth), and his sense of smell (he felt himself surrounded by a pleasing sweet smell as if he were in a garden). Said he, "this man of God managed to create for me a distinct sense of being in sacred space."[10]

Bradd Shore calls this equation of "sensory modalities" synesthesia, or "sensory metonymies" (1991: 18). Thus the sacred is experienced as "radiation of something" from an iconic leader, and this radiation is taken to be the cause of the strong association of sight and smell with body temperature. In short, the iconic leader, as a concrete representation or revelation of the "holy," engages exactly those perceptive powers that we usually associate with art. Indeed, he is art.

More generally speaking, in the charismatic Christian fold, the path from "Christ" to art and science is through the "Holy Spirit." The "task of the Holy Spirit" is to make available to, or awaken in, the human being those gifts of mind, spirit, imagination, and sensory perception that most directly connect the human being to "God" through disclosure or revelation. Every interviewed scientist who joined an independent charismatic church said, for example, that he joined it because he *sensed* something different. All commented that they used their intellectual talents more intensely, and indeed their careers did seem to justify this claim. And all commented that to the intellectual dimension were added "heart" and "reflection"; the latter especially through prayer, the former through increased community service.

By looking at scientists who are charismatic Christians, we see that doing science, and "knowing God through the Holy Spirit," are intimately connected by metonymic patterns of thought that are grounded in one and the same ontology and epistemology (Horton 1967: 51; Poewe 1989). Specifically, all interviewed scientists argued that the point of union between science and religion happened during a major proleptic or assumption-changing experience.[11] While some atheistic scientists searched for proof of the existence of "God" before this experience, the proleptic experience made any such search irrelevant, and it was abandoned. Proleptic experiences are described in great detail and seem to consist of a concentration of numerous delicate and small existential moments that even years later call forth strong emotion and vivid images in the telling.

PROLEPTIC EXPERIENCE AS THE KEY TO A SPECIFIC SENSE OF REALITY: A LOOK AT HAMANN

Evidence indicates that the second half of the twentieth century is a turning point (Drucker 1989). One can perhaps agree with the view that science is being reborn not through the head but through the "soul" and "heart" (see Bebbington 1989; Drucker 1957; Luhrmann 1989; Richardson 1967; Wuthnow 1988; and Kepel 1991, among others, for similar remarks). An analogous statement about philosophy during the second half of the eighteenth century was put forth by Erwin Metzke. In 1967 Metzke published a prize-winning essay on J. G. Hamann, a charismatic Lutheran Pietist, empiricist and philosopher, and a compatriot and adversary of Kant, as the man who symbolized and articulated such a turning point for philosophy of the eighteenth century. If we look at Hamann here, it is because he can help us with the question why these scientists do not regard Christianity to be an illusion. Why instead they insist that it is the anchor or foundation of knowledge.

According to Metzke, the key to Hamann's thought is a specific happening or proleptic experience. Hamann himself called it *Bekehrung*, or conversion, and argued that it gave a permanent direction to his life and view. This happening is the source of the peculiar "constitution" of Hamann's understanding of being and the world. While some people see Hamann as having deliberately set himself against the Enlightenment for the sake of argument (Unger 1968), Metzke insists that Hamann's outlook is the result of a positive disclosure. His outlook on life, the constitution of his thought, has its source in a specific *Bekehrung*-experience. His intentions can not be understood as having their source in the thought world of his immediate environment. They have their source, emphasizes Metzke, in the totality of his own new experience (3).[12]

While the "atheistic intellectus" of the late twentieth century is rooted in the antisystem thinking and the radical relativism of postmodernism (Richardson 1967), and while this thinking takes place largely within the old categories of being, body, life, and metaphor, the source of Hamann's intellectus (Metzke 1967: 3) and of charismatic scientists is a radical breakthrough to a new experience, perception, and conception of reality. It is for this reason that we as researchers must understand their ontology and epistemology.

But why is the very specific happening of a conversion important? The answer is because Hamann was quite aware that it centered his existence, gave it meaning, and, most important for his thought, provided the key, as said, to his perception of reality, to his ontology (Metzke 1967: 6).

According to Hamann, and here I am loosely translating and para-phrasing Metzke's explication (6–7), a *Bekehrung* is not just any happen-ing. It is not a random happening that does not affect the substance of the person's life (see also V. Turner 1986: 35, where he distinguishes between *mere* and *an* experience). Rather, it is a crisis-driven shattering through which a human being becomes another from what he was. The change is radical. It changes not only the meaning, belief, or dealings of a person, but his very being. It is becoming a new person. It does not, of course, change the material nature of the person. Instead, it is a turning of one's whole life history and way of life.

Hamann, and the charismatic scientists I interviewed, were con-vinced that this change is not possible through human effort, will, or wish. It is only possible through divine intervention, through the use, in other words, of metonymic patterns of thought. To them the new life is "an act of God," precisely because it is a sudden *Umbruch* (radical change) that goes against the will of the person and counter to his developmental tendencies.

Metzke (1967: 4) points out that Hamann's thinking, and in my view the thinking of charismatic Christians today, is part of a tradition of German religious and metaphysical thought going back to the Lutheran Pietists Johann Arndt (1555–1621), Philipp Jakob Spener (1635–1705), and August Hermann Francke (1663–1727). In 1687 Francke had a proleptic experience like that of Hamann in 1758. And like Hamann, Francke's thought too is grounded in this experience (Stoeffler 1973: 5, 11–13; Wallmann 1990: 63). One can also not rule out the more controver-sial influence from the "Lutheran mystic" Jakob Böhme (1575–1624), who, in turn, was influenced by Paracelsus (1493–1541) and by another Lutheran mystic, Valentin Weigel (1538–1588).[13] This stream of thought is, therefore, not free of serious dangers, among them the pantheistic and theosophical thinking of, for example, the New Age. Consequently, it is important that revelation remain subject to the strictures of science and orthodox Christianity—instead of, as what usually happens, being ex-cluded from them.

THE RELATIONSHIP BETWEEN METONYM, INVISIBLE REALITY, AND POLANYI'S PHILOSOPHY OF SCIENCE

Since charismatic Christianity and metonym are defined throughout this volume and elsewhere (Csordas 1990: 12; Poewe 1989: 367ff), the definition I give here will be rather brief. Charismatic Christianity is experiential, deconstructive, and restorative because it strongly empha-sizes the use of metonymic patterns of thought. Following Edmund Leach (1976), metonymy consists of sign, index, and signal. In a sign relationship, A stands for B as part for a whole. Index means that A indicates B. And signal refers to the fact that A triggers B so that the relationship between A and B is causal. So far I have but paraphrased Leach. It is my observation, however, based on fieldwork and numerous interviews with charismatic Christians, that people do not carefully distinguish among sign, index, and signal, so that A stands for and indicates B while B is seen to cause A. This is the metonymic process.

To give an example, in the context of a charismatic service a charismatic minister may "pray over" an individual until the individual falls to the floor. She is then said to be "resting in the spirit" and this "resting in the spirit" is taken as a sign that the Spirit is working within this individual. Consequently, the event of "resting in the spirit," (A), stands for and indicates the presence of the Holy Spirit, (B), while the Holy Spirit, (B), is said to have caused the individual to rest, (A). In other words, a simple, visible event in a specific context is part of something much bigger and invisible that is said to have caused it.[14] The observation or experience of this event, "resting in the spirit," is a clue to the apprehension of a reality, "the presence of divinity"; while the apprehension of this reality in turn is a clue to future observations that attest, verify, or disconfirm this reality. As we shall see shortly, this thought pattern, based on metonym, is similar to a certain philosophy of science. Consequently, scientists who are charismatic Christians rely on one and the same faculties and thought whether they practice science or Christianity. Put another way, it is not revelation and reason that separate Christianity from science.

To understand this similarity better, we must look particularly at the philosophy of science of Michael Polanyi. According to Polanyi, *"scientific knowing consists in discerning Gestalten that are aspects of reality"* (1964a: 10). By reality he means that "which is expected to reveal itself indeterminately in the future" (10). And that which is "expected to reveal itself" is "tacitly" known. This philosophical attitude is the attitude par excellence of the scientists I interviewed. It is not very different from the Thomistic philosophy that influenced Wilhelm Schmidt, who did superb scientific work for his time and whose theory of "primeval revelation" made at least as much sense as "Tylor's animism" (Brandewie 1990: 90).

Science, argues Polanyi, "is the understanding of interesting shapes in nature" (14). And both the process of understanding and the shapes are "tacitly" known. The scientist, therefore, like the charismatic Christian, assumes the "possibility of revealing still hidden truths" (17).[15] In fact, the whole process of discovery in science is metonymic. As Polanyi says, science is the "discovery of new facts and the discovery of mechanisms or systems which account for the facts already known" (28). This movement from "known" event to discernment of pattern that explains it, and vice versa, from "known" pattern to formerly unknown events, is metonymic thinking. It is what the American philosopher Charles Peirce called knowledge mediated through signs, and what charismatic Christians mean by revelation. Polanyi summarizes the relationship between reality and revelation this way, "scientific propositions describe something real which may manifest itself" (29). That which manifests itself is part of something real, the whole, in which it is grounded. And that sense of the whole is never absent in the thinking of these scientists anymore than it was absent in "the primitive mind" (Fernandez 1986b: 161).

The unexpected finding that charismatic Christianity and science are united in the process of discovery is clear when Polanyi writes that this process is "guided by the urge to make contact with a reality, which is felt to be there already to start with, waiting to be apprehended" (35). Charismatic Christian students who were also interviewed seemed to experience this kind of knowing in their chemistry classes.[16] They found it radically different from "knowing" biology, algebra, or geometry, which, they argued, are learned logically and step by step. They involve a good deal of "common sense." By contrast, argued one student, "common sense can't get you through chemistry." With chemistry "you have to learn the way things happen. And you can only make things happen when you discover something in the formula that makes it happen." In chemistry, and matters related to chemistry, "things aren't just the way you observe them. What you do and what happens are separate. The teacher tells you, 'if you do this something will happen,' and you learn to expect it and believe it will happen."

In a culture based on doing, testing, and seeing proof, it is surprising to learn that the only reason why something happened as you were doing it is because you "actualized" a schema that was abstract, beyond your doing, and yet made something happen when you did what you did (Rao 1988). What surprised the student was that even doing science involved faith, that if she took the teacher literally, something would happen that was abstract. In other words, here is a charismatic Christian student who learned in her chemistry class that taking things literally, far from being a sign of mental dullness, as is often believed, is a sign of genius. As Polanyi points out, the genius of Columbus "lay in taking it literally and as a guide to practical action that the earth was round, which his contemporaries held vaguely and as a mere matter of speculation" (Polanyi 1964b: 277).

When Polanyi argues that science is "personal knowledge" he means, like Hamann, that the scientist is intimately involved in the discovery of reality. Knowledge is objective, but how it is revealed is personal. Consequently, argues Polanyi, good science requires that scientists apply their scientific conscience, creative impulse, and critical caution.

Every interviewed scientist emphasized conscience, creative impulse, and critical caution.[17] Whether Polanyi intended it or not, this scientific trinity parallels the Christian Trinity of Father, Holy Spirit, and Son invoked by charismatic scientists. These in turn parallel, as one charismatic scientist said, truth (the Father), intuition (the Spirit), and reason (the Son), which parallel light, joy, and restraint, or hidden reality, discovery, and judicial verification. According to Thomas F. Torrance these parallels have to do with "the accord between the laws of our mind and the laws of nature" (1989: 10). However hesitant we may be to agree with Torrance, it is clear that a proleptic experience serves to establish a specific perception of reality, namely, an a priori or tacitly known reality that, in Polanyi's words, is there waiting to be apprehended through revelation. Hamann and Bastian did not oppose the Enlightenment so much as they opposed "rationalist fundamentalism" (Gellner 1992: 80). Science, they argued, should be based on both revelation and reason.[18]

CONSEQUENCES

Implications for Globality

A global attitude is closely linked to, and is usually the direct consequence of, a proleptic or an otherwise intense spiritual experience. The fact that these experiences have become rituals does not detract from their transformative power. As Kathleen Ashley (1990: xvii) points out, Turner too recognized the subversive and creative energy of ritual. It is therefore not surprising to find that these proleptic experiences initiated a paradigm shift. As mentioned earlier, the proleptic experience establishes such a strong link between the individual and "God" that beyond this specific link the individual revels in "diversity," "new insights," "newness," and so on. Here is the simultaneous narrowness and openness of metonymic thought. All interviewed scientists mentioned having a direct and certain relationship with "God." Yet this absolute certainty paradoxically relativized empirical reality and theoretical explanations. They took it to be the source of their power to be completely open and receptive to the "reality" of the universe, which they expected to "reveal itself indeterminately in the future." For lack of a better term, I call this a paradigm-linked globality. The scientist opens up to the universe as it reveals itself and it reveals itself progressively, as one scientist said, through "revelatory experiences." But an important part of a revelatory experience is how it illuminates already existing paradigms or frameworks and how it nudges them to change.

Openness to globality may start in a small way. For example, one surgeon was brought up in a very tight-knit ethnic and language commu-

nity. Then he had a strong spiritual experience and a vision confirming
a new direction in his spiritual life. While he had attended an ethnic
church until this time, he now moved to a nondenominational charismatic one. As he said, "We are Afrikaners. The new church was seventy
to eighty percent English speaking and perhaps ten percent black. But
when we visited there, we sensed love. . . . So first we gave up our
Afrikaans language and then our inculcated racism." When one checked
into the process of giving up racism, one noticed that it moved from
experience to experience along a dialectical exchange whereby an experience illuminated scripture and scripture illuminated an experience. It
is this dialectic, or "reciprocal illumination," (Mühlmann 1984: 44) that
accounts for the "revelatory" aspect of experience.[19]

One surgeon had spent seven years in China and then four years in
a Japanese internment camp. In China he had observed many traditional
exorcisms and, in the desperate conditions of the internment camp,
healing following prayers. When he returned to England, too weak
physically to practice surgery, he retrained as a psychiatrist. He had been
a Christian all of his life. But the Chinese and Japanese experiences
turned him into a charismatic Christian before there was a charismatic
movement. So great was the impact of Chinese thought on his theology
that, during his internship in the mental hospital, he began to experiment
with exorcism prayers when his patients appeared to have religious
problems. Importantly, he adapted Chinese thought and practice to the
English environment and Christian framework. Exorcism became deliv-
ering a person's specific ancestors into "God's kingdom" by way of
family tree research and a specially organized Eucharistic service. During the service, visions of ancestors were reported, but more important,
people began to be healed. Given these visions, he came to interpret the
Eucharistic service as "immersion of the dead into Christ's life," a view
supported by the local Anglican Bishop. He soon combined this interpretation with the Roman Catholic notion of "limbo." The end result was a
relatively successful curative practice that has been documented in
medical journals.

What is important for us is the nature of this globality. The psychiatrist achieved it by placing emphasis on local adaptations of the main
tradition rather than on the main tradition itself (Hannerz 1990: 237).
Because local adaptations were the result of several distinct spiritual
experiences, he arrived at this global "knowing" through these experiences and, importantly, through visual imagery.[20] It should be noticed,
however, that he did not abandon the two major traditions of Christianity and science. Rather, he insisted that each respond to the experiential
illuminations that he gained through his contact with specific local

cultures. He had no difficulty working simultaneously with the global and local aspects of various traditions.

A younger man, a social scientist who became a pastor following a proleptic experience, expressed the nature of globality somewhat differently. He distinguished the "city church" from the "urban church," the latter being an independent charismatic church. To his mind, the city church was conservative, largely homogeneous, and highly structured. His description of the urban church, by contrast, is an apt metaphor for global culture. In his words, the "urban church *is* the heart of the inner city." Its congregation consists of "a few professionals, lots of unemployed single parents, lots of handicapped, lots of black and Oriental people, lots of non-Christians, lots of transients, and some former criminals." All speak different idioms and many are illiterate with respect to Christianity. The major task of this church, therefore, is the liminal one of "spirit renewal." Furthermore, the points of contact between this liminal institution and the city are its professional counselling ministry and medical practice. Through them, the congregation sees all the problems of the inner city: "racial prejudice, those dying of AIDS, sexual abuse, family break-downs, marital violence, former convicts, and so on." It is literally a church that uses guards. Their aim is not to "advertise or promote Christianity" but to "affect that world."

This kind of church is global because it is liminal. Its survival is dependent on the "experiential matrix" of diverse "social dramas" (Ashley 1990: xvi). This is the source of its testimonial narratives and persuasive prayers. The church cannot achieve its globality by simply preaching and hoping people will turn around. It is dependent on "revelatory" experiences mediated through metonymic thought patterns because only these can "effect so deep a penetration of the Word as to rearrange a person's life." Such a church, argued the interviewee, is "not a structure; it's a movement." It requires its members to have a definitive relationship with "God" precisely because they have to be open to all else. Once again belief in "God" relativizes life, but not beyond the fixed point of that relationship.

This church, run by several scientists, is also global because it is iconic. In societies suffering from Christian illiteracy, on one hand, and Christian fundamentalism, on the other, charismatic Christians emphasize finding their way to "God" through all five senses.

Some of these scientists value this emphasis. Thus a urologist and microbiologist described their respective shifts to charismatic Christianity as follows. The first time they went to a charismatic church, the service was led by a musical leader. The "sound of music" and the "storytelling" captured their attention. Their sense of hearing was engaged as never before. Then they were "immensely moved" by Reinhard Bonnke and Edgardo Silvoso—who are kinds of "iconic leader" in the worldwide charismatic Christian fold. Their senses of sight and feeling were engaged in new ways. Although they themselves might not like this description, popular charismatic leaders like Reinhard Bonnke and Yonggi Cho are, in some sense, iconic representations of "the Spirit left by Christ." Iconic leadership is very important in African Initiated Churches (AICs). Yet few academics have commented upon its importance among charismatic Christians in Western societies. But as among Kimbanguists, for example, some of these scientists expressed a clear sense that through these exceptional leaders, or at least the "anointing" upon them, "Jesus Christ" acquired "existential reality." As mentioned earlier, "the Spirit" is said to work through the imagination and senses of individuals enabling them to perceive what was formerly missed (see Daneel 1988: 108, where he discusses Ralph Martin's Kimbangu work).[21]

In secular terms, an iconic leader has the ability to stimulate a client to use formerly repressed sensory perceptions. The iconic leader opposes the Enlightenment mind-set, which censored experience of the transcendent (Roszak 1981: 58). He does not have to be a "magician" or "brainwasher." All he has to do is to represent a tradition that sanctions opening the doors of perception. Charismatic Christians are undoing what Peter Berger called the "shrinkage" of the sacred in reality to the opposition between "a radically transcendent divinity and a radically 'fallen' humanity" (1969: 111–12). They are putting back precisely that which earlier Protestants removed, namely, the sense of the numinous.

One scientist expressed it this way. "To experience a *holy* God is the most important thing about charismatic Christianity, that and its internationalism. A holy God is not one who lacks color, lives in the dust of empiricism, or in the sterile sentence of a biblical scholar. Experiencing God is an actual experience—it's an experience I see in color, I hear in sound, and I feel in touch."

Thus one physician, who was also mayor of his city, described the height of his proleptic experience as follows: "First I heard my full name called [the sense of hearing], then as I lay on the bed with my eyes closed, I felt God's hand on my right thigh. The touch was very distinct and real." Had his wife not prompted him, he would have left this unsaid.

I have already commented on the sense of smell. Even the sense of taste is involved, as when one psychiatrist offered prepared prayers for mental patients at the Eucharistic service in which not just the words of deliverance but the bread and wine are vitally important. The effectiveness of this service depends on a heightened engagement of the senses of hearing, seeing, and tasting.[22] Furthermore, these Eucharistic services were also held for people who were not nor intended to become Christian. The Christian psychiatrist simply appealed to the numinous in any religion and the revelatory faculty in any individual. Services were held for Jews, Buddhists in Taiwan, Parsis and Hindus in India, and so on. Instead of becoming Christians, these people claimed to have become "fulfilled Buddhists, Hindus, and Jews." When he was asked why a Eucharistic service should be effective, the psychiatrist answered, "I don't know the theology. I have come to this purely by revelation and experience, not by theory. When it comes to its theology I ask my bishop."

In short, several things underpin the global nature of charismatic Christianity beyond, most obviously, its internationalism. There is first the proleptic experience that opens an individual to a new and infinitely wider world. The sense of the numinous of the proleptic experience is global because it can be found among peoples anywhere in the world, and its local specificities are global because some of them were implied in the main tradition in the first place.

Then there is the sense of globality centered on the urban or inner city church that is seen as being "the heart of something." Speaking metaphorically, one might say it is "a heart" that pumps the "life" of "renewal" through diverse groups of people who would otherwise live separate lives. Finally, there is the sense of globality that comes from the fact that this form of Christianity is iconic, synesthetic, and metonymic. It is mediated by the five senses of seeing, hearing, smelling, tasting, and touching, and it involves patterns of thought centered on the discovery of that which is expected to be revealed.

Implications for Storytelling and Styles of Writing

Like Hamann, so contemporary scientists and physicians experienced God first in history, especially, their personal histories. Because they experienced the "living presence of God" through the "Holy Spirit" in the events of their own lives, they did not need science or philosophy to prove the existence of "God." Rather, assuming the existence of "God," these scientists were filled with renewed joy in their work almost to a point of playfulness. Sometimes they left their work altogether to go into full-time ministry, more often they integrated work and life into a unified Christian story. How was this done?

Every interviewed scientist described the major turning point of his life, from whatever it was to that of a "spirit-filled" Christian, in terms of a proleptic experience. With this proleptic experience, the scientist's universe of thought shifted to a new (to him or her) foundation. Even for a geologist, Genesis ceased to be outdated science and became a "literary statement." Indeed, following this experience, all interviewed scientists broke into a storytelling mode. Suddenly, it seemed, their life, their work, their troubles, their scientific knowledge, all became part of the big story of a living, experienced "God."

When they thought about healing, evolution, the origin of the cosmos, the beginning and end of human history or the universe, their thought, however competent and knowledgeable, became infinitely playful. Some constructed subtle analogies between scripture and medicine, others crossed disciplinary boundaries to grasp a broader picture, some argued against aspects of evolution and creationism but not against the wonder and skill of science to illuminate "reality." Some argued that the church needs scientists who have become theologians, not M.Div.'s who will never be scientists.

Whatever they argued, they argued *wholes*. They worked within an intellectus of "a God of unity" in which each life has hope and meaning. And they took comfort in the rich images of Psalms, Job, Ecclesiastes, Solomon, and Proverbs. The imagery of the Wisdom Literature was the broad framework from within which their life and work was thought out and conducted.

When I interviewed some noncharismatic fundamentalist scientists about how they reconciled Christianity with science, they often pointed to a poster of a river that several had hanging in their offices. Then they said, "reason takes you to the shore, faith takes you across," or something to that effect. This response was not given by a single charismatic Christian scientist whom I interviewed. Each one talked "experience," "pattern," "holism," "openness," and told a long open-ended story that detailed the events of his life, family, career, and scientific thinking from within a scriptural framework. Each one turned into a good storyteller and each story was told differently, though it was of a pattern. Some worked with analogies, some detailed their proleptic experience at some length, some spoke with humor, others of miracles—all told, as said, fascinating open-ended stories. Why this urge to tell stories? Because all of them knew that there was more than one way of knowing and more than one way to convey knowledge.

At the core of these stories was the unmediated and direct relationship between "God" and human being, so that reality, revealed through direct contact, is personal and relational. But if this knowledge is personal, relational, and revelational, how does it affect writing? The answer to this question puts us on dangerous and controversial ground. It requires much more thought than I offer here.

Metzke argues, and the same is said by Mircea Eliade (1963: vi) about Gerardus van der Leeuw, that Hamann does not think systematically in line with convention nor in logical succession as is required in normal science (see Kuhn 1970): the very thing that Ernest Gellner fears. Hamann's and van der Leeuw's writing, as some of the writing of charismatic scientists, seems impressionistic and paradoxical, and is filled with references to literary works—in the case of Hamann from at least five different languages. Furthermore, with Lavater and Hamann we get the practice of scholars writing formal works as well as in other genres, including biography, journals, travel diaries, letters, and novels.

Like Hamann, so early anthropologists too chose deliberately to follow or invent a style of writing that suited their epistemologies, theories, and experiences. Bastian, for example, intentionally followed the writing style of the great naturalist Alexander von Humboldt. In Humboldtian fashion Bastian attempted "to compose *Naturmalereien*, written descriptions of nature which evoke a painting, a still-life in words" (Koepping 1983: 26).

In the English-speaking world all this changed with the "ethnographic revolution" around 1910 (Langham 1981: xii). It ushered in "the anthropological monograph" that constituted "a comprehensive (and usually single-volume) study of one particular society" (xii). More recently things changed again. There is a general recognition that team work, global linkages, and knowledge of a people's literature and history are indispensable.

CONCLUSION

Most of us who are social scientists were educated in the belief that science and religion or science and Christianity are incompatible. In the introduction to this volume and in this chapter I reviewed some of the literature that showed, however, that the methods of anthropology and other social sciences were not invented by secular but by Catholic and Pietist scholars (Mühlmann 1984; Koepping 1983; Kohl 1987; Stoeffler 1973; Brecht 1993; Wallmann 1990). It would seem, therefore, that the assumed incompatibility between science and Christianity is an illusion.

Chapter one and various chapters thereafter showed that the incorporation of experiences and oral witness into normal Christian practice paralleled a similar incorporation of experiences and "told stories" in normal social-science practice. It would appear, therefore, that the assumed incompatibility between written conceptualization and oral narrative is also an illusion (Hollenweger 1979a; chapter nine of this volume).

Finally, this chapter showed that some hard and soft scientists who were trained to separate science from faith had strong religious experiences that reaffirmed their unity. Consequently, this research persuades me to ask why Christianity (or religion) and science were separated in the first place? Given our findings, two answers suggest themselves. One answer has to do with the politics of knowledge and with the fact that Christian scholars were often, and continue to be, in conflict with the official church (Brandewie 1990; Thiel 1984; Tempels 1959; Fabian 1971; Metzke 1967). A second answer is more complicated. It has to do with the fact that scholars who favored the separation of science from Christianity were primarily French and English philosophers of the seventeenth and eighteenth centuries who were part of what came to be known as the Enlightenment, which occurred at a time when English and French were the dominant languages of Europe. In this environment it was easy to ignore scholars who opposed the science-faith separation. They were at any rate primarily German Pietists from unknown and remote cities like Königsberg and Halle, of whom the English and French were "almost wholly unaware" (Neill and Wright 1988: 2–3).

This brings us back to scientists who are charismatic Christians. Whatever else their proleptic experiences did, they put together what was parallel and separate so that science and religion came to sit on the same foundation. What seemed to change during conversions or awakenings were worldviews and the relationship to, and perception of, reality. What changed was the big story and how this big story integrated little stories about science, service, nations, and individuals. Academically speaking these scientists changed their epistemologies and ontologies because conversion affirmed their trust in a largely invisible, independent, but personally knowable reality. It also affirmed their sense that there is more than one way of knowing and conveying knowledge. If they separated anything it was not science and faith but certain procedural rules that helped them act responsibly and wisely in their chosen professions.

NOTES

I thank SSHRCC for funding the research, conducted between 1989 and 1991, on scientists in charismatic independent churches, and I thank the University of Calgary for funding a pilot project in Germany, summer 1991.

1. Londa Shembe is the grandson of Isaiah Shembe, the founder of the African Christian Amanazaretha Church. The Amanazaretha are one of many African Independent Charismatic churches which emphasize *umoya*, or Spirit, and healing. Londa Shembe, well educated and well read, with a degree in law, was leader of one of two factions of Amanazaretha. He was brutally murdered in 1989. I quote him here because no Western charismatic Christian could so simply defend his faith and hope to be taken seriously.
2. Metonymic pattern of thought will be further defined later. The aim of this chapter is, on the one hand, to get away from the fixation with metaphor ("an

assertion based on similarity of relation"), and, on the other, to move beyond the view that metonym, a trope, is but "an assertion of an association based on contiguity of relation" (Fernandez 1986b: 173). The contiguity is causal. James W. Fernandez also recognizes the presence of metonymy in revitalization (172). Metonym is a turn of thought that is used to express a relationship between an aspect of experienced reality and the larger reality, visible or invisible, of which the experience is a manifestation. Experience and interpretation are two sides of the same coin.

3. Interviewed scientists argued that, at any rate, their research, medical work, and writing were part of the "Kingdom of God." "Kingdom of God" and the "Holy Spirit" seemed to express an attitude of surrender to a living relationship with God; otherwise doctrines were played down. One might say that under the "holy canopy"—to play with Peter Berger's words—scientists who are charismatic Christians, like any other scientists, preserve their loyalty to certain procedural rules (see Gellner 1992: 80). Furthermore, as for Ernest Gellner's "rationalist fundamentalism," so for charismaticism, "all facts and all observers are equal" and the source and affirmations are always subject to query. And yet what is not done is to desacralize, to disenchant (81). In fact, quite the opposite is the case. The same sentiment was expressed by Wilhelm Schmidt, the German Catholic anthropologist who founded *Anthropos*. Addressing missionaries, he wrote: "Everything must be handled with religious reverence: nothing must be glossed over or *prettified*. If missionaries describe the facts falsely, they falsify the ways of God and put obstacles in the way of deriving any great benefit from their descriptions" (quoted in Brandewie 1990: 55–56).

4. Turner had of course converted to Catholicism.

5. It should be noted that Hamann, Herder, and Lavater were affected by Pietism and, in turn, were widely read among Pietist groups (Stoeffler 1973). The introduction to this volume also describes many Catholic links.

6. Likewise, Josef Franz Thiel wrote, and I translate loosely, "Those who have never personally experienced the religious, who have never grappled with it existentially, are not in a position to grasp the nature of religion; they must perforce be content with external appearances" (1984: 14).

7. Among the German thinkers listed one should include the French Jesuit P. Matteo Ricci (1552–1610), inventor of participant observation, and Joseph François Lafitau (1670–1740). The latter made explicit the meaning of the comparative method as reciprocal illumination (*Wechselseitige Erhellung*), by which he meant that native customs and institutions illuminate antiquity (or current Western ones) while antiquity (or Western customs and institutions) illuminate native (or non-Western) ones. As Marcus and Fischer (1986) point out, this method has never been systematized. Mirroring, which is associated with the Jesuit Louis le Comtes (1656–1729), meant that one presents or writes up one's findings in such a manner as to show that the ethnographic other (for example the Chinese) find our customs as peculiar as we find theirs.

8. Polanyi does not make reference to Hamann's work in the eighteenth century, but in fact Polanyi's thinking is anticipated by Hamann. Hamann talked about personal knowledge and personal reality, thereby opposing the

Dingmetaphysik. Hamann was totally against the objectification of God as, for example, the "highest Being," whose condition and qualities lead inevitably upon contemplation to certain truths. He trusted instead in the primacy of experience that came from a relationship to God. Hamann emphasized the inadequacy of doctrinally established categories of thought (see Metzke 1967).

9. It will be noted that the charismatic Christian notion of revelation is quite different from Gellner's notion of revelation as "a Revelation" that seems to consist of "the idea of a unique and final Message, delivered at one place and one time, exempt from scrutiny, from disaggregation into its constituent claims, and from the need to subject those claims to question" (1992: 84). Charismatic Christian revelations are always subject to question, disaggregation, and scrutiny. Indeed, these are part of as solid a set of procedural constraints as are those of the scientific method. Where charismatic Christians differ from Gellner's "rational fundamentalists" is in the "fixed point" of their worldview. For Gellner that fixed point is "the rules of the Kantian or Enlightenment ethic of cognition" to which a social scientist becomes committed (84); for charismatic Christians it is their experienced "relationship with God."

10. This kind of response to iconic leaders does not happen all the time. Most scientists, especially those returning to the Christian fold or becoming Christian, experienced it at least once. Usually, the first such experience of an iconic leader constitutes a turning point or a point of entrance into a "wider universe" (see Daneel 1988).

11. Following the proleptic experience, thirty-eight became more intensely involved with their professional career, ten radically changed their career from science to full-time ministry, nine intensified both their scientific career and their Christian lay activities by using their scientific knowledge in Christian environments. All increased the service aspect of their work. Their increased service-consciousness and deep sense of responsibility is remarkable. If there is one philosophical implication or "ethic" that emerged from all interviews it is an "ethic of service." All interviewees changed quite radically how they thought about and related to people, be these patients, colleagues, friends, spouses, the poor, or people of different ethnic origins.

12. Hamann is difficult to read because, among other things, he makes reference to numerous small local events, the meanings of which are lost to us, as well as various literary works from the English, French, Spanish, Greek, and Slavic-speaking world. His mentality was a global one. Because Metzke's prizewinning essay is truly superb, and I have read back and forth between Hamann and Metzke, I rely on it here. What I say is of course my translation from the German. My affinity for Hamann stems from the fact that I was born in the same city, Königsberg, and into the same tradition, which combined Pietism and empiricism, or a "mystical" (charismatic) Lutheranism, and science. Hamann, though religious, admired the thought of Kant and Hume, although he argued with it. He did not, as is thought in the English-speaking world, oppose the Enlightenment, nor did he reject science. At the same time, he was not blind to the partial blindness of the Enlightenment, nor to its dangers.

13. This tradition that combines Pietism and science can be traced forward from Hamann to Jacobi (1743–1819) and Herder (1744–1803), and to Lotze (1817–

1881), who argued that intellect and scientific knowledge were the means and tools of feeling, emotion, and intuition, thoughts that led to a theory of *Einfühlung*, or empathy, which was fully developed by Lipps (1851–1914). Lotze argued that the fusion of science and religion, reason and feeling, knowledge and value occurred only at particular moments that I here call proleptic experiences. Lotze, precisely because he showed that in a specific happening Christianity (or religion) and the methods and conclusions of science were reconciled, influenced various American philosophers, including B. P. Browne, G. T. Ladd, Josiah Royce (who studied under Lotze and later taught at Harvard), and Charles Peirce. Royce, especially, but also Peirce, developed a theory of interpretation that argued that all knowledge is mediated through signs. This is the link, by the way, to what I call metonymic patterns of thoughts, discussed later. More importantly one can detect the influence of Hamann and Herder in the work of such largely ignored German anthropologists as Gutmann (1876–1966) and Adolf Bastian (1826–1905), who insisted on the union of science, or British empiricism, and religion. Indeed, Bastian argued that without this union, empiricism would become sterile. Was he wrong?

14. This is simply the other faculty that is as universal as is the human ability to reason. It is more compatible with Schmidt's (see Brandewie 1990) notion of "primeval revelation" than with Tylor's notion of "animism." Together, one might say, these two scholars recognized the two major faculties that make for human creativity: metonymic patterns of thought, which is nothing other than revelation, and reason.

15. All interviewed scientists emphasized the importance of personal revelations or of revealing still hidden truths through revelatory experiences. This anticipation of discovery is the reason for their excitement about this form of Christianity.

16. Six eleventh-grade students, age seventeen, were interviewed in the school run by Chapel Hill Harvester, Atlanta, Georgia. The students and their parents belonged to this church.

17. Good science requires conscience in that all mentioned a greater awareness of right and wrong, so that the universe of science is a moral universe; it requires creative insight in that all mentioned revelatory experiences as one of the most important aspects of charismatic Christianity and their work; it requires critical caution in that all used scientific knowledge to check the abuses of, for example, faith healing, just as they used Christianity to check the abuses of science. One specialist saw it this way: "Infections require antibiotics. Not to use antibiotics would be irresponsible. If there is no conflict here with divine knowledge it is because knowing antibiotics is in my philosophy divine knowledge." In other words, "we have been given talents, certain gifts, and accumulated medical knowledge which are divine, and it is our responsibility to put them into practice. At the same time, there is healing which I cannot explain as a doctor. But then planes fly and I can't explain that either." This kind of literalness has to do with working quite consciously within a tradition based on the cosmological principle of a contingent and inherently rational and orderly universe.

18. That this position is still rejected can be seen in Raymond Scupin's introductory text, where he radically separates scientific knowledge, as the scientific method, from other knowledge, such as religion and faith (1992: 17). And yet revelation is as subject to verification or falsification as reason is.

19. It is fascinating that the French Jesuit missionary Joseph Francois Lafitau (1670–1740), who is regarded by W. E. Mühlmann (1984: 44) to be the founder of modern comparative ethnology, developed a comparative method based on "reciprocal illumination," whereby Iroquois customs and institutions were seen to illuminate antiquity just as customs and institutions of antiquity were seen to illuminate contemporary indigenous customs and institutions. This "comparative method" is an inherent aspect of Christian, especially Catholic thought, so that one need not be surprised that it is not only found in Lafitau, but also Wilhelm Schmidt, among others.

20. He gave many examples of "knowing" through visual imagery. In his words, during one Eucharistic healing service he and his assistants "*saw* an RAF man in his uniform fighting against the angels who were pulling him down to make him look at the bread and wine and what we were doing. And I said to the Lord, 'there is no RAF person in the family.' And He just said, 'his name is Keith.'" Three days later the psychiatrist said to the client, "does the name Keith mean anything?" She said, "How do you know?" And he said, "Well he was there in his RAF uniform." And she said, "Good gracious you know that too." This knowing is similar to that described by Jean-Guy Goulet for the Dene Tha to whom "dreams and visions are seen as a source of knowledge" (forthcoming). Goulet points out that "a person with religious experience is described not as a believer, but as someone who 'knows'" (3). This attitude is very similar to that of well-educated Western charismatics.

21. Daneel says that an "iconic leader is a reflection and concretization of Christ without necessarily usurping Christ's place."

22. For example, services were held for people who had undergone an abortion, suffered from anorexia nervosa, epilepsy, manic depression, paranoia, obsession, and schizophrenia. All of these conditions involved "imbalance," or some sense of distortion or malfunction of the five senses: touch, taste, sight, sound, and smell. A charismatic Christian psychiatrist described the following example (this is an abridged version of his story). The patient was a hospitalized classified schizophrenic who "heard" swearing, clashing swords, and the roaring sea. He also then "saw" blood, "felt" the wind on his face, and "tasted" the salt of sweat. The Christian psychiatrist, following interviews and historical research, promised to get a bishop's permission to have a Eucharistic service for the patient's ancestors. The following morning the patient called the psychiatrist saying that all sensations had gone except for the wind on his face. So he and his family were taken to the Eucharistic service to deliver the patient's seafaring ancestors into the "Kingdom of God." When the patient received the bread (taste), the wind sensation ceased. As well, during the service, the patient and others present had visual images in which they saw the deliverance of the patient's ancestors. The patient is now a college lecturer.

Bibliography

BOOKS AND JOURNAL ARTICLES

Abuor, Christopher Ojwando. 1971. *White Highlands No More*. Nairobi: Pan African Researchers.

Adams, Daniel J. 1991. "Reflections on an Indigenous Christian Movement: The Yoido Full Gospel Church." *Japan Christian Quarterly* 57 (1): 36–45.

Aloo, Albert. N.d. "Maria Legio of Africa. Lemo Mar Katena." Typescript.

Alvarez, Carmelo E. 1987. "Latin American Pentecostals: Ecumenical and Evangelical." *Pneuma* 9 (1): 91–95.

Alves, Rubem. 1984. *What Is Religion?* Maryknoll, N.Y.: Orbis Books.

Amin, Mohammed. 1983. *Portraits of Africa*. Text by Peter Mol. London: Harvill Press.

Ammerman, Nancy T. 1990. "North American Protestant Fundamentalism." In *Fundamentalisms Observed*, edited by Martin E. Marty and R. Scott Appleby, 1–65. Chicago: University of Chicago Press.

Amuka, Peter. 1978. *Ngero As a Social Object*. M.A. thesis. University of Nariobi, Kenya.

———. 1991. "Pakruok: The Art of Naming and Praising among the Luo of Kenya." In *Spring Conference on the Translations of Africa*. March 15–17. Center for Cultural Studies, Rice University.

Anderson, Robert Mapes. 1979. *Vision of the Disinherited: The Making of American Pentecostalism*. New York: Oxford University Press.

Ankele, John. 1982. *Rise Up and Walk*. Film, written and directed by Ankele. Available through University of California, Berkeley, Extension Media Center.

Anyumba, H. Owuor. 1971. "Spirit Possession among the Luo of Central Nyanza." In *Occasional Papers in African Traditional Religion* 3: 1–46. Makerere University, Department of Religious Studies and Philosophy.

———. 1974. "The Historical Dimensions of Life-Crisis Rituals: Some Factors in the Dissemination of Juogi Beliefs among the Luo of Kenya up to 1962." Paper presented at the Limuru Conference on the Historical Study of East African Religions, June 26.

Anzai, Shin. 1977. "Iesu no Mitama Kyokai—Okinawa dendo no shoso" (The Spirit of Jesus Church—Aspects of Evangelism in Okinawa). In *Shukyo to rekishi* (Religion and History), edited by Wakimoto Tsuneya, 18–43. Tokyo: Yamamoto Shoten.

Arrington, F. L. 1988. "Historical Perspectives on Pentecostal and Charismatic Hermeneutics." In *Dictionary of Pentecostal and Charismatic Movements*, edited by Stanley M. Burgess, Gary B. McGee, and Patrick H. Alexander, 376–89. Grand Rapids, Mich.: Zondervan.

Ashley, Kathleen. 1990. Introduction to *Victor Turner and the Construction of Cultural Criticism*, edited by Ashley, ix–xxii. Bloomington: Indiana University Press.

Atieno Odhiambo, E. S. 1975. "A Note on the Chronology of African Traditional Religion in Western Kenya." *Journal of Eastern African Research and Development* 5 (2): 119–22.

———. 1977a. "Rebutting 'Theory' with Correct Theory: A Comment on the Trial of Dedan Kimatha." *Kenya Historical Review* 5 (20): 385–88.

———. 1977b [1970]. "The Rise and Decline of the Kenya Peasant, 1888–1922." In *African Social Studies*, edited by Peter Gutkin and Peter Waterman, 233–40. New York and London: Monthly Review Press.

———. 1984. "The Historical Perspective of Socio-cultural Development in the Third World." Lecture at the Ramogi Cultural Festival, Kisumu, Kenya, January 27.

———. 1988. "Democracy and the Ideology of Order in Kenya." In *Democratic Theory and Practice in Africa*, edited by Walter Oyugi, et al., 111–37. Portsmouth: Heinemann; London: James Currey.

Ault, James. 1987. "Family and Fundamentalism: The Shawmut Valley Baptist Church." In *Disciplines of Faith: Studies in Religion, Politics and Patriarchy*, edited by Jim Olbekevich, Lyndel Roper, and Raphael Samuel, 13–36. London: Routledge and Kegan Paul.

Ayany, Samuel. 1964. *Kar Chakruok Mar Luo*. 3d ed. Nairobi: Equatorial Publishers.

Baal, J. van. 1981. *Man's Quest for Partnership: The Anthropological Foundations of Ethics and Religion*. Assen, The Netherlands: Van Gorcum.

———. 1989. *Mine Eyes Have Seen the Glory: A Journey into the Evangelical Subculture in America*. New York: Oxford University Press.

———. 1990. *Mysterie also Openbaring* (Mystery as Revelation). Utrecht: ISOR Occasional Papers.

Bames, Sandra. 1989. *Africa's Ogun: Old World and New*. Bloomington: Indiana University Press.

Barnett, Donald L., and Karari Njama. 1966. *Mau Mau from Within*. New York: Monthly Review Press.

Barr, James. 1978. *Fundamentalism*. Philadelphia: Westminster Press.

Barrett, David B. 1968. *Schism and Renewal in Africa: An Analysis of Six Thousand Contemporary Religious Movements*. Nairobi: Oxford University Press.

———. 1971. "Who's Who of African Independent Church Leaders." *Risk* 3 (7): 23–34.

———. 1973. *Kenya Churches Handbook: The Development of Kenyan Christianity 1498–1973*. Kisumu, Kenya: Evangel Publishing.

———. 1979. "Legio Maria." In *Encyclopedic Dictionary of Religion*, edited by Paul Kevin Meagher, Thomas C. O'Brien, and Consuelo Maria Aberne, 2087. Washington, D.C.: Corpus Books.

————, ed. 1982. *World Christian Encyclopedia*. New York: Oxford University Press.

————, ed. 1984. *Beyond Fundamentalism*. Philadelphia: Westminster Press.

————. 1990. "Annual Statistical Table on Global Mission." *International Bulletin for Missionary Research* 14 (January): 26–27.

Barrett David B., and T. John Padwick. 1989. *Rise Up and Walk! Conciliarism and the African Indigenous Churches, 1815–1987. A Sequel to Schism and Renewal in Africa (1968)*. Nairobi: Oxford University Press.

Barrett, Michèle. 1988. *Women's Oppression Today: The Marxist-Feminist Encounter*. London: Verso.

Barron, Bruce. 1987. *The Health and Wealth Gospel*. Downers Grove, Ill.: InterVarsity Press.

Barth, Karl. 1918. *Der Römerbrief*. Bern: G. A. Baschlin. Translated by Edwyn C. Hoskyns as *The Epistle to the Romans*. London: Oxford University Press, 1957.

Bartleman, Frank. 1925 [1980]. *How "Pentecost" Came to Los Angeles—How It Was in the Beginning*. Republished as *Azusa Street*. Plainfield, N.J.: Logos International.

Bastian, Adolf. 1860 [1968]. *Der Mensch in der Geschichte: Zur Begründung einer Psychologischen Weltanschauung* (The Human Being in History: Toward the Establishment of a Psychological Worldview). 3 vols. Leipzig: Verlag Otto Wiegand. Reprinted Osnabrück: Biblioverlag.

Bastian, Jean Pierre. 1979. "Protestantismo y política en México" (Protestantism and Politics in Mexico). *Taller de Teología* (Journal of Theology) 5: 7–23.

Beaman, Jay. 1989. *Pentecostal Pacifism: The Origin, Development, and Rejection of Pacific Belief among the Pentecostals*. Center for Mennonite Brethren Studies: Hillsboro, Kans.

Bebbington, D. W. 1989. *Evangelicalism in Modern Britain*. London: Unwin Hyman.

Beck, Brenda E. F. 1978. "The Metaphor as a Mediator Between Semantic and Analogic Modes of Thought." *Current Anthropology* 19 (1): 83–97.

Bennett, Dennis J. 1970. *Nine O'Clock in the Morning*. Plainfield, N.J.: Logos.

————. 1991. "[Benny] Hinn's Book Clarified." *Charisma* 16 (28 April): 9.

Berger, Iris. 1976. "Rebels or Status Seekers: Women as Spirit Mediums in East Africa." In *Women in Africa*, edited by Edna Bay and Nancy Hafkin, 157–82. Stanford, Calif.: Stanford University Press.

Berger, Peter L. 1959. "Sectarianism and Religious Sociation." *American Journal of Sociology* 64: (1) 41–44.

————. 1969. *The Sacred Canopy: Elements of a Sociological Theory of Religion*. New York: Anchor Books.

Berg-Schlosser, Dirk. 1984. *Tradition and Change in Kenya*. Paderborn: Ferdinand Schöning.

Best, Gary. 1990. Personal interview by Karla Poewe, Langley, B.C., Canada.

Bettray, Johannes P. 1955. *Die Akkomodationsmethode des P. Matteo Ricci in China* (The Accommodation Method of P. Matteo Ricci in China). Rome: Apud Aedes Universitatis Gregorianae.

Bhutta, A. R. N.d. *Was Jesus Buried?* Nairobi: E. A. Ahmadiyya Muslim Mission.

Bittlinger, Arnold. 1981. *The Church is Charismatic: The World Council of Churches and the Charismatic Renewal*. Geneva: World Council of Churches.

Bickle, Mike. 1990. Personal interview by Karla Poewe and Irving Hexham, Decatur, Ga.

Blackstone, William E. 1980. *Jesus is Coming.* New York: Fleming H. Revell.

Blattner, John. 1981. "Report From North America: The Kansas City Conference." In *The Church is Charismatic,* edited by Arnold Bittlinger. Geneva: World Council of Churches.

Blue, Ken. 1990. Personal Interview by Irving Hexham and Karla Poewe, Calgary, Alt., Canada.

Blumhofer, Edith L. 1989. *The Assemblies of God: A Chapter in the Story of American Pentecostalism,* 2 Vols. Springfield, Mo.: Gospel Publishing House.

Bock, Claudia de. 1987. Personal interview by Gerard Roelofs, Antwerp, Belgium.

Boff, Leonardo. 1985. *Church, Charisma and Power: Liberation Theology and the Institutional Church.* London: SCM.

Bourdieu, Pierre. 1977. *Outline of a Theory of Practice.* Cambridge: Cambridge University Press.

Boyd, Carolyn. 1991. *The Apostle of Hope: The Dr. Kriengsak Story.* West Sussex: Sovereign World.

Brandewie, Ernest. 1990. *When Giants Walked the Earth.* Fribourg: Switzerland University Press.

Branover, Herman. 1982. *Return.* Jerusalem and New York: Feldheim Publishers.

Brecht, Martin. 1993. *Der Pietismus vom siebzehnten bis zum frühen achtzehnten Jahrhundert* (Pietism from the Seventeenth to the Early Eighteenth Century). Göttingen: Vandenhoeck & Ruprecht.

Brereton, Virginia L. 1990. *Training God's Army: The American Bible School.* Bloomington: Indiana University Press.

Brittain, Victoria. 1983. Preface to *Barrel of a Pen: Resistance to Repression in Neo-Colonial Kenya,* by Ngugi wa Thiong'o, iii–ix. Trenton, N.J.: Africa World Press.

Buckingham, Jamie. 1979. *Kathryn Kuhlman: A Glimpse into Glory.* Plainfield, N.J.: Logos.

Buijtenhuijs, Robert. 1982. *Essays on Mau Mau: Contributions to Mau Mau Historiography.* Research Reports. No. 17. Leiden, The Netherlands: African Studies Center.

———. 1985. "Dini ya Msambwa: Rural Rebellion or Counter-Society?" In *Theoretical Explorations in African Religion,* edited by Wim Van Binsbergen and Matthew Schoffeleers, 323–45. London: Routledge and Kegan Paul.

Burdick, John. 1988. *Dictionary of Pentecostal and Charismatic Movements.* Regency Reference Library. Grand Rapids, Mich.: Zondervan.

———. 1990. "Gossip and Secrecy." *Sociological Analysis* 51 (2): 153–70.

Burgess, Stanley M., Gary B. McGee, and Patrick H. Alexander, eds. 1988. *Dictionary for Pentecostal and Charismatic Movements.* Grand Rapids, Mich.: Zondervan.

Burridge, Kenelm. 1969. *New Heaven, New Earth.* Oxford: Basil Blackwell.

Burton, John. 1988. "Nilotic Studies: Some Past Problems and Prospects." *Anthropos* 83: 453–68.

Byrne, James. 1971. *Threshold of God's Promise: An Introduction to the Catholic Pentecostal Movement.* Notre Dame, Ind.: Ave Maria Press.

Catherall, Gordon. 1978. "Jesuits (Society of Jesus)." In *The New International Dictionary of the Christian Church*, edited by J. D. Douglas, 531. Grand Rapids, Mich.: Regency/Zondervan.

Cecile, Sister. 1987. Personal interview by Gerard Roelofs, Antwerp, Belgium.

Cesara, Manda. 1982. *Reflections of a Woman Anthropologist*. London: Academic Press.

Chappell, Paul G. 1988. "Roberts, Granville Oral (1918–)." In *Dictionary of Pentecostal and Charismatic Movements*, edited by Stanley M. Burgess, Gary B. McGee, and Patrick H. Alexander, 759–60. Grand Rapids, Mich.: Regency/Zondervan.

"Charismatic Unity in Kansas City." 1977. *Christianity Today*. 21 (August 12): 36–37.

Chidester, David. 1992. *Religions of South Africa*. London: Routledge.

Chikane, Frank. 1988. *No Life of My Own*. Braamfontein, South Africa: Skotaville Publishers.

Cho, Paul Yonggi, with John W. Hurston. 1983. "Ministry Through Home Cell Groups." In *Korean Church Growth Explosion*, edited by Ro Bong-Rin and Marvin L. Nelson, 270–89. Seoul: Word of Life Press.

Cho, Paul Yonggi. *The Fourth Dimension*. South Plainfield, N.J.: Bridge Publishing.

———. 1984. *More Than Numbers*. Waco, Tex.: Word Books.

———. 1990. Personal interview by Karla Poewe, Virginia Beach, Va.

Choi, Syn-Duk. 1986. "A Comparative Study of Two New Religious Movements in the Republic of Korea: The Unification Church and the Full Gospel Central Church." In *New Religious Movements and Rapid Social Change*, edited by James Beckford, 113–45. Beverly Hills, Calif.: Sage Publications.

Choueiri, Youssef. 1990. *Islamic Fundamentalism*. Twayne's Themes in Right-Wing Politics and Ideology Series. Boston: Twayne.

Christenson, Larry. 1972. *A Message to the Charismatic Movement*. Minneapolis, Minn.: Bethany Fellowship.

———. 1976. *The Charismatic Renewal among Lutherans*. Minneapolis, Minn.: Lutheran Charismatic Renewal Services.

Clark, Donald N. 1986. *Christianity in Modern Korea*. New York: University Press of America.

Clark, Stephen B. 1970. *Baptized in the Spirit*. Pecos, N.M.: Dove Publishers.

———. 1971. "Charismatic Renewal in the Church." In *As the Spirit Leads Us*, edited by Kevin and Dorothy Ranaghan, 17–37. Paramus, N.J.: Paulist Press.

———. 1978. "Response to Dr. J. Massyngberde Ford." *New Covenant* 7 (April): 14–20.

Cleary, A. S. 1990. "The Myth of Mau Mau in its International Setting." *African Affairs* 89 (355): 227–45.

Clifford, James. 1986. "Introduction: Partial Truths." In *Writing Culture*, edited by Clifford and George Marcus, 1–26. Berkeley: University of California Press.

Clifford, James, and George Marcus. 1986. *Writing Culture*. Berkeley: University of California Press.

Clouse, Robert. 1978. "Pietism." In *The New International Dictionary of the Christian Church*, edited by J. D. Douglas, 780. Grand Rapids, Mich.: Regency/Zondervan.

Cohen, Anthony P. 1985. *The Symbolic Construction of Community*. Chichester and London: Ellis Horwood/Tavistock.

Cohen, David William. 1981. "Pim's Work: Some Thoughts on the Construction of Relations and Groups—the Luo of Western Kenya." Paper presented to the History of the Family in Africa Conference. School of Oriental and African Studies, London, September.

———. 1983. "The Face of Contact: A Model of A Cultural and Linguistic Frontier in Early Eastern Uganda." In *Nilotic Studies,* edited by R. Vossen and M. Bechhaus-Gerst, 339–55. Berlin: Dietrich Reimer Verlag.

———. 1988. "The Cultural Topography of a 'Bantu Borderland': Busoga, 1500–1850." *Journal of African History* 29: 57–79.

Cohen, David William, and E. S. Atieno Odhiambo. 1989. *Siaya: The Historical Anthropology of an African Landscape.* London: James Curry; Athens: Ohio University Press; Nairobi: Heinemann Kenya.

Coleman, Simon. 1959. *The Official Handbook of the Legion of Mary.* Shepherdsville, Ky.: Publishers Printing Co.

———. 1991. "Faith Which Conquers the World." *Ethnos* 56 (1–2): 9–18.

Connelly, James T. 1985. "Not in the Reputable Churches? The Reception of the Charismatic Movement in the Mainline Churches in America." In *Essays on Apostolic Themes,* edited by Paul Elbert, 184–92. Peabody, Mass.: Hendrickson.

Connerton, Paul. 1989. *How Societies Remember.* Cambridge: Cambridge University Press.

Crazzolara, J. P. 1950–1954. *The Lwoo: Parts I–III.* Museum Cobonianum, Collana di Studi Africani. Verona: Missioni Africane.

Cronje, Carel. 1987. Personal interview by Karla Poewe and Irving Hexham, Durban, South Africa.

Csordas, Thomas J. 1987. "Genre, Motive and Metaphor: Conditions for Creativity in Ritual Language." *Cultural Anthropology* 2 (4): 445–69.

———. 1990. "Embodiment as a Paradigm for Anthropology." *Ethos* 18: 5–47.

Dale, Kenneth J. 1975. *Circle of Harmony: A Case Study in Popular Japanese Buddhism.* Tokyo: Seibunsha.

DaMatta, Roberto. 1988. "Soccer: Opium for the People or Drama of Social Justice?" In *Social Change in Contemporary Brazil,* edited by Geert Banck and Kees Koonings, 125–33. Providence, R.I.: Foris.

Daneel, M. L. 1988. *Old and New in Southern Shona Independent Churches.* Gweru, Zambia: Mambo Press.

Davis, Winston. 1980. *Dojo: Magic and Exorcism in Modern Japan.* Stanford: Stanford University Press.

Dayton, Donald W. 1987. *Theological Roots of Pentecostalism.* Metuchen, N.J.: Scarecrow Press.

Dayton, Donald W., and Robert K. Johnston, eds. 1991. *The Variety of American Evangelicalism.* Knoxville: University of Tennessee Press.

De Bisschoppen van België. 1987. *Geloofsboek* (Book of Faith). Tielt, Belgium: Lannoo.

De Craemer, Willy. 1977. *Jamaa and the Church: A Bantu Movement in Zaire.* Oxford: Clarendon Press.

De Gruchy, John. 1989. Personal interview by Irving Hexham and Karla Poewe, Cape Town, South Africa.

De Haas, Mary. 1986. "Is Millenarianism Alive and Well in White South Africa?" *Religion in Southern Africa* 7 (1): 37–45.

Dempster, Murray A. 1987. "Pentecostal Social Concern and the Biblical Mandate of Social Justice." *Pneuma* 9 (2): 129–53.

———. 1991. "Cross Borders: Arguments Used by Early American Pentecostals in Support of the Global Character of Pacifism." Paper read at the Conference on Pentecostal and Charismatic Research in Europe, Kappel, Switzerland.

Deng, Francis. 1988. "Dinka Response to Christianity: The Pursuit of Well-Being in a Developing Society." In *Vernacular Christianity: Essays in the Social Anthropology of Religion Presented to Godfrey Lienhardt,* edited by Wendy James and Douglas Johnson, 157–69. New York: Lilian Barber.

de Soto, Hernando. 1989. *The Other Path: The Invisible Revolution in the Third World.* New York: Harper & Row.

de Wet, C. 1989. *The Apostolic Faith Mission in South Africa 1908–1980. A Case Study in Church Growth in a Segregated Society.* Ph.D. dissertation, Cape Town University, South Africa.

Dieter, Melvin E. 1990. "The Wesleyan/Holiness and Pentecostal Movements: Commonalities, Confrontation, and Dialogue." *Pneuma* 12 (Spring): 4–13.

Dilthey, Wilhelm. 1974. *Dilthey: Selected Writings,* edited by H. P. Rickman. Cambridge: Cambridge University Press.

Dirven, Peter J. 1970a. *The Maria Legio: The Dynamics of a Breakaway Church among the Luo in East Africa.* Ph.D dissertation, Pontificia Universitas Gregoriana, Rome.

———. 1970b. "A Protest and Challenge." *AFER. African Ecclesial Review* 12 (2): 127–33.

Dorst, John D. 1989. *The Written Suburb: An American Site, an Ethnographic Dilemma.* Philadelphia: University of Pennsylvania Press.

Droogers, André. 1990a. *Macht in zin: Een drieluik van Braziliaanse religieuze verbeelding* (Power in Meaning: A Triptych of Brazilian Religious Imagination.) Inaugural lecture, Vrije Universiteit, Amsterdam.

———. 1990b. "Power and the Construction of Religion: Levels and Modes." Paper prepared for the sixteenth congress of the International Association of the History of Religions (IAHR), Rome, 3–8 September.

———. 1991. "Visiones paradójicas sobre una religión paradójica." In *Algo más que opio: Una lectura antropológica del pentecostalismo latinoamericano y caribeño* (Paradoxical Views on a Paradoxical Religion. *In* Somewhat more than Opium: An Anthropological Reading of Latin American and Carribean Pentecostalism), edited by Barbara Boudewijnse, André Droogers, and Frans Kamsteeg, 19–41. San José, Costa Rica: DEI.

Droogers, André, and Hans Siebers. 1991. "Popular Religion and Power in Latin America." In *Popular Power in Latin American Religions,* edited by André Droogers, Gerrit Huizer, and Hans Siebers, 1–25. Nijnegen Studies in Development and Cultural Change. Vol. 6. Saarbrucken and Fort Lauderdale: Breitenbach.

Drucker, Peter F. 1957. *Landmarks of Tomorrow.* New York: Harper & Row.

———. 1985. *Innovations and Entrepreneurship.* New York: Harper & Row.

———. 1989. *The New Realities.* New York: Harper & Row.

Dulles, Avery. 1992. *Models of Revelation.* Maryknoll, N.Y.: Orbis.

Dunn, James D. G. 1984. "Models of Christian Community in the New Testament." In *Strange Gifts? A Guide to Charismatic Renewal,* edited by David Martin and Peter Mullen, 1–18. Oxford: Basil Blackwell.

Dunne, George H. 1962. *Generation of Giants.* Notre Dame, Ind.: University of Notre Dame Press.

Du Plessis, David J. 1970. *The Spirit Bade Me Go.* Plainfield, N.J.: Logos.

———. 1973. "Holy Spirit in Ecumenical Movement." *Jesus, Where Are You Taking Us? Messages from the First International Lutheran Conference on the Holy Spirit,* edited by Norris L. Wogen, 223–50. Carol Stream, Ill.: Creation House.

———. 1975. "A Pentecostal and the Ecumenical Movement." *What the Spirit is Saying to the Churches,* edited by Theodore Runyon, 91–103. New York: Hawthorn Books.

Dussel, Enrique, 1986. *Hipotesis para una historia de la teología de la América Latina* (Hypothesis for a History of Latin American Theology). Bogotá, Colombia: Ind-American Press Service.

Earhart, Byron H. 1974. "The New Religions of Korea: A Preliminary Interpretation." *Transactions of the Korea Branch of the Royal Asiatic Society* 49: 7–25.

Edgerton, Robert. 1989. *Mau Mau: An African Crucible.* New York: Free Press.

"Editorial." 1975. *Kenya History Review* 3: N.p.

Eliade, Mircea. 1963. Preface to *Sacred and Profane Beauty,* by Gerardus van der Leeuw, v–ix. Translated by David E. Green. London: Weidenfeld and Nicolson.

Elliot, Gil. 1972. *Twentieth Century Book of the Dead.* London: Penguin.

Emmert, Athanasios F. S. 1976. "Charismatic Developments in the Eastern Orthodox Church." In *Perspectives on the New Pentecostalism,* edited by Russell P. Spittler. Grand Rapids, Mich.: Baker Book House.

Engbrecht, Dennis D. 1985. "The Americanization of a Rural Immigrant Church: The General Conference Mennonites in Central Kansas, 1874–1939," 199–200. Ph.D. dissertation, University of Nebraska, Lincoln.

Erb, Peter. 1983. *Pietists: Selected Writings.* New York: Paulist Press.

Ervin, Howard M. 1968. *These Are Not Drunken As Ye Suppose.* Plainfield, N.J.: Logos.

———. 1971. *And Forbid Not to Speak With Tongues.* Plainfield, N.J.: Logos.

———. 1972. *This Which Ye See and Hear.* Plainfield, N.J.: Logos.

Evans, William I. 1946. "This River Must Flow." *Pentecostal Evangel* (3 August 1946): 2–3.

Evans-Pritchard, Edward E. 1964. *Social Anthropology and Other Essays.* New York: Free Press of Glencoe.

———. 1965. *Theories of Primitive Religion.* Oxford: Clarendon Press.

Ewart, Frank J. 1947. *The Phenomenon of Pentecost.* Houston: Herald Publishing House.

Fabian, Johannes. 1971. *Jamaa: A Charismatic Movement in Katanga.* Evanston, Ill.: Northwestern University Press.

———. 1979. "Text as Terror: Second Thoughts About Charisma." *Social Research* 46 (1): 166–203.

————. 1983. "Anthropological Approaches to Religious Movements." In *Religion, Sect and Cult*, edited by David A. Halperin, 131–62. Boston: John Wright.

————. 1985. "Religious Pluralism: An Ethnographic Approach." In *Theoretical Explorations in African Religion*, edited by W. van Binsbergen and M. Schoffeleers, 138–63. London: Kegan Paul.

————. 1991. "Charisma: Global Movement and Local Survival." Paper presented at the Conference on Global Culture: Pentecostal/Charismatic Movements Worldwide, May 9–11, University of Calgary.

————. 1993. "Jamaa: A Charismatic Movement Revisited." In *Religion in Africa: Experience and Expression*, edited by Thomas D. Blakely and Walter E. van Beek. London: James Currey.

Farah, Charles. 1981. "A Critical Analysis: The 'Roots and Fruits' of Faith-Formula Theology." *Pneuma* 3 (Spring): 3–21.

Featherstone, Mike. 1990. "Global Culture: An Introduction." In *Global Culture*, edited by Featherstone, 1–14. London: Sage.

Fernandez, James W. 1965. "Politics and Prophecy." *Practical Anthropology* 12 (2): 71–75.

————. 1975. "The Ethnic Communion: Inter-ethnic Recruitment in African Religious Movements." *Journal of African Studies* 2 (2): 131–47.

————. 1977. "The Performance of Ritual Metaphors." In *The Social Use of Metaphor: Essays on the Anthropology of Rhetoric*, edited by J. David Sapir and J. Christopher Crocker, 100–31. Philadelphia: University of Pennsylvania Press.

————. 1979. "Africanization, Europeanization, Christianization." *History of Religions* 18 (3): 284–92.

————. 1982. *Bwiti: An Ethnography of the Religious Imagination in Africa*. Princeton, N.J.: Princeton University Press.

————. 1986a. *Persuasions and Performances: The Play of Tropes in Culture.* Bloomington: Indiana University Press

————. 1986b. "The Argument of Images and the Experience of Returning to the Whole." In *The Anthropology of Experience*, edited by Victor W. Turner and Edward M. Bruner, 159–87. Urbana: University of Illinois Press.

Ferry, Anne. 1988. *The Art of Naming.* Chicago: University of Chicago Press.

Finke, Roger, and Rodney Stark. 1992. *The Churching of America, 1776–1990.* New Brunswick, N.J.: Rutgers University Press.

Fleisch, D. Paul. 1983. *Geschichte der Pfingstbewegung in Deutschland von 1900 bis 1950* (A History of Pentecostalism in Germany from 1900 to 1950). Marburg: Verlag der Francke-Buchhandlung GmbH.

Ford, J. Massyngberde. 1966. "Was Montanism a Jewish-Christian Heresy?" *Journal of Ecclesiastical History* 17 (October): 145.

————. 1970. *The Pentecostal Experience.* Paramus, N.J.: Paulist Press.

————. 1976a. *Six Pentecosts.* Pecos, N.M.: Dove Publishers.

————. 1976b. *Which Way For Catholic Pentecostals?* New York: Harper and Row.

————. 1988. "Mary and the Holy Spirit." In *Dictionary of Pentecostal and Charismatic Movements*, edited by Stanley M. Burgess, Gary B. McGee, and Patrick H. Alexander, 376–89. Grand Rapids, Mich.: Zondervan.

Fosdick, Harry Emerson. 1922 [1988]. "Shall the Fundamentalists Win? A Sermon Preached at the First Presbyterian Church, New York, 21 May 1922." Reprinted in *The Fundamentalist-Modernist Conflict: Opposing Views on Three Major Issues*, edited by Joel Carpenter. Vol. 23 of *Fundamentalism in American Religion, 1880–1950*. Hamden, Conn.: Garland.

Foucault, Michel. 1986. "Of Other Spaces." *Diacritics* 16 (1): 22–27.

Frame, Randy. 1991a. "Benny Hinn: Best-Selling Author Admits Mistakes, Vows Changes." *Christianity Today* (28 October) 35(12): 44–46.

———. 1991b. "Canadian Scholars Form Association." *Christianity Today* (19 August) 35 (9): 43, 45.

Frankl, Razelle. 1987. *Televangelism: The Marketing of Popular Religion*. Carbondale: Southern Illinois University Press.

Freud, Sigmund. 1938. *Totem and Taboo*. Harmondsworth, Eng.: Penguin.

Friedrich, Paul. 1992. "Interpretation and Vision: A Critique of Cryptopositivism." *Cultural Anthropology* 7 (2): 211–31.

Frobenius, Leo. 1933. *Kulturgeschichte Afrikas* (A Cultural History of Africa). Zürich: Phaidon Verlag.

Frodsham, Stanley H. 1928. "Disfellowshipped!" *Pentecostal Evangel* (18 August): 7.

The Fundamentals: A Testimony to the Truth. 1910–1915. Chicago: Testimony Publishing Company.

Furedi, Frank. 1989. *The Mau Mau War in Perspective*. London: James Currey; Nairobi: Heinemann Kenya; Athens: Ohio University Press.

Furley, O. W. 1972. "The Historiography of Mau Mau." In *Hadith 4*, edited by Bethwell A. Ogot, 105–33. Nairobi: EAPH.

Garlock, Ruthanne. 1981. *Benson Idahosa: Fire in his Bones*. Tulsa, Okla.: Praise Books.

Geertz, Clifford. 1973. *The Interpretation of Cultures*. New York: Basic Books.

———. 1983. *Local Knowledge*. New York: Basic Books.

———. 1986. "Making Experience, Authoring Self." In *The Anthropology of Experience*, edited by Victor M. Turner and Edward M. Bruner, 373–80. Urbana: University of Illinois Press.

———. 1988. *Works and Lives*. Stanford: Stanford University Press.

Gellner, Ernest. 1992. *Postmodernism, Reason and Religion*. London: Routledge.

Gelpi, Donald L. 1971. *Pentecostalism: A Theological Viewpoint*. Paramus, N.J.: Paulist Press.

Geraets, David. 1977. "Power in Pecos." *Catholic Charismatic* 2 (August–September): 20–23.

Gerard, Bernice. 1988. *Bernice Gerard: Today and For Life*. Burlington, Vt.: Welch.

Gerlach, Luther, and Virginia Hine. 1970. *People, Power, and Change*. Indianapolis: Bobbs-Merrill.

Giddens, Anthony. 1984. *The Constitution of Society: Outline of the Theory of Structuration*. Berkeley: University of California Press.

Gifford, Paul. 1988. *The Religious Right in Southern Africa*. Harare, Zimbabwe: Baobab Books.

———. 1989. "Theology and Right Wing Christianity." *Journal of Theology for Southern Africa*. 69 (December): 28–39.

———. 1990a. "Prosperity: A New and Foreign Element in African Christianity."
  Religion 20: 373–88.

———. 1990b. *Christianity: To Save or Enslave?* Harare, Zimbabwe: Ecumenical
  Documentation and Information Center for Southern Africa.

Glazier, Stephen, ed. 1980. *Perspectives on Pentecostalism: Case Studies from the
  Caribbean and Latin America.* New York: University Press of America.

Goff, James R., Jr. 1983. "Pentecostal Millenarianism: The Development of
  Premillennial Orthodoxy, 1909–1943." *Ozark Historical Review* 12 (Spring):
  14–24.

———. 1988. *Fields White Unto Harvest.* Fayetteville: University of Arkansas
  Press.

Goldenberg, David. 1982. "Liel—The Kenya Luo Funeral: Central Ritual in the
  Maintenance of Urban-Rural Ties." Paper presented at the Twenty-Second
  Annual Meeting of the Northeastern Anthropological Association, Princeton
  University, March 20.

Goldsworthy, David. 1982. *Tom Mboya—The Man Kenya Wanted to Forget.* New
  York: Africana Publishing.

Gordon, A. J. 1889. *Ecce Venit.* New York: Fleming H. Revell.

———. 1905. *The Holy Spirit in Missions.* London: Hodder & Stoughton.

Goulet, Jean-Guy. 1994. "Ways of Knowing: An ethnography of Dene-Tha
  Experiences." *Journal of Anthropological Research.* Forthcoming.

Grassi, Ernesto. 1980. *Rhetoric as Philosophy.* University Park: Pennsylvania State
  University Press.

Grayson, James Huntley. 1985. *Early Buddhism and Christianity in Korea: A Study
  in the Emplantation of Religion.* Leiden, The Netherlands: E. J. Brill.

———. 1989. *Korea: A Religious History.* New York: Oxford University Press.

Green, Maia. 1990. "Mau Mau Oathing Rituals and Political Ideology in Kenya:
  A Re-analysis." *Africa* 60 (1): 69–87.

Gros, Jeffrey. 1987. "Confessing the Apostolic Faith from the Perspective of the
  Pentecostal Churches." *Pneuma* 9 (1): 5–16.

Grubb, Norman. 1933 [1983]. *C. T. Studd: Cricketer and Pioneer.* Guildford, Eng.:
  Lutterworth Press.

Guerlich, Robert A. 1991. "Spiritual Warfare: Jesus, Paul and Peretti." *Pneuma* 13
  (1): 33–64.

Gustafsson, Ove. 1987. "Örnen har landat-utkast till ett forskningsproject" (The
  Eagle Has Landed: An Outline for a Research Project). *Svensk Missionstidskrift*
  75 (3): 45–59.

Hammond, Phillip E., ed. 1985. *The Sacred in a Secular Age: Toward Revision in the
  Scientific Study of Religion.* Berkeley: University of California Press.

Hampsch, John. 1988. "Can a Catholic Be a Fundamentalist?" *Chariscenter USA
  Newsletter* 13: 3–6.

Hanegraaff, Hank. 1993. *Christianity in Crisis.* Eugene, Oreg.: Harvest House.

Hannerz, Ulf. 1990. "Cosmopolitans and Locals in World Culture." In *Global
  Culture,* edited by Mike Featherstone, 237–52. London: Sage.

Harper, Michael. 1965. *As at the Beginning.* London: Fountain Trust.

———. 1971. *As at the Beginning,* revised version. Plainfield, N.J.: Logos.

———. 1979. *Three Sisters*. Wheaton, Ill.: Tyndale House.

Harrell, David Edwin. 1975. *All Things Are Possible*. Bloomington: Indiana University Press.

———, ed. 1981. *Varieties of Southern Evangelicalism*. Macon, Ga.: Mercer University Press.

———. 1985. *Oral Roberts: An American Life*. New York: Harper & Row.

Hart, Keith. 1990. "Swimming into the Human Current." *Times Higher Education Supplement* 915 (May 5): 13–14.

Hastings, Adrian. 1979a. *A History of African Christianity 1950–1975*. Cambridge: Cambridge University Press.

———. 1979b. "A Discussion Relating to the Typology of New Religious Movements in Africa." Paper presented at the international conference entitled Recent African Religious Studies: Towards an Evaluation, 11–14 December, Leiden, Afrika-Studiecentrum.

Hauman, Father Fred. 1987. Personal interview by Gerard Roelofs, Antwerp, Belgium.

Hay, Margaret Jean. 1972. *Economic Change in Luoland: Kowe, 1890–1945*. Ph.D. dissertation, University of Wisconsin.

———. 1976. "Luo Women and Economic Change During the Colonial Period." In *Women in Africa. Studies in Social and Economic Change*, edited by Nancy J. Hafkin and Edna G. Bay, 87–109. Stanford: Stanford University Press.

Hayashi, Minoru. 1988. "Learning from the Japanese New Religions." Doctor of Missiology thesis. Fuller Theology Seminary, Pasadena, California.

Hayes, Stephen. 1990. *Black Charismatic Anglicans*. Pretoria: University of South Africa.

Herring, Ralph S. 1978. "The Joluo Before 1900." Paper presented to the University of Nairobi History Seminar.

Hexham, Irving, ed. Forthcoming. *Some Prayers and Writings of the Servant of Sorrows: Thumekile Isaiah Shembe*. Calgary: University of Calgary Press.

Hexham, Irving, and Karla Poewe. 1986. *Understanding Cults and New Religions*. Grand Rapids, Mich.: Eerdmans. 159–63.

Hill, Clifford. 1989. *Prophecy Past and present*. Crowborough, Eng.: Highland Books.

Hill, Michael. 1973. *A Sociology of Religion*. London: Heinemann Educational Books.

Hill, Samuel S., Jr. 1976. "A Typology of American Restitutionism: From Frontier Revivalism and Mormonism to the Jesus Movement." *Journal of the American Academy of Religion* 44 (March): 65–76.

Hiro, Dilip. 1989. *Holy Wars: The Rise of Islamic Fundamentalism*. New York: Routledge.

Hodges, Melvin. 1953. *The Indigenous Church*. Springfield, Mo.: Gospel Publishing House.

Hogue, Wilson T. 1916. *The Holy Spirit: A Study*. Chicago: William B. Rose.

Hollenweger, Walter J. 1974. *Pentecost between Black and White. Five Case Studies on Pentecost and Politics*. Belfast: Christian Journals.

———. 1979a. *Erfahrungen der Leibhaftigkeit: Interkulturelle Theologie* (Experiences of Embodiment: Intercultural Theology). München: Chr. Kaiser Verlag.

———. 1979b. *Erfahrungen in Ephesus* (Experiences in Ephesus). München: Kaiser.

———. 1987. "Interaction between Black and White in Theological Education." *Theology* 90 (September): 341–50.

———. 1988a [1969]. *The Pentecostals*. 3d ed. Peabody, Mass.: Hendrickson.

———. 1988b. *Geist und Materie* (Spirit and Matter). München: Kaiser.

———. 1990. "The Koinonia of the Establishment." *Pneuma* 12 (2): 154–57.

———. 1991. "The Discipline of Thought and Action in Mission." *International Review of Missions* 80 (317): 91–104.

Holthaus, Stephan. 1993. *Fundamentalismus in Deutschland* (Fundamentalism in Germany*)*. Bonn: Verlag für Kultur und Wissenschaft.

Hood, Ralph W. 1985. "Mysticism." In *The Sacred in a Secular Age: Toward Revision in the Scientific Study of Religion,* edited by Phillip E. Hammond, 285–97. Berkeley: University of California Press.

Hori, Ichiro. 1968. *Folk Religion in Japan: Continuity and Change,* edited by Joseph M. Kitagawa and Alan L. Miller. Chicago: University of Chicago Press.

Horn, J. N. 1989. *From Rags to Riches.* Pretoria: University of South Africa.

Horner, Winifred B. 1988. *Rhetoric in the Classical Tradition.* New York: St. Martin's Press.

Horton, Robin. 1967. "African Traditional Thought and Western Science." *Africa* 37 (1, 2): 50–71, 155–87.

Houston, James. 1991. "Spirituality, Tradition and Culture in a Post-Modern World." Paper presented at the Conference on Global Culture: Pentecostal/ Charimatic Movements Worldwide, May 9–11, University of Calgary.

Huffman, J. A. 1920. *History of the Mennonite Brethren in Christ Church.* New Carlisle, Ohio: Bethel.

Hughes, Richard T. 1976. "From Primitive Church to Civil Religion: The Millennial Odyssey of Alexander Campbell." *Journal of the American Academy of Religion* 44 (March): 87–103.

———. 1988. "Introduction: On Recovering the Theme of Recovery." In *The American Quest for the Primitive Church,* edited by Hughes. Urbana and Chicago: University of Illinois Press.

Idahosa, Benson. 1990. Personal interview by Karla Poewe and Irving Hexham, Decatur, Ga.

Iglehart, Charles W. 1959. *A Century of Protestant Christianity in Japan.* Tokyo: Charles E. Tuttle.

Ileffe, John. 1987. *The African Poor: A History.* Cambridge: Cambridge University Press.

Irungu, James, and James Shimanyula. 1982. *The Black Prophet. A Play.* Nairobi: Kenya Literature Bureau.

Jacobs, Cindy. 1991. *Possessing the Gates of the Enemy.* Grand Rapids, Mich.: Chosen Books.

Jacquet, Constant H., Jr., and Alice M. Jones, eds. 1990. *Yearbook of American and Canadian Churches: 1991.* Nashville: Abingdon Press.

Jahr, Mary Ann. 1976. "The First Pentecostal Abbey." In *The Spirit and the Church,* edited by Ralph Martin, 261–65. Paramus, N.J.: Paulist Press.

James, Joan. 1986. *Please Talk to Me, God*. Burlington, Vt.: Welch.

———. 1990. Personal interview by Karla Poewe, Vancouver, B.C., Canada.

James, William. 1902 [1985]. *The Varieties of Religious Experience: A Study in Human Nature*. Cambridge, Mass.: Harvard University Press.

Johannesen, Stanley. 1988. "The Holy Ghost in Sunset Park." *Historical Reflections/Reflexions historiques* 15 (3): 543–77.

———. 1990. "Remembering and Observing: Modes of Interpreting Pentecostal Experience and Language." In *Continuity and Change in the Pentecostal and Charismatic Movements*, Proceedings of the Twentieth Annual Meeting, the Society for Pentecostal Studies, 8–10 November, Dallas, Texas, 11–21.

———. 1991. "Language and Experience in a Pentecostal Church: An Historical and Critical Perspective." Paper read at the Tri-University Conference, 26 January, Wilfrid Laurier University, Waterloo, Ont., Canada.

Johnson, Mark. 1987. *The Body in the Mind: The Bodily Basis of Meaning, Imagination, and Reason*. Chicago and London: University of Chicago Press.

Jones, Charles E. 1983. *A Guide to the Study of Pentecostalism*. 2 Vols. Metuchen, N.J.: Scarecrow Press.

Jorgensen, Sven-Aage, ed. 1968. *Johann Georg Hamann: Sokratische Denkwürdigkeiten*(Socratic Memoirs). Stuttgart: Philip Reclam.

Jorstad, Erling. 1974. *Bold in the Spirit*. Minneapolis, Minn.: Augsburg Publishing House.

Jules-Rosette, Bennetta. 1975. *African Apostles*. Ithaca, N.Y.: Cornell University Press.

Jung, Carl. 1938. *Psychology and Religion*. New Haven, Conn.: Yale University Press.

Kaggia, Bildad. 1975. *Roots of Freedom, 1921–1963*. Nairobi: East African Publishing House.

Kanai, Shinji. 1987. "The New Religious Situation in Japan." In *New Religious Movements and the Churches*, edited by Allan R. Brockway and J. Paul Rajashekar, 30–36. Geneva: World Council of Churches Publications.

Kang, Wi Jo. 1987. *Religion and Politics in Korea under Japanese Rule*. Lewiston, N.Y.: Edwin Mellen Press.

Kanogo, Tabitha. 1977. "Rift Valley Squatters and Mau Mau." *Kenya Historical Review* 5 (2): 243–52.

———. 1987a. *Squatters and the Roots of Mau Mau*. London, Nairobi, and Athens, Ohio: James Currey.

———. 1987b. "Kikuyu Women and the Politics of Protest: Mau Mau." In *Images of Women in Peace and War*, edited by Sharon MacDonald, Pat Holden, and Shirley Ardener, 78–99. Madison: University of Wisconsin Press.

Kariuki, J. M. 1963. *Mau Mau Detainee: The Account by a Kenyan African of his Experience in Detention Camps, 1953–1960*. London: Oxford University Press.

Keating, Karl. 1988. *Catholicism and Fundamentalism: The Attack on "Romanism" by "Bible Christians."* San Francisco: Ignatius Press.

Kelley, Dean M. 1977. *Why Conservative Churches Are Growing*. New York: Harper & Row.

Kelsey, Morton. 1978. *Discernment*. New York: Paulist Press.

———. 1981. *Tongue Speaking*. New York: Crossroad.

———. 1986. *Christianity as Psychology*. Minneapolis, Minn.: Augsburg.

Kenyatta, Jomo. 1938 [1965]. *Facing Mount Kenya*. New York: Vintage.

Kepel, Gilles. 1991. *Die Rache Gottes* (The Revenge of God). Translated from the French by Thorsten Schmidt. München: Piper.

Kerr, Daniel W. 1922. "The Basis for Our Distinctive Testimony." *Pentecostal Evangel* (2 September 1922): 4.

Kibbey, Ann. 1986. *The Interpretation of Material Shapes in Puritanism: A Study of Rhetoric, Prejudice and Violence*. Cambridge, Eng.: Cambridge University Press.

Kibuye Parish. 1971. *Kitap Wer*. N.p., n.d. [Imprimatur, J. de Reeper, Bishop of Kisumu].

Kim, Byong-Suh. 1985. "The Explosive Growth of the Korean Church Today: A Sociological Analysis." *International Review of Mission* 74 (293): 61–74.

Kim, Kwang-il. 1988. "Kut and the Treatment of Mental Disorder." In *Shamanism: The Spirit World of Korea*, edited by Chai-Shin Yu and R. Guisso, 131–61. Berkeley, Calif.: Asian Humanities Press.

Kimulu, D. N. 1967. "The Separatist Churches." *Dini na Mila, Makerere* 2 (2–3): 11–61.

Kipkorir, B. E. 1976. Review of Bildad Kaggia's *Root's of Freedom, 1921–1963. The Autobiography of Bildad Kaggia. Kenya Historical Review* 4 (1): 140–43.

———. 1977. "Mau Mau and the Politics of Transfer of Power in Kenya, 1957–1960." *Kenya Historical Review* 5 (2): 313–28.

Koepping, Klaus-Peter. 1983. *Adolf Bastian and the Psychic Unity of Mankind*. St. Lucia: University of Queensland Press.

Kohl, Karl-Heinz. 1987. *Abwehr und Verlangen* (Aversion and Desire). Frankfurt/M.: Qumran.

Kramer, Fritz. 1986. *Bronislaw Malinowski: Schriften zur Anthropologie* (Bronislaw Malinowshi: Anthropology and Text) Frankfurt/M.: Syndikat.

Kuhn, T. S. 1970. *The Structure of Scientific Revolutions*. Chicago: University of Chicago Press.

Kuzmic, Peter. 1990. "Pentecostal Ministry in a Marxist Context." *Epta Bulletin* 9 (1): 4–32.

Laan, C. V. D. 1991. *Sectarian Against His Will: Gerrit Roelof Polman and the Birth of Pentecostalism in the Netherlands*. Studies in Evangelicalism, No. 11. Metuchen, N.J., and London: The Scarecrow Press.

Laan, P. N. V. D. 1988. "The Question of Spiritual Unity: The Dutch Pentecostal Movement in Ecumenical Perspective. Ph.D. dissertation, University of Birmingham.

Lane, Ralph, Jr. 1976. "Catholic Charismatic Renewal." In *The New Religious Consciousness*, edited by Charles Y. Glock and Robert N. Bellah, 162–79. Berkeley: University of California Press.

Langham, Ian. 1981. *The Building of British Social Anthropology*. London: D. Reidel.

Latourette, Kenneth Scott. 1929 [1970]. *A History of Christian Missions in China*. New York: Paragon Book Gallery.

Laurentin, René. 1977. *Catholic Pentecostalism*. Garden City, N.Y.: Doubleday.

Lawless, Elaine. 1988. "The Night I Got the Holy Ghost. . . ." *Western Folklore* 47 (1): 1–20.

Lawrence, Bennett F. 1916. *The Apostolic Faith Restored.* St. Louis, Mo.: Gospel Publishing House.

Leach, Edmund. 1976. *Culture and Communication, the Logic by which Symbols are Connected: An Introduction to the Use of Structuralist Analysis in Social Anthropology.* Cambridge: Cambridge University Press.

Lederle, H. I. 1988. *Treasures Old and New: Interpretations of "Spirit Baptism" in the Charismatic Renewal Movement.* Peabody, Mass.: Hendrickson.

Lee, Jae Bum. 1986. "Pentecostal Type Distinctives and Korean Protestant Church Growth." Ph.D. dissertation, School of World Mission, Fuller Theological Seminary, Pasadena, California.

Lee, Robert. 1967. *A Stranger in the Land: A Study of the Church in Japan.* London: Lutterworth.

Lee, Yohan. 1985. "An Analysis of the Christian Prayer Mountain Phenomenon in Korea." Ph.D. dissertation, School of World Mission, Fuller Theological Seminary, Pasadena, California.

Lefebvre, Henri. 1971. *Everyday Life in the Modern World.* Translated by Sacha Rabinovitch. London: Allen Lane.

Lévi-Strauss, Claude. 1978. *Myth and Meaning.* London: Routledge and Kegan Paul.

Leviton, Daniel, ed. 1991. *Horrendous Death, Health, and Well-Being.* New York: Hemisphere Books.

Lewis, I. M. 1971. *Ecstatic Religion.* Harmondsworth, Eng.: Penguin.

Lienhardt, Godfrey. 1982. "The Dinka and Catholicism." In *Religious Organization and Experience,* edited by J. Davis, 81–95. A.S.A. Monograph 21. London: Academic Press.

Linn, Dennis, and Matthew Linn. 1974. *Healing of Memories.* New York: Paulist Press.

Lipps, Theodor. 1893–1897. *Raumästhetic* (Aesthetics of Space). Leipzig: J. A> Barth.

Lodge, David. 1977. *The Modes of Modern Writing: Metaphor, Metonymy, and the Typology of Modern Literature.* London: Edward Arnold.

Lonsdale, John. 1990. "Mau Maus of the Mind: Making Mau Mau and Remaking Kenya." *Journal of African History* 31: 393–421.

Lovett, L. 1988. "Black Holiness Pentecostalism," "Black Theology," and "Positive Confession Theology." In *Dictionary of Pentecostal and Charismatic Movements,* edited by Stanley M. Burgess, Gary B. McGee, and Patrick H. Alexander, 76–84, 84–86, 718–20. Grand Rapids, Mich.: Zondervan.

Luckmann, Thomas. 1990. "Shrinking Transcendence, Expanding Religion?" In *Sociological Analysis* 50 (2): 127–38.

Luhrmann, T. M. 1989. *Persuasions of the Witch's Craft.* Cambridge, Mass.: Harvard University Press.

Lyall, Leslie. 1978. "China." In *The International Dictionary of the Christian Church,* edited by J. D. Douglas, 217–18. Grand Rapids, Mich.: Regency\Zondervan.

McAlister, Robert. 1990. Personal interview by Karla Poewe and Irving Hexham, Decatur, Ga.

McAll, Kenneth. 1985. *Healing the Family Tree.* London: Sheldon Press.

————. 1990. Personal interview by Karla Poewe and Irving Hexham, Calgary, Alt., Canada.

McCauley, Ray. 1987. Interview by Karla Poewe and Irving Hexham, Johannesburg, South Africa.

McConnell, D. R. 1987. *A Different Gospel: A Historical and Biblical Analysis of the Modern Faith Movement*. Peabody, Mass.: Hendrickson.

MacDonald, W. 1982. "The Cross Versus Personal Kingdom." *Pneuma* 3 (2): 26–37.

McDonnell, Kilian. 1970. "Catholic Pentecostalism: Problems in Evaluation." *Dialog* 9 (Winter): 35–54.

————. 1973. "Statement of the Theological Basis of the Catholic Charismatic Renewal." *Worship* 47 (December): 611–20.

————. 1974. "The International Roman Catholic-Pentecostal Dialogue: The Meeting of a Structural Church and a Movement." *One in Christ* 10 (1): 4–6.

————. 1976. *Charismatic Renewal and the Churches*. New York: Seabury Press.

————, ed. 1980. *Presence, Power, Praise: Documents on the Charismatic Renewal*. Vol 1. Collegeville, Md.: Liturgical Press.

McFague, Sallie. 1983. *Metaphorical Theology: Models of God in Religious Language*. London: SCM Press.

MacGaffey, Wyatt. 1983. *Modern Kongo Prophets*. Bloomington: Indiana University Press.

————. 1986. *Religion and Society in Central Africa*. Chicago: University of Chicago Press.

McGuire, Meredith B. 1982. *Pentecostal Catholics*. Philadelphia: Temple University Press.

————. 1985. "Religion and Healing." In *The Sacred in a Secular Age: Toward Revision in the Scientific Study of Religion*, edited by Phillip E. Hammond, 268–84. Berkeley: University of California Press.

————. 1988. *Ritual Healing in Suburban America*. New Brunswick, N.J.: Rutgers University Press.

————. 1990. "Religion and the Body: Rematerializing the Human Body in the Social Sciences of Religion." *Journal for the Scientific Study of Religion* 29 (3): 283–96.

McLoughlin, William G. 1978. *Revivals, Awakenings, and Reform: An Essay on Religion and Social Change in America, 1607–1977*. Chicago: University of Chicago Press.

MacNutt, Francis, O. P. 1974. *Healing*. Notre Dame, Ind.: Ave Maria Press.

McPherson, Aimee Semple. 1923. *This is That*. Los Angeles: Echo Park Evangelistic Association.

————. 1925. "The Holy Spirit in Old Testament Types and Shadows and New Testament Power." *Bridal Call* 9 (June): 9–13, 25–28.

————. 1926. "It Was Never So Seen." *Bridal Call*. 10 (October): 24.

————. 1927a. "A Voice from Heaven." *Bridal Call* 10 (January): 15–17.

————. 1927b. "The March of Christianity." *Bridal Call* 10 (February): 5–16, 28–29.

————. 1927c. "Heavenly Gales." *Bridal Call* 11 (December): 10, 22–23.

————. 1929. "God's Pattern for a Model Revival." *Bridal Call*. 12 (February): 7–8, 30–31.

MacRobert, Ian. 1988. *The Black Roots and White Racism of Early Pentecostalism in the USA*. London: Macmillan.

Maes, Daniel. 1983. "Charismatische Vernieuwing: Een dubbele uitdaging" (Charismatic Renewal: A Second Blessing). Unpublished document.

Maillu, David G. 1988. *Our Kind of Polygamy*. Nairobi: Heinemann Kenya.

Maina wa Kinyatti. 1977. "Mau Mau: The Peak of African Nationalism in Kenya." *Kenya Historical Review* 5 (2): 287–311.

———. 1983. "Mau Mau: The Peak of African Political Organization and Struggle for Liberation in Colonial Kenya." *Ufahamu* 12 (3): 90–123.

———, ed. 1987. *Kenya's Freedom Struggle: The Dedan Kimathi Papers*. London: Zed Press.

———. 1990. *Thunder from the Mountains: Poems and Songs from the Mau Mau*. Trenton, N.J.: Africa World Press.

Malinowski, Bronislaw. 1935. *Coral Gardens and their Magic*. London: Kegan Paul.

Manney, James. 1985. "Father Michael Scanlan and the University of Steubenville." *New Covenant* 15 (September): 10–14.

Manuel, David. 1977. *Like a Mighty River*. Orleans, Mass.: Rock Harbor Press.

Marcus, George F., and Michael M. J. Fischer. 1986. *Anthropology as Cultural Critique*. Chicago: University of Chicago Press.

Marks, Vera. 1991. "Cultural Pastiches: Intertextualities in the Moncrabeau Liars' Festival Narratives." *Cultural Anthropology* 6 (2): 193–211.

Marsden, George M. 1980. *Fundamentalism and American Culture: The Shaping of Twentieth-Century Evangelicalism 1870–1925*. New York: Oxford University Press.

———. 1988. "Fundamentalism." In *Encyclopedia of the American Religious Experience: Studies of Traditions and Movements*, edited by C. H. Lippy and P. W. Williams, II:948–54. New York: Scribners.

———. 1991a. "Fundamentalism." In *The New 20th Century Encyclopedia of Religious Knowledge*, 2d edition, edited by J. D. Douglas, 346. Grand Rapids, Mich.: Baker Book House.

———. 1991b. *Understanding Fundamentalism and Evangelicalism*. Grand Rapids, Mich.: Eerdmans.

Martin, Ralph. 1974a. "David Wilkerson's Vision." *New Covenant* 3 (January): 11–12.

———. 1974b. "How Shall We Relate to Church?" In *Pentecostal Catholics*, edited by Robert Heyer, 9–16. Paramus, N.J.: Paulist Press.

———. 1978. "Parish Renewal or Covenant Community?" *New Covenant* 8 (July): 20–22.

Martin, David. 1990. *Tongues of Fire: The Explosion of Protestantism in Latin America*. Oxford: Basil Blackwell.

Marty, Martin E., and R. Scott Appleby, eds. 1991. *Fundamentalisms Observed*. The Fundamentalism Project, Vol. 1. Chicago: University of Chicago Press.

Maswanganyi, Elijah. N.d. *How You Can Be Free From Fear*. White River: Emmanuel Press.

Matta, Judith A. 1984. *The Born-Again Jesus of the Word Faith Teaching*. 2d edition. Fullerton, Calif.: Spirit of Truth Ministries.

Maxwell, Arthur. 1957. *The Bible Story*. Vol. 10. Alma Park, Grantham, Lincolnshire, Eng.: Stanborough Press.

Mazibuko, Bongani. 1987. *Education in Mission/Mission in Education: A Critical Comparative Study of Selected Approaches*. In *Studies in the Intercultural History of Christianity*, no. 47. Frankfurt/M., Berne, Paris, New York: Lang.

Mazrui, Al-Amin. 1987a. "Ideology, Theory and Revolution: Lessons from the Mau Mau." *Race and Class* 27 (4): 53–61.

———. 1987b. "Ideology, Theory and Revolution: Lessons from the Mau Mau of Kenya." *Monthly Review* 39 (4): 20–30.

Mazrui, Ali. 1967. *On Heroes and Uhuru Worship*. London: Longmans.

———. 1973. "Mau Mau: The Men, the Myth and the Moment." Foreword to *Mau Mau Twenty Years After*, edited by R. Buijtenhuijs, 7–13. The Hague: Mouton.

———. 1978. *Political Values and the Educated Class in Africa*. Berkeley and Los Angeles: University of California Press.

———. 1979. "Casualties of an Underdeveloped Class Structure: The Expulsion of Luo Workers and Asian Bourgeoisie from Uganda." In *Strangers in African Society*, edited by William Shack and Elliot Skinner, 261–78. Berkeley: University of California Press.

Mbete, Paul. 1989. Personal interview by Karla Poewe, Johannesburg, South Africa.

Mboya, Tom. 1963. *Freedom and After*. Boston: Little, Brown.

Meares, John. 1990. Personal interview by Karla Poewe and Irving Hexham, Decatur, Ga.

Meeking, Basil. 1974. "The Roman Catholic/Pentecostal Dialogue," *One in Christ* 10 (2): 106–9.

Merkel, Franz Rudolf. 1920. *G. W. von Leibniz und die China Mission* (G. W. Leibniz and the China Mission). Leipzig: Hinrichs.

Metzke, Erwin. 1967. *J. G. Hamanns Stellung in der Philosophie des 18. Jahrhunderts* (J. G. Hamanns and Eighteenth-Century Philosophy). Darmstadt: Wissenschaftliche Buchgesellschaft.

Michell, Justin. 1988. *Church Ablaze: The Hatfield Story*. London: Marshalls.

Middleton, John. 1967. "Luo." In *Encyclopaedia Britannica*. XIV:432. Chicago: William Benton.

Milingo, Emmanuel. 1984. *The World In Between*. Maryknoll, N.Y.: Orbis Books.

"The Millennium." 1906. *Apostolic Faith* 1 (September): 3.

Miller, Robert Moats. 1985. *Harry Emerson Fosdick: Preacher, Pastor, Prophet*. New York: Oxford University Press.

Miyake, Hitoshi. 1972. "Folk Religion." In *Japanese Religion*, edited by Hori Ichiro, et al., 121–43. Tokyo: Charles E. Tuttle.

Moerman, Daniel. 1979. "Anthropology of Symbolic Healing." *Current Anthropology* 20 (1): 59–80.

"Moi's Mau Mau." 1984. *Economist* 293 (December 22): 26–27.

Montague, George T. 1979. "Hermeneutics and the Teaching of Scripture." In *Scripture and the Charismatic Renewal*, edited by George Martin, 77–95. Ann Arbor, Mich.: Servant Books.

Moos, Felix. 1967. "Leadership and Organization in the Olive Tree Movement." *Transactions of the Korea Branch of the Royal Asiatic Society* 43: 12–25.

Morphew, Derek. 1989. *South Africa: The Powers Behind*. Cape Town: Struik.

———. 1989. Personal interview by Karla Poewe and Irving Hexham, Cape Town, South Africa.

Morran, Elda Susan, and Lawrence Schlemmer. 1984. *Faith for the Fearful?* Durban: Diakonia.

Morris, Brian. 1987. *Anthropological Studies of Religion*. Cambridge: Cambridge University Press.

Mueller, Susan. 1984. "Government and Opposition in Kenya, 1966–9." *Journal of Modern African Studies* 22 (3): 399–427.

Mühlmann, W. E. 1968 [1984]. *Geschichte der Anthropologie* (History of Anthropology). Wiesbaden: Aula Verlag.

Mullins, Mark R. 1989. "The Situation of Christianity in Contemporary Japanese Society." *Japan Christian Quarterly* 55 (2): 78–90.

———. 1990a. "The Transplantation of Religion in Comparative Sociological Perspective." *Japanese Religions* 16 (2): 43–62.

———. 1990b. "Japanese Pentecostalism and the World of the Dead: A Study of Cultural Adaptation in Iesu no Mitama Kyokai." *Japanese Journal of Religious Studies* 17 (4): 353–74.

———. 1991. "Perspective: Magic, Ancestors, and Indigenous Christianity." *Japan Christian Quarterly* 57 (1): 60–62.

———. 1992. "Japan's New Age and Neo-New Religions: Sociological Interpretations." In *Perspectives on the New Age*, edited by James R. Lewis and J. Gordon Melton, 232–46. Albany: State University of New York Press.

Murdoch, Iris. 1970. *The Sovereignty of Good*. London: Routledge and Kegan Paul.

Myerhoff, Barbara. 1985. *In Her Own Time*. Video. Los Angeles: Center for Visual Anthropology, University of Southern California.

Myland, D. Wesley. 1910. *The Latter Rain Covenant and Pentecostal Power*. 2d ed. Chicago: Evangel Publishing House.

Nagahara, So. 1983. "Nihon ni okeru 'karisuma sasshin undo' juyo ni tsuite no shukyo shakaigakuteki kosatsu" (The Acceptance of the Charismatic Movement in Japan: A Sociology of Religion Inquiry). M.A. thesis, Tokyo Union Theological Seminary.

Naipaul, V. S. 1991. "Our Universal Civilization." *New York Review of Books* 38 (January 31): 22–15.

Neill, Stephen, and Tom Wright. 1988. *The Interpretation of the New Testament: 1861–1986*. Oxford: Oxford University Press.

Nelson, Douglas J. 1981. *For Such a Time as This: The Story of Bishop William J. Seymour and the Azusa Street Revival*. Ph.D. dissertation, University of Birmingham.

"New Hope for the OAU of Churches." 1984. *Viva* October: 9.

Newsinger, John. 1985. "Mau Mau—30 Years Later." *Monthly Review* 37 (1): 12–21.

———. 1990. "A Counter-Insurgency Tale: Kitson in Kenya." *Race and Class* 31 (4): 61–72.

New Wine 9 (October 1977).

Ng'anga, D. Mukaru. 1977. "Mau Mau, Loyalists and Politics in Murang'a, 1952–1970." *Kenya Historical Review* 5 (2): 365–84.

Ngugi wa Thiong'o. 1983. *The Barrel of a Pen: Resistance to Repression in Neo-Colonial Kenya*. Trenton, N.J.: Africa World Press.

———. 1987a. Foreword to *Kenya's Freedom Struggle. The Dedan Kimathi Papers*, edited by Maina wa Kinyatti, xiii–xvi. London and N.J.: Zed Books.

———. 1987b. *Matigari*. London: Heinemann.

Ngugi wa Thiong'o and Micere Mugo. 1977. *The Trial of Dedan Kimathi*. London: Heinemann.

Nichols, Gladwyn N. 1926. "A Dangerous Voyage." *Bridal Call* 10 (October): 21–23.

Nipper, Leonard. 1970. "Full Gospel Work in Japan." In *Japan in Review* (Japan Harvest Anthology), edited by Arthur Reynolds, 99–100. Tokyo: Japan Evangelical Missionary Association.

Nishiyama, Shigeru. 1986. "Shin shin shukyo no shutsugen" (The Appearance of the 'New' Religions). In *Nihon no shakaigaku: shukyo* (Japanese Sociology: Religion), edited by Jun Miyake, Komoto Mitsugu, and Shigeru Nishiyama, 198–204. Readings, vol. 19. Tokyo: University of Tokyo Press.

———. 1991. "Youth, Deprivation, and New Religions: A Sociological Perspective." Translated by Mark R. Mullins. *Japan Christian Quarterly* 57 (1): 4–11.

Nussbaum, Martha C. 1986. *The Fragility of Goodness: Luck and Ethics in Greek Tragedy and Philosophy*. Cambridge: Cambridge University Press.

Obudho, Robert A. 1974. "Urbanization and Regional Planning in Western Kenya." In *Urbanization and Regional Planning in Africa*, edited by Salal El-Shakhs and Robert Obudho, 161–76. New York: Praeger.

Ochieng', William R. 1975. *The First Word: Essays on Kenya History*. Nairobi: East Africa Literature Bureau.

———. 1976. Review of *Roots of Freedom, 1921–1963: The Autobiography of Bildad Kaggia. Kenya Historical Review* 4 (1): 135–40.

———. 1977. *The Second Word: More Essays on Kenya History*. Nairobi: East African Literature Bureau.

———. 1985. "Autobiography in Kenyan History." *Ufahamu* 14 (2): 80–101.

———. 1989. "Migrations and the Emergence of Societies." In *Themes in Kenyan History*, edited by Ochieng', 1–13. Athens: Ohio University Press.

O'Connor, Edward. 1971. *The Pentecostal Movement in the Catholic Church*. Notre Dame, Ind.: Ave Maria Press.

———. 1978. *Pope Paul and the Spirit*. Notre Dame, Ind.: Ave Maria Press.

Odinga, Oginga. 1954. *Dweche Ariyo e India*. Kisumu, Kenya: Ramogi Press.

———. 1967. *Not Yet Uhuru: The Autobiography of Oginga Odingaba*. New York: Hill and Wang.

Odingo, Richard. 1971. "Human Migrations in East and Central Africa: The Case of the Nilotics." *Past and Present* 1 (4): 3–9.

O'Donnell, Christopher. 1983. "Nieuwe Charismatische Bewegingen in Noord-Amerika en Europa" (New Charismatic Movements in North America and Europe). *Concilium* 19 (1): 51–59.

Ogot, Bethwell A. 1967. *History of the Southern Luo. Volume 1: Migration and Settlement 1500–1900*. Nairobi: East African Publishing House.

———. 1972. "Revolt of the Elders: An Anatomy of the Loyalist Crowd in the Mau Mau Uprising 1952–1956." In *Hadith* 4, edited by Ogot, 134–48. Nairobi: EAPH.

―――. 1974. "A Community of Their Own: A Study of the Search for a New Order by the Maria Legio of Africa Church." Paper presented at the Historical Study of East African Religion, Limuru, Kenya, June.

―――. 1976. "Towards a History of Kenya." *Kenya Historical Review* 4 (1): 1–9.

―――. 1977a. "Introduction." *Kenya Historical Review* 5 (2): 169–72.

―――. 1977b. "Politics, Culture and Music in Central Kenya: A Study of Mau Mau Hymns, 1951–1956." *Kenya Historical Review* 5 (2): 275–86.

―――. 1981. *Historical Dictionary of Kenya*. African Historical Dictionaries, No. 29. Metuchen, N.J.: The Scarecrow Press.

―――. 1983. "Language, Culture and Ethnicity in the Precolonial History of Africa." In *Nilotic Studies*, edited by R. Vossen and M. Bechhaus-Gerst, 23–32. Berlin: Dietrich Reimer Verlag.

Ogot, Bethwell A., and Tiyambe Zeleza. 1988. "Kenya: The Road to Independence And After." In *Decolonization and African Independence*, edited by Paul Gifford and W. R. Louis, 401–26. New Haven, Conn.: Yale University Press.

Okoth, P. Godfrey. 1985. "Autobiography in Kenyan History: A Critique." *Ufamhamu* 14 (2): 102–12.

Olivier de Sardan, Jean-Pierre. 1992. "Occultism and the Ethnographic 'I': The Exoticizing of Magic from Durkheim to 'Postmodern' Anthropology." *Critique of Anthropology* 12 (1): 5–25.

Oloo Aringo, Peter. 1969. *History of Settlement: An Example of Luo Clans in Alego, 1800–1918*. B.A. graduation essay, University of Nairobi.

Olson, William G. 1974. *The Charismatic Church*. Minneapolis, Minn.: Bethany Fellowship.

O'Meara, Thomas F. 1990. *Fundamentalism: A Catholic Perspective*. Mahwah, N.J.: Paulist Press.

Ong, Walter. 1982. *Orality and Literacy*. London: Methuen

Onyango-Ogutu, Benedict, and A. A. Roscoe. 1974. *Keep My Words: Luo Oral Literature*. Nairobi: East African Publishing House.

OAIC (Organization of African Independent Churches). 1982. *OAIC 2nd Conference 6–13th November, Nairobi*. Nairobi: Kenya.

Oosthuizen, G. C., et al. 1988. *Afro-Christian Religion and Healing in Southern Africa*. Lewiston, N.Y.: Edwin Mellen Press.

Ortner, Sherry B. 1984. "Theory in Anthropology Since the Sixties." *Comparative Studies in Society and History* 26 (1): 126–66.

Orwig, A. W. 1916. "My First Visit to the Azuzu [*sic*] Street Pentecostal Mission, Los Angeles, California." *The Weekly Evangel* March 18: 4–7.

―――. 1989. *High Religion: A Cultural and Political History of Sherpa Buddhism*. Princeton, N.J.: Princeton University Press.

Otto, Rudolf. 1923. *The Idea of the Holy*. London: Oxford University Press.

Overing, Joanna. 1987. "Translation as a Creative Process: The Power of the Name." In *Comparative Anthropology*, edited by Ladislav Holy, 70–87. Oxford: Basil Blackwell.

Pala Okeyo, Achola. 1980. "Daughters of the Lake and Rivers: Colonization and Land Rights of Luo Women in Kenya." In *Women and Colonization: Anthropological Perspectives*, edited by Mona Etienne and Eleanor Leacock, 186–213. New York: Praeger.

Palma, Marta. 1985. "A Pentecostal Church in the Conciliar Movement." *Ecumenical Review* 37 (2): 223–29.

Parham, Charles. 1902 [1985]. *The Sermons of Charles Parham*, edited by Donald W. Dayton. New York: Garland.

Parham, Sarah E. 1930. *The Life of Charles F. Parham, Founder of the Apostolic Faith Movement*. Joplin, Mo.: Tri-State Printing Co.

Parkin, David. 1978. *The Cultural Definition of Political Response: Lineal Destiny Among the Luo*. London: Academic Press.

———, ed. 1982. *Semantic Anthropology*. London: Academic Press.

Paulk, Clariece and Don. 1990. Personal interview by Karla Poewe, Decatur, Ga.

Paulk, Earl. 1989. Personal interview by Karla Poewe, Decatur, Ga.

Perrin Jassy, Marie-France. 1966. "Religious Situation in North Mara District—Tanzania." Report to the Maryknoll Fathers Mission, December.

———. 1973 [1970]. *Basic Community in the African Churches*. Translated by Jeanne Marie Lyons. Maryknoll, N.Y.: Orbis Books.

Pierson, Arthur. 1984. *George Müller of Bristol*. Grand Rapids, Mich.: Zondervan.

Plowman, Edward. 1975. "The Deepening Rift in the Charismatic Movement." *Christianity Today* 20 (10 October): 52, 53–55.

Plüss, Jean-Daniel. 1988. *Therapeutic and Prophetic Narratives in Worship: A Hermeneutic Study of Testimonies and Visions. Their Potential Significance for Christian Worship and Secular Society*. Frankfurt/M.: Peter Lang.

Poewe, Karla. 1985. *The Namibian Herero: A History of Their Psychosocial Disintegration and Survival*. Lewiston, N.Y: Edwin Mellen Press.

———. 1988. "Links and Parallels between Black and White Charismatic Churches in South Africa and the States." *Pneuma* 10 (2): 141–58.

———. 1989. "On the Metonymic Structure of Religious Experiences: The Example of Charismatic Christianity." *Cultural Dynamics* 2 (4): 361–80.

———. 1992. "Max Weber and Charismatic Christianity." In *Twentieth-Century World Religious Movements in Neo-Weberian Perspective*, edited by William H. Swatos, 159–73. Lewiston, N.Y.: Edwin Mellen Press.

———. 1993a. *South Africa: Existential Themes and Religious Solutions*. In preparation.

———. 1993b. "Theologies of Black South Africans and the Rhetoric of Peace Versus Violence." *Canadian Journal of African Studies* 27 (1): 43–65.

Polanyi, Michael. 1964a. *Science, Faith, and Society*. Chicago: University of Chicago Press.

———. 1964b. *Personal Knowledge: Towards a Postcritical Philosophy*. New York: Harper Torchbooks.

Poloma, Margaret. 1989. *The Assemblies of God at the Crossroads*. Knoxville: University of Tennessee Press.

Potash, Betty. 1978. "Some Aspects of Martial Stability in a Rural Luo Community." *Africa* 48 (4): 380–96.

Pratt, Thomas. 1991. "The Need to Dialogue: A Review of the Debate on the Controversy of Signs, Wonders, Miracles and Spiritual Warfare Raised in the Literature of the Third Wave Movement." *Pneuma* 13 (1): 7–32.

Prince, Derek. 1976. *Discipleship Shepherding Commitment*. N.p.: privately published.

Pullinger, Jackie. 1980. *Chasing the Dragon*. London: Hodder and Stoughton.

Pulkingham, W. Graham. 1972. *Gathered for Power*. New York: Morehouse-Barlow.

———. 1973. *They Left Their Nets*. New York: Morehouse-Barlow.

Quebedeaux, Richard. 1983. *The New Charismatics II*. San Francisco: Harper & Row.

Rabinow, Paul. 1986. "Representations Are Social Facts: Modernity and Post-Modernity in Anthropology." In *Writing Culture*, edited by James Clifford and George Marcus, 234–61. Berkeley: University of California Press.

Radin, Paul. 1957. *Primitive Religion: Its Nature and Origin*. New York: Dover.

Ranaghan, Kevin M. 1971. "Catholics and Pentecostals Meet in the Spirit." In *As the Spirit Leads Us*, edited by Ranaghan and Dorothy Ranaghan, 114–25. Paramus, N.J.: Paulist Press.

———. 1973a. "The Liturgical Renewal at Oral Roberts University." *Studia Liturgica* 9 (3): 122–36.

———. 1973b. *The Lord, the Spirit, and the Church*. Notre Dame, Ind.: Charismatic Renewal Services.

Ranaghan, Kevin M., and Dorothy Ranaghan. 1969. *Catholic Pentecostals*. Paramus, N.J.: Paulist Press.

Randall, Claire. 1987. "The Importance of the Pentecostal and Holiness Churches in the Ecumenical Movement." *Pneuma* 9 (1): 50–60.

Randall, John. 1973. *In God's Providence*. Plainfield, N.J.: Logos International.

Ranger, Terence O. 1985. *Peasant Consciousness and Guerilla War in Zimbabwe: A Comparative Study*. London: James Currey.

———. 1986. "Religious Movements and Politics in Sub-Saharan Africa." *African Studies Review* 29 (2): 1–69.

Rao, B. Narahari. 1988. "Science: Search for Truths, or Way of Doing?" *Cultural Dynamics* 1 (3): 336–58.

Reed, D. A. 1988. "Oneness Pentecostalism." In *Dictionary of Pentecostal and Charismatic Movements*, edited by Stanley M. Burgess, Gary B. McGee, and Patrick H. Alexander, 644–51. Grand Rapids, Mich.: Zondervan.

Reichel, Jorn. 1969. *Dichtungstheorie und Sprache bei Zinzendorf*. (On the Poetic Theory and Language of Zinzendorf). Bad Homburg: Gehlen.

Report of the General Synod of the Presbyterian Church of Southern Africa. 1986. The Presbyterian Church, Johannesburg.

"Report of the Tenth Annual Convention of the World's Christian Fundamentalist Association: Chicago, 13–20 May." 1928. *Christian Fundamentalist* 12 (1 June): 3–10.

Rhee, Kang Hun. 1989. *Nihon issenman kyurei wa kano da* (The Salvation of Ten Million Japanese Souls is Possible). Tokyo: Division of Mission of the Tokyo Full Gospel Church.

Richardson, Herbert W. 1967. *Toward an American Theology*. New York: Harper & Row.

Richter, D. Julius. 1924. *Geschichte der Berliner Missionsgesellschaft 1824–1924* (History of the Berlin Mission Society 1824–1924). Berlin: Verlag der Buchhandlung der Berliner ev. Missionsgesellschaft.

Riss, Richard. 1987. *Latter Rain*. Etobicoke, Ont., Canada: Honeycomb Visual Productions.

Robeck, C. M. 1970. "Specks and Logs: Catholics and Pentecostals." *Pneuma* 12 (2): 77–83.

———. 1982. "Signs, Wonders, Warfare and Witness." *Pneuma* 3 (2): 1–5.

———. 1987. "David Du Plessis and the Challenge of Dialogue." *Pneuma* 9 (1): 1–4.

———. 1988. "Pentecostal World Conference." In *Dictionary of Pentecostal and Charismatic Movements*, edited by Stanley M. Burgess, Gary B. McGee, and Patrick H. Alexander, 707–10. Grand Rapids, Mich.: Regency/Zondervan.

Roebert, Ed. 1987. 1989. Personal interviews by Karla Poewe and Irving Hexham, Pretoria, South Africa.

Roelofs, Gerard. 1990. "Woorden van Kennis: Gebedsgenezing bij Charismatische Katholieken" (Words of Knowledge: Faith Healing of Charismatic Catholics). In *Medische Antropologie* (Medical Anthropology), 2:195–209.

Roh, Raymond V. 1972. *The Pentecostal Movement and Church Unity*. Pecos, N.M.: Dove Publications.

Rollman, Hans. 1991. "From Yankee Failure to Newfie Success: Indigenization and Cultural Participation of the Newfoundland Pentecostal Movement." Paper for the Conference on Global Culture: Pentecostal/Charimatic Movements Worldwide, University of Calgary, May 9–11.

Rosaldo, Renato. 1986. "From the Door of His Tent." In *Writing Culture*, edited by James Clifford and George Marcus, 77–97. Berkeley: University of California Press.

———. 1989. *Culture and Truth. The Remaking of Social Analysis*. Boston: Beacon.

Rosberg, Carl, and John Nottingham. 1970. *The Myth of "Mau Mau" Nationalism in Kenya*. New York: World.

Ross, Thomas, and Adolf Hampel. 1992. *Gott in Russland: Ein Bericht* (God in Russia: A Report). München: Carl Hanser Verlag.

Roszak, Theodore. 1981. "In Search of the Miraculous." *Harper's* 262 (January):54–62.

Rothkug, Lionel. 1980. *Religious Practices and Collective Perceptions: Hidden Homologies in the Renaissance and Reformation*. Waterloo, Ont., Canada: *Historical Reflections/Reflexions historiques* vol. 7.

Ruether, Rosemary R. 1989. "Christian Zionism is a Heresy." *Journal of Theology for Southern Africa* 69 (December): 60–64.

Rusch, William G. 1987. "The Theology of the Holy Spirit and the Pentecostal Churches in the Ecumenical Movement." *Pneuma* 9 (1): 17–30.

Ryu, Tonshik. 1987. *Kankoku no Kirisutokyo* (Korea's Christianity). Tokyo: University of Tokyo Press.

Sahlins, Marshall. 1985. *Islands of History*. London and New York: Tavistock.

Samarin, William J. 1972a. "Tongues of Men and Angels: The Religious Language of Pentecostalism." New York: Macmillan.

———. 1972b. "Language in Religion and the Study of Religion." *Linguistica Biblica* 20: 18–19.

———. 1976. "The Language of Religion." In *Language in Religious Practice*, edited by Samarin, 3–13. Rowley, Mass.: Newbury House Publishers.

Sandeen, Ernest. 1974. "Millennialism." In *The Rise of Adventism*, edited by Edwin S. Gaustad, 104–18. New York: Harper and Row.

Sandidge, J. L. 1976. *The Origin and Development of the Catholic Charismatic Movement in Belgium*. M.A. thesis, Katholieke Universiteit Leuven.

———. 1985. "Roman Catholic/Pentecostal Dialogue: A Contribution to Christian Unity." *Pneuma* 7 (Spring): 41–60.

Sandor, Andras. 1986. "Metaphor and Belief." *Journal of Anthropological Research* 42 (2): 101–22.

Sapir, J. David. 1977. "The Anatomy of Metaphor." In *The Social Use of Metaphor: Essays on the Anthropology of Rhetoric*, edited by Sapir and J. Christopher Crocker, 3–32. Philadelphia: University of Pennsylvania Press.

Schaeffer, Edith. 1969. *L'Abri*. Wheaton, Ill.: Tyndale House.

———. 1981. *The Tapestry*. Waco, Tex.: Word Books.

Schäfer, Heinrich. 1989. "Dualistische Religion aus gesellschaftlichen Gegensätzen: gesellschaftliche Krise und religiöse Nachfrage im Protestantismus Mittelamerikas" (Religious Dualism and Social Opposition. . .). *Wege Zum Menschen* (Ways Toward Humanity) 41 (2): 52–70.

———. 1990. "...Und Erlöse Uns Von Den Bösen" (. . . And Save Me from Evil). In *Gottes einzige Antwort* (God's Only Answer) edited by Uwe Birnstein. Ubstadt-Weiher: Hammer.

Schmidt, Wilhelm P. 1913. "Die Uroffenbarung als Anfang der Offenbarungen Gottes" (Primitive Revelation . . .). In *Religion, Christentum, Kirche* (Religion, Christianity, Church), edited by Gerhard Esser and Joseph Mausbach, 481–636. Kempten: Verlag der Jos. Kösel'schen Buchhandlung.

———. 1923. *Menschheitswege zum Gotterkennen* (Ways Toward Knowing God). München: Kösel und Pustet.

———. 1931. *The Origin and Growth of Religion*. London: Methuen.

Schwartz, Nancy L. 1989a. "World Without End: The Meanings and Movements in the History, Narratives, and 'Tongue-Speech' of Legio Maria of African Church Mission Among Luo of Kenya." Ph.D. dissertation, Princeton University.

———. 1989b. "Legio and Spirit: Intentionality, Illocutions, and Power in the 'Speaking in Tongues' of Legio Maria of African Church Mission." Workshop on Anthropology and Philosophy, Smithsonian Institution, April 18–19.

———. 1990. "Words on the Wind: Some Uses of Oral Literature Narratives and Proverbs by Legio Maria of African Church Mission among Kenya Luo." Twenty-first Annual Conference on African Linguistics, 13 April.

Scupin, Raymond. 1992. *Cultural Anthropology: A Global Perspective*. Englewood Cliffs, N.J.: Prentice Hall.

Seidenberg, Dana. 1983. *Uhuru and the Kenyan Indians: The Role of a Minority Community in Kenya Politics, 1939–1963*. New Dehli: Vitas Publishing House.

Sellers, Ian. 1978. "Leibniz, Gottfried Wilhelm (1646–1716)." In *The New International Dictionary of the Christian Church*, edited by J. D. Douglas, 589. Grand Rapids, Mich.: Zondervan.

Seymour, William J. 1907. "Behold the Bridegroom Cometh." *Apostolic Faith* 1 (January 1907): 2.

Shack, William. 1979. Foreword to *African Christianity: Patterns of Religious Continuity*, edited by George Bond, Walton Johnson, and Sheila Walker, xi–xvi. New York: Academic Press.

Shakarian, Demos. 1989. Personal interview by Karla Poewe, Calgary, Alt., Canada.

Shantz, Ward M. 1977. *A History of Bethany Missionary Church, 1877–1977.* Kitchener, Ont., Canada: Bethany Missionary Church.

Shembe, Londa. 1987. Personal interview by Karla Poewe, Ekuphakameni, South Africa.

Sheppard, Gerald T. 1984. "Pentecostals and the Hermeneutics of Dispensationalism: The Anatomy of an Uneasy Relationship." *Pneuma* 6 (2): 5–33.

Sherrill, John. 1965. *They Speak with Other Tongues.* New York: Pyramid-McGraw Hill.

Shils, Edward. 1981. *Tradition.* Chicago: University of Chicago Press.

Shimanyula, James Bandi. 1978. *Elijah Masinde and the Dini ya Musambwa.* Nairobi: Transafrica Publications.

Shipton, Parker. 1987. *Bitter Money: Cultural Economy and Some African Meanings of Forbidden Commodities.* American Ethnological Society Monograph Series, Number 1. Washington, D.C.: American Anthropological Society.

Shore, Bradd. 1991. "Twice-Born, Once Conceived: Meaning Construction and Cultural Cognition." *American Anthropologist* 93 (1): 9–27.

Shorten, Richard. 1987a. *The Legion of Christ's Witnesses.* Cape Town: Center for African Studies, University of Cape Town.

———. 1987b. "An Anglican Renewal Movement in Relation to its Zulu Context." *Journal of Theology for Southern Africa* 58 (March): 32–41.

Shorter, Alyward. 1985. *Jesus and the Witchdoctor: An Approach to Healing and Wholeness.* Maryknoll, N.Y.: Orbis Books.

Sisson, Elizabeth. N.d [ca. 1918]. *A Sign People.* Springfield, Mo.: Gospel Publishing House.

Siu, Helen. 1990. *Furrows, Peasants, Intellectuals and the State.* Stanford: Stanford University Press.

Slosser, Bob. 1979. *Miracle in Darien.* Plainfield, N.J.: Logos International.

Smith, Uriah. 1946. *The Prophecies of Daniel and the Revelation.* Nashville: Southern Publishing Association.

Snyder, Arnold. 1991. "Oral Dimensions of the Reformation in St. Gall." Paper read at the Anabaptist Colloquium, Conrad Grebel College, Waterloo, Ont., Canada, 19 April.

Son, Bong-Ho. 1983. "Some Dangers of Rapid Growth." In *Korean Church Growth Explosion*, edited by Ro Bong-Rin and Marlin L. Nelson, 337–41. Seoul: Word of Life Press.

Soskice, Janet Martin. 1985. *Metaphor and Religious Language.* Oxford: Clarendon Press.

Southall, Aidan. 1952. *Lineage Formation Among the Luo.* International African Institute, Memorandum 26. London: Oxford University Press.

———. 1970. "The Illusion of Tribe." *Journal of Asian and African Studies* 5 (1-2): 28–50.

———. 1971. "Cross-Cultural Meanings and Multilingualism." In *Language Use and Social Change. Problems of Multi-lingualism with Special Reference to Eastern Africa,* edited by W. H. Whiteley, 376–96. London: Oxford University Press for International Africa Institute.

———. 1986. "The Illusion of Nath Agnation." *Ethnology* 25: 1–20.

Spaetzel, Roy. 1974. *History of the Kitchener Gospel Temple 1909–1974.* Kitchener, Ont., Canada: KGT.

Spencer, John. 1977. "Kau and Mau Mau: Some Connections." *Kenya Historical Review* 5 (2): 201–24.

Spittler, Russell P. 1983a. "Suggested Areas for Further Research in Pentecostal Studies." *Pneuma* 5 (1): 39–57.

———. 1983b. "Bat Mitzvah for Azusa Street: Features, Fractures, and Futures of a Renewal Movement Come of Age." *Theology News and Notes* (Fuller Seminary Alumni Publication) 1: 13–35.

———. 1988. "Du Plessis, David Johannes (1905–87)." In *Dictionary of Pentecostal and Charismatic Movements,* edited by Stanley M. Burgess, Gary B. McGee, and Patrick H. Alexander, 250–54. Grand Rapids, Mich.: Zondervan.

———. 1991. "Theological Style Among Pentecostals and Charismatics." In *Doing Theology in Today's World: Essays in Honor of Kenneth S. Kantzer,* edited by John D. Woodbridge and Thomas Edward McComiskey, 291–318. Grand Rapids, Mich.: Eerdmans.

Spong, John Shelby. 1991. *Rescuing the Bible from Fundamentalism: A Bishop Rethinks the Meaning of Scripture.* San Francisco: Harper Collins.

Stamp, Patricia. 1983. "Kenya's Year of Discontent." *Current History* 482 (March 1983): 102–4, 126.

Stark, Rodney, and William Sims Bainbridge. 1985. *The Future of Religion: Secularization, Revival and Cult Formation.* Berkeley: University of California Press.

Steele, Ron. 1986. *Reinhard Bonnke: Plundering Hell and Populating Heaven.* Chichester: Sovereign World.

Steinecke, O. 1902. *Zinzendorf und der Katholizismus* (Zinzendorf and Catholicism). Halle-A.S.: R. Mühlmann.

Stocking, George. 1987. *Victorian Anthropology.* New York: Free Press.

Stoeffler, F. Ernest. 1971. *The Rise of Evangelical Pietism.* Leiden, The Netherlands: E. J. Brill.

———. 1973. *German Pietism during the Eighteenth Century.* Leiden, The Netherlands: E. J. Brill.

Stoll, David. 1990a. *Is Latin America Turning Protestant? The Politics of Evangelical Growth.* Berkeley: University of California Press.

———. 1990b. "A Protestant Reformation in Latin America?" *Christian Century* 107 (2): 44–48.

Stoller, Paul, and Cheryl Olkes. 1987. *In Sorcery's Shadow.* Chicago: University of Chicago Press.

Stoneham, C. T. N.d. *Mau Mau.* Museum Press.

Storms, Everek Richard. 1958. *History of the United Missionary Church.* Elkart, Ind.: Bethel.

Suenens, Léon Joseph. 1974. *A New Pentecost?* New York: Seabury Press.

Suh, David Kwang-Sun. 1985. "Forty Years of Korean Protestant Churches: 1945–1985." *Korea and World Affairs: A Quarterly Review* 9 (4): 788–817.

————. 1991. *The Korean Minjung in Christ.* Hong Kong: Christian Conference of Asia.

Sundkler, Bengt. 1961. *Bantu Prophets in South Africa.* London: Oxford University Press.

————. 1976. *Zulu Zion and Some Swazi Zionists.* London: Oxford University Press.

Swanson, Tod. N.d. Unpublished paper on conversion among the Quechua.

Swyngedouw, Jan. 1988. "The Awakening of a Local Church: Japanese Catholicism in Tension Between Particularistic and Universal Values." In *World Catholicism in Transition,* edited by Thomas M. Gannon, 379–92. New York: Macmillan.

Synan, Vinson. 1971. *The Holiness-Pentecostal Movement in the United States.* Grand Rapids, Mich.: Eerdmans.

————, ed. 1975. *Aspects of Pentecostal-Charismatic Origins.* Plainfield, N.J.: Logos International.

————. 1976. "Reconciling the Charismatics." *Christianity Today* 20 (9 April): 46.

————. 1984. *In The Latter Days.* Ann Arbor, Mich.: Servant Books.

————. 1988. "W. J. Seymour." In *Dictionary for Pentecostal and Charismatic Movements,* edited by Stanley M. Burgess, Gary B. McGee, and Patrick H. Alexander, 778–80. Grand Rapids, Mich.: Zondervan.

Taylor, George F. 1907 [1985]. *The Spirit and the Bride.* Falcon, N.C.: Falcon Printing Co.; reprinted, with two other documents, under the title *Three Early Pentecostal Tracts,* edited by Donald W. Dayton. New York: Garland.

Taylor, Howard. 1911 [1943]. *Hudson Taylor in Early Years.* London: China Inland Mission.

Tempels, Placide. 1959. *Bantu Philosophy.* Paris: Présence Africaine.

ter Haar, Gerrie. 1987. "Religion and Healing: The Case of Milingo." *Social Compass* 34 (4): 475–93.

Teshima, Ikuro. 1984. *Nihon Minzoku to Genshi Fukuin* (The Japanese People and the Original Gospel). Tokyo: Kirisuto Seisho Juku.

Tezuka, Masaaki. 1989. *Kirisutokyo no daisan no nami—karisuma undo to wa nani ka* (The Third Wave of Christianity: What is the Charismatic Movement). Tokyo: Kirisuto Shinbunsha.

Thiel, Josef Franz. 1984. *Religionsethnologie.* Berlin: Dietrich Reimer Verlag.

Throup, David. 1987. *Economic and Social Origins of Mau Mau, 1945–1953.* Athens: Ohio University Press.

Tinney, J. 1978. "William J. Seymour: Father of Modern-day Pentecostalism." In *Black Apostles at Home and Abroad,* edited by David W. Wills and Richard Newman. Boston: G. K. Hall.

Tomlinson, A. J. 1910. "More About the Church." *Evening Light and Church of God Evangel* 1 (July 1, 1910): 1–2.

Torrance, Thomas F. 1989. *The Christian Frame of Mind.* Colorado Springs, Colo.: Helmers & Howard.

Trinh, Minh-ha T. 1989. *Woman, Native, Other.* Bloomington: Indiana University Press.

Trollinger, Jr., William V. 1991. *God's Empire: William Bell Riley and Midwestern Fundamentalism*. Madison: University of Wisconsin Press.

Turner, Harold W. 1974. "Maria Legio." *Encyclopaedia Britannica. Micropaedia* VI:617.

———. 1979. *Religious Innovation in Africa. Collected Essays on New Religious Movements*. Boston: G. K. Hall.

———. 1984a. "Maria Legio." In *The Penguin Dictionary of Religions*, edited by John R. Hinnels. Harmondsworth, Eng.: Penguin.

———. 1984b. "Maria Legio." In *The Facts on File Dictionary of Religions*, edited by John R. Hinnels. New York: Facts on File.

Turner, Victor. 1967. *The Forest of Symbols*. Ithaca, N.Y.: Cornell University Press.

———. 1974. *The Ritual Process*. Harmondsworth, Eng.: Penguin.

———. 1986. "Dewey, Dilthey, and Drama: An Essay in the Anthropology of Experience." In *The Anthropology of Experience*, edited by Turner and Edward M. Bruner, 33–44. Urbana: University of Illinois Press.

Tydings, Judith. 1977. *Gathering a People: Catholic Saints in Charismatic Perspective*. Plainfield, N.J.: Logos.

Tylor, Edward Burnett. 1871. *Primitive Culture: Researches into the Development of Mythology, Philosophy, Religion, Language, Art and Custom*. London: J. Murray.

Unger, Rudolf. 1968. *Hamann Und Die Aufklärung* (Hamann and the Enlightment). Tübingen: Max Niemeyer Verlag.

van der Heyden, Ulrich. 1991. "Alexander Merenskys Beitrag zur ethnographischen und historischen Erforschung der Völkerschaften Südafrikas" (A. M.'s Contribution . . .). In *Ethnographische-Archäologische Zeitschrift* 32: 263–68.

van der Leeuw, Gerardus. 1963. *Sacred and Profane Beauty*. London: Weidenfeld and Nicolson.

Vanvelderen, Marlin. 1991. "Pentecostal World Conference." In *Dictionary of the Ecumenical Movement*, edited by Nicholas Lossky, 792. Geneva: World Council of Churches.

Venter, Bushy. 1989. Personal interview by Karla Poewe, Johannesburg, South Africa.

Verryn, Trevor. 1983. *Rich Christian, Poor Christian: An Appraisal of Rhema Teachings*. Pretoria: Ecumenical Research Unit.

Vickers, Brian. 1989. *In Defense of Rhetoric*. Oxford: Clarendon Press.

Villafane, Elvin. 1990. "A Pentecostal Call to Social Spirituality." Paper read at the Conference of the Society for Pentecostal Studies, Dallas.

Volf, Miroslav. 1987a. "Divine Spirit and New Creation: Toward a Pneumatological Understanding of Work." *Pneuma* 9 (2): 173–93.

———. 1987b. *Zukunft der Arbeit—Arbeit der Zukunft: Das Marsche Verständnis der Arbeit und seine theologische Wertung* (The Future of Work—Work of the Future) Munich and Mainz: Kaiser/Grünewald.

———. 1989. "Kirche als Gemeinschaft. Ekklesiologische Ueberlegungen aus freikirchlicher Perspektive" (Church as Community ...). *Evangelische Theologie* 49: 52–75.

Wacker, Grant. 1984. "The Functions of Faith in Primitive Pentecostalism." *Harvard Theological Review* 77 (July–October): 353–75.

———. 1985. *Augustus H. Strong and the Dilemma of Historical Consciousness.* Macon, Ga.: Mercer University Press.

———. 1986. "Are the Golden Oldies Still Worth Playing? Reflections on History Writing among Early Pentecostals." *Pneuma* 8 (Fall): 81–100.

———. 1990. "Wild Theories and Mad Excitement." In *Pentecostals from the Inside Out,* edited by Harold B. Smith, 19–28. Wheaton, Ill.: Victor Books.

Walker, Andrew. 1984. "The Orthodox Church and the Charismatic Movment." In *Strange Gifts,* edited by David Martin and Peter Mullen, 163–71. Oxford: Basil Blackwell.

Wallace, Anthony F. C. 1966. *Religion: An Anthropological View.* New York: Random House.

Wallerstein, Immanuel. 1974. *The Modern World System.* New York: Academic Press.

———. 1987. "World-Systems Analysis." In *Social Theory Today,* edited by A. Giddens and J. Turner, 309–24. Oxford: Polity Press.

Wallmann, Johannes. 1990. *Der Pietismus* (Pietism). Göttingen: Vandenhoeck & Ruprecht.

Wanjala, Chris. 1977. "In Search of a Revolutionary Hero: A Review Essay." *Kenya Historical Review* 5 (2): 389–95.

Watson, Graham. 1991. "Rewriting Culture." In *Recapturing Anthropology,* edited by Richard G. Fox, 73–92. Santa Fe, N.M.: School of American Research Press.

Watts, Frank, and Mark Williams. 1988. *The Psychology of Religious Knowing.* Cambridge: Cambridge University Press.

Weaver, C. Douglas. 1987. *The Healer-Prophet: William Marrion Branham.* Macon, Ga.: Mercer University Press.

Weber, Max. 1964. *Wirtschaft und Gesellschaft. Studienausgabe herausgegebenvon Johannes Winckelman* (Economy and Society). Köln: Kiepenheuer and Witsch.

Weber, Timothy P. 1983. *Living in the Shadow of the Second Coming.* Chicago: University of Chicago Press.

Weeks, Tricia. 1989. 1990. Personal interviews by Karla Poewe, Decatur, Ga.

Welbourn, Fred, and Bethwell A. Ogot. 1966. *A Place to Feel at Home: A Study of Two Independent Churches in Western Kenya.* London: Oxford University Press.

Welch, John W. 1916. Introduction to *The Apostolic Faith Restored,* by Bennett F. Lawrence, 7–8. St. Louis: Gospel Publishing House.

———. 1919. "The Power of Apostolic Days for You in the Twentieth-Century." *Pentecostal Evangel* (1 November): 2–3.

Welime, J. D. W. 1967. "Dini ya Msambwa." Paper read at East African Institute of Social Research Conference, Makerere University, Kampala, January.

Were, Gideon S. 1967. "Dini Ya Msambwa: A Reassessment." Makerere Institute of Social Research. Conference Paper 441, January.

———. 1972. "Politics, Religion and Nationalism in Western Kenya, 1942–1962: Dini ya Msambwa Revisited." In *Hadith 4,* edited by Bethwell A. Ogot, 85–104. Nairobi: East African Publishing House.

———. 1977. "Interaction of African Religion with Christianity in Western Kenya." In his *Essays on African Religion in Western Kenya,* 60–71. Nairobi: East African Literature Bureau.

Whisson, Michael G., and John Lonsdale. 1975. "The Case of Jason Gor: A Luo Succession Dispute in Historical Perspective." *Africa* 45 (1): 50–66.

White, Ellen G. 1957. *The Triumph of God's Love: The Story of the Vindication of the Character of God and the Salvation of Mankind.* Nashville: Southern Publishing Association.

Whiteley, Wilfred H. 1971. Introduction to *Language Use and Social Change: Problems of Multilingualism with Special Reference to Eastern Africa,* edited by Whiteley, 1–23. London: Oxford University Press for the International African Institute.

"Whose Faith Follow" [editorial]. *Pentecostal Evangel* (8 July 1922): 1–3.

Wienans, Chris. 1987. Personal interview by Karla Poewe, Durban, South Africa.

Williams, J. Rodman. 1972. *The Pentecostal Reality.* Plainfield, N.J.: Logos.

Wilson, Bryan R. 1959. "The Pentecostal Minister: Role Conflicts and Status Contradictions." *American Journal of Sociology* 64 (5): 494–502.

Wilson, D. J. 1988. "Pacifism." In *Dictionary of Pentecostal and Charismatic Movements,* edited by Stanley M. Burgess, Gary B. McGee, and Patrick H. Alexander, 658–60. Grand Rapids, Mich.: Zondervan.

Wilson, Everett A. 1987. "Latin American Pentecostals: Their Potential for Ecumenical Dialogue." *Pneuma* 9 (1): 91–95.

Wimber, John, and Kevin Springer. 1985. *Power Evangelism: Signs and Wonders Today.* London: Hodder and Stoughton.

———. 1986. *Power Healing.* London: Hodder and Stoughton.

Wipper, Audrey. 1971. "The Rise and Decline of a Folk Hero, Elijah Masinde." In *Hadith 3,* edited by Bethwell A. Ogot, 157–89. Nairobi: EAPH.

———. 1977. *Rural Rebels: A Study of Two Protest Movements in Kenya.* Nairobi: Oxford University Press.

———. 1983. "Lofty Visions and Militant Action: A Reply to Jan de Wolf." *Canadian Journal of African Studies* 17 (2): 277–94.

———. 1988. "Rural Rebels and Colonial Kenya: The Argument Against Buijtenhuij's Re-Analysis." *Africa* 58 (3): 353–63.

Wolf, Eric. 1982. *Europe and the People Without History.* Berkeley: University of California Press.

Wolf, Jan Jacob de. 1977. *Differentiation and Integration in Western Kenya: A Study of Religious Innovation and Social Change Among the Bukusu.* The Hague and Paris: Mouton.

———. 1983. "Dini ya Msambwa: Militant Protest or Millenarian Promise?" *Canadian Journal of African Studies* 17 (2): 265–76.

Wolmarans, Theo. 1989. Personal interview by Karla Poewe and Irving Hexham, Johannesburg, South Africa.

Wuthnow, Robert. 1988. *The Restructuring of American Religion.* Princeton, N.J.: Princeton University Press.

Yeomans, Lilian B. 1926. *Healing From Heaven.* Springfield, Mo.: Gospel Publishing House.

Yoo, Boo Woong. 1986. "Response to Korean Shamanism by the Pentecostal Church." *International Review of Mission* 75 (297): 70–74.

———. 1988. *Korean Pentecostalism: Its History and Theology*. New York: Peter Lang.

Yoshiyama, Hiroshi, ed. 1979. *Mitama ni michibikarete—soritsu 30 nenshi* (Led by the Holy Spirit—A 30 Year History). Tokyo: Japan Assemblies of God.

Zegwaart, Huibert. 1988. "Apocalyptic Eschatology and Pentecostalism: The Relevance of John's Millennium for Today." *Pneuma* 10 (1): 3–25.

Zerubavel, Eviatar. 1981. *Hidden Rhythms: Schedules and Calendars in Social Life*. Chicago: University of Chicago Press.

———. 1985. *The Seven Day Circle: The History and Meaning of the Week*. New York: Free Press.

NEWSPAPERS AND PERIODICALS

Daily Nation, Kenya

East African Standard, Kenya

Jezus Leeft! (Jesus Lives!). Monthly magazine of the Flemish Catholic Charismatic Renewal. Schoten, Belgium: G. Colpaert.

Kenya Times

Nairobi Times

Natal Mercury, South Africa

Reporter, Kenya

Sunday Nation, Kenya

Contributors

André Droogers is professor of anthropology of religion, department of cultural anthropology/sociology of development, Free University, Amsterdam, the Netherlands.

Irving Hexham is professor, department of religious studies, University of Calgary, Alberta, Canada.

W. J. Hollenweger is emeritus professor of missions, University of Birmingham, Birmingham, England.

Stanley Johannesen is associate professor of history, history department, University of Waterloo, Waterloo, Ontario, Canada.

David Martin is emeritus professor of sociology, London School of Economics, London University, London, England.

Mark R. Mullins is associate professor, Meiji Gakuin University, Tokyo/Yokohama, Japan.

Charles Nienkirchen is professor of church history and formation, Rocky Mountain College, Calgary, Alberta, Canada.

Karla Poewe is professor of anthropology, department of anthropology, University of Calgary, Calgary, Alberta, Canada.

Gerard Roelofs is graduate in cultural anthropology, University of Amsterdam, Amsterdam, the Netherlands.

Nancy Schwartz is assistant professor, department of sociology and anthropology, Southwest Missouri State University, Springfield, Missouri.

Russell P. Spittler is professor of New Testament, Fuller Theological Seminary, Pasadena, California.

Index